JOURNEY TOGETHER

JOURNEY TOGETHER

49 Steps
to Transforming a Family

SARAH HERMELIN

URIM PUBLICATIONS
Jerusalem • New York

Excerpts from ArtScroll books are reproduced from: *Tehillim Treasury* by Avrohom Chaim Feuer; *The Pirkei Avos Treasury* by Moshe Lieber; *Conversations with Yourself* by Zelig Pliskin; *Rabbi Yissocher Frand in Print* by Yissocher Frand in collaboration with Yonason Rosenblum; *Iggeres HaRamban, Ramban: A Letter for the Ages* by Avrohom Chaim Feuer; and, *Perek Shirah: The Song of the Universe, Translation and Insights* by Nosson Scherman, with permission of the copyright holders, ArtScroll/Mesorah Publications, Ltd.

Excerpts from *The Garden of Emuna*; *The Garden of Wisdom*; and *Women's Wisdom* (all by Rabbi Shalom Arush) are reproduced with permission of the copyright holders, Chut Shel Chessed Institution (Israel).

Journey Together: 49 Steps to Transforming a Family

by Sarah Hermelin

Typeset by Ariel Walden

Printed in Israel

First Edition

ISBN 978-965-524-159-4

Urim Publications, P.O. Box 52287,
Jerusalem 9152102 Israel

www.UrimPublications.com

Library of Congress Cataloging-in-Publication Data
Hermelin, Sarah.
Journey together : 49 steps to transforming a family / Sarah Hermelin.
pages cm
ISBN 978-965-524-159-4 (hardback)
1. Sefirah period. 2. Self-actualization (Psychology)–Religious aspects–Judaism. 3. Jewish way of life. I. Title.
BM695.S4H47 2014
296.7'4–dc23 2014002201

To HaKadosh Baruch Hu, the source of all life, light, inspiration, and oneness.

To my husband, Reuven Moshe Shlomo, the most wise-hearted person I have ever met – may Hashem continue to bless our love with *chesed, gevurah, tiferet, netzach, hod,* and *yesod* in order that the symphony of *malchut* we have worked diligently to attain can continue to play until 120.

To our Children and Grandchildren – each of you represents a unique and precious star with the potential to illuminate the entire world.

To the *Journey Together* Explorer – may you capture the essence of the Omer count and may your journey become a yearly ascent towards connection and greater harmony with self, with others, and with Hashem.

Contents

Week Three: *Tiferet* (Harmony/Truth)

Week Four: *Netzach* (Endurance/Eternity)

Week Five: *Hod* (Humility)

Week Six: *Yesod* (Bonding)

Week Seven: *Malchut* (Leadership/Nobility)

Author's Note

An amazing gift! That is the best way to describe the opportunity God has given us, when He commanded us to count the Omer for 49 days between Pesach and Shavuot. During this period, when we connect with the guiding attributes according to which God created the entire world, each of us has an opportunity to enhance who we are, to actualize our full potential, and to advance radically in our personal growth – as Jews have done for thousands of years.

It was more than 3,300 years ago, that our ancestors had gathered at Mount Sinai, having first purified and elevated themselves in advance of the awesome moment when they would merit an encounter with God. Every year since then, for the 49 days between Pesach and Shavuot, we have striven to elevate ourselves, as our ancestors did, to be worthy of again receiving the greatest revelation of all time – our holy Torah.

These 49 days are truly magical. And this easy-to-use guide to counting the Omer has been formulated to help one and all turn this exercise into a highly spiritual, meaningful, and growth-enhancing experience. Through this process, we can uncover root causes to thorny problems, untie tangled knots, achieve better life outlooks, improve our character traits and, as a result, help each other. We can alter the future. We can not only become worthy of receiving the Torah, but also learn how to embody it and collectively become a living Torah ourselves. We can all turn the cycle of these seven weeks into a transformative experience for ourselves and for those we love, and we can repeat it every year as we continue to evolve higher and higher.

We are meant to utilize these 49 days to become worthy servants of

God while, at the same time, achieving a mastery over our lives, which entails the complete integration of the attribute of *malchut* (kingship). It may sound paradoxical that a servant can also be a king, but our extraordinary religion teaches that this is precisely what we each can achieve. In the *Hallel* prayers we say, "I am Your servant . . . You have released my bonds."[1] Through service to God we are liberated from that which enslaves us and are freed to become the best we were created to be. The annual Omer count provides us with the roadmap for this worthy adventure, and all we have to do is dedicate genuine effort in order to achieve this goal.

The process by which we achieve *malchut* in our relationship with ourselves, with others, and with God requires an honest inner search to discover and reinforce our strengths and find a counterbalance to our weaknesses. What a marvelous opportunity it is to examine our habits, character traits, and unconscious choices that may have caused dissonance in the pure soul we were given by God when we were created.

As we do this, we ask ourselves whether our thoughts, speech, and actions display the appropriate amount of gratitude, kindness, consistency, and closeness, or is the opposite true? Do we cause pain and distance between ourselves and others because of the way we think, speak, and conduct ourselves? We ponder what God must think of our life-choices up until now, and ask: Is our relationship with Him close, meaningful, and filled with complete faith that everything He does is for our best?

This self-examination is all part of a frank and probing *cheshbon hanefesh*. And we are privileged to be given the opportunity to use each of the 49 days of the Omer count to perform laser surgery on ourselves – to repair any unsatisfactory gaps between the person we are and the person we want to be, between the person we are and the person God would want to see as part of His Chosen People.

Each year, by working on all three levels of the relationship between ourselves and our soul, between ourselves and others, and between ourselves and God, we are able to climb the ladder, step-by-step, towards becoming a balanced, fully-actualized person, who is worthy of the World to Come.

1. *Tehillim* 116:16.

WHY A FAMILY GUIDE?

We have all come to know how family units have the potential to bring out the best and worst in us. Each of us has experienced the inexplicable reality of people we love displaying their best and worst, sometimes within the hour. We are often amazed and baffled by how complex human behavior and family dynamics can be. Although the family deserves the best of our thoughts, speech, and actions, it can become mired in a mixed bag of behavioral problems and dissatisfactions and even outright dysfunctionality.

In a sense, the family is the ultimate laboratory in which we mature, develop, and grow. It is no wonder that the evolving family is how God chose to define Avraham's sacred mission. Avraham is not only the first Jew but the "father of nations." The entire first book of the Torah (*Bereshit)* is devoted to sharing intimate details of the first extended Jewish family, describing how spouses, parents, siblings, children, grandparents, uncles, and stepchildren relate to each other, to the outside world, and to God.

At the end of *Bereshit*, we read that Yaakov descended into Egypt with the entire Jewish family consisting of only seventy souls. It is not until 210 years later that this family grew into and emerged as a Jewish nation of three million former slaves, freed from bondage by the hand of God. We were rescued from the furnace of Egyptian enslavement only to enter the wilderness, a no man's land where God fashioned us into the first religious and ethical social unit ever created. Every year since then, we are called upon to re-enact this incredible experience. We observe the festival of Pesach and, beginning on the second day of this holiday, we begin a 49-day period of preparation to become servants of God, deserving of receiving God's greatest gift to man – His Torah.

But times have changed. Over the three millennia since Sinai, we have seen drastic change in family life, and never more than today. It is an understatement to say that today's families are under a frontal assault, as rapid technological changes have altered the way people communicate and spend time. Family members may sit at a dinner table together but, while doing so, they may be texting, sending e-mails, or surfing the net on a variety of handheld devices. Psychologists warn that our children are "at risk," citing distressing statistics that point to the breakdown of the family. Many are asking what are we to do about it?

The solutions and tools are found in the Torah. The 49-day Omer count offers a "firewall" to protect our families from these dangers while, at the same time, enhancing our lives. God's antidote for what ails us is this amazing spiritual gift of counting and understanding the content of each day's count, as well as the cumulative holistic significance of the Omer exercises. The family that communicates and devotes time to discussing together the importance of each day's Omer count will inevitably become closer, stronger, happier, calmer, and more balanced.

Let's begin together and stay together as a Jewish family, in loving service to the Creator and Sustainer of the world.

In gratitude for all of Hashem's infinite gifts,

Sarah Hermelin
Jerusalem, Israel
journeytogether49steps@gmail.com

Introduction

It is nothing short of awesome to prepare ourselves each year for Pesach in order to re-experience our exodus from Egyptian bondage. We expend significant energy to remove the *chametz* from our lives physically, emotionally, mentally, and spiritually. Beyond the four corners of our home, it is also as if we are being asked to take our body and soul to the cleaners to remove any trace of arrogance from the content of our thoughts, speech, and actions.

Pesach night arrives and we all experience close family bonding, as we gather around a table upon which the Seder plate has pride of place along with the matzah and wine. We try to make *Leil HaSeder* a memorable experience for our children and everyone present. These cherished moments connect us to our rich history, to our ancestors who escaped from Egypt more than 3,000 years ago, and to God's absolute sovereignty over our lives ever since.

The next day something very unusual happens. We begin a 49-day process of elevating ourselves to be worthy of receiving the Torah at Mount Sinai through the mitzvah of *Sefirat ha'Omer*. This transformational mitzvah is fulfilled on each of the 49 days, comprising roughly one-seventh of the calendar year. Each day we count, we focus on one of the divine attributes with which God created the world.

Some fulfill this mitzvah of counting the Omer in a perfunctory way that merely satisfies the basic obligation. Others, desiring to take advantage of this God-given opportunity to examine, repair, and enhance who they are, go deeper. They seek to explore their strengths and weaknesses, trying to actualize their full potential for personal growth. Combining the mitzvah obligation of counting the Omer with self-evaluation becomes a bold, mature, life-enhancing step that redeems thought, speech, and action.

There is also a third approach that engenders even greater fulfillment and takes this mitzvah to the highest level. This approach entails involving the entire family in the process of transformation. *Journey Together* expands the mitzvah of counting the Omer by demonstrating how family members can participate in a meaningful dialogue on the significance of each day's count which is bound to impact one and all.

This approach is designed to bring about remarkable behavior transformation for family members of all ages. Those who have discovered the value of counting and discussing the Omer together end up helping each other develop and mature. In the process, they can resolve any chronic stumbling blocks in their relationships.

The result is an improved interpersonal dynamic within the family that includes more frequent and deeper expressions of love, harmony, honesty, humility, bonding, and respect – all leading to a heightened understanding of self and others that is bound to be felt by each family member.

Journey Together is also intended as an aide in identifying concrete, proactive steps to help rectify harmful influences, thought patterns, emotional outbursts, bad habits or other behaviors that are counterproductive or destructive.

Journey Together challenges its readers to evaluate the ways their thinking, speech, and actions serve them well or poorly in the areas of physical, mental, emotional, and spiritual health. Individuals who partake of this process will find that they have taken a huge step towards becoming both calmer and happier, as they discover a life of greater meaning, purpose, personal integrity, and closeness to God and His creation.

Counting the Omer in a family setting is an intriguing and engaging life experience. At different times, it can be a source of entertainment, a source of learning, an opportunity to improve communications, sort out problems, build self-esteem and mutual respect, while at the same time fulfilling a very important mitzvah.

How can such dramatic change possibly happen in just 49 days? Because it has happened before, and it has the potential to happen every year. It's just that many of us have not taken full advantage of this annual opportunity to help maximize our potential as human beings.

FROM ENSLAVEMENT TO FREEDOM IN SEVEN WEEKS

Try to visualize the drama that unfolded over 3,300 years ago. After some 210 years of harsh enslavement, roughly three million Jewish men, women, and children left Egypt and embarked on a journey which would take them seven weeks or 49 days. As we all know, on the fiftieth day, they stood at the foot of the flaming Mount Sinai and encountered God. This day upon which our nation received the priceless eternal gift of Torah is the special holiday of Shavuot to which we return with anticipation and preparation each year.

We recall how hundreds of thousands of Jewish families, who until recently were beaten-down slaves, walked united toward a common destiny, and how – during the 49-day journey that spanned Pesach and Shavuot – God helped them remove all the vestiges of their brutal enslavement.

Although they had been abused and debased, although they had sunk to the forty-ninth level of impurity, God, through His infinite mercy, made it possible for them to gradually reverse the effects of their enslavement, and purify and elevate themselves in only 49 days.

On the fiftieth day, God gave Israel the Torah, the greatest gift ever received by any nation, a blueprint for how we can establish a close, loving and respectful relationship with Him, with each other and with ourselves. The Torah teaches us how to obey the will of God, not as slaves, but as servants who freely choose to align their will with their God, Master, King, and Redeemer.

But what exactly happened in those 49 days to transform slaves into a free people worthy of direct communication with the Creator and Master of the Universe?

Rabbi Eliyahu Kitov, in the classic *Book of Our Heritage*, answers this question as follows:

> . . . once Israel left Egypt and became a part of God's portion, a gate of purity was opened for them – a gate that the people of that era entered and through which they became purified over a period of 49 days. They rose from the status of brick makers and straw gatherers serving the Pharaoh of Egypt, to become a holy people chosen by God, a nation of *kohanim*, kings, and ministers, all devoted to His service.

Rabbi Kitov continues, explaining how we can connect with that awesome spiritual energy which permeated that period of time and which is available to us during the Omer count:

> This path of purification was paved then, and each year when this period arrives, the gate is once again opened and the road made clear for all those who seek to assume the seven attributes in their completeness . . . We find that the Torah mentions the Exodus from Egypt 50 times, demonstrating God's great kindness to Israel. When we count the Omer for 49 days from the first day of the Festival, it reminds us that on each day He brought Israel another step away from the defilement of Egypt and led them to enter the gate of purity so that they would be worthy of receiving the Torah.[2]Those first 49 days thousands of years ago introduced a new paradigm, and it has guided all the subsequent generations of Jews in our annual Omer counting process. The overarching dynamic is movement from darkness to light, incorporating within it the movement from enslavement to freedom, from impurity to holiness, from descent to ascent, from constriction to expansion, from stagnation to growth. In the words of Rabbi Eliyahu Dessler: "The Exodus was an abrupt transition from forced enslavement by the power of evil to willing submission to the absolute good – the kingdom of God."[3]

The Omer count is meant to help us in making the same essential transition. Much like the first 49 days when our ancestors journeyed into the wilderness in order to learn to depend upon and freely choose to serve God, all future generations have the same amount of time to discover their worthiness, and once again be ready to accept the Torah on Shavuot.

It is through the daily Omer count that we are able to elevate ourselves. We do so by engaging in a genuine and serious assessment of our character and by evaluating objectively the direction of our life. If we do this introspection honestly, our lives will be forever changed for the better.

---

2. Eliyahu Kitov, *The Book of Our Heritage*, Vol. 2 (Jerusalem: Feldheim, 1997), 683, 686.
3. Eliyahu Dessler, *Sanctuaries in Time* (Jerusalem: Feldheim, 1994), 29–30.

WHAT ENSLAVES US TODAY?

This is a question that is as relevant today as it was for our ancestors: What enslaves us today? Sadness? Spiritual apathy? Overwork? Worry? Anger? Insecurities? Unhealthy relationships? Loneliness? Jealousy? Weak personal boundaries? Depression? Resentments? Arrogance? Negative thinking? Poor self-image? Societal influences? Lack of faith? Alcohol, drugs, nicotine or food addictions?

The list is endless. Today, we may not live as "slaves" of a foreign nation, but each of us is enslaved by some "alien behavior or power." And each of us needs to figure out what it is. The truism is as simple as it is obvious: *We cannot be free as long as we are still enslaved.*

Once we discover and acknowledge what enslaves us, we need to apply effort to uncover the sources of our personal bondage. *Journey Together* not only provides examples in the form of true stories and insights to inspire character refinement, but it also provides thought-provoking questions for adults and children to help assess and confront issues and problems in their conduct and interpersonal relationships. The goal throughout is to use Torah lessons about our ancestors in combination with impactful stories from modern life in order to stimulate dialogue within families. By engaging in such discussions, we can identify which of our behaviors require attention and improvement. Each day of the Omer, then, enables us to become healthier, because we are seeking to emulate the attributes of God as we progress on the path toward our goals.

Getting into the habit of doing this every day will help us eliminate, or at least start to weaken, the bonds that enslave us. With practice and commitment, we and every member of our family, can achieve this very lofty goal of growth and refinement.

Because the stakes are so high – personal freedom versus a life of continued entrapment – we are motivated to maximize the God-given opportunity of the Omer count. Although some may choose to continue counting the Omer in a rote or perfunctory manner without any serious reflection and study, and some may even rationalize not counting at all, those who do so are making a terrible mistake. They miss an opportunity of a lifetime, with repercussion in this world and in the next.

Those who don't delve into the meaning of the count forfeit the potential spiritual and emotional benefits of personal expansion that *always* occur when the count is done with deep concentration and focus. We all should treasure this time in the Jewish calendar and make a meaningful effort to recreate the 49-day ascent that culminated in our ancestors reaching the highest spiritual level ever achieved by humankind.

It is such a shame when a person quickly rattles off the blessing and counts the day without ever reflecting on what God is asking us to rectify on that particular day. Much like the beautiful butterfly emerging from its dark cocoon, we could all be experiencing the birth of a newly refreshed personality if only we chose to put in the effort.

What a missed opportunity! It should be the most spiritually-charged moment in time. It should be a moment of meaningful change in all our relationships. What a loss!

These 49 days were given to us by God to launch our own personal journey of self-development and self-actualization, and yet this opportunity will disappear if we race through the mechanics of the count without nary a thought as to what it all means.

THE IMPORTANCE OF COUNTING THE OMER

What does it mean? And what is so important about counting the Omer?

The 49 days of the Omer are evenly divided into seven weeks. In the Jewish mystical literature – better known as the Kabbalah – these seven weeks were meant to correspond to the reality of the seven *sefirot*. Therefore, when we count the Omer we are recognizing, identifying, and internalizing the seven *sefirot*, and their combinations which are the attributes – or guiding principles – with which the temporal world was created by God, who embodies these attributes.

Each of the seven *sefirot* will be described in detail in subsequent chapters, and the following is a useful cursory definition, adapted from *Endless Light*, by Rabbi David Aaron, founder of the Isralight Institute and dean of Orayta Yeshiva in Jerusalem. There, Rabbi Aaron states that there are "six guiding principles to life and love" according to Kabbalah, and these are expressed in two groups of three and arranged in a triangular fashion to mirror the human body:

- *chesed* (loving-kindness) as the right arm
- *gevurah* (strength/discipline/restraint) as the left arm
- *tiferet* (truth/harmony) as the torso that connects them
- *netzach* (endurance) as the right leg

- *hod* (humility) as the left leg
- *yesod* (bonding/foundation) as the reproductive system[4]

This Kabbalistic understanding has best been illustrated by the well-known teacher of mystical Judaism and author of several books on the subject, Sarah Yehudit Schneider:[5]

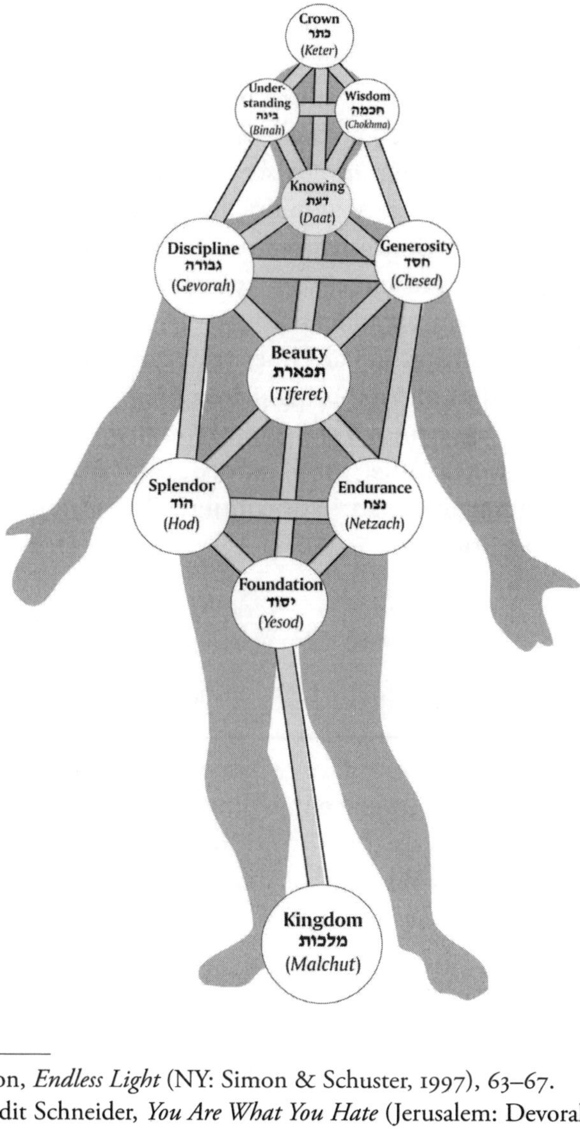

4. David Aaron, *Endless Light* (NY: Simon & Schuster, 1997), 63–67.
5. Sarah Yehudit Schneider, *You Are What You Hate* (Jerusalem: Devorah/A Still Small Voice, 2009), 27.

From this diagram, we see that *tiferet* and *yesod* – falling in the center of our bodies – are the "balancing principles" that "create harmony in living and loving." When we live and love in accordance with *tiferet,* we are true to ourselves. When we live and love in accordance with *yesod,* we enjoy peace with others.

These six guiding principles – along with the seventh, *malchut* – comprise our work for the seven weeks of counting of the Omer. They guide us in becoming people who are true to themselves and who enjoy peace with others.

What about the culmination of this process? In the seventh week, the *sefirah* of *malchut* will emerge naturally *if* we have done our work during the previous six weeks. *Malchut* represents "kingship," which in modern language translates into dignity, nobility, leadership, sovereignty, and independence. Our success in this regard will be measured by how ready we will be to stand before God and again receive the Torah on the fiftieth day, and not only receive but live by its precepts.

If we elect to make the annual Omer count meaningful, we can seize the opportunity to discover and bring proper balance to these seven critical attributes that correspond to the seven *sefirot* or principles with which God created and sustains the world. Indeed, each week of the Omer is spent working on a different attribute, until the forty-ninth day brings us to a fulfilling transformation.

THE PURPOSE OF THE SEVEN-WEEK OMER CYCLE

In *Sefer Vayikra* we find the following commandment:

> You shall count for yourselves – from the morrow of the *rest day,* from the day when you bring the Omer of the waving – seven weeks, they shall be complete. Until the morrow of the seventh week you shall count, fifty days; and you shall offer a new meal-offering to God.[6]

The Jewish Oral Tradition defines this "rest day" not as Shabbat, but as the first day of Pesach. Rabbi Dessler expounds on why God chooses to equate the first day of Pesach with Shabbat:

6. *Vayikra* 23:15–16.

> The root meaning of "Shabbat" is "cessation" . . . The day of the Exodus is here called "Shabbat" because our association with the defilement of Egypt then ceased. The following weeks, too, are called "Shabbat" to remind us that the keynote of these weeks of preparation is the complete removal of all defilement from our midst by constant and unremitting effort.

Rabbi Dessler concludes:

> Each day of this "supercycle" of seven-times-seven needs to be carefully examined for possible re-entry of moral pollution. There are cracks in each person's defenses through which evil can penetrate, unless close watch is maintained. This is the meaning of the expression "you shall count for yourselves." The counting – or accounting – must take place in the depths of our being.[7]

Rabbi Dessler's last point – that the counting, or accounting, must take place in the depths of our being – bears emphasis. For, if we have not been successful in achieving the desired level of behavioral refinement from our previous year's Omer count, then the *Journey Together* can be an indispensible guide that can help close, as he put it, the "cracks in each person's defenses through which evil can penetrate."

As mentioned earlier, *Journey Together* relies on Kabbalistic teachings which say that there are seven attributes upon which the temporal world is based: *chesed* (loving-kindness); *gevurah* (strength/restraint); *tiferet* (harmony/truth); *netzach* (endurance); *hod* (humility); *yesod* (foundation/bonding); and *malchut* (leadership/nobility).

The sin of Adam and Eve in Gan Eden resulted in these seven attributes becoming damaged. Rabbi Kitov, in summarizing the teachings of Jewish mysticism, states that these attributes were later reconstituted in this world by our great ancestors who merited, by their *middot*, to repair this deficiency. They are called the "Seven Shepherds" and they are:

- Avraham who personified *chesed*
- Yitzchak who personified *gevurah*
- Yaakov who personified *tiferet*

7. Dessler, *Sanctuaries in Time*, 30–31.

- Moshe who personified *netzach*
- Aaron who personified *hod*
- Yosef who personified *yesod*
- David who personified *malchut*

These Seven Shepherds stood up to extreme tests and challenges in their lives and thus they purified these marred attributes. And, in turn, they gave over these attributes to us.

All the stories from Tanach about each of the Seven Shepherds and the tests they endured are eye-opening and form the basis for a lifetime of discussions for each and every one of us, and at all age levels.

Journey Together will reference and weave in relevant life stories of these great men to illustrate the attributes they exhibited in meeting various life challenges. *Journey Together* will also draw on contemporary stories of "everyday heroes" depicting various attribute combinations in the events of their lives.

REPAIRING THE SEVEN ATTRIBUTES

Although the Seven Shepherds did a great deal of work to repair the damage done to the seven attributes, more work remains to be done. This work is evident in many of today's behaviors:

For example, if a person displays insufficient *gevurah*, then he or she is also lacking healthy *chesed*, because the latter attribute is nothing more than soft-heartedness if not balanced by *gevurah*. If *chesed* lacks *tiferet*, then it can degenerate into sins of excess. Conversely, none of the other six attributes are considered complete if they lack some element of loving-kindness. As Rabbi Kitov advises: "Each attribute has a light of its own that shines forth from its combination with the others."[8]

The masters of Jewish mysticism see the seven weeks of the counting of the Omer as a period where we, too, can rectify the defects that have marred the seven attributes by focusing on one attribute per week.

When the Torah declares: "And Hashem saw all that He had done and behold it was very good,"[9] it depicts what a "good" world will look like, once each and every one of us has completed our part in its rectification.

8. Kitov, *The Book of Our Heritage*, Vol. 2, 683–686.

9. *Bereshit* 1:31.

The path of purification was paved then by our ancestors as they walked from Egypt to Mount Sinai, and each year – as we count the Omer – the same gate they entered reopens once again and, as noted earlier, "the road [is] made clear for all those who seek to assume the seven attributes in their completeness."[10]

In short, we are being asked to do our part in the rectification of all of creation known as *Tikkun Olam*.

This is amazing. God has designated the 49 days of counting the Omer as a period in which we can repair any flaw in every attribute in its combination with the other six. And just as the Seven Shepherds played their role, we are likewise mandated to engage in this process of spiritual burnishing and purification.

THE DEEP WISDOM OF THE COUNT

Ramban advances the Kabbalistic thought contained in the Zohar that these 49 days of the Omer count provide an essential daily opportunity to do *teshuvah*, thus cleansing the blemishes that our previous behavior has produced.

Indeed, there is a magnificent prayer which we can elect to recite after the Omer count that, sadly, many skip. It captures the depth and levels of meaning alluded to by Ramban:

> Master of the Universe, You commanded us through Moshe, Your servant, to count the Omer in order to cleanse us from our encrustations of evil and from our contaminations, as You have written in Your Torah: "You are to count from the morrow of the rest day, from the day you brought the Omer-offering that is waved – they are to be seven complete weeks. Until the morrow of the seventh week you are to count fifty days, so that the souls of Your people Israel be cleansed of their contamination." Therefore, may it be Your will, God, our God and the God of our forefathers, that in the merit of the Omer that I have counted today, may there be corrected whatever blemish I have caused in the *sefirah* — [insert that day's *sefirah* combination]. May I be cleansed and sanctified with the holiness of Above, and through this may abundant bounty flow in all the worlds. And may

10. Kitov, *The Book of Our Heritage*, Vol. 2, 683.

> it correct our lives, spirits, and souls from all sediment and blemish; may it cleanse us and sanctify us with Your exalted holiness. Amen, *Selah*![11]

Astonishing! What an opportunity for us to thank and serve God by resolving to remove the encrustations of evil from the world polluted by the sin of Adam and Eve. What a chance to elevate ourselves through such personal spiritual cleansing and at the same time contribute to bettering the world.

ADVICE FROM *SEFER HACHINUCH*

Sefer HaChinuch provides a different – yet complementary view – from the Zohar. It states that the purpose of the Omer count is to bridge Pesach with Shavuot. We are marching to Mount Sinai, but our exodus from Egypt is not enough. Freedom means nothing unless it emerges from and is defined by the engravings on the Tablets of the Covenant.

Pesach only has meaning when it leads to Shavuot. The point is that it is incumbent upon us to make the journey. The path to Shavuot, the path to receiving the Torah, is followed one step each day for 49 days by counting the Omer in a deep, honest, insightful effort in order to change, to improve, to develop. When we do this, we can help to bring Mashiach in our day.

Rabbi Yochanan, one of the great Talmudic sages, taught that it was because of the mitzvah of counting the Omer that Avraham merited inheriting the Promised Land[12] and that the Jewish People were saved in the days of Gideon, Chizkiyahu, and Yechezkel.[13] We must ask ourselves: Can we do no less in our lives by contributing to the salvation of the Jewish people and allowing them to become – in the words of Yeshayahu[14] – a "light unto the nations"?

Rabbi Levi, another noted sage from the Talmud, taught that this mitzvah of counting the Omer saved the Jews of Persia in the days of

11. The prayer is from the ArtScroll Pesach Machzor.
12. *Bereshit* 17:8 and 17:10.
13. *Vayikra Rabbah* 28.
14. *Yeshayahu* 42:6.

the Purim story – the days of Haman, Queen Esther, and Mordechai.[15]

There are countless times in our history that underscore again and again the importance of this mitzvah when observed with true meaning and intent.

THE IMPORTANCE OF TIME

Rabbi Joseph B. Soloveitchik, a leading twentieth century Torah and halachic authority better known as "the Rav," captures the essence of the spiritual meaning of the Omer count:

> When the Jews were delivered from the Egyptian oppression, and Moshe rose to undertake the almost impossible task of metamorphosing a tribe of slaves into a nation of priests, he was told by God that the path leading from the holiday of Pesach to Shavuot, from initial liberation to consummate freedom . . . leads through the medium of time. The commandment of *sefirah* was entrusted the Jew; the wondrous test of counting 49 successive days was put to him. These 49 days must be whole. If one day [is] missed, the act of numeration is invalidated. A slave who is capable of appreciating each day, of grasping its meaning and worth, of weaving every thread of time into a glorious fabric . . . is eligible for Torah. He has achieved freedom.[16]

The Rav's understanding here is gripping in its description of the supreme importance of every one of the 49 days leading to Shavuot. This relatively simple-to-do command of counting the Omer appears paramount in achieving mastery over our own lives, as well as forging a unified nation.

He points out that "qualitative time-consciousness" is made up of two elements. First, the free person appreciates that "no fraction of time . . . should slip through the fingers, left unexploited; for eternity may depend upon the brief moment." The second aspect of this acute

---

15. *Vayikra Rabbah* 28.

16. Joseph B. Soloveitchik, "Sacred and Profane: Kodesh V'Chol," an essay found in David Shapiro, *Rabbi Joseph B. Soloveitchik on Pesach, Sefirat ha-Omer and Shavu'ot* (Jerusalem: Urim Publications [in cooperation with the Rabbi Josef B. Soloveitchik Institute], 2005), 147.

time-consciousness is an awareness "while in the present, of the past and the future."

Rabbi Soloveitchik poetically extols that no distance should ever separate "one's time-consciousness from the dawn of one's group or from the . . . destiny and infinite realization of one's cherished ideals." A former slave, therefore, will always remember that he was taken out of Egyptian bondage so that God could be his God and so that he will know that one day the Mashiach will come to redeem the world and proclaim God's name as One.[17]

A student of Rabbi Soloveitchik and a pulpit rabbi for forty years, Rabbi Jeffrey Bienenfeld, writing in his weekly *parsha* sheet, *Chizuk*, describes another dimension of counting the Omer. Commenting on *Parshat Tazria* – which usually falls during the Omer – he notes that a woman who had just given birth was required to bring an offering in the Mishkan, and he shares this insight:

> . . . this cannot be emphasized enough – when we do return to the normality of our lives [after giving birth to a child], we are and ought not to be the same person as before. Each of these God-like moments transforms us ever so slightly, so that, in sum and over time, we experience a rhythm of spiritual growth and consolidation of that growth into our lives. Hopefully, we become better and stronger.[18]

Following childbirth, or any life-altering event, we are not to be same person as before. But even if we do not experience such dramatic changes, counting the Omer is an annual opportunity given to us by God to transform our lives just the same.

We must each ask ourselves whether we are counting the Omer in the life-transforming manner our Sages have called for. If not, do we deserve receiving the Torah anew this year for ourselves, our children, and the generations that follow?

---

17. Ibid., 147–48.
18. Jeffrey Bienenfeld, *Chizuk*, *Parshat Tazria*, April 27, 2012.

WHY THE COMMANDMENT TO COUNT THE OMER?

In addition to the above explanations as to why we count the Omer, might there be other reasons?

Before Pesach we removed not only the physical *chametz* but also, hopefully, the *chametz* in our thoughts, actions, and deeds as well. But, the moment Pesach ends, *chametz* is re-introduced into our lives. If we are to receive the Torah in seven weeks, we need to take a fresh look at any spiritual, emotional, and mental *chametz* that may remain in the corners of our lives. It is precisely during these seven weeks that we are commanded to count the Omer and emulate the behavior of a dignified, refined, free person soon to have an audience with the Creator of the World at Mount Sinai. The Omer count can focus us on this process. It is an invaluable, proactive way of taking an inventory of ourselves, of examining what we should be doing, thinking about it, and then electing to apply, on each day of the Omer and beyond.

What happens after the Omer count ends?

Not long after Shavuot comes the hot summer filled with the memories of tragic events in our history – events that took place between the Seventeenth of Tammuz and the Ninth of Av – events which were all brought about by Jewish disunity and needless hatred. Then, when the month of Elul is ushered in, we are again asked to introspectively reflect upon our character traits and actions and prepare ourselves – through the *Selichot* and *teshuvah* in advance of Rosh Hashana – for the Ten Days of Awe and Yom Kippur.

Thus we might say that the 49-day Omer count launches a period of extensive and intensive personal examination that, although climaxing on Shavuot, really readies us for rebirth in the New Year. When we successfully navigate this 49-day period, we grow and ascend, reaching closer toward the fulfillment of our individual and collective missions.

THE SIGNIFICANCE OF THE OMER OFFERING

Without the Temple, we merely count the Omer without bringing the prerequisite *omer* offering. And, therefore, we tend to ignore its significance.

Interestingly, the *omer* offering was a measurement of flour (approximately 2.5 kilograms) from the newly-ripened barley harvest that was brought to the Holy Temple in Jerusalem on the second night of Pesach.

Until one measure (*omer*) was brought to the Temple, none of the new barley harvest could be consumed or used for one's own purposes.[19] But, when the offering was brought, the entire barley harvest was endowed with special significance. Thus, this mitzvah taught a fundamental lesson – "that we are not to use anything in this world except as a means to serve God," as noted by Rabbi Dessler.[20]

The ultimate goal of our Omer count is to reach the fiftieth day, Shavuot, the day of Revelation. On Shavuot, we are commanded to bring a "new offering" of two wheat loaves of bread to the Holy Temple, which is the first offering brought from the new wheat crop.[21]

The question is obvious: Why do we start by bringing barley, which is basically fodder for animals, and then must bring two loaves of wheat bread, a food associated with humankind? What is there about barley that makes it such a fascinating symbol? Why barley and not, say, coins or strands of cloth or oranges? All were available in the Middle East in ancient times. Why was barley specifically selected for the omer offering? And what is the significance of two wheat loaves offered fifty days later?

The song of barley in *Perek Shirah* ("Chapter of Song") provides a possible clue to its selection on Pesach as well as the selection of the two wheat loaves on Shavuot. Referenced in the Talmud, *Perek Shirah* is a collection of eighty-five biblical verses that are sung by all elements of creation – including the heavens, moon, sun, wind, clouds, seas, streams, birds, fish, creeping creatures, and various animals, as they fulfill their purpose intended by their Creator. It is must reading. While humans are not able to entirely hear their daily songs, we *are* still able to gain insights from their respective messages.

Chapter Three of *Perek Shirah* describes the various songs of plant life. What is the song of barley? The sheaf of barley sings a verse from *Tehillim*: "A prayer of the afflicted man when he swoons, and pours forth his supplications before God."[22] Rabbi Nosson Scherman offers a penetrating insight in ArtScroll's beautiful rendition of *Perek Shirah:*

19. *Vayikra* 23:9–14.
20. Dessler, *Sanctuaries in Time*, 31.
21. *Vayikra* 23:17.
22. *Tehillim* 102:1.

> Barley is planted with its shell. There, in the ground, it disintegrates, and only then does a new stalk begin to grow. So, too, a destitute starving man . . . pours out his supplication to God. Outwardly, he is shriveled and forlorn – like barley that is animal feed – but within himself is the seed of a new growth, the faith that as long as he can pour out his heart to God, he has more than hope, he has the strongest Power in the universe.[23]

Is this a reminder of the work we are meant to do during the seven-week cycle of counting the 49 days? We are being asked to look inside of our "shell" to examine what paralyzes, defiles, and darkens our life and then apply those insights to stimulate a new beginning filled with growth, light, and ascent. Symbolically, we are likened to a kernel of barley planted in the dark ground, an apt metaphor for our Egyptian servitude. We emerge at Mount Sinai 49 days later after purifying our thoughts, speech, and actions. We are then ready to receive the Torah and take our lives to the next level of spirituality.

And what about the symbolism of the wheat used in the two loaves brought on Shavuot? What song does wheat sing each day?

The sheaf of wheat also sings a verse from *Tehillim*: "A song of the ascents. From the depths I called you, God."[24] About wheat, Rabbi Scherman writes:

> How often does it happen that a person feels he has hit bottom, that there is no hope, that his most objective analysis shows that his prospects are nil . . . [In answer comes] the message of the wheat sheaf. Its future is brightest when it is smashed and dismembered – because that is when its kernels are gathered from the chaff and are milled to make the flour that will nourish man.[25]

When wheat was converted, through human ingenuity, into nourishing loaves of bread and brought on Shavuot as an offering to the Beit HaMikdash in Jerusalem, where it was eaten by the *kohanim* who served

23. Nosson Scherman, *Perek Shirah: The Song of the Universe, Translation and Insights* (Brooklyn, NY: Mesorah Publications, 2004), 55.

24. *Tehillim* 130:1.

25. Scherman, *Perek Shirah: The Song of the Universe*, 54.

in the Holy Temple, then the wheat fulfilled the purpose for which it was created.

In a similar fashion to this process of turning wheat into bread, when we take the raw material and potential that is "us" – our personality traits, our strengths, our limitations, all the elements that require further development – and work to separate the "wheat from the chaff," we achieve the completion intended at Shavuot by metaphorically turning ourselves into nourishing loaves of bread to serve God.

When we meaningfully count the Omer over 49 days – correctly working through the various combinations of the *sefirot* and the attributes they represent – we recalibrate ourselves to deepen our understanding of ourselves and improve our relationship with others and God. This emotional "spring-cleaning" readies us and each member of our family to receive the many benefits that Torah brings to our lives.

BORN TO WIN

The following chapters examine each of the seven weeks individually and in combination with each of the other *sefirot*. There are a total of 49 different combinations that we are striving to understand in their delicate balance with each other and to apply one per day.

When we display physical, emotional, mental, and spiritual health and balance in our dealings with ourselves, others, and God, we then help rectify imbalances in the seven *sefirot* of *chesed*, *gevurah*, *tiferet*, *netzach*, *hod*, *yesod*, and *malchut*, along with their various combinations. The result is an experience of wholeness – we manifest an integrated personality that expresses our love, humility, and gratitude as well as our respect for ourselves, for our families, for others and for God.

In their famous book, *Born to Win*, Dr. Muriel James and Dorothy Jongeward remind us that each person "is born with what he needs to win at life . . . Each has his own unique potentials – his capabilities and limitations. Each can be a significant, thinking, aware, and creatively productive person in his own right – a winner."[26]

This is true. Each of us is created in the image of God, each of us is born *b'tzelem Elokim*, embodying a divine soul. Sadly, numerous other

26. Muriel James, and Dorothy Jongeward, *Born to Win, Transactional Analysis with Gestalt Experiments* (Reading, MA: Addison-Wesley, 1971), 1.

influences begin to bombard us from the moment we arrive in this world. By adulthood, and sadly sometimes long before, many of us no longer think, speak or act as if we were "Born to Win."

How can we reclaim this sense of positive self-esteem? One way is by counting the Omer as commanded by the Torah and then serving God as a balanced, self-actualized person.

If we no longer feel that we are "Born to Win," then we can do the work of integration that the Omer count offers us, and we can become "Balanced to Win." This term best describes our goal – the ideal state of wholeness that we want to achieve. It brings to mind *malchut*, which is dignity, nobility, and sovereignty over our lives.

"Balanced to Win" expresses a marvelous, sacred blending of all aspects of our newly-minted personality. We can feel it in every pore of our body as the light of our *neshamah* pours through.

BALANCED TO WIN

We will become "Balanced to Win" as we strive to achieve the appropriate balance by knowing how to live a life of worth and meaning in all situations. Notice that the criterion is "strive to achieve" – not "achieve" – because the end goal does not define success. The process, the struggle, the effort is what defines success.

We will not achieve perfection in our lifetimes, as only God is perfect. But we can steadily progress year after year if we consistently work each and every day to achieve appropriate balance in our lives, physically, mentally, emotionally, and spiritually.

One of the reasons *Journey Together* aims to encourage the entire family to observe a meaningful Omer count is that sometimes family members unwittingly play a role in "enslaving" each other. A mother may become enslaved by the stress that comes from her trying to be the perfect parent or child or spouse. A father can become enslaved by the stress that comes from being the provider, the teacher, the perfect model for his children – especially when he knows he constantly falls short. Parents may feel that their children continually make demands on them and otherwise violate their personal boundaries, to their detriment and to the detriment of their own health, yet they may not know how to reverse this pattern which the family has fallen into. Perhaps a daughter or son loves a parent who is too controlling and, as a result, is stifled either in his or her self-development.

The complexities of the family dynamic and their dysfunctionalities are endless.

Journey Together aims to help families grow closer and learn to communicate better through the process of the 49-day Omer count. We can all discover what we can productively bring into the rest of the year that can optimize love, respect, harmony, endurance, humility, bonding, and dignity in our homes.

Of course, we should at least count. But we can do much more than that. We can boldly seize the extra spiritual aspects of this seven-week cycle and take action to strengthen not only our own character and emotional traits, but also those of our family members as well. We can discover, in the process, that our own well-being and that of our loved ones are closely interlocked. Anyone who has just one dysfunctional family member, or only one less-than-optimum communication style, knows how much time this consumes and grief this involves for the entire family. Some families are eaten up emotionally by the constant bickering and fighting, or walking on eggshells to prevent the former. Nerves are frayed. Mealtimes are full of tension. But it doesn't have to be that way.

You can do something about it. And you can do it now. You can use the Omer count to open the door to create a new balance to your family. You can become "Balanced to Win" personally and you can bring this dynamic into your family as well.

When possible, the family unit should physically "stand together" and fulfill the commandment to count together. There are many families that do so and to see it is an inspiration. As well, the family unit is encouraged to read together the carefully selected contemporary stories and Torah passages that correspond to the *sefirah* for each day.

Journey Together presents thought and discussion-provoking questions for each day that apply to thoughts, speech, and actions. It contains steps that are geared to balance and strengthen each individual and the bonding within the family unit.

It is suggested that, after reading the section for each day of the Omer count, the participants take a little time to go through the questions for adults or for children and discuss whatever topics arise as a result. Of course, participants can propose their own questions. Children should be encouraged especially to make suggestions. And everyone should listen to the answers, for a great deal can be gleaned from them. The goal is to open communications and increase interpersonal insight and bonding.

It is important to give the process the time it needs each day without a stopwatch. No multitasking by anyone should be permitted. The goal is to achieve higher levels of emotional and spiritual functioning for each family member and the family as a whole. The benefits are guaranteed if the family simply commits to the schedule.

THE OMER COUNT AS A RE-CALIBRATOR

In summary:

The annual 49-day Omer counting cycle functions as a recalibrator. We each *are* "Born to Win," but many of us have lost that feeling. Too much is burdening us. But starting today, we can search deeply, perform a *cheshbon hanefesh* and choose to begin a process of becoming "Balanced to Win," physically, mentally, emotionally, and spiritually. The Omer count is tailor-made to help us achieve this goal.

During each of the 49 days that make up these mystical seven weeks, God gives us the opportunity to understand and focus on a unique aspect of self-development, but *only if* we choose to count the Omer and think about the meaning of that day's Omer count.

By counting every day and spending the necessary time to reflect on that day's inner meaning, we can reach a high degree of balance and harmony. By counting every day with our family and spending time afterwards discussing how our family unit can achieve greater harmony in our dealings with each other, we can add exponentially to the experience of what God had in mind for us when He commanded us in the Torah to count these 49 days.

Remember that our focus during the Omer count should be to cure any deficiencies within us, in our relationships with each other, and in our relationship with God. Remember, too, that many Jews, the world over, will be focusing on the same *sefirot* and attributes for that day, collectively combining to create a powerful spiritual force. Just thinking about it can help us catch a glimpse of God's plan which uses this sacred mitzvah to make a difference in the world and bring about the coming of Mashiach.

Let us begin our seven-week *Journey Together* through the spiritual gateway of the Omer count with the goal of tapping into the breadth, depth, and significance of each of the *sefirot* and their combinations with each other. One week at a time, let's extract meaning, find the proper application and balance, and work to integrate these attributes into our lives. Through this process we will elevate ourselves to be worthy servants of God entitled to receive the holiest of all gifts, the living Torah, and thus align ourselves with God's Oneness.

Our journey begins with Week One, *chesed* (loving-kindness) which, in the words of our Sages, is the foundation upon which the world is built.[27]

27. *Tehillim* 83:3; *Pirkei Avot* 1:2; *Sotah* 14a.

WEEK ONE

Chesed

(Loving-Kindness)

OVERVIEW

Chesed (Loving-Kindness)

Counting the Omer begins with *chesed* because it was with this attribute that the world and everything in it, including humanity, was created. And immediately we are moved to ask: Why? Why did God – who lacks nothing, who is perfectly complete – choose to create an "other" and a space for that "other" to exist?

He created an unparalleled level of unknowable diversity, plant life, mineral life, and star life – indeed there are billions of galaxies that we know exist out there. This vast expanse of creation includes the constellations, the heavens, the seas, the lands, the diverse varieties of vegetation, birds and fish, animal and insect life. And if all that was not enough, He chose to create human life with the capacity for speech.

He did so to be able to reveal His mercy and *chesed*. In each act of creation, He displayed His *chesed* in a pure and balanced form, and no less so when He created humanity:

> And God saw all that He had made and, behold, it was very good . . . And Hashem formed the man of dust from the ground, and He blew into his nostrils the soul of life; and man became a living being.[28]

To man, whom He endowed with free will, God assigned a unique mission to tend to all of creation, as the Torah tells us:

> And God said: "'Let us make mankind in Our image, after Our likeness. They shall rule over the fish of the sea, the birds of the sky, and over the animal, the whole earth, and every creeping thing that

28. *Bereshit* 1:31 and 2:7.

> creeps upon the earth." So God created Man in His image, in the image of God He created him; male and female He created them.[29]

From this reservoir of *chesed*, God decided to give every human being a part of Himself, a Divine spark – what the Torah calls *tzelem Elokim*. The lesson is clear. If, through an act of *chesed* we were created, then we must manifest this essential quality in our life events and relationships.

Bottom line: *chesed* is vital, for *chesed* sustains all of life. Without *chesed*, all of creation and all of life would find its way to quick oblivion. *Chesed* is a powerful overarching principle upon which all life operates and depends. It is the foundation of the world and therefore must be the foundation of our own personal lives.

KNOWING GOD THROUGH *CHESED*

In the Torah, God tells us clearly: "You shall love your fellow as yourself, for I am God."[30] And, "You shall love Hashem, your God, with all your heart, all your soul, and with all your resources."[31]

Further, we know from the Prophet Yirmeyahu that God has infinite love for us: "And I have loved you with an eternal love, therefore I have extended kindness to you. I shall yet rebuild you and you shall be rebuilt."[32]

How we experience and express this *chesed* is depicted in the beloved and moving *Tehillim* of King David which we read every day of our lives. Consider these verses:

> Oh God: You are my God, I seek You. My soul thirsts for You, my flesh longs for You; in a parched and thirsty land with no water . . . For Your kindness is better than life, my lips shall praise You. Thus shall I bless You all my life; in your Name I shall lift my hands . . . For You have been a help for me; in the shelter of your wings I joyously sing.[33]

29. Ibid., 1:26.
30. *Vayikra* 19:18.
31. *Devarim* 6:5.
32. *Yirmeyahu* 31:2–3.
33. *Tehillim* 63:2–9.

Without question, God loves us, and we are meant to reflect that love. But as we are only rays of God's infinite light, we need help learning about love, so that we may learn to both give it and receive it in our relationship with others.

Consider the advice of Rabbi Moshe Chayim Luzzatto, the great eighteenth century Kabbalist and author of *The Path of the Just* (*Mesillat Yesharim*):

> . . . If we do not make an effort to implant [love of God] in our hearts, utilizing all of the means which direct us towards it, how will it exist within us? Whence will enter intimacy into our souls, intimacy with and ardor towards the Blessed One and towards His Torah if we do not give heart to His greatness and majesty which engender this intimacy in our hearts?[34]

In our effort to emulate God's attributes, we must inculcate within ourselves a nucleus of *chesed* that reaches both out and in. And this is what all of Week One is about.

In the first week, we seek to understand exactly what it means to achieve balance in the area of loving-kindness, and just how *chesed* needs to be harnessed and directed to be a healthy, vital, and sustaining force in our lives.

AN IMBALANCE OF *CHESED*

There are several faces to *chesed*. It is not only endless kindness. It can also be tough love. Yes, *chesed* can be manifested through unrestrained giving, spontaneity, and an undisciplined extension of oneself, but these traits are not always positive. As we shall learn, it depends on the situation.

Too much *chesed* can result in a spoiled child and, if not restrained, can produce a selfish, self-centered adult. But too little *chesed* can deprive a person of the necessary level of love and security that every human being needs. Babies raised without love suffer from a "failure to thrive" and may be delayed in the essential area of speech and in normal growth patterns.

What about modern households? Are they defined by too little or too

34. Moshe Chayim Luzzatto, *The Path of the Just* (*Mesillat Yesharim*), (Jerusalem: Feldheim, 1990), 7–9.

much *chesed*? When parents and children hardly see each other for meals, long talks, or the transmission of values for normal healthy living – because both parents and children are distracted by other issues that consume their time and energy – *chesed* is clearly absent.

And what about marital relationships? There, too, *chesed* is lacking. Too many marriages worldwide suffer from insufficient expressions of love. How are we to address the hectic crush of our daily lives which seem to constantly pull couples in opposite directions?

According to Rabbi Yissocher Frand, the Chazon Ish, the Torah giant of the last generation,[35] advised couples to "find those few moments every day for talking to one another . . . Two people marry to share their lives. But to share your lives, it is first necessary to share your days."[36]

In Judaism, the husband is commanded to honor his wife more than himself and to love her as himself. The Rambam states that the wife should do the same.[37]

Week One, *chesed*, is designed to help husband and wife, parent and child, each member of the family, to determine the best formula for them individually as well as for the family unit as a whole. The lessons of this week alone, if properly analyzed and applied, can open up every mind, heart, and soul to an entirely new way of relating that will reap rewards for all concerned.

AVRAHAM, THE FIRST SHEPHERD

We can discern – from reading hundreds of truly astonishing Torah stories – how God went about teaching us the proper balance of *chesed*. Each story, each example, each lesson is tailored to teach us how *chesed* should be combined with other attributes, depending upon the ethical choices before us.

Avraham was unique and certainly merits being called "the first" of the Seven Shepherds. And he, more than anyone, repaired the deficiency in love. In a popular sixteenth century work of Mussar, *The Ways of the*

35. Avraham Yeshaya Karelitz (1878–1953) is popularly known by the name of his magnum opus, *Chazon Ish*.

36. Yissocher Frand (with Yonason Rosenblum), *Rabbi Yissocher Frand in Print* (Brooklyn, NY: Mesorah Publications, 1995), 93.

37. Rambam, *Hilchot Ishut*.

Righteous (*Orchot Tzaddikim*), the author writes under "The Gate of Love" that:

> [One] who serves out of love occupies himself with Torah and *mitzvot* and walks in the paths of wisdom for no worldly reward whatsoever, nor from fear of evil or expectation of good, but he pursues the truth because it is true, the good coming in its wake. This quality is an extremely exalted one, which not every sage can attain. It is the quality of Avraham our father, whom the Holy One Blessed be He called "my friend" (Yeshayahu 41:8), for he served only out of love.[38]

It is said that Avraham had no cruelty, jealousy, or hatred in his character. Look at how he treated his nephew Lot, despite Lot's many deficiencies. Look at how he converted Eliezer, whom the Midrash describes as none other than Og, into a servant of God, and then how, upon his death, Eliezer returned to his evil ways when no longer anchored to the *middot* of his master.[39] Look at how Avraham rushed to greet and host three strangers even though it was the third and most painful day after his circumcision at age 99.

Indeed, the three identifying marks of his descendants, the Jewish people, are that they are merciful, bashful, and do acts of kindness – just like Avraham.[40]

The Torah and the Midrash are full of stories about the endless *chesed* of Avraham. He loved humankind, and he loved God with a full heart, and God loved him back, as He Himself said:

> For I have loved him, because he commands his children and his household after him that they keep the way of God, doing charity and justice . . .[41]

Despite this, God tested Avraham – each test perfectly tailored to help him balance his naturally dominant trait of *chesed* with more *gevurah*

---

38. *The Ways of the Righteous* (*Orchot Tzaddikim*), The Gate of Love (Jerusalem: Feldheim, 1995), 127.

39. *Yalkut Shimoni*, *Chukat* 765; *Pirkei d'Rabbi Eliezer* 16.

40. *Yevamot* 79a.

41. *Bereshit* 18:19.

(restraint), as when he had to keep silent when Sarah sent Hagar and Ishmael away, or when he had to offer his beloved Yitzchak in the *Akeidah*.

"HERE I AM"

Rebbetzin Esther Jungreis, the indefatigable and dynamic founder of Hineni, describes the final test of Avraham in her excellent work, *Life Is a Test*, applying it to our tests as well:

> If it is to be truly a test, it must hit you where you feel most challenged, where it really hurts. If you can pass such a test, you will have proven that you are truly in charge of your life, capable of fulfilling the higher purpose for which you were created.[42]

She notes that it would be an ordeal for any parent to offer up their child as a sacrifice, but for Avraham, who was the epitome of *chesed* and who had also spent sixty-three years telling the world that God did not want human sacrifice, it was the ultimate test.

When Avraham took up the knife to slaughter Yitzchak, the angel of God called to him twice, "Avraham! Avraham!" And he answered, "Here I am (*Hineni*)."[43] From this Rebbetzin Jungreis drives another message about our tests and missions:

> Our Sages teach that the repetition of Avraham's name was both an expression of love, but also confirmation that Avraham had fulfilled his mission, that the two Avrahams, the one here on earth and the one whose portrait hangs in the Heavenly Gallery, were not only in perfect harmony, but were one and the same. The most terrifying pain, the most hellish experience, is to arrive at the Heavenly Court and behold God's portrait of you – to see what you were meant to be, and contrast that with what you actually became.[44]

We, too, are being asked to stand ready to say "Here I am" with each test God delivers our way. These tests come as a *chesed* from Him so that we

---

42. Esther Jungreis, *Life Is a Test*, (Brooklyn, NY: Shaar Press), 28–29.
43. *Bereshit* 22:11.
44. Jungreis, *Life Is a Test*, 29.

can improve our character and succeed in fulfilling our unique personal mission. We may resent them bitterly at the time they come our way, or even for many years later, but all are ultimately for our good.

CUSTOM-DESIGNED TESTS

Of course, we are not at the level of Avraham, and this is why we are given different tests. But each test is exactly what is required to balance our naturally dominant attributes and tendencies. Our challenges – and there are bound to be some very difficult ones – are intended to help us learn how best to actualize our true potential.

We are not likely to be asked to bind one of our children on an altar, but we may be tested to see if we are going to give sufficient independence to our children as they grow up and not smother their individuality. We are not likely to be asked to send our maidservant and her son away, but we may be tested to see if and how we choose to keep harmful people or influences away from our children.

We will certainly be tested in small areas of *chesed* every day. Will we greet others, including strangers, with a smile or will we react with apathy and indifference? Will we be short-tempered or impatient with the long line at the checkout counter, or with a co-worker, or with our child who is getting dressed far too slowly to make it to school on time? As Rebbetzin Jungreis writes:

> God places us in situations and relationships in which we are provoked and tempted. It's all part of our test. If you are easily given to losing your temper, you may discover that there is someone in your life who is always pushing your buttons, be it a spouse, a child, a neighbor, or even a stranger. Be aware that this is no coincidence. These situations and people have been placed in your path so that you might master your emotions. Just as you are custom-made, so too are your tests uniquely designed by God to challenge you.[45]

The tests mentioned above are likely to be the smaller, less consequential tests, easy to pass with flying colors. Others will be more difficult. Ultimately, if we ever feel defeated by a painful challenge in our lives, we

45. Ibid., p. 28.

must keep in mind that we should never give up, not as long as we have life. Whether it's a lesson to learn, or an insight to apply, or a tragedy to overcome, the gift of our life itself is a *chesed*, and we are meant to live it until our dying breath.

Consider Rebbetzin Eva Sandler of Toulouse, France, whose husband, Rabbi Yonatan Sandler and their two sons, Aryeh and Gavriel, were murdered in cold-blood by an Islamic terrorist in March 2012. Accepting an invitation from Chief Rabbi Warren Goldstein of South Africa, she spoke at the Sinai Indaba Convention later that summer to affirm her "determination and commitment to continue to promote Torah values in the world so that the terrorists who attacked these values will not be granted victory . . . to continue the mission of teaching Torah values and bringing a message of faith and loyalty to God."[46]

God wants each of us to grow, to mature, to thrive, and succeed in the mission He designed for us to complete in our lifetime. And this is why every new day is filled with tests.

Such tests may open the door for us to humble our conceit, thus bringing closer the reality of *malchut*, a "Balanced to Win" state of being. Humbling events may occur that ultimately force us to curb the arrogant belief that we have all the answers or that somehow we are wiser than others. Through such tests, we come to realize that it is actually wise to be considerate and show appropriate loving-kindness to others – to our spouses, children, subordinates, students, clients, family, and peers.

Reading in the Torah how our ancestors worked through their issues and improved themselves gives us the inspiration to do likewise. Their lives were nothing short of miraculous, just as ours are. Let's learn together how to pass our tests by activating the attribute of *chesed* and relating to everyone with loving-kindness, including God, for this is how we grow close to Him, and this is how we ensure He will hopefully respond in kind.

We learn in *The Palm Tree of Devorah* (*Tomer Devorah*), written by the great sixteenth century Kabbalist, Rabbi Moshe Cordovero, that "when a person cleaves to his Creator in total love from the depths of his heart and

46. Warren Goldstein, "Message of Strength and Faith," *The Jerusalem Post Magazine*, June 29, 2012.

soul, the Holy One, Blessed be He, showers him with love, kindness, and benevolence."[47]

From this, an honest self-introspection might reveal that if we don't experience enough loving-kindness in our lives that imbalance may be the result of our own inability to cleave to God. We may be blocked. We may feel distant. We may feel unworthy. Whatever the source, it is good to know that God is always with us, and all we have to do is reach out to Him. Doing so will open up the flow of *chesed* into our lives. We will experience ourselves and everyone we love as more open and giving.

It is a matter of choice. While God does only good, humankind is free to choose both "good" and "evil," both "right" and "wrong." And yet, out of the goodness of God's enduring kindness comes *teshuvah* – the ability to undo our mistaken choices. When we ignore the path of Torah, God gives us many opportunities to return to the path from which we have strayed. Some of these opportunities arise from experiencing difficult challenges and learning from life's many tests, which can range from minor disappointments to painful losses. Major tests require our heartfelt prayers, genuine soul-searching, and persistent effort to change ourselves in order to restore a loving relationship with God.

Each test should be recognized for what it is – a "wake up call" sent directly from God, our Father in Heaven. Just like good parents will provide some form of warning before they turn a child out of their home, God does so as well. This is all part of the intricate system of *teshuvah*, which in itself is a gift of *chesed*.

SEVEN DAYS TO BALANCE THE TRAIT OF *CHESED*

The task before us in Week One is to emulate God in our deeds of *chesed* and incorporate elements of each of the other *sefirot* in their proper balance to achieve the optimal expression of the *chesed* attribute.

To that end, all this week, we will examine the attribute of *chesed* and how it intersects with itself, with *gevurah* (strength/discipline), with *tiferet* (harmony/truth), *netzach* (endurance), *hod* (humility), *yesod* (bonding), and *malchut* (leadership/nobility). By the end of seven days, we should have at least identified our current level of *chesed* and the level we aspire to

47. Moshe Cordovero, *The Palm Tree of Devorah (Tomer Devorah)*, (Jerusalem: Targum/Feldheim, 1993), ix.

achieve in balance with the other dimensions. We should have identified any combinations that require adjustment. And we should have created a plan, outlining what action we intend to take to bringing about the desired change.

As we follow this *Journey Together*, we will repeat this pattern with each of the subsequent *sefirot*, week by week. If we apply ourselves, we should experience a snowball effect. And we should expect significant personal change. Then, whatever spiritual work we do throughout the rest of the year will reinforce the gains of each cycle.

I would like to end this overview of Week One: *Chesed* with a message of profound importance beautifully penned by Rebbetzin Jungreis at the close of *Life Is a Test*:

> There are no barriers between ourselves and God. There is no act or deed that could consign us to doom. The only wall that exists between ourselves and our "sweet Father" is the one that we ourselves build in our hearts and minds. If we will it, each and every one of us has the ability to make a difference in our personal and in our national destiny. We need only call out to God and He will walk us through all our tests, from the most trivial to the most difficult. So never despair – never give up. Be assured that God knows you better than you know yourself, and He will never challenge you with tests that are beyond you.[48]

If we keep this message in mind with each day of the Omer count, it will help us succeed in taking advantage of this awesome, God-given opportunity for insight, growth, and becoming "Balanced to Win."

---

48. Jungreis, *Life Is a Test*, 270–80.

היום יום אחד לעומר

(Ha'yom yom echad la'Omer)

"TODAY IS THE FIRST DAY OF THE OMER."

DAY 1

Chesed sh'b'Chesed (Loving-kindness within Loving-kindness)

***Chesed* within *chesed* is love in its pure form. It includes giving, receiving, and expressing loving-kindness in all relationships – with ourselves, with others, and with God.**

Every human is created in the image of God (*b'tzelem Elokim*) and, therefore, every human being has the capacity to demonstrate and express love. That said, we all know people who are either unaware of their capacity to express love (in their thoughts, speech, and actions) or who don't exert the effort to love another, or, who don't even love themselves. Many of those who are unable to experience and/or express the essence of affection and loving-kindness are usually alienated from God.

For Day 1 of the Omer count, our task is to examine how we give, receive and express love in relationships with ourselves, with others, and with God.

While millions of books have been written about love, almost all of them acknowledge two important, interlocking truisms: The first is that love inspires us to give. The second is that love grows from acts of giving on the part of both the giver and the receiver. As stated by Rabbi Shalom Arush, the dean of the Chut Shel Chesed Yeshiva in Jerusalem and a best-selling author: "Unconditional giving arouses emotion that only grows and develops in both the giver and in the recipient . . . Therefore, if you want more love, start giving right away!"[49]

What follows are some amazing examples of people who have given to others in truly inspiring ways.

NADAV BEN-YEHUDA'S EXTRAORDINARY ACT OF *CHESED*

In 2012, 24-year-old Israeli mountain climber, Nadav Ben-Yehuda, was climbing Mt. Everest and was nearing the summit. It was a culmination of years of training, self-discipline, and indescribably demanding work. He was about to triumph. And yet, in order to save the life of a fellow climber – a Turkish Muslim, by the way – Ben-Yehuda turned back, just as he was about to reach his goal. He selflessly carried the climber back down the mountain, foregoing his ascent to the top.

In response to a moving article in *The Jerusalem Post Magazine*, "A Personal Triumph," that described Ben-Yehuda's heroism, numerous readers were compelled to write Letters to the Editor. Unanimously, they were touched by what some called "pure *chesed*" on the part of Nadav Ben-Yehuda. Consider the letter from Yitzchak Ben-Shmuel who wrote: "Perhaps in these days of intense trepidation, we can still be moved by acts of holiness and love, and thereby redeem both ourselves and mankind before it is too late."[50]

Pure *chesed* applied towards worthy causes is all around us. Let's look for it and applaud it whenever we can. Let's teach it to our children. Let's never overlook an opportunity to contribute and never take for granted the efforts of others to help us.

YOSEF GITLER AND THE LEKET FOOD BANK

I am repeatedly inspired by the stories shared by journalist Barbara Sofer, whose regular feature in *The Jerusalem Post Magazine* is called "The Human Spirit." Indeed, she never fails to capture an aspect of the indomitable human ethos that reflects the *tzelem Elokim* within us.

---

49. Shalom Arush, *Women's Wisdom* (Jerusalem: Chut Shel Chessed Institutions, 2010), 51.

50. Letters to the Editor, *The Jerusalem Post Magazine*, June 15, 2012, 6.

In one such story, she tells about Yosef Gitler, a North American-born attorney who made *aliyah* and founded an organization first called Table to Table and later Leket. Gitler was disturbed by the vast quantities of food wasted in dining halls, restaurants, and bakeries, while so many in Israel went hungry. And he went to work. Barbara Sofer relates:

> [Over ten years he has turned] a simple food resource idea into the National Food Bank, centralizing donations and providing meals to thousands of needy people every day . . . Every day Leket provides 7,000 sandwiches for hungry children, more than a million a year . . . If the food provided by Leket's volunteer field near Rehovot has fruit and vegetables available to be tucked in as well, there might be an apple or a whole tomato. In Natanya . . . the sandwich-makers are mostly Holocaust survivors.[51]

All the people who participate in this effort – from Gitler to the sandwich-makers – are displaying *chesed* within *chesed*, while fulfilling a vital Torah commandment. "Leket is a biblical idea," Sofer notes, "a key concept in Jewish values." She goes on to explain:

> We are commanded in Deuteronomy that the sheaves that fall shouldn't be gathered. This provides food for the poor who come to glean the remains and educates us to curb our innate selfishness . . . Rabbi Yisrael Salanter taught that a pious person is not one who worries about his fellow's soul and his own stomach; a pious person worries about his own soul and his fellow's stomach.[52]

HOSPITALITY TO GUESTS

Surely the mitzvah of hospitality to guests (*hachnasat orchim*) – the mitzvah that made Avraham and Sarah famous – demands that we practice *chesed*. But as Rabbi Joseph B. Soloveitchik points out, this mitzvah can be inspired by either genuine kindness or simply by good manners and courtesy.

---

51. Barbara Sofer, "A Roll This Side of Heaven," *The Jerusalem Post Magazine*, December 24, 2010, 12.
52. Ibid.

Rabbi Soloveitchik contrasts these two motivations in his monumental book, *Abraham's Journey*, which movingly describes the very first Jew and God's special friend. He points out that the kind person has unlimited patience and tolerance to help the needy over years and years, even helping people who are "vulgar and coarse." Such a person even "takes abuse," and "nothing can alienate him from the person in need." In contrast, a polite person has limited patience and will harshly reject any pleas for help that appear illogical or exaggerated.[53]

As revealed in Torah commentaries, Avraham and Sarah welcomed everyone regardless of how poor, uneducated or unkempt they were. Such *chesed* enabled them to fulfill their mission of introducing humankind to the belief in one God.

Rabbi Soloveitchik asks why Avraham's *hachnasat orchim* is emphasized so much in the Torah, where Avraham is described as running to greet, bow, serve, cleanse, water, feed, and entertain three strangers who happened upon his tent on the painful third day after his circumcision at age 99. Rabbi Soloveitchik also asks how hospitality to guests is different from *tzedakah*. He answers that hospitality to guests "is symbolic of our personal relationships," and that is why the Torah takes the time to paint this picture of Abraham in order to supply us with a vivid model:

> [When one gives charity,] it demonstrates sympathy, but not a philosophy of human equality . . . It is much easier to give someone money and send him away than to invite him under your own roof. If I invite him in, that means that no matter what his station in life, I am treating him with respect, as an equal.[54]

If we give to others, but think we are superior to them at the same time, we have failed to achieve this level of altruistic behavior. Avraham did not fail – he excelled.

---

53. Joseph B. Soloveitchik, *Abraham's Journey* (NY: Toras HoRav Foundation, 2008), 169–195.

54. Ibid., 169.

THE EXAMPLE OF RACHEL

Another Torah example of *chesed* within *chesed* is embodied by Rachel, the beloved of Yaakov who worked seven years for her demanding father, Lavan, in order to earn her hand in marriage. Meanwhile, Lavan schemed to switch the bride on the wedding night, and substitute Leah, Rachel's older sister.

Learning of her father's plot, what did this young girl do, even though she wanted nothing more than to marry her true love?

She responded with pure *chesed*. The Talmud tells us that Rachel gave her sister the "signals" that she and Yaakov had devised. She did this in order to spare her sister any embarrassment. She knew with certainty that her father intended to make the switch, and she acted with pure *chesed* to preserve her sister's dignity. Believing that, in so doing, she was giving up her love, Rachel was still willing to make this sacrifice to ensure that her sister would come to no shame. She could not know that Yaakov would be willing to work another seven years in order to marry her as well.[55]

How many of us would be able to do something like that?

I am fairly certain that I would not have been capable of such pure *chesed*. But I am also fairly certain that I can learn from Rachel and rise to the occasion when a critical moment arrives demanding something selfless of me. And we all can.

For example, there are times when we, as parents, act selflessly for the benefit of our children, even if they may have disappointed us tremendously. Parents and siblings have donated one of their kidneys to save another's life. Soldiers have sacrificed their lives in order to save their comrades in arms or innocent civilians.

These are acts of pure *chesed*, and I marvel at them. Words cannot describe the selflessness of these acts.

It was only because of her act of pure *chesed* that Rachel's appeal to God to show mercy to the Jewish people was answered. The appeals of Avraham, Yitzchak, and Yaakov at that time were not compelling, because the sins of Israel during the period of the First Temple were damning. Only Rachel's simple argument won the day. She pointed out to God that if she could do what she did and not be jealous of her sister, then surely

55. *Bereshit* 29:16–26; *Bava Batra* 123a.

God could have mercy on the wayward Jewish people and not be jealous of their worship of false gods. The Midrash relates:

> "I performed an act of kindness for her [Leah], was not jealous of her and did not expose her to shame. I, who am flesh and blood, dust and ashes, was not jealous of my rival and did not expose her to shame. You, O Eternal, Merciful King – why were You jealous of idolatry, which has no substance? Why did You exile my children and let their enemies slaughter them and do with them as they pleased?"
>
> [At this,] the compassion of the Holy One, Blessed be He, was aroused and He said, "For Rachel, I will return the people of Israel to their place."[56]

THE *CHESED* OF MARRIAGE

Rabbi Dr. Akiva Tatz, who is both a physician and accomplished teacher, explains that when husband and wife both approach their relationship as an experience of pure giving, the marriage will succeed and flourish. In contrast, when they each expect reciprocity, the outcome is marital strife. Rabbi Tatz states categorically: "Marriage is the main learning experience in the area of giving and taking. It is here, perhaps more than anywhere else, that being a giver is all-important."[57]

Rabbi Tatz goes on to say that beyond marriage, in any relationship, the same principle applies:

> When everyone is giving, everyone receives. A society which focuses on rights is a society which develops takers. A society which focuses on obligations develops givers . . . The great secret of political and social stability is that the individuals within a system must be givers. The Torah insists on this; a child raised in a Torah environment is a child who is trained to be conscious of his obligations. Such a member of society can be relied upon, even when no-one is watching . . .
>
> Taking is related to the present – when I take, I have what I want now. Giving is an investment in the future – when I give, apart from

56. *Pesikta Eichah Rabbati* 24.

57. Akiva Tatz, *The Thinking Jewish Teenager's Guide to Life* (Southfield, MI: Targum/Feldheim, 1999), 98–99.

> the pleasure of giving, I may not see the effects for a long time; in fact, all I may experience now is the sacrifice of that which I am giving away.
>
> A Jewish life is invested in the future; that is the meaning of *emunah*, faith. I do what I must because it is correct, because I am obliged; I am not looking for an immediate result. The focus on giving and obligation is a focus on another time and another world. Just as the farmer plants seeds and tends them while the crop is yet a season distant, so too, the person of *emunah* plants in this world and knows that in another time and another season the fruits will result. This is the path of maturity . . .[58]

So on Day 1, the day of *chesed* within *chesed*, our most important task is to honestly examine where we stand on the continuum of "giving" versus "taking." The scope of what we choose to give can be tangible or intangible, or both.

TANGIBLE AND INTANGIBLE GIVING

Beyond a gift, there are many other ways to give through profoundly meaningful deeds that have a long-lasting impact: making telephone calls to say "I love you," or "I remember you," or "I care about how you feel"; cooking a meal for someone unable to do so for himself or herself; helping with chores or errands; listening; reading aloud to a blind person or a child; taking someone lonely for a walk around the block in fresh air.

Children can express love by creating art projects or writing letters that express their love for their parents, siblings, or grandparents. A framed photograph of a child blowing out birthday candles becomes an ever-present reminder of love and shared memories. So many memories captured by a camera's lens have been lost in these days of e-mail when digital photography gets either deleted, or stored on a disc or in a computer without being printed and framed. Good reason to restore letter writing and photos to their rightful place as an expression of love and preserver of memories.

Intangible giving is captured with a smile, eye contact, a loving hug, or a gentle touch on the shoulder. How many of us have felt the glow from

58. Ibid., 100–104.

a warm greeting, or an expression of appreciation, or words of praise for worthy actions, or a demonstration of loyalty? Why not return this intangible gift that we so much like to receive? When pitched an intangible gift, why not swing the bat to hit a home run that repays these *chesed* overtures a hundred times over?

We do so when we provide emotional support to someone during a difficult time. Intangible gifts cost nothing, but leave both the giver and receiver richer as a result of the *chesed* interchange that brought the two together.

People of all ages can learn to exercise their "giving" muscles in a variety of ways, none of which cost anything, but for time and desire to make someone else feel good.

For the very best example of giving, we need to look no further than the giving of Torah at Mount Sinai by God. It was freely offered. It did not cost anything to buy it. And yet it was – and is – priceless. To be given a guidebook to help us lead worthy and meaningful lives, to be named partners of God in the redemption of the world, was simply the most quintessentially important gift a human being could ever be blessed to receive.

What do we learn from this event about how to give?

Gifts do not need to be expensive or cost anything at all, but they need to have inherent value. The gift of time is as important as anything tangible. God spent forty days with Moshe communicating directly with him, transmitting both the Written and Oral Law so that Moshe would then be able to convey it to all of Israel.

That gift still keeps giving today with millions learning Torah more than 3,300 years later.

VOLUNTEERING

Almost one-third of all Israelis volunteer for one cause or another, participating in 24,000 organizations. Although statistics for Jewish volunteerism outside of Israel are hard to come by, it is known that this type of giving appeals to the Jewish heart.

When one volunteers, without pay, to help another person, what an act of *chesed* within *chesed* it is! In virtually all cases, the beneficiary is a complete stranger. Consider just a few examples of how individual Jews and Jewish communities have elected to give to others:

- The Jerusalem Hills Therapeutic Center in Moshav Neve Ilan is a residential village for about 100 children who have been victims of emotional, physical or sexual abuse. For many, it is the "last stop" after unsuccessful experiments with family foster care or other group homes. The Center, while a safe haven, is nevertheless an institution which cannot replace the love of a nuclear family. But a giving and visionary group of neighborhood residents decided to find a way to make it less so. Learning that about 20 percent of the children at the Center have no families who visit them, the residents of Neve Ilan decided to collectively "adopt" these children. Armin Grunewald, manager of the Neve Ilan Hotel, started by helping provide kosher meals at Pesach. This expanded to inviting the children for a day of fun that included a swim and a movie. Others pitched in. One Neve Ilan mother says she volunteers at the Center to teach her own children to appreciate what they have. And moshav children fund-raise for Jerusalem Hills.[59]
- Yachad, an exemplary agency of the Orthodox Union, was founded in 1983 with a clear goal – to address the needs of all individuals with disabilities and include them in the Jewish community. Whether through vocational services, elementary and upper schools, family Shabbatons, sensitivity training, Team Yachad races, summer programs, or Yachad Birthright Israel trips, the organization has engaged 40,000 participants in one year (2011–2012) of operation. For example, ninety racers aged 13 to 71 raised more than $50,000 for Yachad by participating on Team Yachad in the Jerusalem Marathon in 2012. And the 135 runners for Team Yachad in Miami's 2012 Marathon and Half-Marathon raised more than $400,000, with fourteen Yachad "members" completing the race themselves.[60]
- American Friends of MADA (Magen David Adom, the equivalent of the Red Cross in Israel) proudly shows off a photograph of two 16-year-old MADA volunteers who delivered "Yocheved's twins" inside of the ambulance. The smiles on the face of these two young men, as they gaze at the babies they had just delivered, are indescribable.

59. Ruth Eglash, "It Takes a Village," *The Jerusalem Post Magazine*, February 10, 2012, 10–11.
60. *Belong: The Yachad Magazine*, 2012, a supplement to *Jewish Action*.

- Aleh is an organization with a mission to provide a high level of medical and rehabilitative care and live-in facilities for 650 children with severe physical and cognitive disabilities in four locations across Israel. The organization is heavily dependent on volunteers such as Susie Engel, who came to Israel from Australia twenty years ago and became involved with Aleh after learning about a toddler who suffered severe brain damage in an accident in his home. Susie and more than a dozen other women organize major events – such as galas and concerts – to raise money for Aleh, which makes up 30 percent of its budget from private donations. Another special volunteer at Aleh is Curtis Sparks, a Christian from Alaska, who comes to Israel for one month every summer to spend time with the children living in Aleh's facility in Jerusalem. In turn, the parents' auxiliary for each Aleh location hosts barbeques and gives holiday gifts to Aleh volunteers and staff. Alon Chasid, the head of the organization's Jerusalem parents' auxiliary, summed up what these volunteer efforts mean to him: "I don't have the ability to give my child what he needs . . . but I can help the staffers give their best to my child . . . I couldn't imagine what life would be like without this place."[61]

If encouraged by their parents, children can understand from an early age that giving to others is a value to be cherished. Once inculcated in young people, it becomes a trait that they carry with them into adulthood. This is *chesed* within *chesed.*

61. Josh Hasten, "A Second Home," *The Jerusalem Post Magazine,* June 29, 2012, 18.

DISCUSSION TOPICS FOR *CHESED* WITHIN *CHESED*

The following questions/suggestions are meant to be used by adults as well as children to trigger the process of self-introspection and stimulate family discussion.

For adults

1. Ask yourself: Am I more of a "giver" or "taker"? (If you answer "giver," describe using specific examples the way you give to others. If you answer "taker," describe using specific examples the way you take from others.)
2. Do I express the love I feel for others, or do I keep it bottled up inside, all the while assuming they know how I feel? Am I responsive when others give of their love to me? If so, how do I respond and reciprocate?
3. Do I violate the personal boundaries of others, and do others violate my boundaries? If I want to change this, what specific actions do I need to initiate?

For children

1. How do I show kindness to my parents, sisters, and brothers? What else can I do to show even more kindness?
2. How do I express appreciation to God, my parents, sisters and brothers, grandparents, teachers and friends, when they do something nice for me?
3. Do I share my time? My things? My friendship? Or, do I mainly think about myself? Can I think of specific examples of how I can improve in this area?

היום שני ימים לעומר

(Ha'yom shnei yamim la'Omer)

"Today is the second day of the Omer."

Day 2

Gevurah sh'b'Chesed
(Strength/Discipline within Loving-kindness)

***Gevurah* within *chesed* recognizes that, for optimal health and growth, there must be times when love is restrained by discipline.**

Healthy love requires respect for those you love. Respect for their boundaries. Respect for their mission. Respect for their thoughts and feelings. Respect for their individuality. Too much love given by a parent to a child smothers and suffocates. Too much love given by one person to many people can lead to an inability to commit, or even infidelity. An overly-developed expression of love – without the self-restraint of *gevurah* – can lead to an unhealthy love which lacks consideration for the ones we claim to love.

Gevurah focuses and directs our love in proper proportions and directions for the mutual benefit and betterment of all.

CHESED NEEDS *GEVURAH* FOR BALANCE

God first created Adam and Chava as one being, but later separated them and created Chava to be an *ezer kenegdo* to Adam. *Ezer kenegdo* literally means "a helpmate opposite of him,"[62] implying equality and a face-to-face stance. From this we learn that there must be a degree of honor and respect for the other. This is where *gevurah* (discipline/restraint) comes in to refine the expression of pure *chesed*.

When *chesed* is undisciplined, tragedy can result. For example: A husband can conclude that he does not have to be loyal to his wife. A mother can spoil her children in the name of love, allowing them to believe they can engage in negative or addictive behavior without any consequences. A grandparent can suffocate an adult grandchild with too many intrusive telephone calls or too many unwanted opinions.

We all know how – in our unbounded goodness – we can and sometimes do shower money and other generosities (*chesed*) so freely on young children that they do not learn to distinguish between what they want and what they need. We have all been guilty of this, and the Omer counting process helps us discover how to check this abuse. Our Sages ask, "Who is rich?" and answer, "He who is happy with his lot."[63] Children learn this lesson when the love they receive is restrained by *gevurah*.

In the last third of the twentieth century and accelerating into the twentieth-first century, as affluence and television advertising increased, "keeping up with the neighbors" became a phenomenon mimicked by parents to the detriment of their children. Children learn to imitate what they see around them, including their parents' actions. If what they see is unbridled indulgence, and selfish and envious behavior, they will grow up to be adults who behave likewise.

In an article in *Jewish Action*, the magazine of the Orthodox Union, entitled "Are Too Many Toys Bad for Our Children?" – author Jack Botwinik reminds us that it is our responsibility as parents to educate our children:

> Reducing the amount of toys in our homes can have certain benefits: it can force our children to be more creative and resourceful, causing them to play outdoors more and experience nature; and – depending on the kinds of toys that are eliminated – it can help increase their attention spans. Perhaps most importantly, limiting the amount of toys helps convey the important message that material possessions

62. *Bereshit* 2:18.
63. *Pirkei Avot* 4:1.

> don't buy happiness. Having too many playthings clutters not only the house, but also the spirit.[64]

What Botwinik is describing is a perfect example of how parents with wisdom and forethought can apply *gevurah* to *chesed.*

Ramban in his Torah commentary wrote that we become holy by limiting even those things we are permitted to enjoy. The Torah restricts the number of horses that a Jewish king may own and admonishes him not to "greatly increase silver and gold for himself."[65] If a Jewish king was limited in acquiring only that which was needed for public service, the army or for personal use, then what about us?

RECOVERING FROM ADDICTIONS REQUIRES *GEVURAH*

Rabbi Dr. Abraham Twerski, the founder of the Gateway Rehabilitation Clinic who has helped more than 40,000 addicts recover from their addiction, uses the metaphor of "herd instinct" to explain the sometimes dangerous effects of peer pressure. He points out that the herd instinct helps animals band together either for defensive or offensive purposes. This is why a child can lead a herd of sheep, goats, cows, and the like. In a herd, each animal does what the others do.

As for human beings, if they need to be united to defend themselves or to fight an evil enemy, then herding is useful. But, when the herd phenomenon displaces individual judgment, it can be most destructive. Says Rabbi Twerski:

> Many young people have entered into the lethal cycle of addiction as a result of peer pressure, surrendering their judgment to the group . . . [But] the message of the scriptural story of Noah is precisely that one individual may be virtuous in defiance of the corrupt values of his entire culture . . .
>
> Moral and ethical values should be established in the home, and this is primarily a parental responsibility. If one fails to exercise one's inalienable right to establish spiritual standards of right and wrong

64. Jack Botwinik, "Are Too Many Toys Bad for Our Children?" *Jewish Action*, Winter 2011, 80.
65. *Devarim* 17:16–17.

> independent of public opinion, one should not be surprised if one's children succumb to peer pressure and use drugs because "everyone else is doing it." Preaching values will have no impact. Living according to one's principles and sacrificing for one's beliefs and principles is the only hope of providing children with the necessary fortitude to resist peer pressure.[66]

Our work as parents then – through our prayers and consistent efforts, and most of all, through our example – is to ensure that our children have healthy self-esteem and are thinking clearly, so that they can resist dangerous peer pressure. This requires coupling *gevurah* with *chesed* as best we can.

But if, God forbid, either we or someone we love is already addicted to something harmful, what are we to do? It's important to understand this undisputed truism – only the addict can begin the process of recovering from his addiction, a process that starts when the addict displays *gevurah* within *chesed*. Those who live around an addict need to also display *gevurah* within *chesed* by not making excuses or becoming enablers for the addict, which simply allows him to continue upon his self-destructive path.

We may want to think of addictions as isolated problems, but the national statistics in the United States are horrifying. The Centers for Disease Control and Prevention report that heavy drinking is the third leading cause of preventable death, following smoking and the combination of lack of exercise and bad eating habits. According to the National Center on Addiction and Substance Abuse at Columbia University, 34 percent of Americans age 12 and older are either addicted to alcohol or indulge in what is considered to be "risky drinking" by public health officials. And what about other harmful addictions? The World Health Organization reports that, in 2011, a billion people worldwide smoked tobacco and 80 percent of them lived in the poorer regions of the world. Up to half of these smokers will eventually die from some tobacco-related disease. As well, 10 percent of those who will die each year will be non-smokers who were exposed to secondhand smoke. Non-smokers who live around smokers should consistently display enough *gevurah* within *chesed* to forbid smokers to ever smoke around them or their children.

---

66. Abraham J. Twerski, *I'd Like to Call for Help . . . But I Don't Know the Number* (NY: Pharos Books, 1991), 109–111.

And then there are new addictions. In particular, I am speaking here about the non-stop electronic overload, internet gaming, texting, and the like. And religious Jews, who eschew all electric and electronic devices on Shabbat, are not immune. They face a distinctive crisis which has come to be known as "Half Shabbat." This term describes a practice among some Orthodox youth who violate the sanctity of the day because they cannot refrain from sending text messages to friends on Shabbat. What brought this about?

Rabbi Stewart Weiss, director of the Jewish Outreach Center of Ra'anana, offers some keen insight with emphasis on the conflict between restraint and permissiveness resulting from free-wheeling love. He writes:

> [Today] . . . there is the syndrome of extreme entitlement, whereby all restraints are rejected and all limits are lost. Tradition is fine, but not when it gets in my way; I want what I want when I want it, and no one can tell me otherwise. Instant gratification – once reserved for infants and toddlers – has been encouraged for far too long . . . Controlling our passions and proclivities is an essential part of growing up, and it is precisely that kind of discipline that defines our Torah and spiritual lifestyle.[67]

Importantly, Rabbi Weiss notes:

> . . . we parents, must be intellectually honest and completely consistent . . . If *we* fudge on our *own* religious integrity, if we bend the rules when it suits us, why shouldn't they? More than one dad has become addicted to his "Crack-Berry," ignoring his family every time the phone rings or an e-mail arrives . . . And what is Shabbat, if not a way to remind us to be more than collectors of material things, more than slaves to commerce and competition? Patiently but firmly, these ideas must be broached and explored. Parents . . . must still be parents, and we cannot abdicate our obligations to our children. Timid as we may sometimes be about confronting our kids, they still value our words and consistently vote us as their favorite heroes.[68]

---

67. Stewart Weiss, "Shabbat – The Day to Text?" *The Jerusalem Post Magazine*, July 8, 2011, 38.
68. Ibid.

There is no question that for *chesed* to be healthy, it must be balanced with thoughtful and wise *gevurah*, which is the essence of the second day of the Omer count.

WISE ADVICE FROM A MASTER EDUCATOR

In one of the best essays I have ever read on early childhood education, Rabbi Samson Raphael Hirsch reminds parents of two essential facts. First, that the very early years of a child's life are the preparatory state for that child's moral training, and second, that it is the parent, and not the school, who has the primary responsibility for moral education of their child. Indeed, Rabbi Hirsch believes that one must start moral education in the very first year of a child's life.

Rabbi Hirsch describes the benefit to every child and to every parent of this approach to early childhood education. He adds:

> If you follow intelligently these basic principles from the very first years of your child's life, he will grow accustomed at an early date to subordinate his likes and dislikes to a higher authority. He will, therefore, become adept, according to his age, at precisely that skill on which the success of his training in the art of morality so crucially depends. If you will do this, then your child's intelligence and his emotions will develop under your hands in the spirit of serenity and joy . . .
>
> Our children can learn to walk and talk only by seeing us walk and talk. How else, then, should they be able to learn from us patience, equanimity, gentleness, sincerity, honesty, moderation, humility, justice, and loving-kindness if not through our example?[69]

What else is there to say? His advice reflects Day 2 of the Omer count, *gevurah* within *chesed*. Knowing when to be strong and when to show restraint is how we maturely and thoughtfully express love for our children, and this requires us to fully apply basic educational principles in a consistent manner.

69. Samson Raphael Hirsch, "On the Role of Education in the First Years of a Child's Life" included in the *Collected Writings of Rabbi Samson Raphael Hirsh*, Vol. 7 (Jerusalem: Feldheim, 1997), 121–137.

What are these basic educational principles? First, Rabbi Hirsch advises us to train our children "from the very first year of his life" to obey all reasonable directions given by the parents. Second, he advises breaking our children "as early as possible" of the habit of staging temper tantrums or outbursts of impatience in order to get something that would not be healthy for them. Third, he instructs parents to train themselves to be able to endure their child's outbursts and tantrums, and he stresses:

> [Do not,] out of a selfish desire for some peace and quiet, grant [your child] a wish that you would otherwise deny him out of your unselfish love for him. Your child must learn to do whatever you tell him to do and, above all, he must never – even once would be too often – be allowed to think that if he torments and annoys you sufficiently, he can get you to permit what you originally forbade him.[70]

Rabbi Hirsch then adds the following brilliant insight:

> In view of the foregoing, be reasonable, circumspect, and sparing with your commands and prohibitions. Never give your child orders that are unnecessary or unimportant. Never forbid him anything that is not harmful to him and involves no wrongdoing. Think carefully before you issue a prohibition to your child. Permit him to do anything you can safely let him do without endangering his physical or moral welfare. Never let your moods of the moment influence you to permit or forbid your child anything. Do not tell him to do anything that you may permit him at some other time. These are the ABC's of moral training which you cannot begin to pursue too early with your child.[71]

Pretty simple, and yet how many of us have been able to consistently apply this fundamental advice?

70. Ibid., 132.
71. Ibid.

HEALTHY LOVE

Gevurah within *chesed* means knowing that – with those we love and the world around us – we must exercise the strength, restraint, and discipline when appropriate. Indeed, this is a more honest form of loving-kindness than pure *chesed.* Unfortunately, although there are countless examples of situations in our lives that require *gevurah* within *chesed,* we often fail to exercise this important *sefirah* combination. Here are some examples of what we do instead:

- We do our children's homework for them
- We call our spouse repeatedly while he/she is busy at work
- We call the boss of our addicted spouse to make excuses for him/her
- We procrastinate starting a necessary diet/exercise program
- We buy cigarettes/alcohol for our loved one who smokes/drinks
- We attempt to control the actions of those around us
- We micro-manage our subordinates
- We offer unwanted opinions when no one has asked us

Each one of us should make a list of the unhealthy practices and habits we have exhibited "in the name of love." Such a list is bound to make us aware of the damaging effects of these practices and what we need to change immediately. With practice and discipline, we can free ourselves from these harmful behaviors.

DISCUSSION TOPICS FOR *GEVURAH* WITHIN *CHESED*

For adults

1. Looking at how my children behave, what can I say about how my own behavior has impacted them? How should I alter what I am doing?
2. As I assess my children's ability to make wise and independent decisions on their own, are there any adjustments I should be making now in the way I relate to them?
3. Do I exhibit the proper amount of restraint in how I express love toward my family, friends, others?

For children

1. Do I remember to show appreciation and love to my parents, grandparents, brothers, sisters, and God, or do I keep it inside of me? How can I express my love and appreciation more completely?
2. Have I been spoiled by my parents/grandparents? If so, how has this affected my personality? What are the behaviors I want to change?
3. Do I choose friends who have a good influence on me? Have some people taken advantage of me? What changes should I make in my current friendships?

היום שלושה ימים לעומר

(Ha'yom shlosha yamim la'Omer)

"TODAY IS THE THIRD DAY OF THE OMER."

DAY 3

Tiferet sh'b'Chesed (Harmony/Truth within Loving-kindness)

***Tiferet* within *chesed* helps us to determine the proper balance in giving and receiving love. It teaches us how much love to give, to whom, when and where, and what type of love it is proper to give and receive in particular circumstances.**

On Day 1, we learned that daily acts of loving-kindness are vital to any human being who is focused on giving and not taking. On Day 2, we learned the importance of displaying some restraint in how we express love, so we don't smother others with overindulgence. On Day 3, *tiferet* within *chesed*, we discover how to harmonize the inherent tug between *chesed* and *gevurah* to achieve a healthy, balanced love.

God is our best model for achieving this balance. Indeed, how our individual life story plays out depends on the delicate balance with which God determines exactly how much, and in which moment, to manifest His *chesed* or His *gevurah* toward us as individuals, toward the Nation of Israel as a whole, and toward the world.

Each of us has faced complex challenges sent to us by God. During the ordeal, we may have wondered how we would survive and then, much to our surprise, we have discovered that the challenge actually made our lives better. For some of us, the outcome may even appear miraculous.

For example: A person who had learning disabilities as a child is inspired by that experience to seek a degree in special education in order to help children with similar challenges. That one individual's personal struggle goes on to provide a new perspective and to open new windows on treatment and interventions.

There are countless examples of those who lose their job, only to later find a better one, more suited to their talents; or those who leave an abusive marriage, only to find a spouse who is far kinder and who lovingly spurs them toward their optimal potential; or those who, after years of struggle, overcome an addiction and become a much stronger, wiser, well-adjusted, complete human being, capable of helping other addicts pave the way to an addiction-free life.

Our long lives can only be understood in retrospect. It is the totality of our experiences that tell our whole story.

MODERN-DAY STORIES OF *TIFERET* WITHIN *CHESED*

Nefesh B'Nefesh, founded in 2002 to simplify the process of making *aliyah* to Israel for North American Jews, celebrated its tenth anniversary with a collection of moving stories entitled "Israel Inspired" and issued as a supplement to *The Jerusalem Post*. I selected this one story from many amazing stories, because it appears that the family involved intuitively perceived that Divine Providence propelled them to move to Israel:

Herman and Mia Weiss, from West Hempstead, New York, always said they couldn't make *aliyah* because they had "too much stuff." But when their house burned down with all its contents, they took this as a strong message "to rethink where they were living and what they were doing with their lives." They moved to Israel in 2008 and found that "stuff" does not matter so much. Today Herman works as an OB-Gyn, and Mia has started a computer job placement company. The photograph of their family in 2012 includes a lot of beaming smiles.[72]

The Weiss's story reminds me of the story of Alan and Bonnie Cohen, formerly of Los Angeles and now of Jerusalem. In the early 1990s, the Cohens became interested in leading a Torah-observant life, which in turn led to their spending a great deal of time in Israel, although they continued

72. "Israel Inspired: Nefesh B'Nefesh Celebrates a Decade of Aliyah." Supplement to *The Jerusalem Post*, July 6, 2012, 31.

going back and forth to the U.S. for Alan's business. On one visit, as they were getting ready to return to Los Angeles, Bonnie convinced Alan to stay a while longer in Jerusalem. That very week, on the morning of January 17, 1994, they were stunned to learn that a major earthquake had devastated LA during the night and the epicenter was close to their neighborhood. A friend who surveyed the damage reported that while their whole street was hard hit, their home "took the prize." Their bedroom alone was a disaster area – a 350-pound track-lighting system had fallen on their bed, a large shattered mirror sliced through their pillows like a guillotine, and a heavy wardrobe fell on top of it all. Had Alan and Bonnie been asleep in Los Angeles at the time, they would have both been killed. Like the Weiss family, they understood these events as a message from God about a new direction their life should take. They ended up making *aliyah* and staying in Israel permanently.[73]

When God gives us such messages, it is His highest form of love for us. Let's learn to keep our eyes and ears open for them because they are constantly coming at us, albeit in much subtler form than fires and earthquakes.

The Weiss's based their excuses for not moving to Israel to the quantity of their possessions. Well, a fire got rid of all that, but did not harm them at all. They connected the dots, read the implied message from God, and moved forward. Today they live where they want to live, connected to the Land and their dreams. As with the Weiss family, God rewarded the Cohens with a new life in Jerusalem and with continued success in Alan's business (albeit from a distance) with a partner on site in the US.

There is the "hidden" and the "revealed" in all of life. The key is to recognize all the signs and try to read them accurately as *chesed* from God.

IDEAL EXPRESSION OF *TIFERET* WITHIN *CHESED*

How should the ideal expression of harmony, balance, and truth within loving-kindness look like? Are we meant to imagine a fairytale ending of love and peace, accompanied by the soft singing of birds in clear blue skies? Or, are we meant to strive for something altogether different? What is the deeper understanding of *tiferet* as it relates to what constitutes a true act of loving-kindness?

---

73. Interview with Alan and Bonnie Cohen, April 10, 2013.

The Torah, by describing in detail the lives of Yaakov's children, gives us the answer.

On the surface, it would appear that God was not displaying *chesed* in the events that caused Yosef to be sold into slavery by his own brothers, that brought him into the house of an Egyptian master whose wife tried to seduce him, that got him sent to prison for a crime he did not commit, and that separated him from his beloved father for twenty-two years. But a deeper study of the Torah allows us to connect the dots, discover the big picture and behold God's grand plan.

God had earlier told Avraham that the Jewish people were destined to leave the Promised Land and become slaves in another country, before their eventual return to the Land of Israel. This was going to happen one way or another. Had Yosef not been sold into slavery, the period of Jewish bondage in Egypt would have played out differently. It would have been harsher and longer, but it would have occurred either way because the Jewish soul had to experience enslavement both on an individual and national basis. Only through this experience could the Jewish people fully appreciate freedom, learn to make free will choices, and be able to provide a model to the rest of the world.

Thus the surface events belied what was really happening on a deeper level. The drama unfolding within Yaakov's household would ultimately serve to shield all twelve brothers from destruction, reunify the family and make it possible for a nation of three million men, women, and children to be whisked out of Egypt in a single day. In a mere 49 days from that moment, the new Jewish nation of former slaves, now twelve united tribes, would hear the voice of God and receive the Torah.

There were unparalleled "highs" and "lows" in this saga – the sale of Yosef and Yaakov's heartbreak, the elevation of an imprisoned slave to the position of Viceroy, the joyful reunion of brothers, two centuries of cruel enslavement of a nation, the drama of the Exodus and journey from bondage to freedom. On the surface, all this might appear to be a haphazard collection of events – many of them disastrous and the opposite of *chesed*. And yet what emerges down the road is the greatest act of *tiferet* within *chesed* in history, for the tiny Jewish nation, once it has embraced the Torah, has gone on to influence virtually the entire world to reject paganism and adopt monotheistic beliefs. And individual Jews have impacted and continue to impact the moral and legal codes of most nations, thus advancing the cause of human decency over barbarism.

When all the dots are connected in this amazing story, a perfect portrayal of *tiferet* within *chesed* is revealed.

THE DIVINE CANVAS

If we were to observe any great painter at work just putting the first stroke of paint onto a blank canvas, we could not possibly know what the final painting will look like. When only a splotch of blue or a smear of red appears, we cannot know how the picture will evolve, let alone whether it will be a masterpiece, or a waste of time and effort. We experience the same confusion when looking at isolated patches of the Divine Painter's canvas.

The dark act of selling a brother into slavery miraculously turns out to ensure the physical survival of the Jewish people. Ultimately, there is an escape from enslavement, the encounter with God at Mount Sinai, the giving of the Torah, and an eventual reclaiming of the Promised Land.

Only when the Divine painting is finished can we understand the Great Painter's masterpiece and master plan.

When truth and harmony emerge from a place of loving-kindness, this then is the amazing gift of *tiferet* balancing *chesed.*

DISCUSSION TOPICS FOR *TIFERET* WITHIN *CHESED*

For adults

1. Can I recall events/experiences that I thought were a great misfortune or disappointment at the time only to see them turn out for the best? What lesson did I learn from this?
2. How can I establish a more balanced, truthful, and loving relationship with people in my life, so that we all know when and how to give to the other in the most optimal way? What changes can I make to bring about an immediate improvement?
3. Does my circle of loving-kindness need to be enlarged to include strangers, worthy causes, and/or more one-on-one time with my spouse, each of my children, or my parents? If so, in what areas will I make changes?

For children

1. When have people I love let me down? Can I describe how I felt at the time in a clear but calm way, and share this with them so they know what they did?
2. When have I let someone down who relied on me? What should I have done so that I did not disappoint them? Did I ever discuss the subject with the other person and resolve the problem? What did I learn from this experience?
3. Why does God give us tests in our lives? What are some of the tests that God has given to me or my family? Has something good come out of each challenge, even though it was difficult?

היום ארבעה ימים לעומר

(Ha'yom arba'a yamim la'Omer)

"TODAY IS THE FOURTH DAY OF THE OMER."

DAY 4

Netzach sh'b'Chesed (Endurance within Loving-kindness)

***Netzach* within *chesed* is the attribute of enduring consistency and permanence in love relationships. This attribute should shine when we demonstrate our love for God, ourselves, our family, and others.**

When we see one spouse lovingly and devotedly care for another who might suffer from a terminal illness, we are witnessing endurance within loving-kindness.

When Gilad Schalit's parents Noam and Aviva, sat for two years in front of the house of the Prime Minister in Jerusalem – miles from their own home – as part of a respectful, yet visible, campaign for their son's release from captivity in Gaza, that was endurance within loving-kindness.

When we adhere to a healthier way of eating, stick to our decision to quit smoking, spend more time exercising rather than sitting in front of a computer screen, force ourselves to go to bed on time so we get at least seven hours of sleep at night, we display *netzach* within *chesed* in terms of how we regulate the quality of our lives.

It is vital that those we love the most know that our love for them endures no matter what challenges, needs or tests come our way. And conversely, it is vital for us to know that those whom we love the most will also provide enduring love to us in our times of greatest need. If we are lacking in this area, we must learn from and emulate God, who does not give up on us until our final dying breath.

There are endless examples throughout Tanach of this *sefirah* combination – *netzach* within *chesed.* The importance of endurance within loving-kindness is illustrated most consistently by God in His love of humankind. Despite our sins, many of them willful, God chooses to allow for *teshuvah* to give us endless opportunities for sincere soul-searching and cleansing, and for returning to the formerly close relationship we'd had with Him. His love endures, even when we have strayed from the path. He never stops loving us and waits until our dying breath for us to come back.

THE STORY OF RUTH

One of my favorite stories that so beautifully describes *netzach* within *chesed* is found in the Book of Ruth, which we read every Shavuot, the holiday when we celebrate receiving the Torah and when we are reminded of the inspirational manner in which Ruth embraced the Word of God. Though a convert, Ruth merited to become the progenitor of the line from which came King David, and from which Mashiach ben David will come.

The story begins when Elimelech, a wealthy man from the tribe of Yehuda, leaves the Land of Israel when famine strikes, taking his wife Naomi and their two sons to settle in the fields of Moab. There Elimelech dies, the two sons marry Moabite women – both Moabite princesses, Ruth and Orpah – and then the two sons also die. Devastated by her sons' death, the widowed Naomi decides to return to the Land of Israel, regretting ever having left.

Initially both daughters-in-law follow Naomi although she attempts to dissuade them. She finally succeeds in convincing Orpah to turn back, but Ruth clings to Naomi, so great is her love and loyalty to her. In the touchingly famous lines, Ruth tells Naomi:

> Do not urge me to leave you, to turn back and not follow you. For wherever you go, I will go; where you lodge, I will lodge; your people

> are my people, and your God is my God; where you die, I will die, and there I will be buried. Thus may God do to me – and more! – if anything but death separates me from you."[74]

What more is there to say? Ruth personifies complete love for and enduring commitment to Naomi's Torah way of life. This pure example of *netzach* within *chesed* earns Ruth the merit of a key link leading up to Mashiach.

And now let us look at some modern-day examples of this attribute.

THE STORY OF ADI HUDJA

On the night of December 1, 2001 when Adi Hudja was 14, she and her cousins went to the popular Ben Yehuda Pedestrian Mall in Jerusalem for a bite of ice cream. Tragically, just as had happened so many times – in 1948, 1970, 1975, 1976, 1979, 1981, 1984, and 1997 – terrorists struck Ben Yehuda. On that fateful night, a young Arab man blew himself up, followed by a second a couple minutes later; and then, twenty minutes later, a booby-trapped car exploded. The carnage was indescribable. Eleven teenagers were murdered and a hundred others were wounded and rushed to hospitals.

Adi had been close to one of the terrorists and she suffered severe shrapnel wounds all over her body, particularly her legs. She lay unconscious on the ground and was rushed to Hadassah Ein Kerem. Professor Rami Mosheiff, the orthopedic trauma expert who saw her that night recalls that "Adi's case was the most serious of those who survived." Mali, her mother, saw her in the hospital, and "understood that she was dying." The riveting *netzach*-within-*chesed* story which follows was captured by Barbara Sofer in her regular feature in *The Jerusalem Post Magazine*:

> No matter how many blood products were infused she was still bleeding out. Professor Avi Rivkind suspected that the nuts and bolts had been soaked in rat poison to increase the bleeding. Rivkind got permission to use an expensive-as-platinum experimental medicine, NovoSeven, a clotting agent used for hemophiliacs, as yet unproven

---

74. *Megillat Ruth* 1:16–17.

> for trauma cases. Since the drug was still in trial stages, Adi's mother also had to give the okay. "I was willing to try anything to save my daughter," said Mali, "I never stopped praying."[75]

After two doses of NovoSeven, the bleeding slowed. But Adi's ordeal was hardly over, neither was the *netzach* within *chesed* demanded of her mother and her carers:

> The staff [at Hadassah] had decided that her chances of survival, which were slim at best, would improve if her right leg was amputated. Mali Hudja had tearfully agreed to the amputation. "Above all, I wanted my daughter to live," she said.

The head of Hadassah's Orthopedics Department, Professor Meir Liebergall, was at a medical conference in Europe, but, upon hearing about Adi's case, he immediately rushed home. Writes Sofer:

> Liebergall . . . is modest and reserved. He doesn't like to talk about his personal Israeli story, how he decided to become a doctor after recovering from his war wounds in the IDF, how his parents survived the Shoah. But how else can you explain his urgency to come home and weigh in on Adi's case . . . In one of the toughest calls of his professional life, Liebergall overruled his staff. They would fight for Adi's leg. Day after day, Adi survived. Two and a half weeks later, she woke up.
>
> Her mother spent every day in the hospital, not only to see her daughter, but also to give birth to Adi's brother. Adi was wheeled into the delivery room. "Let's call him Osher (joy)," suggested Adi. "The joy of being alive."

Although it is now many years later, Adi is still undergoing various treatments, but the occasion that prompted Sofer's touching essay was the October 2012 Centennial Celebration of Hadassah, the Women's Zionist Organization of America. With 2,000 people in a Jerusalem audience, Adi

---

75. Barbara Sofer, "Adi Judja's High Heels," *The Jerusalem Post Magazine*, October 26, 2012, 36.

Hudja, a "beautiful, confident young woman" about to begin university studies walked across the stage in an elegant long dress "wearing high heels."

The audience responded with a spontaneous outburst of wild applause. In the audience were her mother, 10-year-old Osher, two other siblings, and Professor Liebergall. What a story of *netzach* within *chesed* displayed by Adi, Mali, the Hadassah staff, and the attending physicians in particular, the state of Israel with its medical excellence and health coverage, and of course, God, the Master of Healing.

UNITED HATZALAH OF ISRAEL

Speaking of all those who play a role in the saving of life, the role of the first responder is critical. Let's examine the *netzach* within *chesed* needed to found and sustain one of the best emergency responders, United Hatzalah of Israel.

Eli Beer, a Jerusalem native born to American parents who had made *aliyah* in 1969, spent his first month of life in a bomb shelter as he was born on the eve of the 1973 Yom Kippur War. At the age of five, he saw "six people killed before my very eyes, and many kids from my school injured," when a bus was blown up in Jerusalem. Ever since then, all he wanted to do was save lives. Inspired by the Hatzalah organizations in New York, Los Angeles, and elsewhere, he founded United Hatzalah of Israel in 1989.

He started with 20 volunteers and now has 1,800 first responders throughout Israel ranging in age from 21 to 78. Their average response time is three minutes, and their goal is to trim that to ninety seconds. Most of their annual budget of $5 million comes from charitable contributions. United Hatzalah does not charge for its services.

Beer, an Orthodox Jew, initiated a program four years ago whereby *haredim* can satisfy their national service or army duty as volunteers with United Hatzalah. In Jerusalem, while most Hatzalah volunteers come from the religious community, secular Jews and Israeli Arabs also volunteer. One Israeli Arab volunteer notes:

> "Some of our volunteers work in the Old City [of Jerusalem] . . . If we have a CPR [call] we – Arabs, *haredi*, and secular Jews – meet

> each other in the house of the patient. We work in harmony, in a wonderful way, to do all the treatments together."[76]

Both the mission of United Hatzalah and how it is implemented by each of its volunteer first responders demonstrate *netzach* within *chesed*, a commitment to care for all of God's children while at all times respecting the value of life.

DISCUSSION TOPICS FOR *NETZACH* WITHIN *CHESED*

For adults

1. Do I demonstrate enduring commitment to my Judaism like Ruth did? Is being Jewish as important to me as it was to Ruth?
2. With whom and how have I demonstrated throughout my life that I am capable of giving and receiving enduring love? Do I display enduring commitment and love toward the members of my family like Ruth did toward Naomi?
3. Can I describe three examples of times when I demonstrated a strong level of endurance within love?

For children

1. Can I describe how God shows His love of me? How do I show God that I love Him?
2. How do I show that I am a good and loyal friend?
3. Do I switch moods a lot, being happy one moment and upset the next? What do I need to do to be consistent in maintaining a good mood?

76. Felice Friedson, "Every Second Counts," *The Jerusalem Post Magazine*, July 27, 2012, 12–17.

היום חמישה ימים לעומר

(Ha'yom chamisha yamim la'Omer)

"TODAY IS THE FIFTH DAY OF THE OMER."

DAY 5

Hod sh'b'Chesed (Humility within Loving-kindness)

Humility within loving-kindness means giving genuine consideration to the feelings, needs, rights, or perspective of others, and being willing to place their needs ahead of our own, whenever appropriate.

We are given multiple opportunities to display humility in loving-kindness every day, principally by submerging our concerns, desires and wants out of a deeper concern for others. For example: When we give an older person or a pregnant woman our seat on a crowded bus, despite our being tired and worn out from a long day at work, that is *hod* within *chesed.* When our spouse burns dinner and we say nothing about it, that is *hod* within *chesed.* When we acknowledge we were thoughtless and lost our temper, and we sincerely apologize for our behavior and any discomfort we caused others, that is *hod* within *chesed.*

Searching for more numerous ways we can perform acts of *hod* within *chesed* in our relationships and in our communities would make the world we live in a much kinder place.

THE BOISSEVAIN FAMILY

The tests and challenges we face in life are meant to reveal our true character and highlight aspects of our life mission – what we were put on earth to do. Accordingly, we can learn much from events which occurred in Jewish history and which tested our people – as well as the people of other nations – again and again.

During World War II, many individuals and nations were given an opportunity to react ethically when they were presented with the reality of horrific cruelty and barbarism aimed at the Jewish people. Needless to say, with rare exceptions, they did not, and the world failed to prevent the death and devastation that Nazism visited upon the Jewish people and humankind.

The Boissevains were that rare exception. As related by Esther Boissevain Grinberg, the members of her extended family, all gentiles, refused to stand by while Jews were being persecuted in their native Holland. (After the war, Esther converted to Judaism and today she is a retired nurse and grandmother, living in Kiryat Tivon, Israel.)

In 1943, Esther's father, Robert, brought home "dinner guests," a Russian-Jewish couple and their daughter. They remained hidden in their home until the war was over in 1945. Esther could never have a friend over to their home, lest the identity of their guests would be discovered and revealed. Later a Jewish dentist joined them in hiding. Esther's mother had ration cards for seven, but she had to feed eleven including her guests. For a period of seven months, they all survived by eating tulip bulbs.

Altogether, eighteen members of the Boissevain family were involved in rescuing Jews during the war, but each kept the secret so well that none knew what others in the family were doing. Seven of the eighteen did not survive, including Esther's father who died in Buchenwald as Allied soldiers were arriving. When asked why her relatives risked their lives, Esther explained that "they just believed that what the Nazis were doing was absolutely wrong and wanted to do anything they could to keep Jews alive."[77]

Esther's relatives sacrificed their comfort and security for the Jewish people they saved – their conduct personifies *hod* within *chesed*. They put

---

77. Abigail Klein Leichman, "Honoring Altruism," *The Jerusalem Post Magazine*, June 1, 2012, 21.

the needs of others ahead of their own in order to save lives. They passed the test.

But what about the rest of the world? We will return to this subject during the remaining weeks of the Omer count.

GOD'S VISIT TO AVRAHAM

The best source for gaining insight into the attribute of *hod* within *chesed* is the Torah. It teaches us that we were created in the image of God and must, therefore, emulate His ways and attributes. Astonishingly, God, who is the all-powerful, omniscient, creator of the world, actually relates toward us, His creation, with love and humility. The key example that illustrates this is the episode of Avraham's *brit milah*.

When Avraham was 99 years old, God commanded him to circumcise himself, and to circumcise all the male members of his household.[78] Immediately after this event, we read that "God appeared to him." None other than God Himself paid Avraham a sick call because he was in pain after the circumcision. The Talmud says the Almighty appeared to Avraham to ask about the state of his health.[79] Rabbi Soloveitchik, in *Abraham's Journey*, provides a glimpse into this astonishing act:

> There is no *va-yomer*, no message, no command, no law, no promise. God simply came to see him . . . Before this visit, the relationship between God and Abraham was a formal one; it did not involve friendship. There was a contractual relationship between employer and employee, between master and servant. Every *va-yera* was accompanied by a *va-yomer*. But, after Abraham was circumcised and the covenant established, there was a new intimacy, a new kind of friendship . . . God came because Abraham was ill, but even if Abraham had been well, God would have been there.[80]

One can well imagine that the Creator of the Universe was quite busy and had lots of other things to do on the day He made a house call to Avraham. But He did so anyway, displaying for us *hod* within *chesed*.

---

78. *Bereshit* 17:23–27; 18:1.
79. *Bava Metzia* 86b.
80. Soleveitchik, *Abraham's Journey*, 160–161.

Now let us take a look at how Avraham displayed this attribute:

While God was paying the sick call on the third, most painful day after the *brit milah,* Avraham, who was sitting at the entrance of his tent in the searing heat of a mid-day sun, saw three travelers approaching. He didn't know them; they were not friends, family or acquaintances.

And what did Avraham do?

Although he was 99 years old and in a great deal of pain, although the Master of the World was communing with him at that very moment, Avraham jumped up and ran to greet the strangers. He bowed to them and addressed them with great humility:

> My Lord, if I find favor in Your eyes, please pass not away from Your servant. Let some water be brought and wash your feet and recline beneath the tree. I will fetch a morsel of bread that you may sustain yourselves, then go on – in as much as you have passed your servant's way.[81]

Listen to the humility in his language as he speaks to them. While bowing and referring to himself as "your servant," he puts the travelers' needs for water, rest, and food before his own need to rest and heal. This is humility within loving-kindness.

Our Sages list this as one of the tests Avraham had to pass in order to demonstrate that he was worthy of becoming the father of the Jewish nation, as Rabbi Soloveitchik notes:

> Thus *Hazal* said that to receive lonely travelers on a hot day and give them water to drink, tell them to wash up, and serve them food, is greater than being in the company and presence of the Almighty.[82]

Avraham actually interrupted God's visit to attend to the strangers. He saw to their needs, served the meal that Sarah had prepared for them, and only then returned to his visitor, God, who had waited patiently for him this entire time![83]

---

81. *Bereshit* 18:2–5.
82. Soloveitchik, *Abraham's Journey*, 168, referring to *Shabbat* 127a.
83. *Bereshit* 18:22.

THE STORY OF RIVKA

Another amazing Torah story that reveals *hod* within *chesed* is the story of Rivka.

When Avraham's servant, Eliezer was assigned the task of finding a wife for Yitzchak, he asked that God assist him in this important duty and help him find a candidate who can demonstrate the attribute of *chesed.* And God did.

As the Torah relates, upon reaching his destination, Eliezer stopped at a well, weary and disheveled from his lengthy trip. A very young Rivka saw him and brought him water to drink. Despite his asking her to crudely pour the water directly into his mouth, she did so without complaining or embarrassing him, notwithstanding the fact that she had no knowledge of who he was or the mission he was on. On top of it all, she lugged jug after jug to water his thirsty camels as well, in an amazing display of *hod* within *chesed.*[84]

After observing Rebecca's impressive character, Eliezer thanked God for the signs that assured him she was the right wife for Yitzchak and thus would continue the sacred tradition started by Avraham and Sarah.[85]

---

84. Ibid., 24:15–22.

85. Ibid., 24:26–27.

DISCUSSION TOPICS FOR *HOD* WITHIN *CHESED*

For adults

1. When I am in an argument or fight, how likely am I to take the first steps towards compromise or reconciliation? Can I give examples of times when I yielded to another?
2. Honestly, do I consider myself superior to a person who looks dirty, disheveled, or has bad teeth? Do I make it a practice to smile and look into the face of the person to whom I am giving *tzedakah*?
3. Do I give *tzedakah* (or my time) to worthy causes in order to receive honor, or do I give purely to help others?

For children

1. Do I seem to get into fights in order to have my way, or am I pretty easy going?
2. When have I ever yielded to others but kept an attitude of loving-kindness?
3. Do I tend to judge or look down on people who are different from me?
4. Have I ever offered water or refreshments to a stranger who appeared to need it?

היום ששה ימים לעומר

(Ha'yom shisha yamim la'Omer)

"Today is the sixth day of the Omer."

Day 6

Yesod sh'b'Chesed (Bonding within Loving-kindness)

***Yesod* within *chesed* is the formation of relationship where one bonds with another so that each can always count on the other. This applies whether the relationship is with God, with our spouse, with our parents, with our children, or with our friends, teachers, students, or co-workers.**

A relationship takes on emerging or permanent elements of bonding when we are able to rely on another person with unspoken trust. We both know the relationship will weather the ups and downs of life and will not be undermined by difficult or turbulent times. Such bonding allows us to count on each other in a loyal and lasting way. We know that we can always rely on God, and by emulating God's ways, we can allow others to rely upon us through both good times and bad.

If we want to achieve *yesod* within *chesed* in a relationship with another person, we must begin by asking how involved we are in the meaningful aspects of the other's life. We must ask ourselves if we encourage and support the other's efforts, dreams and work, whatever that may be. Do we pray every single day for God to bless our spouse – or our children, or our dearest friend – with protection and *mazal*? Do we treat our loved ones with deep and abiding respect at all times in our thoughts, speech, and actions? Do we hold back from complaining about matters that cannot be changed? Are we dedicated and loyal employees who feel a strong sense of belonging to our employer?

Yesod within *chesed* begins with us. And the opportunities to display this trait are around us, every day.

We should not wait for someone else to move first or give more. We should not spend even a moment tallying the scorecard each night to make sure we are not being taken advantage of. God is aware of everything we think, say and do. So let's begin modeling unconditional loving-kindness that also displays loyalty, care, concern, and the desire to bond in positive, supportive, and nourishing ways.

Besides the positive opportunities to display *yesod* within *chesed* during good times, there are also opportunities to do so when bad things happen to those we love. When others experience personal or financial losses, great disappointments, tragedy, upheaval, embarrassment, humiliation, illness, shocking news, or any of a long list of sad events, what do we do? Are we there for them, or do we not want to hear too much about it?

None of us appreciates fair-weather friends who disappear once clouds begin to form on the horizon of our lives, when we need them the most. *Yesod* within *chesed* asks that we withstand the tests of life at all times – not just when it is pleasant for us.

YEHUDA MESHI-ZAHAV AND ZAKA

Anyone tired of the divisive and shrill debate that pits one group of Jews against another can derive inspiration from the story of ZAKA, the rescue and recovery organization of Israel which brings together large groups of volunteers from all ranks of Israeli society (from ultra-Orthodox to secular) to work together for an important common cause.

ZAKA founder Yehuda Meshi-Zahav says the name stands for *Zeh Kiruv Achim*, which literally means "this is the bringing together of kin." It all began in 1989 when, as a yeshiva student, Meshi-Zahav helped to gather the remains of the sixteen people killed in the terrorist attack on Bus #405 near Jerusalem. This became an epiphany for Meshi-Zahav, who in the years prior had been arrested thirty-four times during various anti-Zionist demonstrations. But the Bus #405 bombing showed him that terrorists do not discriminate between the Jews they kill; he realized that such attacks are aimed at the *entire* Jewish people, remembering from his yeshiva learning that the Jewish people are all bound to the same fate regardless of their level of religious conviction. Six years later, he founded ZAKA as a volunteer group of (initially) *haredi* men who could both provide an essential service, but also give back to Israeli society.

Today, ZAKA has 1,650 volunteers around Israel who respond to terrorist attacks, accidents, and disasters. In accordance with Jewish law to honor the dead, the ongoing task of volunteers is to help identify and collect the remains in order to bury as much of the body as is possible. ZAKA also has a fleet of motorbikes driven by paramedics who provide a rapid response to about 7,000 incidents each year. It also has a search-and-rescue branch – whose members dive, climb, and rappel and also work with canine partners – responding to 2,000 incidents per year.

A special article in *The Jerusalem Post* captured the essence of ZAKA:

> It's clear that Meshi-Zahav sees within his work a mission not just to help society practically, but also break down barriers, to unite people, to build bridges, and bring disparate sectors of the public together . . . ZAKA and Meshi-Zahav will keep doing what they excel at: providing services to honor the dead and save the living, as he eloquently puts it. And in so doing, the goals of both Jewish and human unity can also be advanced.[86]

When we conduct ourselves with the spirit akin to that of ZAKA volunteers, we are living life committed to *yesod* within *chesed*.

RABBI ARYEH LEVIN AND HIS BELOVED HANNAH

Many have heard of the saintly Rabbi Aryeh Levin, whose acts of loving-kindness during the years of the British Mandate – to Jewish patients in the leper hospital of Jerusalem, to Jewish inmates imprisoned for political activity, and to Jews of all kinds, both observant and non-religious – are virtually without precedent. He touched tens of thousands of lives just within Israel. Indeed, *yesod* within *chesed* permeated his entire being.

But he, himself, gave all the credit to his wife Hannah. He told people that she never complained, that she never worried about tomorrow, that hers was a power of faith that knew no bounds. "If not for her, I could not

86. Jeremy Sharon, "Bringing Kin Together," *The Jerusalem Post*, February 10, 2012, 15.

possibly have withstood the days of hunger during the First World War," he said, adding, "When it came to trusting the Holy One, Blessed be He, she was greater than I was; she surpassed me."[87]

Hannah was learned and fluent in many languages. The daughter and granddaughter of famed and learned rabbis, she had moved from Lithuania to Eretz Yisrael. The match between Hannah and Reb Aryeh was suggested by Rabbi Avraham Yitzchak HaCohen Kook. A month after meeting, they were married, "forming a lifelong bond" as he put it.

Together they faced extreme challenges of hunger, poverty, war, and even the early death of some of their young children. When he began visiting Jewish prisoners of the British Mandate, she sewed deep hidden pockets into his clothes where he could carry secret messages to and from the men of the underground movement. She knew everything, but never questioned her husband about his activities and only encouraged him. And in return, she was blessed with a devoted husband who, while accompanying her to a doctor's appointment, announced to the doctor that "my wife's leg is hurting *us*" – so deep and abiding was their loving connection.[88]

Their relationship is a stellar example of bonding in love.

AVRAHAM AND SARAH

The biblical model for *yesod* within *chesed* is that of Avraham and Sarah, a relationship without which there would be no Jewish people today. As Rabbi Soloveitchik explains:

> . . . the fact that Sarah was married to Abraham was not enough to give her a permanent place in the Jewish historical household. Rather, Sarah in her own right was a major figure, as important as Abraham – as a matter of fact, *Hazal* say she was *superior* to him.
>
> When Sarah ordered Abraham to send away Hagar and her son, Yishmael, Abraham – the prince of *chesed* did not want to do it. God instructed Abraham, ". . . in all that Sarah has said to you, listen to her voice." Abraham would not have succeeded without Sarah's

87. Simcha Raz, *A Tzaddik in Our Time* (Jerusalem: Feldheim: 1989), 55.
88. Ibid., 150.

> cooperation; all his efforts would have been in vain had Sarah not stood by him . . .
>
> Abraham cannot be *av hamon goyim*, the father of many peoples, if Sarah is not simultaneously crowned as the mother of those peoples. There was an existential interdependence between Abraham and Sarah.[89]

Their bonding and loyalty to each other, perhaps more than any other example, captures *yesod* within *chesed*.

DISCUSSION TOPICS FOR *YESOD* WITHIN *CHESED*

For adults

1. Can I think of three occasions when was I was accessible and helpful to a loved one during his or her time of great need? What in particular did I do?
2. Do I believe there can be deeper bonding with my spouse, more than what we have already achieved in our marriage thus far? What changes can I make to foster a closer relationship?
3. Am I bonded with all of the Jewish people, or do I pick and choose only certain Jews to interact with, relate to, and assist in their time of need? What can I do to reach out to more Jews?

For children

1. Has a friend ever needed me to make him or her feel better after something "bad" happened? What did I do to help?
2. Do I feel a closeness with all of my sisters and brothers? How do I show it? How can I improve my bond with each of my siblings?
3. When something sad has happened to me, did I remember to turn to God for help? What could I say to God about such an unhappy event?

89. Soloveitchik, *Abraham's Journey*, 114–117, referring to *Shemot Rabbah* 1:1 and *Bereshit* 21:10–12.

היום שבעה ימים לעומר

(Ha'yom shiva yamim, she'hem shavuah echad la'Omer)

"TODAY IS THE SEVENTH DAY, OR ONE WEEK, OF THE OMER."

DAY 7

Malchut sh'b'Chesed (Leadership/Nobility within Loving-kindness)

When we have mastered how to consistently give and receive love in a manner that is balanced with respect to ourselves, others, and God, *malchut* within *chesed* is the natural outgrowth, for an element of nobility comes from our breadth of experience in giving and receiving love in positive and constructive ways.

When we have achieved *malchut* within *chesed*, we can be relied upon to factor in the correct amounts of loving-kindness, restraint, harmony, endurance, humility, and bonding called for in any given situation. For then, our love is mature and highly developed, and we are expressing dignity and nobility in all our decisions and actions. When we have arrived there, we are "Balanced to Win" in the *sefirah* of *chesed*.

The following are some remarkable stories from biblical and modern times that illustrate the *malchut* within *chesed*.

RESPONDING TO SODOM

The three travelers who came by on the third day after Avraham's circumcision were angels masquerading as men, each sent on a different assignment. One came to heal Avraham, one came to announce the birth of Yitzchak, and one came to destroy Sodom and Gomorrah.[90]

The twin sin cities were very prosperous and strong, but also immoral and licentious.[91] And their very existence made Avraham's and Sarah's mission of spreading the truth of One God of loving-kindness very difficult. So, anyone would think that Avraham would be glad.

If we were told that our arch competitor in business was going to be completely destroyed in a matter of days, making our life's mission easier to achieve, many of us would be thanking God from the bottom of our hearts for this incredible good fortune. But not Avraham. Instead, when told what was about to happen, he forcefully argued with God to spare his neighbors. Amazingly, God agreed! Had the angel been able to find ten righteous men there, Sodom would not have been destroyed, and it would have continued to be a powerful force of evil in the world.[92]

Avraham's actions surrounding this event reflect a complete mastery of the previously discussed six *sefirot* balanced with *chesed*:

- As much as Avraham despised evil, he did not want to see the destruction of human life (*chesed*)
- He expressed compassion for the Sodomites who never showed any reciprocal compassion or any ethical value system (*tiferet*)
- He displayed endurance in the negotiations with God (*netzach*)
- He showed humility in his language while making his case with the Creator of the Universe (*hod*)[93]
- He displayed deep bonding with the entire human race, despite their wickedness (*yesod*)
- And finally, he accepted that it is God's world, and he restrained his own opinions in view of God's decree (*gevurah*)

Avraham showed us how to combine all the *sefirot* in *malchut* within *chesed*.

---

90. *Bereshit Rabbah* 50:2 and *Bava Metzia* 86b.

91. *Bereshit* 18:17–20.

92. Soloveitchik, *Abraham's Journey*, 170.

93. "Avraham answered and said: 'I am aware that I have just begun to speak to God, and that I am dust and ashes'" (*Bereshit* 18:27).

AVRAHAM'S LEGACY

We might be inclined to say at this point, "Well, I am not Avraham, nor the caliber of any of the *Avot* and *Imahot*." But, actually, the Kabbalah teaches us that each of us has a part of the *Avot* and *Imahot* within us.

How is that possible?

Each of us has a divine gift of soul (breathed into us by God as the *tzelem Elokim*) as well as a divine gift of free will. What we choose to do with these gifts is completely up to us, just as it was up to the *Avot* and *Imahot*.

And look what they accomplished even though they started from nothing. Avraham was a convert, who grew up in a house of idol worship, yet he rejected it. Virtually alone in his belief in the One God, he withstood attempts to kill him. Through all his travails, he persevered. Finally, when he was 75 years old, God determined that he was worthy of a visit, and God spoke to him for the first time.

God's opening words were "*Lech lecha*" – an instruction to Avraham to leave his homeland and "go to a place that I will show you."[94] And Avraham did. With a small entourage, including Terach his father who by now had also come to reject his idolatrous lifestyle, Avraham left Ur and traveled to the Promised Land.

Although most of the people he encountered throughout his life rejected him as *Ish Ivri*, the Hebrew, a man "from the other side," Avraham nevertheless earned tremendous respect from the nations around him, even those who both feared and hated him.

Those of us who are born Jewish, or those of us who convert to Judaism, inadvertently follow in the footsteps of Avraham. When we choose to stick to our Jewish beliefs and practices despite their unpopularity, we walk in the footsteps of our *Avot* and *Imahot* – Avraham and Sarah, Yitzchak and Rivka, Yaakov, Rachel, Leah, and their children. It is not easy to travel such a path. When we make that choice, however, we are acting exactly like our *Avot* and *Imahot*, and we ought to be proud of it.

94. *Bereshit* 12:1.

RABBI LAU'S MOTHER

The autobiography of Rabbi Israel Meir Lau's life – entitled *Out of the Depths* in the English version and *Al Tishlach Yadcha el HaNaar* in the Hebrew – is a "must" addition to every Jewish home library. His story has relevance for all ages and backgrounds. Families should read and discuss it together, a chapter at a time, in order to appreciate and learn from all the beautiful lessons of his astonishing life.

I doubt I will ever forget the following story which captures the essence of *malchut* within *chesed.*

Rabbi Lau was the third son of Rabbi Moshe Chaim Lau and Rebbetzin Chaya, a "member of the thirty-eighth generation of two rabbinic dynasties that have continued uninterrupted for more than one thousand years." His father, the Chief Rabbi of Petrikev, Poland, volunteered himself in the first Nazi round up, hoping that the capture of a community leader would result in fewer others being taken, which proved the case. He died in Treblinka. Chaya Lau and two of her sons – Israel Meier (Lulek) and Naphtali (Tulek) remained behind, hiding in Poland.

However, they too were eventually captured and shipped to a concentration camp. Rabbi Lau was only six years old at the time and very small for his size because of the deprivations he endured while in hiding. His mother saw that men and youths like Tulek, who was 16 at the time, were being directed to one group of railroad cars, while women and small children were sent to another. She understood that the latter meant death, but the former might mean life, as able-bodied men were often selected for hard labor.

Within seconds, Chaya Lau knew what she had to do to save her little boy. As Rabbi Lau tells it:

> She grasped my back with both hands and shoved me in the direction of the men . . . I only heard her say, "Tulek, take Lulek. Good-bye, Tulek; good-bye, Lulek." And I never saw her again.[95]

That was it. It took less than a minute for her to analyze the situation and take the necessary action to save her son's life because she already

95. Israel Meir Lau, *Out of the Depths* (NY: Sterling Publishing Co., 2011), 20–21.

embodied *malchut* within *chesed*. Let us examine what went into that split-second decision:

First she acted out of total love (*chesed*) and she restrained (*gevurah*) any personal need to have him with her and not be alone when she faced her own certain death. She displayed complete faith (*yesod* and *hod*) in God that He would somehow protect her sons from the Nazis. She did not waste any breath wailing about her own fate (*hod*). She weighed the situation and immediately acted with complete resolve and strength (*tiferet* and *gevurah*). Her act of selflessness ensured that the life of her smallest child would be spared, and also that the proud rabbinic dynasty of her family would remain unbroken (*netzach*). Rabbi Lau sums it up touchingly:

> Her maternal instinct was honed to its sharpest in those few seconds . . . [But I didn't understand that then.] Never before and never since did I cry as I did on that day of my separation from Mother. To separate from your mother is inconceivable; it hurts your whole being all the years of your life. It took me a long time to understand that when Mother pushed me toward Naphtali, she saved my life.[96]

Rebbetzin Chaya Lau never lived to know whether or not her Lulek or Tulek survived, but it is certain that all of her prayers until her death were pleas to God to save them both. Chaya Lau never lived to know that Tulek went on to save the lives of many others in his efforts to help Jews in the Displaced Persons Camps after the war. She never lived to learn that Lulek became the Chief Ashkenazi Rabbi of Israel, or that grandsons she never met have also been ordained, continuing the family's unbroken rabbinic legacy, and that one of those grandsons would also become the Chief Ashkenazi Rabbi of Israel in 2013. But it is in her merit that all of this became a reality. She displayed nobility, dignity, and sovereignty in her life and in her death. No Nazi barbarian could ever take that away. As a result of her mastery of *malchut* within *chesed*, the Lau family lives on.

She is inside of and part of the "self" that is Rabbi Lau, his brother, and all their children and grandchildren for all the generations to come, just as Avraham and Sarah are inside of and part of the "self" of each and every Jew.

96. Ibid., 21–22.

BARON DE ROTHSCHILD

What a rich heritage we have! If you have ever visited the central and northern parts of Israel – places such as Rishon LeTzion and Zichron Yaakov – your ability to do so is in large measure due to the leadership and groundbreaking efforts of one family: the Rothschilds. Around the turn of the twentieth century, they almost single-handedly insured that Jews would have a place to live and work in Israel. Theirs was another example of *malchut* within *chesed*.

Baron Edmond Benjamin James de Rothschild of France did not invest in populating Israel because he thought it would be financially profitable, nor because he wanted to become the first Prime Minister, nor because of any prestige he sought. Indeed, his contributions were largely anonymous, and he shunned publicity.

Born to privilege, he seemed uninterested in the French banking business which his family founded, caring more about art. But in his late 30s, he decided to curtail his art purchases and put his money behind the Zionist cause – the creation of a Jewish homeland. He began to buy land in what was then called Palestine. Known as "the Great Benefactor," he spent $50 million supporting Jewish settlements, promoting industrialization and economic development of Israel, and backing research in the generation of electricity for the country.[97] (Following in his footsteps, his son provided funds to construct the Knesset building in his father's memory.)

Although the Baron and his wife, Adelheid, died and were buried in France, their bodies were re-interred in Ramat HaNadiv memorial gardens near Zichron Yaakov, another community they founded.

The Rothschilds were fully committed to the Jewish homeland. Leaving a legacy that displayed his acts of *malchut* within *chesed*, Edmond de Rothschild and his family helped secure the pre-state Israel for Jews. Their commitment to Eretz Yisrael was both a visionary and a generous expression of *malchut* within *chesed* that few can match.

---

97. See Wikipedia, http://en.wikipedia.org/wiki/Edmond_James_de_Rothschild.

DISCUSSION TOPICS FOR *MALCHUT* WITHIN *CHESED*

For adults

1. Can I think of a time when I took a complicated situation, involving someone very close to me, and applied just the right amounts of love, restraint, truth/harmony, endurance, humility and bonding to resolve a matter that otherwise could have resulted in a breakdown of the relationship? Can I describe a situation in my life right now that calls for this approach and explain how I plan to resolve it?
2. Do I display my love in a way that helps others achieve a sense of freedom to be who they are? What successful examples of this can I name?
3. Is there someone close to me who expresses his or her love for me in a way that tends to demoralize me? How can I change this situation?

For children

1. Do I feel secure knowing that I am loved by my family? What could make me feel even better?
2. Do I demand that people show their love for me by entertaining me, playing with me or giving me presents? If so, what can I do to change this behavior?
3. Do I remember to thank God in my daily prayers for the family He gave me? What do I thank God for?

WEEK TWO

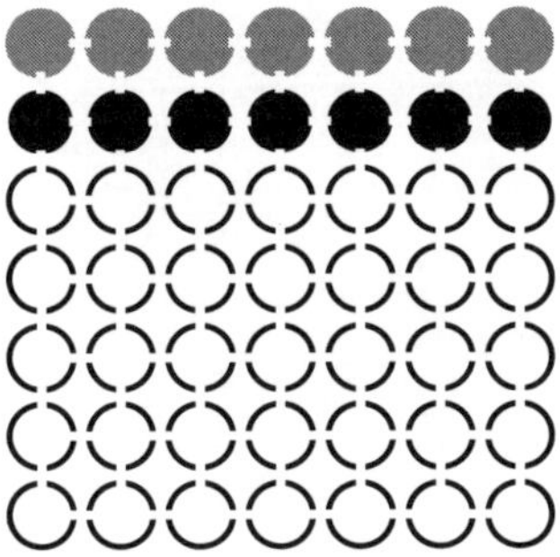

Gevurah (Strength/Discipline)

OVERVIEW

Gevurah (Strength/Discipline)

We learned a little about *gevurah* on Day 2 of Week One in the Omer count, when we established that restraint in *chesed* (loving-kindness) is sometimes necessary and healthy. Now that we have left Week One, we hopefully have a small taste of how to balance love with each of the other six *sefirot*.

In Week Two, we will focus on *gevurah* and learn to balance strength, discipline, and restraint with the right levels of the other *sefirot* – loving-kindness (*chesed*), harmony/truth (*tiferet*), endurance/ambition (*netzach*), humility (*hod*), bonding/foundation (*yesod*) and leadership/nobility (*malchut*).

Gevurah is related to the Hebrew word *gibor*, which means "strong." Thus *gevurah* is chiefly about strength and power, but also about discipline and restraint, as it sometimes can take a great deal of strength to restrain ourselves and our desires. And it can take a great deal of discipline to react to life situations in a measured, sound manner rather than with unbridled emotion.

God is mighty and strong, as our prayers testify. For example, at the very beginning of the thrice-daily *Shemoneh Esrei* (Eighteen Benedictions), we say: "Blessed are You, God . . . the great, mighty, and awesome God, the supreme God." And then we say: "You are eternally mighty, my Lord" and go on to describe God as He "who makes the wind blow and the rain descend, who sustains the living with kindness, resuscitates the dead with abundant mercy, supports the fallen, heals the sick, releases the confined . . . causes death and restores life . . ."[98]

This list is insightful. There appears, though, to be a glaring omission from this enumeration of mighty and powerful forces that God commands

98. *The Seif Edition ArtScroll Transliterated Linear Siddur*, 372–374.

– there is no mention of the universe, or the galaxies, or other wonders of nature. Wouldn't their inclusion make more sense that wind, rain, and kindness?

The Sages who formulated our prayer service more than 2,000 years ago were wise, and they emphasized what God wanted us to understand. True might is shown by *restraining* the power we have. God's strength is demonstrated when He sustains the living with kindness even though some may deserve punishment or death; when He resuscitates the dead with abundant mercy; when He makes dew fall in the summer and rain in the winter (especially in Israel), and when He makes that happen at the right time, in the right quantities, and in the right places so there is neither flood nor famine; when He heals the sick even if they have not done complete *teshuvah* for their sins; and on and on.

God's *gevurah* is revealed in the following Mishna, which describes how He has demonstrated His strength through restraint:

> There were ten generations from Adam to Noah to show the degree of His [God's] patience, for all those generations angered Him increasingly until He brought upon them the waters of the Flood. There were ten generations from Noah to Avraham to show the degree of His patience, for all those generations angered Him increasingly, until our forefather Avraham came and received the reward of them all.[99]

Examples of God's *gevurah* in the form of restraint are numerous. At creation, He restrained Himself from finishing the job, so that humankind could contribute to its completion. Every day He restrains Himself from destroying us when we violate His commandments. He restrains Himself from giving us the immediate punishment we deserve as a result of our misdeeds. Instead, His way is to provide us with wake-up calls and tests, giving us the opportunity to return to Him through *teshuvah* after our poor choices and mistakes, for that is what our sins really are.

The Hebrew the word *chet*, which is almost always translated into English as "sin," really means to "miss the mark." We miss the mark when we slip and act contrary to God's will. Fortunately for us, God has given

99. *Avot* 5:2–3.

us the mitzvah of *teshuvah* whereby we can leave our sins behind and begin anew.

Since we are created in God's image, we must emulate His ways and restrain ourselves as He does. For example, He expects us to show restraint from living an unbridled life of sin. He expects us to display elevated *derech eretz* in our choices, our conduct, and in how we treat others. Just because we *can* squash a bug or kick a small animal doesn't mean we should do it. Just because we are strong enough to physically harm an infant or child doesn't mean we are allowed to. Just because we are able to steal something doesn't mean we are ever to act in such a manner. Human beings are not supposed to imitate animals in the jungle. We are meant to discipline our behavior. In the words of King Shlomo, considered the wisest person who ever lived: "Hold fast to discipline; do not let go. Guard it, for it is your life."[100]

GEVURAH AS A POWER SOURCE

Too much power can be destructive. Too little power can be ineffective. Every situation in life requires just the right amount of strength. Sometimes the strongest display of power is the restraint of power, in emulation of God's ways. The Creator of the Universe can do anything He wishes including destroy the entire world in a nanosecond by just failing to will its existence each moment of the day. Instead, He restrains His power, teaching us humans how to use our free will in a balanced way, bringing us closer to Him, and helping us build a relationship with Him.

Our relationship with God grows through the *mitzvot* He has given us. This is the path toward strengthening our ethical qualities and disciplining our *yetzer hara*.

In his book *Endless Light*, Rabbi Aaron equates *gevurah* with terms like justice, control, restraint, maintaining borders, and selfishness. Any of these involve strength, discipline and restraint to execute. Applied properly, they appear as positive manifestations of *gevurah*; when applied inappropriately, they may not be. The Omer count helps us to better apportion our responses to draw upon the right combination of *sefirot* in a measured way, at the right time and in the right place. When we achieve this, we exemplify God's ways in our own behaviors.

---

100. *Mishlei* 4:13.

But let's be honest. It is not simple to discipline ourselves and our nature. It is hard to deny ourselves something we may want, or to work on correcting bad habits and defects.

If I am addicted to something, I want it even if I know that having it will eventually affect my health, ruin my life, and might even kill me. If I am spoiled, I want what I want, when I want it, how I want it, and from whom I want it. If I am lazy, I don't want to hear when to get up for work even if my family's security is on the line. If I am a perfectionist, I want others to do it my way.

And yet, to be fully actualized human beings, we must find ways to restrain our natural drives if they are detrimental to our continued growth – even if it is hard work. Truly, it is no different from the fight of a recovering addict who each and every day chooses to refrain from a harmful substance.

For example: Perfectionists among us might be reminded that even God, who is perfect, restrained Himself from perfecting creation in order to allow us imperfect human beings to become His partners in this process. Even though we have made many wrong choices, which have introduced elements of evil and chaos into creation, God continues to restrain Himself from doing the work of humankind. This is a lesson to all perfectionists among us who might recognize that becoming "control freaks" is not applying God's strategy of allowing others to contribute to God's ultimate plan for man's redemption. The truth is that no one is perfect, and we cannot expect perfection from those with whom we interact and love.

The fight to control our tendency to criticize or give advice on almost everything that does not meet our perfectionist standards is a struggle requiring self-control for our own sake and for the sake of the others around us. It is a far better approach for teachers or parents to hold back and let their students or children discover the answer on their own. Many family imbalances stem from issues in *gevurah* and an inability of those in authority to "mix-out" by showing restraint, self-control, and discipline.

Some of us are born with a natural ability to exude power, strength, and dominance. Used constructively, these can be good attributes. But if unchecked, these traits can lead to us being overly judgmental, assertive, and controlling. In the process, we may unintentionally intimidate our co-workers, subordinates, students, our children, our spouses, and our friends from sharing their good ideas or from even asking questions.

We sometimes think that strength, power, and might are proven by loud boasting, chest beating, yelling, screaming, or wielding the biggest guns. Unfortunately, many world leaders have been confused about what true strength is and what it should not be. It is none of the above. The highest form of strength is control and restraint of power. This is an important insight into *gevurah*.

When we yell loudly and berate someone, we demonstrate that we are unable to control our speech or temper. But, when we have a dispute with someone and are able to speak respectfully in a normal tone, we demonstrate a far higher form of inner strength than yelling irrationally. A proper display of conduct may actually model for others how to act with respect and self-control; it may cause them to choose to emulate us and try to control themselves. Such modeling is a high level of demonstrating *gevurah* in a constructive manner, and it can bring us closer to achieving our goal, especially when our restraint leads others to restrain their temper.

Every counselor or psychologist will advise a person who is in a verbal confrontation to talk softly and calmly. Why? Because of the well-established adage that "it takes two to fight." Within minutes of one party to the argument talking calmly and softly, the other party will also begin talking more softly. A person who is screaming and yelling but getting no response in kind will eventually run out of steam and will either calm down or leave because it is no use fighting by yourself; it just feels silly. So either those fighting wise up and talk calmly to make their point, or they decide to avoid the situation by silence or disengaging. Either way, it takes two to escalate a situation.

Many people mistakenly believe that a display of anger proves one's strength. Actually, it is just the opposite. Anger is a complete inability to control one's emotions. It is a deficiency in restraint. The Maharal of Prague provides four tools for dealing with the challenge of anger: waiting, humanizing ourselves, humanizing the other person, and appreciating our differences.[101] Refusing to display anger openly and loudly requires tremendous *gevurah*. "Just waiting" until someone else blows off their steam requires maturity, discipline, and restraint, but it is worth it.

101. Tzipporah Heller, *Let's Face It! The 8 Essential Challenges of Living* (Jerusalem: Targum/Feldheim, 2005), 101.

YITZCHAK, THE SECOND SHEPHERD

Avraham's son, Yitzchak, the second of our Seven Shepherds, reintroduced *gevurah* to the world after the sin of Adam. His entire life was devoted to this and to serving God with proper reverence, awe, and fear. In this, he never faltered.

Judaism teaches that it takes the highest form of strength to become a mature, highly disciplined person with a strong sense of self-control and restraint, able to willfully deny instant gratifications, and to recognize when it not the right thing to do. This is why we readily forgive children for their lack of control over their emotions and actions. We consider children weak and immature which is why our expectations of their conduct are less than what we normally expect from a mature adult. Indeed, our tradition teaches that a youth is not held accountable in the heavenly court for his or her misdeeds until age 20.[102]

It takes the highest form of true strength to restrain, to defer, to deny, to be moral and ethical and to serve our Father in Heaven. This is what we learn from Yitzchak. As a 37-year-old man at the time of the *Akeidah*, he was fully committed to a life of service to God and continuing the mission of his father. Rabbi Eliyahu Kitov tells us that "when he was bound on the altar, it was not his faith that was being tested, but Avraham's."[103]

When Avraham was told by God to sacrifice his son, he had to draw upon *gevurah* to restrain his innate abundance of *chesed* in order to carry out the command. Avraham did so without even uttering a word about the apparent senselessness of the act. Yitzchak also displayed *gevurah*, but it was a trait that came more naturally to him. He even asked his father to bind his hands and feet, so that he would be a perfect sacrifice for God, even while knowing that God never wanted a human sacrifice. Yitzchak did not flinch.[104]

Up until the *Akeidah*, Avraham and Yitzchak were a team. Rabbi Joseph B. Soloveitchik writes:

> Together they preached, taught, and tried to embody and inculcate *chesed.* Of course, Avraham was the patriarch of the covenantal

---

102. Yerushalmi, *Bikkurim* 2:1.

103. Kitov, *The Book of Our Heritage*, Vol. 2, 683.

104. *Bereshit* 22:1–19.

> community, Yitzchak, the junior partner. Nevertheless, they constituted a harmonious whole.[105]

But after the *Akeidah*, the unity implied in "they both went together"[106] ended. Rabbi Soloveitchik goes on:

> [The *Akeidah*] fashioned a new personality, a new soul, for Yitzchak, and a new covenantal reality . . . The two ideas that Avraham and Yitzchak respectively represented were not merged . . . Avraham symbolized *chesed*, an overflowing love that rises like a river in springtime and inundates its environs. Avraham wanted to convert all of mankind. He was concerned with the whole world. He sat by the highway waiting for travelers; he carried his morality to the people and wanted to proselytize everyone. Yitzchak symbolized *gevurah*, self-limitation and self-concentration, heroic action and withdrawal . . . "Avraham returned to his young men," but Yitzchak belonged to a world of his own.[107]

What was that world?

Not much is written in Torah about the life of Yitzchak, but one major event stands out – the dispute over the wells.

Avraham had dug many wells and entered into treaties with his neighbors. When the neighbors broke the treaty and filled up the wells with dirt to assert their control, Yitzchak re-opened his father's wells and continued to make use of them without budging from the land. While Yitzchak did not fight, he also did not give an inch.[108]

We can learn volumes from Yitzchak about how to refrain from fighting while, at the same time, not giving up our rightful claims. His actions concerning the wells reflect *gevurah*. He firmly held onto the tradition of his father, and he firmly held onto the land that God had promised. He did not leave when threatened; he stayed and prevailed. Remember it takes two to fight. This principle gives one person a great deal of potential control, if he or she chooses to exercise it.

105. Soloveitchik, *Abraham's Journey*, 193.
106. *Bereshit* 22:8.
107. Soloveitchik, *Abraham's Journey*, quoting *Bereshit* 22:19, 193.
108. *Bereshit* 26:15, 19–25.

The greatest act of *gevurah* displayed by Yitzchak was his self-restraint. He did not feel any need to be a pioneer like his father – to strike out on his own with new ideas about God, life and divine service. Yitzchak's greatest contribution – and indeed, his mission on earth – was to be true to what his father Avraham had established. Yitzchak never left the borders of Israel, the land given to Avraham and his progeny by God Himself. He didn't have to go anywhere to prove himself. He was secure enough to understand and fulfill his mission. He was committed to his father's *mesorah* of belief in and service to the One God, and he made sure that it would not change but endure. Because of his efforts, today, some 4,000 years later, we have virtually the same traditions, beliefs, and practices.

The path forged by Yitzchak took true strength, restraint, and discipline. It takes a person of immense spiritual proportions to contain his true power and channel it to the service of the true God. That was Yitzchak's way!

UNRESTRAINED *GEVURAH* AND WORLD EVENTS

Now let us consider two world leaders who took the opposite path: the Roman Emperor Titus, and Adolf Hitler.

Hitler, *yimach shemo*, was feared as one of the most powerful people in the twentieth century. His armies conquered most of continental Europe and North Africa. To realize his evil plan to dominate the world and exterminate the entire Jewish race, he killed twelve million people (six million of them Jews) in forced labor/death camps and caused the death to hundreds of thousands of others on the battlefield.

And yet, in the end, Hitler's megalomanic schemes only brought unspeakable ruin to the world, and he committed suicide thirteen years after assuming power, leaving Germany desolate and broken. His Final Solution failed, and only three years after his death, Jews established a state of their own. God has miraculously ensured that they would survive. Despite the indescribable devastation of the Holocaust, a worldwide *ba'al teshuvah* movement has brought thousands of lost Jewish souls back to the fold. And Jews from all over the world are making *aliyah* to Israel which God has blessed with success.

So how truly "strong" was Hitler? He is dead, his empire is gone, and his evil ideology has been exposed for what it was.

Another figure in history whose actions illustrate the concept that true power comes from restraint and discipline requires us to look back 2,000 years to Roman times. When the Roman general, Vespasian, was declared emperor, he transferred military control to his son Titus, who waged the final battle for Jerusalem. Tragically, because of baseless hatred among the Jews, his army was successful on Tishah B'Av of the year 70 CE. The Romans entered the Beit HaMikdash, emptied its treasures, offered sacrifices on its premises to their pagan gods, and finally set it on fire. Rabbi Yosef Eisen vividly describes this calamity in his monumental work, *Miraculous Journey*:

> Titus himself entered the *Kodesh HaKodashim*, committed a lewd and despicable act, and disdainfully slashed the holy curtain, the *paroches*, with his sword. Miraculously, blood spurted from the curtain, causing Titus to believe that he had killed the Almighty, God forbid. The destruction was so complete that only the Western Wall, the *Kosel HaMa'aravi*, was left standing, for God had promised that the Holy Temple would never be entirely destroyed . . . those that remained alive envied the dead, for the survivors were sent to the mines of Egypt or became gladiators, fighting each other or wild beasts for the amusement of the Romans. Finally, so many Jews were available as slaves that there was no need for slave markets. Overall, Jewish casualties were enormous – more than one million killed in Jerusalem alone, with nearly 100,000 taken captive."[109]

Titus, the mighty destroyer of Jerusalem, succeeded his father as the Roman Emperor several years later. And what happened next? It seems that a tiny gnat ate away at his brain, bringing on a degenerative condition that brought upon a personality change within Titus – his cruelty turned into benevolence. Despite the change, he died. The Talmud explains that "Titus was punished in such an unnatural manner because he blasphemed the Almighty when he destroyed the Beit HaMikdash."[110]

So who had more power in the long run? Was it Titus or the little gnat that patiently fulfilled its God-given mission on earth by killing the seemingly invincible destroyer of the Temple in Jerusalem?

---

109. Yosef Eisen, *Miraculous Journey* (Jerusalem: Targum Press, 2009), 89–98.
110. *Gittin* 56b.

Good or Evil? More or Less Power?

To understand the importance of *gevurah* and its role, we need to understand some basic principles which are best described in lay terms by Rabbi Dr. Akiva Tatz: "Things themselves are not good or bad; only the manner in which they are used is good or evil . . . *Things are not good or bad, only more or less powerful.*"[111]

As part of his explanation, Rabbi Tatz provides a useful analogy:

> The electrical current supplying your home is enough to power a household of appliances. On the other hand, if you accidentally put your finger into the socket the result is unpleasant and dangerous. But the high tension lines supplying a city carry enough power for the entire city, much more energy than the current in your home and able to achieve much more. If you touched one of those lines, you would be fried. More power means more can be done, but the danger increases in proportion to the potential for good.

Rabbi Tatz links power directly to what authentic *gevurah* really is and what we hope to achieve in this week of the Omer count:

> Money, good looks, charismatic personality, powers of persuasion – all of these are neutral. The more one has, the more powerful one is. But not better or worse: that depends on the purposes and ends to which one applies those gifts and talents. And that is your true measure: not how talented you are, *but rather the degree of control that you exert* over your talents. For what purpose do you use your looks, your intelligence? Good or bad? That decision is, in fact, the real you. *You are your free choices.*[112]

We saw this in the earlier example of Hitler, who was given immense powers of persuasion but who used them for death and destruction. Mahatmas Ghandi, Reverend Martin Luther King, Jr., Senator Robert Kennedy, and many others were also gifted with powers of persuasion, but they channeled them in a completely different direction.

---

111. Tatz, *The Thinking Jewish Teenager's Guide to Life*, 22–23.
112. Ibid.

What we freely choose to do with the strengths we have and how we decide to channel and discipline our natural abilities is up to us. That is the power our loving Creator gave to us. Will we use it for good, moral/ethical outcomes, or not? Will we cut ourselves off from God, which means cutting ourselves off from our own selves as well, or not?

Remember that your true measure is not how talented you are, but – to borrow the words of Rabbi Tatz – "the degree of control that you exert over your talents."

The key to balancing every single emotional characteristic (or *sefirah*) in these seven weeks is to exert the proper "degree of control" in order to make sure that the energy of each *sefirah* is channeled toward good. To learn to do this takes true power.

During this week of *gevurah*, we will learn to exert an improved degree of control over the way we express love, power, harmony/truth, endurance/ambition, humility, bonding/foundation and leadership/nobility over our lives.

היום שמונה ימים, שהם שבוע אחד ויום אחד, לעומר

*(Ha'yom shemonah yamim,
she'hem shavuah echad v'yom echad la'Omer)*

"TODAY IS THE EIGHTH DAY, OR ONE WEEK AND ONE DAY, OF THE OMER."

DAY 8

Chesed sh'b'Gevurah (Loving-kindness within Strength/Discipline)

***Chesed* within *gevurah* provides the opportunity for love to temper pure strength and power, so that the end result will be constructive and not destructive.**

Oftentimes, how we express ourselves defines the outcome of our communication with others. Consider some of these commonly used expressions in their abrasive or less-than-respectful form and then consider them again, after they have been softened by the sweet ingredient of *chesed* within *gevurah*:

> *Father to a child:* "Your bedroom is a disaster. What a sloppy mess! I am sick of it. Until your room is spotless, you cannot leave the house."
>
> *Or:* "David, please take the time you need now to make your bedroom orderly and organized so that it will look nice when your friends visit and be a pleasant environment to play in. Call me when you are finished. Thank you, dear."
>
> *Wife to a husband:* "I am sick and tired of you just dropping your shirts and pants on the floor. Why can't you hang things up? We live in a pig pen because of you."

Or: "Honey, I have a small request that would make a big difference to me. When I see clutter in our bedroom, it makes me feel very frustrated. I would appreciate it very much if you could take just a couple of minutes each day to hang up your clothes when you change."

One roommate to another: "What's wrong with you? You are never careful! I just cleaned up in here."

Or: "Can you do me a huge favor and get a rag and wipe up this spill? I'd be forever grateful."

These subtle word changes are the sweet fragrance of *chesed* gently modifying abrasively expressed requests or instructions. Adding the words "please" and "thank you" and speaking calmly is such a nicer way of issuing a directive or making a request of another person.

LOVE IN DISCIPLINE

Rabbi Samson Raphael Hirsch comments that our major task as parents is to guide our children to the goal for which they were created. Our children may not appreciate this concept, but the only reason we insist upon certain standards of behavior from them is because we love them so very much. "Punishment" – or having children face the consequences of something they have done wrong – is how we express our greatest love for them. This is the way we try to correct whatever it is that distances them from *kedushah*.

The same idea applies to our other relationships as well. The deepest form of love means that we want our loved ones to be the best they can be and to achieve their full potential on earth. And this goes for ourselves as well.

It takes maturity to realize that the discipline we choose to apply in our own lives, as well as the discipline that we expect of others, is a strong expression of love. We demonstrate we love ourselves when we set standards and goals, and then work to achieve them, always remembering to be aware that when our conduct starts to drift, we must make course corrections. Ditto for others in our lives.

The best parents, teachers, and bosses set standards and expectations that help those in their charge aim higher, providing them with needed *mussar* when their behavior is wanting. The best parents, teachers, and bosses know they have no right to judge, but they do have a right to show true concern and love for their subordinates in order to help them achieve their highest potential. Rabbi Yissocher Frand counsels wisely:

> When you criticize your child, don't tell him, "You *should* know better." Tell him, "You *know* better." The difference is subtle but crucial. The second way addresses him as a person of discernment and wisdom. The child who is spoken to in that fashion will not experience your criticism as a blow to his self-esteem and walk away feeling worthless.[113]

How do we know this is the preferred model? Because this is exactly how God relates to us, His children.

God has given us 613 *mitzvot* (and Seven Noahide laws for non-Jews) so that we have standards to follow. What God did not do is say to us, His children, "I love you so much, you may do whatever you want." Therefore, as parents neither should we.

GOD'S BLESSING TO YISHMAEL

Sefer Bereshit contains a curious story about Sarah demanding that Avraham send Hagar and Yishmael away because of their negative influence on Yitzchak. Avraham, following the instructions of God to "listen to her voice," does so.

Hagar and Yishmael leave, but soon their provisions are depleted; that is when Hagar abandons her son under a tree and goes away weeping to avoid seeing him die. In response to the anguish of mother and son, God sends an angel who tells her: "Fear not, for God has heeded the cry of the youth in his present state. Arise, lift up the youth and grasp your hand upon him, for I will make a great nation of him."[114]

Various commentaries address the question of why God saved Yishmael despite the knowledge that one day his progeny would murder and wreak havoc on the Jewish people. Yet He did, because, clearly, at that moment in time Yishmael was innocent. God heard his cry, judged his actions then, not later, and determined that he should live.

---

113. Frand, *Rabbi Yissocher Frand in Print*, 73.

114. *Bereshit* 21:11–18.

From this episode, we learn that God will judge us the same way as He judged Yishmael. If we have done *teshuvah* and are innocent at present, then we can hope that God will forgive us now and refrain from allowing other factors to convince Him otherwise. This is *chesed* within *gevurah*.

DISCUSSION TOPICS FOR *CHESED* WITHIN *GEVURAH*

For adults

1. Have I set worthy and reasonable expectations for my children? Or, have I permitted them to drift, spoiling them without expecting much of them either at home or at school? Or, conversely, am I so watchful of them that they do not have enough space to become who they are meant to be? How do I plan to modify my over-protectiveness?
2. Have I ever listened to myself and thought about how I sound to others? How can I modify my directions to members of my family to sound more like respectful requests than arrogant demands? What do I need to change?
3. Do I know what the three most important things in my children's lives are? Once I ask and find out, how am I going to relate to their priorities on their terms?

For children

1. Do I realize that, when my parents ask me to do something around the house or relating to school, it is because they love me and want to help me grow up faster and better? What are the things I could be doing that I am not doing?
2. Is there someone in my family who talks to me in disrespectful ways that hurt my feelings and make me feel bad about myself? How am I going to discuss this issue with that person, or someone else who can help, to see if I can bring about change?
3. When do I make requests of my parents and siblings without using a nice voice? When do I forget to say "please" and "thank you" and communicate in a manner that demonstrates respect and love?

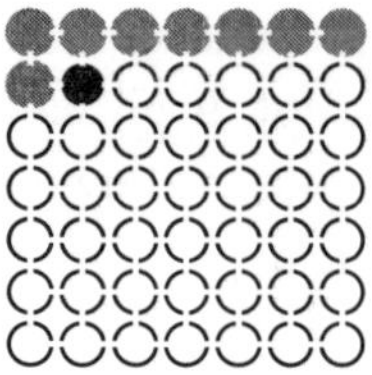

היום תשעה ימים, שהם שבוע אחד ושני ימים, לעומר

(Ha'yom tisha yamim,
she'hem shavuah echad u'shnei yamim la'Omer)

"Today is the ninth day,
or one week and two days, of the Omer."

Day 9

Gevurah sh'b'Gevurah
(Strength/Discipline within Strength/Discipline)

***Gevurah* within *gevurah* is a well of strength that we can harness physically, mentally, emotionally, and spiritually for constructive application in our behavior, relationships, and life. But, we must take caution, for unharnessed, pure *gevurah* within *gevurah* can be dangerous. However, when exercised properly it becomes a source of highly developed discipline and restraint that tempers our actions in all spheres and prevents them from becoming extreme and destructive.**

Pure *gevurah* is extraordinarily powerful and therefore should be used very carefully. It should be applied only when complete and total concentration, discipline, and restraint – without any flexibility or compromise – are required. There are not many of such situations, but there are some that require the power of *gevurah* within *gevurah*. For example:

- when we are seeking to increase in our service to God by becoming highly disciplined and focused in our daily prayers
- when we are taking concrete steps to enhance our physical, emotional, and spiritual health either for the goal of disease prevention and health optimization, or in order to prevent ourselves from

becoming addicted or to break an addiction to a harmful substance (such as drugs, alcohol, food, nicotine, gambling, computer games, the Internet, phone texting, shopping, or other behavioral compulsions)
- when we need to stop ourselves from speaking *lashon hara*
- when we are trying to establish a firm schedule of daily Torah learning
- when we are seeking to control our outbursts of anger
- when we want to commit to living with heightened God awareness
- when we want to consistently display good *middot* and proper *derech eretz*

THE DOWNSIDE OF PURE *GEVURAH*

If we were to constantly display pure discipline in our interactions with others, there is a risk we might become inflexible, judgmental, and overly critical. We might also fall into obsessive compulsive behavior, becoming focused on perfection – which no one can achieve – and as a result, becoming the cause of unhealthy tensions and unnecessary arguments. In the extreme, we might find ourselves so restrained emotionally that we are virtually incapable of expressing love, appreciation, or gratitude.

If we were to apply pure discipline to any area of our lives without balance – such as, for example, when fixing a rigid schedule or mindlessly pursuing a goal – we are likely to find ourselves inconsiderate of others and dealing with unpleasant negative repercussions. We have all seen what happens when high-powered executives over-focus on their jobs, or when Torah students ignore everything in life but their studies, or when well-meaning people take on a just cause which they allow to consume them to the detriment of their families and loved ones. Such people often neglect their own health, their children, seldom visit their aging parents, or are unavailable for other acts of *chesed* when needed by their families or communities. They may be top chemists, attorneys, accountants, or Torah scholars, but distant and uninvolved spouses or parents.

Many years ago, I was impressed with the insight offered in this regard by Dr. Bernie Siegel. After a decade of being a leading oncology surgeon, performing multiple surgeries a day in assembly-line fashion, he was jolted by a note he received that read:

> "Approximately ten years ago [you] operated on my dad and removed a section of his stomach. At this time you found his entire lymph gland system to be cancerous. You advised me, the oldest son, to inform the other members of my family of my father's condition. I chose not to. Last Sunday my dad was surprised with a wonderful birthday party. He was 85 years old and my 80-year-old mom was smiling at his side!"[115]

Contemplating this experience, and others like this, Dr. Siegel began to do research. Eventually, he wrote his famous book, *Love, Medicine and Miracles*, espousing his new balanced treatment approach to help people maximize their chances of cancer survival. It is a must-read for anyone battling cancer and their loved ones, and frankly for anyone who wishes to prevent cancer or any disease. What was Dr. Siegel's insight?

> Our state of consciousness and disease are inseparable . . . Many people don't make full use of their life force until a near-fatal illness goads them into a "change of mind." But it doesn't have to be a last-minute awakening. The mind's power is available to us all the time, and it has more room to maneuver before disaster threatens . . . The ability to love oneself, combined with the ability to love life, fully accepting that it won't last forever, enables one to improve the quality of life. My role as a surgeon is to buy people time, during which they can heal themselves. I try to help them get well and at the same time to understand why they became sick. Then they can go on to true healing, not merely a reversal of one particular disease . . . [My book] is a guide to the part of yourself that can choose your own best advice and then muster the will to follow it. I hope to reach beyond your rational mind, for miracles don't come from the cold intellect. They come from finding your authentic self and following what you feel is your own true course in life."[116]

To translate his insight into our Omer-count parlance: Without balance from the other *sefirot* in the form of being caring and expressive, it is not

115. Bernie S. Siegel, *Love, Medicine and Miracles* (New York Perennial Library, 1988), 21–22.
116. Ibid., x, 4–5.

possible to achieve optimal health and "wholeness" in our professional or personal life.

Unfortunately, examples of lack of that balance abound. We see this particularly on the world stage in leaders who cannot or will not apply *gevurah* within *gevurah* in a constructive manner. Once they begin to perceive themselves as "all mighty," they often cross the line into provocative actions, invading other countries, violating peace treaties, creating discord among their populations (sometimes causing civil wars), arresting dissenters or opposition leaders, curtailing free speech, subjugating women and minorities, and even committing horrific acts of inhumanity. All such negative acts reflect *gevurah* within *gevurah* in an out-of-control display of strength, power, and might.

Let us now examine some examples from the Torah of how a proper expression of *gevurah* within *gevurah* should be like, and how it should not.

GEVURAH WITHIN *GEVURAH* IN TORAH

When, on Day 8, we discussed *chesed* within *gevurah*, we noted that God displayed this attribute in keeping Yishmael alive, after Avraham sent him away at Sarah's urging. But, in that incident, Sarah displayed pure *gevurah* within *gevurah*. Sarah saw that Yishmael posed a threat to her son, Yitzchak, the heir to Avraham's nascent faith, and she demanded that Yishmael and his mother, Hagar, leave. Avraham, balancing his natural *chesed* with *gevurah*, acceded to this demand after being told by God to listen to his wife.[117]

That was an appropriate application of *gevurah* within *gevurah*. The following story – that of Noah – shows the opposite:

When God told Noah about the coming flood and instructed him to build an Ark, He gave him 120 years to do so. Why would God, who could destroy anything He chose in a nanosecond, delay so long?

It seems He had two reasons: First, God was giving humanity 120 years to change their evil, immoral, and selfish ways. He wanted humans to do *teshuvah*, to return to Him, and avoid the catastrophe of the flood. Second, God was giving Noah 120 years to attempt to convince the world that the human race could save itself by giving up evil and acknowledging that there was One God in the world who wants humankind to change

117. *Bereshit* 21:9–14.

and choose "good." But Noah did nothing efffective to save his wayward generation.

Noah focused all his efforts – deploying his strength, determination, and discipline – to build the Ark, following God's instructions to the letter and ignoring the ridicule heaped upon him by the masses.[118] In addition, he used *gevurah* within *gevurah* in searching for the various species of animals. This was a positive illustration of tenacity and resolve in completing an assignment. Yet, even in the face of impending doom, Noah didn't attempt to save anyone other than himself, his family, and the animals. He did not try to get humanity to do *teshuvah*. He did not attempt to apply his *gevurah* to try and change God's mind. Noah was solely focused on only one part of the assignment, while seemingly oblivious to the fact that unless someone did something about it, all of the earth's inhabitants would be obliterated.

Unlike Avraham, who ten generations later would attempt to save the people of Sodom, Noah did not even once try to talk God out of His plan to destroy the world. The absence of effort to apply a constructive aspect of *gevurah* within *gevurah* toward that end tragically resulted in wholesale destruction of the earth.

KORACH'S REBELLION

The Torah tells stories of many disagreements: Kayin and Hevel; Yishmael and Yitzchak; Yaakov and Esav; Lavan and Yaakov; Yosef and his brothers. And then we read about the rebel Korach, who requires an entire *parsha* named after him. What is the lesson in that?

Korach was a Levite, a cousin to Moshe. He was wealthy, highly intelligent, and charismatic. He was one of the few given the privilege by Moshe of carrying the Ark of the Covenant from Sinai. But this was insufficient glory for Korach; he wanted more. Specifically, he wanted to be the *Kohen Gadol*, a role that God selected for Aaron.

Pirkei Avot says to stay away from three things: "jealousy, greed, and the pursuit of honor,"[119] the three self-serving needs which Korach made no effort to control. There are various views as to when he commenced the rebellion which included 250 other "firstborns" whose own jealousies and

118. Ibid., 6:13–7:5.

119. *Avot* 4:21.

insecurities he helped stoke. The result was a full-blown insurrection, the goal of which was to replace the leadership of B'nei Israel.

Parshat Korach immediately follows *Parshat Shelach*, which describes how the Jewish nation was doomed to wander in the desert for forty years. This was the punishment for the Sin of the Spies who disparaged the Promised Land. Korach took advantage of the people's discontent that followed to stage his challenge to Moshe's leadership.

Moshe's efforts to appease Korach and the other rebels were rejected outright. They continued to foment the fires of jealousy among the people. We are told by the commentaries that this was the first and only *machloket* in history where one person (Moshe) was completely blameless and the other person (Korach) was totally in the wrong.

Finally, Moshe asked God: "Do not turn to their gift-offering! I have not taken even a single donkey of theirs, nor have I wronged even one of them." The next day, God instructed Moshe and Aaron: "Separate yourselves from amid this assembly, for I shall destroy them in an instant!" In an act of *chesed*, Moshe and Aaron fell on their faces and pleaded: "O God, God of the spirits of all flesh, shall one man sin and You be angry with the entire assembly?"

God, in an act of restraint, responded: "Speak to the assembly, saying 'Get yourselves up from all around the dwelling places of Korah, Dathan, and Abiram.'" Then, the earth opened to swallow Korach, the worst of his band, and all of their material possessions, while the 250 firstborn were consumed by fire.[120]

The next day, the people complained, accusing Moshe and Aaron: "You have killed the people of God." In response, God brought on an instantaneous plague and before Aaron could intervene, 14,700 perished.[121]

What is the meaning of this astonishing story?

First, we learn here that pure unadulterated *gevurah* within *gevurah* for evil, selfish, egocentric purposes can bring terrible ruin. Second, we learn that serious threats to the Jewish people can not only come from the outside but from the inside as well. Korach was an educated, intelligent Jew with a prestigious lineage. And that made him all the more dangerous because he became the enemy within. Third, we are told that Korach's sons

---

120. *Bamidbar* 16:15–24.

121. Ibid., 17:6–15.

did immediate *teshuvah* and were spared. Indeed, the Prophet Shmuel was their descendant.

According to the Midrash, to this day on each Rosh Chodesh, Korach calls out from his subterranean hell: "Moshe is true and his Torah is true."[122] Thus God orchestrated a perpetual reminder of the error made by Korach in challenging His will and word.

BALANCE IS THE KEY

As noted earlier, being balanced in each of the *sefirot* is the path to "win." We have only one mission, and we are meant to complete it in a manner that is balanced – a manner that leads to spiritual, emotional, mental, and physical health.

Neither "too much" nor "too little" is the preferred path. If we sense we are on the road of having either too much or too little of one dimension, we must work on this area to achieve balance. Otherwise, we will experience the same excess or deficiency each subsequent year, and it may adversely affect the success of our personal mission.

122. *Tanchuma Korach* 11:11.

DISCUSSION TOPICS FOR *GEVURAH* WITHIN *GEVURAH*

For adults

1. In the seven areas listed in the introduction to Day 9, describing instances where it is constructive to apply pure *gevurah*, how do I measure up? In what areas do I need to demonstrate *gevurah* within *gevurah* and improve myself?
2. Do I tend to be too demanding or judgmental of others? How can I apply *gevurah* within *gevurah* to restrain myself from offering constant criticism, verbalizing negative comments, or making wisecracks that put others down in a condescending manner?
3. Am I a person with an addiction? How am I going to apply *gevurah* within *gevurah* to break my addiction?

For children

1. Do I take the time every day to concentrate when I pray to God?
2. Do I think about having proper *derech eretz* in the way I talk and behave around others all the time, or just when I feel like it or when I am reminded?
3. If I had been Noah, would I have tried to save any other people, telling them about God and how He wants us to behave, or would I have only saved my family? What would I have said and done?

היום עשרה ימים,
שהם שבוע אחד ושלושה ימים, לעומר

(Ha'yom asarah yamim,
she'hem shavuah echad u'shlosha yamim la'Omer)

"TODAY IS THE TENTH DAY,
OR ONE WEEK AND THREE DAYS, OF THE OMER."

DAY 10

Tiferet sh'b'Gevurah
(Harmony/Truth within Strength/Discipline)

***Tiferet* within *gevurah* is the ability to achieve the right measure of both loving-kindness and strength/discipline in all life situations. One who has mastered this *sefirah* combination establishes reasonable boundaries and achieves balance and harmony in the use of *gevurah*.**

In all relationships and interactive communications, striving for the correct measure of *gevurah* requires personal insight, empathy for others, and a measure of self-control to ensure that driving passions do not become destructive obsessions or turn into aggression.

Harmony, balance, and truth serve as important modifiers when reacting with too much strength. Applied wisely, they can help to balance both strong positive and negative reactions.

A TRUE STORY

The following true story illustrates how the influence of *tiferet* helped save a teenage girl:

Many years ago, I taught a girl in her last year of high school. She was a doctor's daughter, came from a good family, had many friends, earned excellent grades, and did not behave with chutzpah. In other words, she was a good girl. Yet, one night she was arrested along with her college-age boyfriend when he sold narcotics to an undercover police officer.

I found out the next day at school and was shocked. Furthermore, I learned that her parents, who could certainly afford to bail her out of the county jail, had chosen not to do so and, rumor had it, they were not even going to visit her.

I was floored. I was a young teacher, not yet a parent, and I was working towards my Masters degree in counseling at the time. I began to visit my student in jail, bringing her books and homework as an excuse to spend time with her and talk to her during what turned out to be a two-week stay behind bars.

Sitting in her cell, dressed in the standard-issue orange jumpsuit, she gradually came to terms with the fact that her parents were not going to bail her out (at least not right away). She also had to think about what it meant that they would not even come to visit her. She had to think about this so-called boyfriend. She had to think about her once bright dream of going to university drifting away forever. She had to think about what on earth she had done, and the situation she placed herself in.

Behind the scenes and unbeknown to their daughter or me, the parents were struggling to do the best thing for her. They were consulting night and day with professionals and had retained a good attorney who was later able to successfully argue that their daughter deserved probation for this first-time offense, given her age, her clean record, and, as I recall, the undercover police officer's confirmation that she was not part of the sale. She was able to return to high school and later attended university.

Over the years, I have thought about this girl and her parents many times, and I have concluded that the parents had made the right decision. They had correctly displayed *tiferet* within *gevurah* in a very complex situation to help save their daughter's life.

How many parents could have done what hers did? Most of us would have reacted with the love and tears of *chesed*. Our natural reaction would have been to visit our daughter every day in the jail, make sure she was eating properly, wasn't too hot or too cold; we would have been anxious to let her know how much we loved her. Some of us would have been programmed to only focus on the good in our daughter, ignoring the "elephant sitting in the room" – the fact that our daughter chose a drug-dealer for a boyfriend and indirectly participated in his criminal activities. But any parent who reacted in this manner would have been in total denial. And, at a time like this, coddling may not have been the most constructive way to help a young woman in her formative years.

Alternatively, some of us might have displayed pure *gevurah* to our daughter. We might have taken the position that she broke the law and deserves whatever punishment the law calls for. She doesn't deserve us as parents. She showed a complete lack of regard for us by what she has done and, therefore, she has lost us. Let her have a public defender. We are not going to deal with this.

WISE PEOPLE HAVE THE END IN MIND

Fortunately for my student, her parents chose to do something far wiser. They may have vacillated between these two extremes in their private discussions, as they traveled on the roller-coaster of resolving the crisis. But, instead of choosing either *chesed* or *gevurah* exclusively, they found a way to blend their deep love and concern for their daughter with the realization that she needed to learn a few lifetime lessons from this incident. They sought professional guidance to figure out what message their daughter needed to hear in order to help her decide on her own to make the necessary changes in her life. I imagine that they had to work hard to restrain both their desire to protect her with an outpouring of love, as well as their desire to scream at her in anger and frustration (not to mention disappointment and sadness). For surely they were asking themselves how their child could have done something like this.

The end result? This fortunate girl's parents demonstrated a far more thoughtful reaction by striving to achieve the right balance of *tiferet* within *gevurah* and thus to act in the best interest of their daughter. They wisely arrived at a strategy with their daughter's future in mind. In the short run, she may not have liked sitting alone in a cell in a county jail, but in the long run, this strategy saved her life.

Her parents did not consider, or act upon, such questions as: "How can we try to keep this arrest secret so that our careers won't suffer?" Or, "How can we try to blame this on the boyfriend and protect our sweet, innocent baby who could never do anything wrong?" Or, "How can we send her away to Auntie X in order to spare her any embarrassment?" Instead, her parents served as a model of how to apply the truth and harmony of *tiferet* to the strength, discipline, and restraint of *gevurah* in coming up with an optimum way of helping their daughter.

Stephen Covey, in his best-selling *The Seven Habits of Highly Effective People* and its sequel, *Living the Seven Habits: The Courage to Change*, describes two such habits as "being proactive" and "beginning with the end in mind." Being proactive involves "making choices based on principles and values, rather than on moods or circumstances," while beginning with the end in mind occurs when people mentally identify and commit themselves "to the principles, values, relationships, and purposes that matter most to them."[123] My student's parents did both. They fought for their daughter's life in a way that would, indeed, save her life both now and long into the future. That is what effective people do in all life situations.

BALANCING TWO EXTREMES

It is easier for us to be a parent or teacher or boss who just looks at the positive and never makes the effort to give constructive criticism to help those in our charge. Conversely, it is also easier for us to discipline, judge, or abandon our subordinates rather than determine when and how we might best guide them.

Tiferet within *gevurah* utilizes *gevurah* (first and foremost) with the appropriate amount of *tiferet* to take correct action in any given situation involving family or friends. *Tiferet* within *gevurah* demonstrates that I both care about and love them by contributing my time and efforts to help them achieve their fullest potential, while at the same time dealing constructively and effectively with any negative behavior.

It takes wisdom, patience, and humility to know how to achieve this, but it is essential. Tempering *gevurah* with *tiferet* creates harmony and balance within strength.

---

123. Stephen R. Covey, *Living the Seven Habits* (NY: Fireside, 2000), from the dust jacket narrative.

DISCUSSION TOPICS FOR *TIFERET* WITHIN *GEVURAH*

For adults

1. Am I confronting a family situation right now with either too much or too little *gevurah*? How can I apply the harmony and balance of *tiferet* to be more effective?
2. As I reflect on my own life, was there a time when my parents were either too overprotective or controlling of me (resulting in my reacting negatively), or, conversely, too permissive and indulgent (resulting in my taking too much advantage)? Would it have been more helpful for them to discipline me or otherwise restrain my negative character traits? How can I make sure I don't repeat this mistake with my own children?
3. Is there anyone who regularly violates my personal boundaries? What am I going to do to let this person know that I expect a certain level of *tiferet* within *gevurah* in our relationship?

For children

1. When I misbehave, do my parents discipline me or let me get away with it? What would be the best thing for me?
2. What is a negative trait I have now that I wish I could change? For example, am I selfish, spoiled, moody, lazy, anxious, insecure, or angry? Am I willing to discuss this with my parents and ask them for some suggestions as to how I could change before things get worse and affect my friendships? Or am I afraid to discuss it with them, because my parents might react too strongly?
3. Do I often get into fights? How can I act and react in a more balanced way so that I don't argue and fight so much?

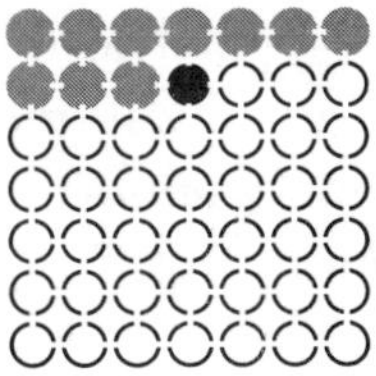

היום אחד עשר יום,
שהם שבוע אחד וארבעה ימים, לעומר

(Ha'yom echad asar yom,
she'hem shavuah echad v'arba'a yamim la'Omer)

"TODAY IS THE ELEVENTH DAY,
OR ONE WEEK AND FOUR DAYS, OF THE OMER."

DAY 11

Netzach sh'b'Gevurah (Endurance within Strength/Discipline)

***Netzach* within *gevurah* is the tenacious effort to persistently and consistently reinforce our commitments to reach our goals or objectives. Without determination, our disciplined efforts may not be sustainable and after a short time can dissipate.**

It takes discipline and strength and *endurance* to achieve any worthy objective or goal. All the commitments we make to ourselves, to our parents, our spouses, our children, our friends and colleagues – and especially those we make to God – require steadfast discipline to carry out. If we fail, we disappoint ourselves and others who counted on us, and who believed we would "cross the finish line." (After all, no one applauds failure or admires a quitter.) But the endurance of *netzach* added to the discipline of *gevurah* can provide the extra impetus to help us succeed.

As previously noted, *gevurah* can be constructive or destructive, depending upon the goal to which it is applied. And so, too, when *gevurah* is paired with *netzach*. If it is applied to the steadfast pursuit of a cause, a belief, or a relationship that is moral, ethical and "right" in the eyes of God, then *netzach* within *gevurah* is an essential combination, virtually ensuring the success of the endeavor. Conversely, if it is applied to the mindless pursuit of a cause, belief or relationship that is unethical, immoral, and "wrong" in the eyes of God, then *netzach* within *gevurah* can generate a harmful spiral that can result in terrible outcomes.

SURVIVAL OF THE JEWS

From an inspirational standpoint, the miraculous survival of the Jewish people through the millennia is a prime example of *netzach* within *gevurah* because it took amazing strength and perseverance.

Consider the crucial role that women played during the 210 years of Egyptian slavery. When their husbands wanted to stop having children because they would be doomed to a life of slavery, the women were determined not to give up, and they succeed in restoring their husbands' resolve.

Consider Rabbi Akiva's reaction, when 24,000 of his students died in a plague because they did not show respect for each other. Rather than succumb to grief over such a huge tragedy, Rabbi Akiva started over with five students, one of whom was Rabbi Shimon Bar Yochai, the future author of the Zohar.

There are so many examples from Jewish history that they are too numerous to mention, but consider:

- the against-all-odds uprising of the Warsaw Ghetto
- the actions of Oskar Schindler, a non-Jew, who saved countless lives and was later named one of the Righteous Among the Nations
- all of those who survived the Nazi horror and those who did not, but whose surviving family members went on to build meaningful lives
- the establishment of the State of Israel, which went from an underdeveloped nation to one of the most technologically innovative and fully-developed nations in the world, in just sixty short years,[124] and which did so while fighting several wars and coping with constant terrorism

---

124. International Monetary Fund findings (Human Development Index) released November 4, 2010. The Index ranks Israel as number 15 among the developed nations of the world, placing it just behind France.

- the *ba'al teshuvah* movement which, starting in the 1960s, has reignited Torah observance among secular Jews
- the story of Gilad Schalit who endured over five years as a prisoner in Gaza and the tenacity of his parents and others dedicated to freeing him

So many amazing and inspiring stories of *netzach* within *gevurah*!

EXAMPLES FROM TORAH

Modern-day Jews have an amazing history and ancestry to draw on when taking on new commitments (whether big or small) that demand endurance in self-discipline. Some of the best models are described in the Torah. Take Yaakov for example:

Needing to flee to escape the murderous rage of his brother Esav, he fled to the home of his uncle Lavan, where he promptly fell in love with his cousin Rachel and agreed to work for seven years in order to earn her hand in marriage. But, to his great dismay, his uncle switched the older Leah for Yaakov's beloved Rachel under the chuppah. Tricked into a marriage he did not want, Yaakov, nevertheless, agreed to work yet another seven years to be able to marry Rachel as well. Altogether, Yaakov ended up working for Lavan a total of twenty years diligently building up his uncle's herd of sheep and goats. During this time, Lavan never once raised his wages and bargained with him over which flocks Yaakov was allowed to keep. To work under these conditions all these years for an untrustworthy conniver and liar took extraordinary *netzach* within *gevurah* on the part of Yaakov.

Yaakov's parting words provide a glimpse at what it took for him to brave the time with Lavan:

> "These twenty years I have been with you, your ewes and she-goats never miscarried, nor did I eat rams of your flock. That which was mangled I never brought you – I myself would bear the loss, from me you would exact it, whether it was stolen by day or stolen by night. This is how I was: By day scorching heat consumed me, and frost by night; my sleep drifted from my eyes. This is my twenty years in your household: I served you fourteen years for your two daughters, and six years for your flocks; and you changed my wage a hundred times. Had not the God of my father – the God of Avraham and the

> Dread of Yitzchak – been with me, you would surely have now sent me away empty-handed . . ."[125]

These words describe the enduring restraint Yaakov had to display and the strength he had to have in order to survive in the house of Lavan.

RABBI ELYASHIV

Rabbi Yosef Shalom Elyashiv, the Torah giant who passed away at age 102 in 2012, is an example of a modern-day Jew whose approach to life emulated his illustrious forefathers.

In a *Jerusalem Post* article, entitled "The Rewards of Diligence," Jonathan Rosenblum chronicles how *netzach* within *gevurah* played a key role in the various elements of Rav Elyashiv's remarkable life:

> The quality that he exemplified above all others – total discipline and self-control – is the rarest, and therefore the hardest for most of us to relate to . . . Even his external appearance conveyed who he was. Tall, ramrod-straight until the very end, he walked purposefully from place to place, staring ahead, his brow furrowed in thought . . .
>
> How could a human being maintain such consistency over a lifetime? For ninety years, he sat alone in the same small synagogue, studying almost all day long except for the hours he answered halachic questions or gave his daily Talmud class, which was open to all . . . He rose every morning between 2 and 3 a.m. to begin his studying, despite suffering from frail health his whole life.

Beyond the physical manifestations of enduring discipline, what about the internal fiber of this rabbinic giant? Rosenblum continues:

> He could be pressured neither from the Right or the Left; *haredi* "political correctness" meant nothing to him. He would not tolerate in his presence any disparagement of Rabbi Avraham Yitzhak HaCohen Kook, the first Ashkenazi chief rabbi, who had proposed Elyashiv's match with his wife and officiated at his wedding. After he put his imprimatur on a certain solution to the problem of building

---

125. *Bereshit* 31:38–42.

> a particular highway over ancient graves, he was pelted by zealots in his own Mea She'arim neighborhood. He was unintimidated.

Rosenblum's conclusion says it all:

> Above all, his life stands as a monument to the power of discipline and determination. For that discipline . . . allowed him to master the vast halachic literature to the extent that the most complicated life-and-death halachic questions over the last thirty years all eventually reached his door without his ever having to say, "I don't know."[126]

INDIVIDUAL ACTS OF DETERMINED DISCIPLINE

While the above examples are remarkable, any ordinary person is capable of great feats when he or she works on the trait of *netzach* within *gevurah*.

When a secular Jew decides to start keeping Torah law – honoring the Shabbat, or abstaining from eating non-kosher food – he or she must rise to an elevated level of *netzach* within *gevurah*. I, for one, am deeply respectful of those who manage to refrain from pursuing activities that they had customarily engaged in on Friday night or Shabbat day. It takes great strength and determination to commit to keep God's laws and stick with it when it is a new practice.

Similarly, when a middle-aged person decides to return to school to learn a new profession and retrain for a new job, it takes great endurance to return to studying habits not put to use in some twenty years or more. Or, when any person of any age undertakes for the first time a nutritional and exercise regimen (in order to lose weight, lower cholesterol or blood sugars), it is no mean feat.

All of the above require applying *netzach* within *gevurah*, a *sefirah* combination which helps each of us to achieve our goals and ultimately our mission while reinforcing our sense of self-worth.

---

126. Jonathan Rosenblum, "Rabbi Yosef Shalom Elyashiv: The Rewards of Diligence," *The Jerusalem Post Magazine*, July 27, 2012.

DISCUSSION TOPICS FOR *NETZACH* WITHIN *GEVURAH*

For adults

1. Can I recall and describe a time in my life when I quit in the middle of an undertaking, which, in hindsight, I wish I had completed? What caused me to quit? Do I have the tenacity to stick with things today?
2. Are there any barriers, self-imposed or other-imposed, standing between me and a goal I would like to achieve at this time in my life? What am I going to do about resolving this problem?
3. If anyone in my family has any addiction of any type, have I taken on the role of an enabler? What can I do to help him or her confront the problem?

For children

1. What projects have I quit before they were finished? How did that make me feel?
2. If I have a hard time finishing homework assignments, reading books to the end, or completing chores assigned to me, what can I do to better discipline myself to finish what I start?
3. Have I ever depended upon others to finish what they were going to do for me, but they failed to do so? How did that make me feel?

היום שנים עשר יום,
שהם שבוע אחד וחמישה ימים, לעומר

(Ha'yom sh'neim asar yom,
she'hem shavuah echad v'chamisha yamim la'Omer)

"TODAY IS THE TWELFTH DAY,
OR ONE WEEK AND FIVE DAYS, OF THE OMER."

DAY 12

Hod sh'b'Gevurah (Humility within Strength/Discipline)

Gevurah* is a powerful force whether in the form of strength, discipline, judgment, or restraint. Whether *gevurah* is expressed in thought, speech or action, it can be severe and even destructive if it originates in arrogance. But when *gevurah* is filtered through *hod* (humility), it is tempered with gentleness and consideration for others.

As we visit the character trait of *hod* each week, we see that it is an essential attribute to cultivate. Whether it is humility within *chesed*, humility within *gevurah*, or humility within any of the other *sefirot*, this trait is critical in leading a meaningful, balanced, grounded, and happy life.

None other than King Shlomo wrote: "The result of humility is fear (awe) of God, wealth, honor, and life."[127] When we realize that God runs the world and everything in it, and that all He does is for our own good, we are rewarded.

Our Sages echoed this lesson when they asked, "Who is rich?" answering, "He who is happy with his lot."[128]

When we understand – through restraining our conceit and humbly

127. *Mishlei* 22:4.

128. *Avot* 4:1.

accepting our life circumstances – that our life is exactly what God intended for us, we demonstrate *hod* within *gevurah.*

Let's take a look at two modern-day stories to learn about this combination of attributes and how two women's lives were enriched by their acceptance of "their lot."

TWO STRONG WOMEN

Meira Bresler Reimer was only 28 when she died in Jerusalem, on Shabbat *Bereshit,* surrounded at home by her loving family after having lost a valiant two-year battle with a lethal form of bone cancer. At the funeral, her husband, Danny, spoke to the hundreds of mourners at Har Menuchot Cemetery in Jerusalem. Through pain, agony and tears, he described Meira's courage in accepting her disease without *any* anger at God.

This remarkable young woman's life had been filled with vibrancy. Born in America, she had worked for the Jewish people and Jewish causes her whole life. She helped Jews in Ukraine. She helped introduce the non-observant to *Yiddishkeit.* Among the many things she did in the final year of life, Meira wrote a letter to her daughter for her every birthday until age 21. And although her strength was ebbing, she also fulfilled a dream within the last few weeks of her life of making *aliyah* to Israel.[129]

Such giving! She left her family a legacy filled with love and inspiration and devoid of bitterness or anger. How did she manage this? The answer is so simple. Meira displayed *hod* within *gevurah,* humbly accepting God's will for her sojourn in this world. The outcome was extraordinary.

Another inspirational story is that of Stella Frankl (Tzuriya Kochevet Bat Sarah), who was diagnosed in her mid-40s with advanced and inoperable stomach cancer. As related by *Jerusalem Post* writer Barbara Sofer, Stella's response to her ordeal is the perfect model of *hod* within *gevurah.*

Stella, who is Japanese, met her Jewish but non-observant husband, Yarden, when both were studying at a US university. Over time, Stella began to explore Judaism and, when she converted, she insisted that her husband start learning about his faith. Ultimately, this led to the entire family becoming Torah-observant and making *aliyah.* As Stella told Sofer,

---

129. Judy Siegel, "Young mother from US with terminal illness achieves dream by becoming new immigrant," *The Jerusalem Post,* September 16, 2011, 10.

"We felt that Israel was the best place to bring up our children as Jews . . . And it would be a chance for spiritual growth for us."[130]

At the time of this writing, Stella is still receiving chemotherapy, and Yarden is raising money for a Gush Etzion sick fund to help families of other patients meet medical expenses. To those around the world who read his blog, "Crossing the Yarden," he gives advice to go out for a walk with someone you love, talk about how amazing it is to love someone, and not to think about the future. He advises to just focus on how good the present is and to take advantage of whatever it is one has. His is a heartfelt demonstration of *hod* within *gevurah* that will last forever in this world and the World to Come.

These two young couples, Stella and Yarden and Meira and Danny, have achieved so very much. Their initial reaction could have been: "Why me God? Why do this to me? You ruined my life!" But these two couples directed their prayers to heaven asking for healing, and accepting the outcome, humbly, as God's will. They were wise and rich in ways that no words can capture. They have provided a legacy to their children, their family, and to all of us who read about them. And, in so doing, they have helped to bring Mashiach that much closer, by living with such pure *emunah* and *bitachon*, the reward for mastering *hod* within *gevurah*, along with all the other *middot* they displayed.

THE EXAMPLE OF YITZCHAK

Such humility and strength has been bequeathed to the Jewish people by none other than Yitzchak, who is the personification of *gevurah* and who exemplifies how to balance all the other attributes within it.

His application of *hod* within *gevurah* is especially apparent in his dealings with his twin sons, Esav and Yaakov. The commentaries make much of the fact that Yitzchak seemingly favored Esav, while Rivka favored Yaakov.[131] When she was pregnant, Rivka had felt "the children agitating within her" and she had received an explanation from God that: "Two nations are in your womb; two regimes from your insides shall be separated; the might shall pass from one regime to the other, and the elder

130. Barbara Sofer, "Riding Through the Long Night," *The Jerusalem Post Magazine*, November 18, 2011, 38.
131. *Bereshit* 25:28.

[Esav] shall serve the younger [Yaakov]."[132] Thus Rivka understood who needed to receive his father's blessing of the firstborn.

Yet Yitzchak was intent on giving the blessing to Esav. Was he really fooled about Esav's true, evil nature, or did he know that one day the world of Esav and the world of Yaakov would work harmoniously together? Regardless, Rivka took matters into her own hands, in order to ensure that the blessing would go to Yaakov. The story of the ruse she devised is well-known.[133]

When Yitzchak learned that he had given the blessing intended for Esav to Yaakov instead, he reacted in a manner that dramatically illustrates the attribute of humility within strength. In the same situation, another person may have complained angrily, "What happened here? Who duped me? How dare you try to pull the wool over my eyes? I am Yitzchak! I am the father! I will give the blessing to whomever I see fit!" But Yitzchak did none of that. When he realized what had happened, He immediately saw the hand of God in the event. As the Torah tells it:

> Then Yitzchak trembled in very great perplexity, and said, "Who – where – is the one who hunted game, brought it to me, and I partook of all when you had not yet come, and I blessed him? Indeed, he shall remain blessed!"[134]

Yitzchak's greatness lies in the fact that he never severed his connection with God. He understood that if someone else got Esav's blessing, it was the will of God. He realized this in an instant, just as he did at the *Akeidah*. His acts are the personification of *hod* within *gevurah*.

THE EXAMPLE OF NAOMI

Earlier we examined the story of Ruth and Naomi with the focus on Ruth. Now let's take a look at Naomi.

When she instructed her daughters-in-law, Ruth and Orpah, to return home to their royal Moabite families rather than accompany her to Eretz Yisrael, Naomi displayed *hod* within *gevurah*:

---

132. Ibid., 25:22–23.
133. Ibid., 27:1–46.
134. Ibid., 27:33.

> "Go return, each of you to her mother's house. May Hashem deal kindly with you, as you have dealt kindly with the dead and with me! May Hashem grant that you may find security, each in the home of her husband."[135]

Naomi gave these instructions although she was a lonely widow bereft of children; she had no one left to care for her at the end of her life. Yet, she humbly restrained what would surely have been a natural inclination to put her needs before those of her daughters-in-law. She did not ask them to stay and care for her in her old age; rather, she did her utmost to send them both home. Orpah obeyed, but Ruth followed Naomi nevertheless. And in her response, Ruth displayed *netzach* within *chesed* as we noted in Week One.

THE EXAMPLE OF MOSHE

Another and quite different example of *hod* within *gevurah* – which brings tears to my eyes every time I read it – is Moshe's reaction to God's verdict that he would not be permitted to enter the Promised Land.

We know that Moshe did not accept this verdict easily, and that he pleaded 514 times that it be overturned.[136] Each time his request was denied. Having done his best to appeal, Moshe accepted the will of God, just as Yitzchak, just as Sarah, and just as so many others. The outcome was not what any of them wanted, nor what they had planned, nor perhaps what they had dreamed of. But once they had given their all, each of them humbly accepted what God decreed.

135. *Megillat Ruth* 1:8–9.

136. *Devarim Rabbah* 11:10.

DISCUSSION TOPICS FOR *HOD* WITHIN *GEVURAH*

For adults

1. Can I describe a situation where I humbly accepted an outcome, even though it was not what I had hoped or prayed for? What did I learn from that experience?
2. When a situation arises – involving my spouse, children, or other family members – do I listen to the quiet still voice that guides me to do what is best for them instead of for me?
3. Do I have the *emunah* to accept outcomes that I didn't intend and still retain my love of, relationship with, and service to Hashem? Can I think of an example?

For children

1. When I don't get to do something I really wanted to do, how do I react? Do I display humility?
2. The last time I was disappointed about something, did I spend any time feeling sorry for myself, getting angry or acting moody? How might I handle matters differently in the future?
3. When people disagree with me, make fun of me or call me names, how do I react? Can I think of other possible ways of responding that won't result in hurt feelings or a fight?

היום שלושה עשר יום,
שהם שבוע אחד וששה ימים, לעומר

(Ha'yom shlosha asar yom,
she'hem shavuah echad v'shisha yamim la'Omer)

"TODAY IS THE THIRTEENTH DAY,
OR ONE WEEK AND SIX DAYS, OF THE OMER."

DAY 13

Yesod sh'b'Gevurah (Bonding within Strength/Discipline)

Without the influence of *yesod* within *gevurah,* breakdowns in relationships can occur. The bonding of *yesod* combined with the strength of *gevurah* makes it possible for people to stick together through thick and thin.

We need to strive to keep relationships strong and lasting, while restraining any tendencies to engage in behavior that whittles away the bond. In applying *yesod* within *gevurah*, we aim to stay connected, refusing to pursue our selfish interests or to throw in the towel at the first sign of trouble.

THE TWELVE SONS OF YAAKOV

The story of the twelve sons of Yaakov illustrates what happens when bonding is weak or absent, but also – and most important of all – how it can be restored and how *yesod* within *gevurah* can triumph.

The twelve sons – who would become the Twelve Tribes of Israel – came from four different mothers, and this caused frictions between them. The situation came to a boil when ten of the brothers decided to sell Yosef, the oldest son of their father's favorite wife, Rachel, into slavery, hoping to be rid of him for good. Some of the brothers actually wanted to kill him, but they were convinced by Yehuda that selling him was the better option. Then they told their father that Yosef had been killed by a wild animal. Obviously, this was a complete breakdown of familial bonding. Brothers simply do not sell, or kill, brothers.

Twenty-two years later the ten brothers who had been involved in the sale of Yosef were sent by Yaakov to Egypt to get food for the entire family, as famine had hit the land of Canaan where they were living. Unbeknown to all, Yosef was no longer a slave. Because of his ability to accurately interpret dreams – an ability which had aroused the jealousy and judgment of his brothers during his youth – he had been appointed the Viceroy of Egypt, second in command only to the Pharaoh.

When Yosef learned that his brothers were in town, he wanted to know if they had changed. He restrained himself from reuniting with them, and instead set up an elaborate test that eventually led Yehuda to play a central role in bringing all the brothers together.

Yosef had demanded that the brothers bring with them the youngest, Binyamin, the other son of Rachel. Yehuda took complete responsibility for doing so, convincing Yaakov to let Binyamin travel with them to Egypt: "I will personally guarantee him; of my own hand you can demand him. If I do not bring him back to you and stand him before you, then I will have sinned to you for all time."[137]

Yehuda's commitment to Yaakov became the first step in the *tikkun* of the brothers' earlier sin, and it was the beginning of the restoration of the balance in the family through *yesod* within *gevurah.*

After seeing his full brother Binyamin alive and well, Yosef restrained his desire to embrace him and reveal his identity. Once again he arranged a test for the brothers: Yosef had his silver goblet planted in Binyamin's sack, making it appear that Binyamin stole it. Riders chased after the brothers, opened the sack, and accused them of theft. It appeared that Binyamin would be imprisoned or enslaved.

Yehuda, in order to honor the commitment to their father to bring Binyamin home safely, first offered to become the Viceroy's slave. In so doing, Yehuda displayed *yesod* within *gevurah.* Yosef, continuing to test his

---

137. *Bereshit* 43:9.

brothers, responded that only the one with the goblet would remain as a slave, and the other brothers should "go in peace to your father."[138]

WHAT WOULD YOU HAVE DONE?

Let us pause in the story to examine the analytical reasoning that many, if not most of us, would have employed if placed in a similar situation. It probably would have sounded like this:

"Binyamin was caught red-handed stealing something of value from the second most powerful person in Egypt, the most powerful empire in the world! He should have known better! He risked getting everyone else in trouble as well. How could he have done this to us?! It is a miracle that the Viceroy is willing to let the rest of us go home. And we should seize this chance, for isn't it better for our father to have ten of his sons back alive, even if it means losing another one? There is nothing else we can do. We are in this man's palace in Egypt, so we can't very well fight it out and prevail. This is a lost cause."

Now consider what the brothers did:

In one of the most stirring scenes in all of Torah, the ten brothers, who had each played a role in the sale of Yosef (except for Reuven) chose to act in a unified manner to bind their fate with that of Binyamin, knowing that their choice could result in their immediate death.

Yehuda's full display of *yesod* within *gevurah* (as well as his noble leadership, *malchut*) emerged. He simply would not permit Binyamin's imprisonment to be their "ticket home." Yehuda had given his word and he meant to keep it, or die trying. And his brothers would be his allies in whatever plan he devised to save Binyamin. They chose to follow his lead and direction. It does not matter what they thought or what they wanted. They voiced no opinion. They just stood together, united as one.

This was the *tikkun* that God and Yosef had been waiting for.

Yehuda approached the Viceroy (Yosef) and humbly repeated his supplication to let his brothers leave, offering himself as the Viceroy's slave. Using all his powers of persuasion, Yehuda tried one final time to influence the Viceroy with words, concluding with another display of *yesod* within *gevurah*:

---

138. Ibid., 44:1–17.

> "For your servant took responsibility for the youth from my father saying, 'If I do not bring him back to you then I will be sinning to my father for all time.' Now, therefore, please let your servant remain instead of the youth as a servant to my lord, and let the youth go with his brothers. For how can I go to my father if the youth is not with me, lest I see the evil that will befall my father!"[139]

Hearing Yehuda's appeal, Yosef realized that the brothers of four mothers have now bonded and were unified to protect Binyamin, the youngest brother. He realized that after twenty-two years, the brothers all cared about how their lack of unity would affect their father, Yaakov. They had reined in their individual differences in order to achieve *yesod*, the foundation of bonding. And so, the time had come to reveal for Yosef to reveal himself:

> No one remained with him when he made himself known to his brothers. He cried in a loud voice that Egypt and Pharaoh's household heard. And Yosef said to his brothers, "I am Yosef. Is my father still alive?'[140]

Yosef's revelation to his brothers is among the most important passages in the Torah. For, in that moment, all twelve brothers stood together and displayed *yesod* within *gevurah* – a model for the future Chosen People.

OUR HEAVENLY MISSION

It is said that when we die and our *neshamah* travels to heaven, we will be asked: "What is your name?" This question is meant to be far deeper than it appears on the surface, for it seeks to discover if our name is aligned with (or cut off from) our heavenly mission. Did we, like Yosef, fulfill our mission on earth, by becoming the best person we could be?

Yosef demonstrated how a Jew could live in exile and yet remain completely faithful to an ethical Jewish life, despite whatever cruelty, injustice, treachery, and hardships were visited upon him. He went from pit and prison to the highest pinnacle of renown. Despite what his brothers had

---

139. Ibid., 44:32–34.
140. Ibid., 45:1–3.

done to him, he forgave them and worked tirelessly to ensure the closeness and continuity of his family once they migrated to Egypt. And finally, in death, he left explicit instructions that his body be taken back to Eretz Yisrael when all the Jews would leave Egypt, reminding us that only Israel is our home, as promised by God Himself.

When he disclosed his identity to his brothers – when he said, "I am Yosef" – he affirmed that he did not cut himself off from God, or his father, or his family tradition, or his own identity.

Can we say the same? Are we one with our name and with our unique mission on earth? If we are not, hopefully, the Omer count can start to clear the fog. The process of counting the Omer, and working at each of the 49 *sefirah* combinations, can help us to see ourselves more clearly.

DISCUSSION TOPICS FOR *YESOD* WITHIN *GEVURAH*

For adults

1. Have I ever worked hard to mend a rift within my family? How did that feel?
2. Is there currently a rift or distance or coldness in my family that has been caused by some disagreement? What steps could I take to help resolve it?
3. How can I practice holding my tongue so that I don't prevent stronger relationships from developing in our family?

For children

1. Am I fighting with someone at school or in my family right now? What caused the fight? What could I do to make peace?
2. When an argument is over, do I forgive and forget easily, or do I remember it and bear a grudge?
3. What is a better way of handling disagreements than having a fight? What else could I practice doing?

היום ארבעה עשר יום, שהם שני שבועות, לעומר

(Ha'yom arba'a asar yom, she'hem shnei shavuot la'Omer)

"TODAY IS THE FOURTEENTH DAY, OR TWO WEEKS, OF THE OMER."

DAY 14

Malchut sh'b'Gevurah (Leadership/Nobility within Strength/Discipline)

Malchut emerges from the balanced integration of the other six *sefirot* – *chesed, gevurah, tiferet, netzach, hod,* and *yesod.* The result is leadership, nobility, dignity, and sovereignty. *Malchut* within *gevurah* introduces an element of maturity and self-composure into relationships and, even more importantly, it consistently and constantly expresses itself with dignity and nobility no matter what is the issue, judgment, interaction, or reaction to a life situation.

The Torah giant, Rabbi Shlomo Zalman Auerbach, routinely displayed *malchut* within *gevurah*. He never compromised his high halachic standards, but he knew how to balance his *gevurah* with *malchut* and treat his fellow Jews with dignity. Writes Jonathan Rosenblum in *The Jerusalem Post Magazine*: "[Rav Auerbach] would not jump up from his seat on the bus if a woman not dressed according to halachic standards sat down next to him, lest she feel insulted. He would simply push the button as if his stop was coming up and get off the bus."[141]

141. Jonathan Rosenblum "My Brothers Do I Seek," *The Jerusalem Post Magazine*, January 6, 2012, 34.

The famous Klausenberger Rebbe, who lost his wife and eleven children in the Holocaust, was another model of *malchut* within *gevurah*. For thirteen years, he worked to raise money in order to build the Laniado Hospital in Natanya to provide a Torah approach to healing. Although he was famous for his stringency regarding the *halachah* to "guard one's gaze," he knew how to balance his views when Jewish souls were at stake. For example, when he learned about a situation involving Jewish prostitutes in the DP camps after World War II, he acted immediately. Writes Rosenblum: "[When the Rebbe] heard that young Jewish girls, dehumanized by what they had been through, had set up a red light district, he personally went to bring them back to their heritage."[142]

These giants restrained themselves from judging, publicly rebuking, or embarrassing others, while working hard work on behalf of the Jewish people. We can learn so much from them in helping preserve the dignity of the Jewish people and the State of Israel in the world. Is it not possible for us to restrain our own need to publicly air our differences with other Jews? What should we do about groups of Jews who are so misguided that they berate their brethren, instead of trying to figure out how to communicate their views more effectively?

Rabbi Aryeh Levin wrote in his Last Will and Testament: "I have tried with all my power to implant in the hearts of the members of my family a love of human beings. Instead of sowing a dislike for the irreligious, I have striven to implant love, respect, and esteem for the devout."[143] How much better our world would be if we learned to emulate this prescription.

The Talmud says that every generation that has not rebuilt the Beit HaMikdash is judged as if it were responsible for its destruction.[144] I, for one, would just as soon not have that on my conscience. What about you? The secret is developing the trait of *malchut* within *gevurah*.

AVRAHAM AND LOT

Avraham taught us how to deal with those we disagree with. For example, when quarrelling broke out between his herdsmen and those of his

142. Ibid.
143. Raz, *A Tzaddik in Our Time*, 465.
144. Yerushalmi *Yoma* 1:1.

nephew Lot, Avraham realized that he and Lot best live apart. He told his nephew:

> "Please let there be no strife between me and you, and between my herdsmen and your herdsmen, for we are kinsman. Is not all the land before you? Please separate from me: If you go left, then I will go right, and if you go right, then I will go left."[145]

This episode illustrates the nobility with which we should attempt to resolve our differences.

A lot was at stake for Avraham. He had been attempting to teach everyone he met about the One God and an ethical way of life where kindness to others was a desirable norm. Avraham did not want his Canaanite neighbors to see any bickering between him and Lot.

Although Avraham must have been sorely disappointed in Lot – he and Sarah were up in years and had no children, so Lot was their most likely successor – he did not reveal how much his nephew had let him down. He was aware that not every thought should be verbalized. He did not waste any energy brow-beating Lot with comments like, "What's gotten into you?" or, "Don't you realize you're killing me with your attitude?" or, "You are throwing your future away!" Instead, he came to terms with the fact that the gap between them was real.

Avraham's mission was focused on spirituality, ethics, and serving the will of the One God. Lot was clearly gravitating towards the material world of money, acquisitions, and pleasure. So, without severing their relationship completely, Avraham arrived at an equitable solution and communicated it in a firm, dignified, yet non-abrasive manner. That is *malchut* within *gevurah* in action.

What Avraham wanted to avoid was any desecration of God's Name by the infighting between himself and Lot. And he did not want their division exposed to the outside world. He displayed *gevurah* by restraining himself. He calmly said to Lot, "Let's separate," and then permitted Lot to have first pick of wherever he wanted to settle.

Wouldn't it be a great and special thing if Jews today could resolve their differences in a similar way? When Jews are divided and then publicly air those divisions, who wins?

145. *Bereshit* 12:8–9.

Malchut within *gevurah* – it is not exactly a lost art, but certainly one we seldom see on display.

MOSHE'S REACTION TO THE GOLDEN CALF

We know the tragic story:

After three million men, women and children experienced an encounter with God at Mount Sinai, Moshe ascended the mountain to receive the rest of the Torah. Moshe was due to return in forty days, but due to an error in counting, the people thought he was not coming back. And so they made the Golden Calf. God responded angrily, telling Moshe:

> "Go, descend – for your people that you brought up from the land of Egypt has become corrupt. They have strayed quickly from the way that I have commanded them . . . I have seen this people, and behold, it is a stiff-necked people. And now, desist from Me. Let My anger flare up against them and I shall annihilate them; and I shall make you a great nation."[146]

What did Moshe do? He refused to accept that harsh verdict; instead, he pleaded with God:

> "Relent from Your flaring anger and reconsider regarding the evil against Your people. Remember for the sake of Avraham, Yitzchak, and Israel, Your servants, to whom You swore by Yourself, and You told them, 'I shall increase your offspring like the stars of the heaven, and this entire land of which I spoke, I shall give to your offspring and it shall be their heritage forever.'"

Since God keeps all promises, He reconsidered. And Moshe's pleas spared the lives of over three million Jews.

Moshe's plea on behalf of the people displayed perfect *malchut* within *gevurah*. From this moment on, Moshe became not just the servant of God who would do everything God commanded. Rather, Moshe became the true leader of the Jewish people.

Of course, God was justified in His fury. The Jews were (and are)

146. *Shemot* 32:1–30.

"stiff-necked." But Moshe did not want them all punished – he himself rounded up and killed the perpetrators most directly responsible, though he defended the people as a whole. What an amazing demonstration of *malchut* within *gevurah!*

GOD AND PHARAOH

God, Himself, is the best model of *malchut* within *gevurah*. In the above example, He restrained Himself from executing the harsh verdict He had in mind. But nowhere is this divine attribute more apparent than in God's dealings with the Pharaoh.

As we know, the ten plagues hit Egypt consecutively over a one-year period. The first, second, fourth, fifth, seventh, eighth plagues were preceded by a personal warning from Moshe and Aaron to Pharaoh. Now, God could have unleashed the plagues simultaneously on one day, or over a much shorter period of time. He could have chosen not to bring down any plagues whatsoever and just wipe out Egypt like He wiped out Sodom – with no warnings or time for repentance.

But, in His divine wisdom – and in a display of *malchut* within *gevurah* – God meted out the ten plagues over a long period of time, which gave the Pharaoh ample opportunity to make the free-will choice to let the Jewish people go. Tragically for him and all of Egypt, Pharaoh did not make this choice until after the tenth plague.

The way God conducts Himself is how we are supposed to conduct ourselves as well. So when we have a child who deserves some form of punishment for his or her misbehavior, it behooves us to attempt to arrive at a mature and self-composed way of handling the matter, so that the child has the opportunity to do *teshuvah*.

The Pharaoh failed to respond to his chances for *teshuvah*. On the one hand, he displayed *gevurah* by stubbornly refusing to give up his power and authority. On the other hand, he was unable to find the type of strength that would allow him to see that he was not "god," but just an earthly king. This was a fatal misuse of *gevurah* and a failure to achieve *malchut*. He threw away the chances he was given to do the "right thing."

We just have to pray that neither we, nor our loved ones, make the same mistakes he did and cut ourselves off from God. Our goal should always be to exercise discipline, make judgments, and take strong action in a way that strengthens the human spirit, preserves our relationships and the dignity of all parties involved.

HOW TO REBUKE

Sadly, many of us don't even have to leave home to have our self-esteem bruised or even slammed. Examples are too numerous to count. How many times have we as parents said very loudly to one of our children in front of the other siblings, "You're impossible!" or, "What am I going to do with you?" or, "When will you stop trying my patience?" or, the most popular catch-all, "What is wrong with you?!"

Such statements are degrading and their effect multiplies when they are repeated constantly.

One of the finest books ever written on this subject – *Your Child's Self Esteem* by Dorothy Briggs – offers superb guidance and issues a loud wake-up call to parents: "Blame – negative judgment – is at the core of emotional disorder and low self-esteem . . . To nurture truly, switch from being a *judge* to being a *reactor*."[147]

The author notes that using the word "you" followed by a noun or adjective when describing a child sends a message of judgment and rebuke. In contrast, the word "I" followed by a statement of our feelings reveals to the child our reaction to his or her behavior. So, for example, if a child (or an adult for that matter) lies to us and we respond, "You are a liar," this message is quite different than saying, "I feel that I cannot rely upon your words when they don't match up with what you do." With the second comment, we are able to address the behavior without destroying the other person's worth and self-image.

Parents must be an example of *malchut* within *gevurah* so that their children grow up with *derech eretz* and the ability to look at themselves and the world-at-large positively. This is how they will come to believe in both, and work to elevate both.

However, parents are not likely to model this attribute, when their dialogue with each other (sometimes in front of the children) goes like this: "Is dinner *ever* going to be ready on time?" or, "Are you going to be late

---

147. Dorothy C. Briggs, *Your Child's Self-Esteem* (Garden City, NY: Doubleday & Company, 1970 and Dolphin Books Edition, 1975), 83–86.

again?" or, "Could you just give me some peace and quiet?" or, "Is nothing ever good enough for you?" or, "When is the last time you said you loved me?" or, "How do you expect me to be happy with you when you _____ [fill in the blank]?"

Such expressions of dissatisfaction work their way into the fabric of the family and eventually ruin the child's self-esteem. They indicate a total absence of dignity combined with a total lack of restraint. A bad mix.

Critical and judgmental words and destructive actions of others impact all our lives in a negative way. For, when dignity disintegrates, self-esteem plummets. No wonder the child comes home saying, "Nobody likes me."

WHY WE FAIL TO BALANCE DISCIPLINE WITH RESPECT

Why is this such a common problem?

Many of us did not have good role models in our childhood that consistently balanced discipline with respect. But that does not excuse us, as adults, from correcting this wrong.

Most of us know that the proper way to rebuke is to label the wrongful "act" but not the "person." This is easiest to accomplish if we ourselves are in a state of emotional control. Unfortunately, many of us rebuke others in moments of anger, or exhaustion, or frustration. That reduces the likelihood that our message will be framed with respect and, consequently, its effectiveness as well. We should each try to live by the rule that rebuke must never be delivered in the heat of anger. Dorothy Briggs, a successful teacher and family counselor, offers this simple and wise advice, which once implemented can bring about an immediate change in family dynamics:

> When anger comes . . . see it for what it is: a code signaling the presence of an earlier emotion. The next time you're angry, look for the underlying emotion. Catch hold of the *first* feeling and share *it* rather than the code. Then, you deal with the cause of your anger . . . this habit makes you a positive model for your children. In addition, sharing primary feelings does less damage to self-esteem than do hot verbal assaults. Anger frightens children; sharing primary emotions reduces their times of fear. When you share those first feelings, send "I-reactions" rather than "you-judgments."[148]

148. Ibid., p. 205.

Another simple piece of advice: never rebuke others publicly.

There may be situations when we literally have no choice, but these should be extremely rare. As a rule, we should quietly and calmly ask the person to step into a private location so that the two of us can talk. This is proper *halachah* and increases the chances of a successful outcome.

Many of us don't take the time or have the patience to plan the right time and place to convey our message. But this is a simple matter of self-discipline. It is essential for us to think about how we would like to be rebuked ourselves and make sure to act accordingly. Perhaps it would help to reflect on the fact that our rebuke – and especially the way it is delivered – will have a lasting impact on the recipient. Again, from the wisdom of Rabbi Yissocher Frand: "If criticism was used as a punishment, a way of withholding love, then when the child grows up, he will react to criticism, from whatever source, with anger."[149]

This does not mean that we have to compromise on discipline. It means that we must choose to exercise it in a context that fosters the self-esteem of another. If we do this, it means the message we are trying to convey will actually be enhanced and maximized to its fullest. King Shlomo writes: "Faithful are the wounds inflicted by a lover; but superfluous are the kisses of a foe."[150] His insight is clear. If a child has earned a punishment, he or she must clearly understand that the parent or teacher is giving it not out of anger, but out of love and for the sake of the child's growth and development. That is a sign of *malchut* within *gevurah*.

149. Frand, *Rabbi Yissocher Frand in Print*, 74.
150. *Mishlei* 27:6.

DISCUSSION TOPICS FOR *MALCHUT* WITHIN *GEVURAH*

For adults

1. Do I consistently, day in and day out, restrain myself from judging other Jews, including those who are different than me? If I cannot say that I do, how have I judged others and separated myself from them?
2. How can I help to foster more age-appropriate decision-making skills in my children? How will that benefit their lives and also relieve me of resulting tensions?
3. Can I describe times when I don't display *malchut* within *gevurah*? What am I going to do to fix this?

For children

1. The next time I feel like yelling at my brother or sister, how can I stop myself and handle it differently?
2. What decisions do I get to make now? How well do I make these decisions?
3. What are some of the bad interactions I have had that resulted in hurt feelings or broken relationships? What can I do differently next time?

WEEK THREE

Tiferet

(Harmony/Truth)

OVERVIEW

Tiferet (Harmony/Truth)

We know that, according to Kabbalah, *chesed* is represented in the physical world by the right arm and *gevurah* by the left arm. Both are important attributes, but too much or too little of either can be harmful. Like an airplane carrying too much weight in one wing or the other, our balance is off, and we cannot operate with the same degree of functionality, if at all.

Our right arm and left arm connect to our torso, which is the location of the heart (which pulsates to send blood throughout the body) and the location of the lungs (which expand and contract to send oxygen to enrich the blood). The torso corresponds to *tiferet*, or harmony, truth and beauty – the blending of loving-kindness (*chesed*) with strength, restraint, and judgment (*gevurah*).

In his special book, *Endless Light*, Rabbi Aaron hones in on *tiferet*:

> *Chesed* and *gevurah* are balanced by *tiferet*, which is translated as "beauty," but it is the principle that negotiates balance and harmony between undisciplined giving and holding back. *Tiferet* is also associated with truth. It ensures we are being honest with ourselves; it integrates the extremes so that we are true to ourselves – not giving more than we can or less than we should. *Chesed* and *gevurah* are extremes, and are harmonized by the principle of *tiferet*.[151]

We have all experienced moments when we have achieved a proper and balanced perspective in our life interactions. *Tiferet* is the balance that represents the truth of that moment. It is beautiful to behold!

Unfortunately, such moments are rare, for it is not easy to achieve *tiferet*. Nevertheless, it should be our aim every single day of our lives.

151. Aaron, *Endless Light*, 64–65.

Tiferet is the attribute that denotes balance through the recognition of truth. Truth is a blend of love and discipline. We sometimes have a skewed view of how to love or how to discipline because of our subjective perspectives. But truth is always objective, and when we are able to rise above our egos, our natural personality tendencies and our prejudices, we can arrive at the truth through a more honest self-awareness.

It is important that we learn to be honest with ourselves, and *tiferet* gives us an honest picture. *Tiferet* considers and weighs our needs, abilities and shortcomings and the needs, abilities, and shortcomings of others. It helps us arrive at the moment of truth, when we reconcile those shortcomings to achieve harmonious relationships with our families and with the world at large.

Harmony and truth are essential to feeling secure and at peace and Torah puts a high premium on both. For example, the laws of Shabbat permit a parent to break down a closet door – an action otherwise forbidden – if a child is trapped behind it, the sole reason being to eliminate the child's fear. For a sense of security is a clearly defined Torah value. Security comes from harmony, and lack of harmony breeds insecurity which is then manifest as discomfort, sadness, depression, frustration, and an entire host of other emotional traumas that can be harmful to our well-being, and which stand in the way to our achieving our optimum potential in life.

But, when our environment is harmonious, we are at peace with ourselves, with our loved ones, and with all the people who are important to us. When our environment is not harmonious, we have a sense of discord, incompleteness, lack of resolution, and we feel unhealthy tensions.

The best analogy is an orchestra. Listening to a well-trained orchestra that harmonizes and delivers melodic music is bliss. But listening to out-of-tune instruments, poorly played, is painful.

As well, when cells in our body are in harmonious balance, we feel healthy. But when an infection invades, we falter. When our cells mutate improperly, they can become destructive, malignant, and toxic to our body as a whole.

Whether physically, mentally, emotionally, or spiritually – whether our eyes, ears, smell, taste, touch, or soul are involved – harmonious balance is essential and a sublime state to aspire to.

YAAKOV, THE THIRD SHEPHERD

Jewish tradition teaches that Yaakov, the third of the Seven Shepherds, models for us this balance. While Avraham models *chesed* in its pure form and Yitzchak models *gevurah* in its pure form, Yaakov (also called Israel) represents the epitome of *tiferet* for he was a man of truth.

The Torah testifies to the stature of Yaakov in the eyes of God and man: "And Yaakov was a perfect man."[152] Yaakov achieved human perfection such as had never been seen before – in his relationship with God, with his parents, and even with his devious uncle Lavan and his bloodthirsty brother Esav.

Yaakov achieved this ideal state by learning to properly balance *chesed* and *gevurah* through the many tests that he experienced in life's school of hard knocks. As a result, he mastered *tiferet* and merited to become the father of twelve righteous sons, who unified to become the Twelve Tribes of Israel. This is why today we are called B'nei Israel. Avraham could not achieve family harmony in his lifetime because his sons (Yishmael and Yitzchak) were not unified; neither could Yitzchak because his sons (Esav and Yaakov) were not unified. But Yaakov inspired twelve dissimilar boys to eventually become twelve unified tribes and their gift of harmony is our proud heritage. Yaakov made this happen because, in all respects, he was the epitome of honesty, morality, and integrity.[153]

It is worthwhile for us to contemplate Yaakov's attribute of *tiferet* as we recite each day the morning *bracha*, "Blessed are you, God, our God, King of the universe, Who gave the heart understanding to distinguish between day and night." Each day we have the opportunity to choose between right and wrong, good and evil, between too much *chesed* and too much *gevurah*. As Jews, our mission is to make these distinctions both for ourselves, in all our relationships, and in all life situations. This is how we achieve *tiferet* and know what truth is.

Psalm 145, which we recite three times daily, reminds us: "God is close to all who call upon Him, to all who call upon Him in truth."[154] When we deceive ourselves, others, or God, we are off the path of truth. If we want to know ourselves, we must be honest with ourselves. If we want a

---

152. *Bereshit* 25:27.
153. Kitov, *The Book of Our Heritage*, Vol. 2, 684.
154. *Tehillim* 145:18.

pure and meaningful relationship with others, we must be honest with them. And honesty certainly applies to our relationship with God since it is impossible to deceive Him. God knows the innermost aspects of our being from our every thought to our every deed, as the Book of Proverbs teaches: "The soul of man is a lamp of God, searching out all the inner rooms of the womb."[155]

Truth is our goal because God is truth, as Moshe taught us, "The Rock! Perfect is His work, for all His paths are justice; a God of faith without iniquity, righteous, and fair is He."[156] As rays of His infinite light, we are expected to emulate his ways.

THE PURSUIT OF TRUTH

The pursuit of personal discovery – which is the object of *Journey Together* – simply cannot be achieved without the attribute of truth. In this context, truth is not just the opposite of lying. Lying is a purposeful distortion of facts or a hiding of the truth. While many of us may not flagrantly lie to ourselves or others, it doesn't mean that we are fully aware of the truth or that we don't subconsciously delude ourselves. And if so, what then is standing in our way in the pursuit of truth and nothing but the truth?

A number of psychological defense mechanisms discourage us from recognizing the truth about ourselves and others and, consequently, keep us from doing *teshuvah* and from meaningful self-improvement. These defense mechanisms include denial, rationalization, projection, habituation, trivialization, and egotism. If we want to be healthy, then we need to deal with these six "cousins of dishonesty" for they block our progress to

155. *Mishlei* 20:27. See also *Bava Kamma* 50a where the Talmud teaches that whoever says that God overlooks things will find his life "overlooked." And *Chagiga* 16a where the Talmud also teaches that "If the Evil Inclination says to you, 'Sin and the Holy One, Blessed be He, will forgive you,' do not trust him." Also note the guidance of Ramchal in *Mesillat Yesharim* (Chap. 4, p. 28): "This is self-evident and clearly spelled out because the Eternal is a God of truth . . . Since the Holy One, Blessed be He, wants [a world of] justice, it would be a violation of justice to turn a blind eye either to merit or to misconduct. Consequently, if there is meant to be justice, He must repay each person in accordance with his conduct and the results of his actions – both for the good and for the bad, with the strictest of precision."

156. *Devarim* 32:4.

achieving truth and harmony. Rabbi Dr. Abraham Twerski, in an article entitled "Six Obstacles to Teshuvah"[157] offers the following insights:

- *Denial* is a defense from accepting a reality that our unconscious psychological system does not want to accept. Says Rabbi Twerski: "Because people are intent on doing whatever they wish, they resort to denial . . . so that they are unaffected by the reality of what they see and hear . . . and block out those realizations that would call for change. The natural state of all matter . . . is inertia, but one must force himself to overcome inertia in order to grow and change. Denial enables a person to maintain the status quo."
- *Rationalization* involves escaping from the truth by providing what we think are plausible reasons, instead of the true ones. "When reality threatens to overcome denial . . . the mind is very clever in . . . justifying one's actions by giving logical-sounding reasons for them . . . Oftentimes one who speaks *lashon hara* may attempt to justify his behavior by claiming 'But it's the truth.' Defamatory speech is *lashon hara*, even if it's true."
- *Projection* is when we place the blame on others for something that we are really responsible for. Projection turns the blame around: "I did not offend him. He offended me. He should really be apologizing to me."
- *Habituation* takes over when one repeats a wrongful act several times, until such time as it becomes habit and one has begun to think such transgressions are permissible.
- *Trivialization* is another impediment to change, *teshuvah*, and truth. "So I chatted with my friend during the reading of the Torah, so what? Doesn't everybody?"
- *Egotism* provides resistance to "humbling oneself, apologizing, and making restitution where required."

All these defense mechanisms serve the function of diverting attention from the truth. And they help preserve the status quo, which may not be a good thing. Rabbi Twerski, who is a world-renowned expert in addictions, notes that "an addict will not agree to change until he hits 'rock-bottom,'

157. Abraham J. Twerski, "The Six Obstacles to *Teshuvah*," *Jewish Action*, Fall 2012, 16–17.

i.e., that the pain incident to the addiction is greater than the pleasure it provides." This, he says, is equally true for the non-addict, who contemplates his life goals and sees that his behavior is jeopardizing their achievement, but nevertheless, he is unwilling to change until some very painful event occurs. Concludes Rabbi Twerski:

> Uncompromised honesty is necessary to see through the psychological defenses that are a barrier to *teshuvah*. Rosh Hashana, the Ten Days of Penitence, and Yom Kippur are days in which one should be inspired to evaluate the meaning of one's life. Only when we are aware that we need "fixing" will we do *teshuvah*.[158]

THE TRICKS WE PLAY ON OURSELVES

The 49 days of the Omer count are perfectly designed to advance the process of truthful self-examination long before we arrive at Yom Kippur, and they can help us circumvent the tricks we play on ourselves. Such as:

We may be in denial about our physical, mental, emotional or spiritual health, or the health of a loved one. We may kid ourselves by thinking that smoking only half a pack a day won't hurt us, or that our spouse still finds us attractive despite our excessive weight gain, or that our job security is assured despite poor performance reviews, or that while our child's friends seem off the path, they won't influence our child at all, or that the constant bickering between spouses is not a threat to the marriage.

We may be using rationalization if we know we have a problem – say a weight problem – yet still seek to justify it in order to preserve the status quo. For example: "I am only a little overweight" or, "It runs in my family" or, "No matter how hard I try, I just can never lose the weight" or, "If it weren't for the stress of my job/family/life, I could start that diet" or, "If I lost weight I would need a new wardrobe and I can't afford that right now" or, "I could lose it in the future at any time I want by just exercising." Each of these is just an excuse to avoid admitting a more blunt reality which is that "I am fat and I don't like myself enough to work hard to lose weight."

Projection is yet one more way to subvert the truth. For example, we may be reluctant to apply for a good job or for entrance to a good school

158. Abraham J. Twerski, *Addictive Thinking* (Center City, MN: Hazelden Foundation, 1997), 41–50.

or to ask someone out on a date because we are afraid of being turned down, so instead, we project onto others a series of "beliefs" to justify not even taking the first step, such as that they probably want someone with more experience/better grades/more potential/taller/smarter/better-looking, etc.

We have all engaged in denial, rationalization, projection, habituation, trivialization, and egotism at some point in our lives. Some of us do it daily. When we deny, rationalize, or project, we are severed from our true selves. Our goal should be honest self-examination and self-awareness in order to eliminate these distorted defense mechanisms and face what is stopping us, blocking us, and preventing us from achieving our true mission in life.

Every human being struggles with this issue, and the Torah relates that even our illustrious ancestors were not immune:

- Although Sarah urged Avraham to send Yishmael away, he was reluctant to do so. Avraham was in denial about the negative influence that Yishmael was having on Yitzchak and the whole family. He did not come to terms with it until God told him directly: "Whatever Sarah tells you, heed her voice, since through Yitzchak will offspring be considered yours."[159] Avraham had to trust God and Sarah to make the painful choice of truth.
- Yitzchak was in denial about Esav. Only Rivka could see the truth about her twin sons, and she proactively intervened to preserve the lineage of the Jewish people through Yaakov, knowing that Esav – whom she also deeply loved – didn't have the wherewithal to insure the transmission of the Avrahamic heritage.[160] While some comment that Yaakov's actions in following his mother's instruction were devious, it is clear that when his character is closely examined, he is the essence of truthfulness and that this was one of those situations when the right thing was to obey his mother, knowing full well that his father would immediately understand why God wanted the blessing to go to him, rather than Esav.
- Following the Exodus from Egypt and while traveling through the desert, the Jewish people rationalized on many occasions how they

159. *Bereshit* 21:12.

160. Ibid., 27:5–29.

were better off when they were slaves in Egypt and why they should return there.[161]

- That slave mentality was also responsible for the Sin of the Spies who were sent on a reconnaissance mission into Eretz Yisrael just before Moshe was to lead the Jewish people across the border. Intimidated by what they found, they rationalized why it was not a good idea to go forward, projecting all kinds of imagined responses on the part of the land's inhabitants. God had to force them to wander in the wilderness for forty years until those who were born in Egypt died along with their slave mentality.[162]

Fundamentally, when we are in denial about the truth, are making rationalizations instead of owning up, or are projecting our problems onto someone/something else rather than accepting responsibility, we betray our true selves. As a result, we may lose our way in the quest to fulfill our unique mission in life. Either way, we could end up wasting years, or even our entire lives, by not letting truth be the guide in our decisions and actions.

Week Three of the Omer, which focuses on *tiferet*, challenges us to strive for truth in all aspects of our lives, particularly in our relationships with ourselves and our loved ones. We are enjoined to identify areas where we may be in denial, employing rationalizations, or projecting blame onto others. Once we have identified these areas, we should try to come to grips with the underlying truth, and then strategize what to do about it.

COMMON TRAPS

If you had a hard time figuring out what "enslaves" you in Week One, that may be an indication that you are stuck, for whatever enslaves you is what keeps you stuck. So let's now examine some common traps that contribute to this condition as well as some solutions.

Many of us cling to a memory of some wrong that was done to us sometime in the past. This memory may be subjectively recalled, but the constant re-examination of the past wrong often keeps us mired in anger and hate. When we hold onto such negative emotions and let them affect

161. *Shemot* 14:11–12; *Bamidbar* 11:1–10.
162. *Bamidbar* 13:27–29.

our emotional, mental, physical, and/or spiritual health, we actually let the person who harmed us years ago continue to harm us today. How tragic to be handcuffed to an old memory!

Pirkei Avot contains this teaching from Rabbi Yehoshua: "An evil eye, the evil inclination, and hatred of others remove a person from the world."[163] Clearly, the stakes are high, and letting go of old memories and hurt feelings is a key to becoming a fully-functioning human being. When we recognize that whatever happens to us, for better or for worse, is an opportunity for growth and is "all for the good," we find an escape hatch from the trap of old memories.

Others among us may be stuck in fears or insecurities. We may have tried something once and, because it didn't turn out well, we are afraid to try it again. Perhaps we were married and the marriage ended in divorce. Perhaps we tried public speaking but got stage fright instead. Perhaps we applied for a driver's license but we kept failing the theoretical test and so now we've given up. Perhaps we tried to swim in the sea, but the waves scared us or we felt an undertow and haven't been in the sea since. Perhaps we cooked a nice meal for our in-laws, but it didn't turn our very well and one of them made a comment that dissuades us from ever doing it again.

Instead of giving up, we should remember that everything that happens to us in life – and especially trial and error challenges – is an opportunity for growth. And that although trying and failing are painful, there is nothing more joyous and sweet than trying again (despite past failures!) and succeeding at last.

A personal example may help illustrate the point: I received a D (the lowest grade next to failing) on my first speech in my high school speech class. The only reason I didn't receive an F was because I completed the assignment on time. And it was only through the mercy of God that other kids in the class didn't fall out of their chairs laughing at how scared I was. My legs were literally shaking uncontrollably for the entire duration of this five-minute exercise. Please believe me when I say that I showed absolutely no promise of ever being a public speaker, but my teacher was patient with me. By the end of the year, because I was determined to improve and equally determined not to get an F for the whole year, I actually became quite comfortable with speaking in front of a group. Years later, I

163. *Pirkei Avot* 2:16.

was able to successful apply all that I learned in this regard and make it a routine part of my job duties.

Why did I succeed? Because I did not blame the teacher for giving me a D, or call her unfair, or project onto her some conspiracy to fail me. Rather than remain in denial about my skills, I accepted the fact that I had spoken very poorly because of my fear. Further, I realized I was the only one who could work on solving this problem. I took responsibility for improving and, as a result, I acquired the skill of public speaking.

I could have rationalized that speaking in front of a group was not an important skill to learn, but I recognized that that probably wasn't true. If I ever wanted to express my opinion about a topic, be able to logically organize my thoughts, and speak with clarity and loud enough for others to hear, I knew it was a skill I would have to acquire or at least try to acquire. I further realized that speaking well correlated to possibly getting into the right university or getting the right job. I didn't want to be passed over or miss out in life just because I was too afraid to speak up or lacked the ability to put together some cohesive thoughts.

I freed myself from the fear of speaking in a group by deciding to see the truth of my limitations and by accepting responsibility for developing myself in this area. To this day, I view the ability to speak up for one's views in a group as an important life skill. I believe it is something that all teenagers and adults should possess. I also believe that speaking in front of groups of all sizes is important for almost all jobs and professions.

THE TRAP OF A BAD SELF-IMAGE

To be stuck in a bad self-image is tragic. After all, our self-image affects our self-concept and self-esteem. A healthy self-esteem is a useful pre-requisite on our path to achieve a sense of *malchut*, and being "Balanced to Win." So if we don't have a positive self-image, it is important to truthfully diagnose what is lacking so that we can grow in those areas that will enable us to change this state of being.

Another personal example: I needed braces as an adolescent, and I was repeatedly called "horse mouth." To add to my problems, I was somewhat chubby. Other kids called me "little fatty" on more than one occasion. Despite the fact that my teeth are now straight, I am not overweight, and more than four decades have past, I still remember those negative labels.

Thank God, my self-image was not permanently scarred, but it took some years for me to understand my real self.

I realized that I had choices to make. In the case of my braces, I had to just endure wearing them, knowing that when they came off, my formerly very crooked teeth (no image builder for sure) would be straight. To this day, I credit my natural tendency to smile to the fact that I am so happy to have my braces off.

But in the case of being overweight, I had a more difficult choice. The statements, though cruel, were truthful. I *was* chubby. I could either resign myself to cruel name-calling for the rest of my life, or I could choose to do something about it. Over the entire summer between eighth and ninth grade, I chose to lose weight by starting to exercise.

I decided to accept responsibility for how I wanted to look for the rest of my life. I chose not to be in denial about the fact that I was chubby. I chose not to blame my mother for cooking things that were fattening nor for the stress I was undergoing at the time. I chose not to rationalize that "it was baby fat" or that "I am not that overweight, only a little bit."

Physical health became a goal for me then, and still remains a goal for me today. Although all name-calling is despicable, I am at least appreciative that it impelled me to decide unequivocally to make a personal choice for optimal physical health.

My self-image was greatly enhanced by the decision to lose the weight and keep it off. My self-esteem was greatly improved by my feeling more mature as a result of having made a personal choice and having had the discipline to stick with it. It made me feel wise and "in control" beyond my age. That feeling is one I remember until this very day. Every time I make a good personal choice and stick with it, I feel great.

I freed myself from a poor self-image and acquired lifelong healthy habits. Over time, I also have come to understand that taking care of my health is something God wishes me to do, although that was not the motivation for my doing so when I was in eighth grade.

I believe that the first step of the Twelve Steps is so successful for all types of addictions because it begins with the need for the addict to say out loud to a group of fellow addicts the following, "My name is —, and I am an alcoholic" or, "My name is —, and I am an overeater" or, "My name is —, and I am a gambler." The first step is to stop lying to yourself and admit who you are right now.

Any change you want to make starts with this process. If you are selfish, you have to first recognize that you are, admit it at least to yourself and then change. If you are arrogant, you cannot be in denial or blame others for it. You have to acknowledge that you are at fault and then determine how to act with greater humility. Truth is always the first step in our recovery, our growth, our future.

THE TRAP OF NEGATIVITY

Negativity is like mud. We get mired in it. We get stuck in bleak thoughts, complaints, ingratitude, and unwillingness to be appreciative about almost everything. Nothing is good enough. We are jealous. We envy others and all their possessions. We do not wish good for others. We try to make ourselves feel better by putting others down. We are secretly, or overtly, happy when misfortune befalls someone else.

Consider the wise advice of our Sages in *Pirkei Avot*:

> He [Rabban Yochanan ben Zakkai] said to them: "Go out and discern which is the proper way to which a man should cling." Rabbi Eliezer said: "A good eye." Rabbi Yehoshua said: "A good friend." Rabbi Yose said: "A good neighbor." Rabbi Shimon said: "One who considers the outcome of a deed." Rabbi Elazar said: "A good heart." He [Rabban Yochanan ben Zakkai] said to them: I prefer the words of Elazar ben Arach to your words, for your words are included in his words."[164]

This wise advice will helps us get out of the mud of our own negativity and despair. For to cultivate a good heart – which encompasses all five suggestions from our Sages – is essential to *tiferet*.

Tiferet is harmony and truth. Everything that happens is ultimately for our own good, and is given to us by a benevolent God who loves us. To see the negative in all of the gifts we have been given is to be stuck in a mire that is poisoned by the evil inclination. The path to getting unstuck is to listen to our good inclination and accept that all that happens, on some level, is for the very best. Such *emunah* reconnects us to our true self and to the essential ray of divine light that we each have within us.

164. Ibid., 2:13.

In his book, *Conversations with Yourself*, Rabbi Zelig Pliskin elaborates on a principle found in Rambam's *Yad HaChazakah*.[165] The Rambam states that if you want to develop positive character traits, then act in ways that are consistent with those positive traits. And to overcome your negative character traits go to the extreme in the opposite direction. After acting consistently in the positive extreme modality for a while, you will arrive at a more balanced state of being and behaving.

Rabbi Pliskin, applying principles from neuro-linguistic programming (NLP) demonstrates how your thoughts and actions work together to create you. He asks his reader: "What do you want to be like? What positive traits and patterns do you really want to master?" He goes on to suggest that if you really aren't sure what you want to be like, at least "start by thinking about these four traits: happiness (including gratitude), kindness, courage, and serenity. These four attributes will have a tremendous effect on your entire life."[166]

In another of his books, *Begin Again Now: A Concise Encyclopedia of Strategies for Living*, Rabbi Pliskin offers this advice for becoming unstuck:

> When you feel stuck, ask yourself, "What inner resources would help me right now to get out of this stuckness?" Remember a time when you had the inner resources you need now. It might be confidence, creativity, resilience, courage, a sense of personal power, assertiveness. Access the inner resource and begin again right now.[167]

This is the work of *tiferet:* to be honest about what enslaves us, what has cut us off from our true self and God, what traps us; to be honest about our strengths and weaknesses; to be honest about our negative thinking patterns that have seeped in and contaminated our efforts to give our best every day of our life.

When we deny, rationalize, blame or project, we are playing psychological games with ourselves. We may be stuck right now in some area of our life, repeating the same patterns and habits that have held us back until

---

165. *Hilchot De'ot*, Chap. 1.

166. Zelig Pliskin, *Conversations with Yourself* (Brooklyn, NY: Mesorah Publications, 2007), 25–26.

167. Zelig Pliskin, *Begin Again Now: A Concise Encyclopedia of Strategies for Living* (Union City, NJ: Gross Bros. Printing Co, 1993), 326.

now, letting them continue their nasty hold. Through *tiferet* (balance/harmony/truth) we can finally arrive at the truth in all life situations and in all relationships, including our relationship with God, with ourselves, with our family members and others.

Week Three, the week of *tiferet*, offers us this opportunity if we choose to be honest.

היום חמישה עשר יום,
שהם שני שבועות ויום אחד, לעומר

(Ha'yom chamisha asar yom,
she'hem shnei shavuot v'yom echad la'Omer)

"TODAY IS THE FIFTEENTH DAY,
OR TWO WEEKS AND ONE DAY, OF THE OMER."

DAY 15

Chesed sh'b'Tiferet (Loving-kindness within Harmony/Truth)

As has been described, *tiferet* in its pure form is harmony/truth–the delicate balance between *chesed* (loving-kindness) and *gevurah* (strength/discipline). Being flooded with the awareness of truth is to experience the awesome, beautiful, harmonious alignment with the light of God. Although truth is positive, it can also be blunt and reveal a harsh negative reality. The window of truth, positive or negative, has no window dressing. Truth is clear and absolute. *Chesed* within *tiferet* endeavors to preserve truth in a loving, kind, and caring manner that considers the individual and his or her relationship with others, promoting acceptance and understanding.

When one's actions embody *chesed* within *tiferet*, beautiful stories of relationship and unity are born. This we see in the example of Rabbi Moshe Sherer.

Long-time president of Agudat Israel of America, a *haredi* organization, Rabbi Sherer worked with both non-religious Jewish politicians as well as other non-*haredi* religious leaders, creating bridges between people. When he passed away in 1998, at age 76, the funeral procession grew so big that traffic was blocked for seven square blocks. Said one mourner, Morton M. Avigdor, that Rabbi Sherer was beloved by so many people because, among other things, he had fought for government benefits and services for children in non-public schools by allying himself with Catholic school advocates. "He felt that people of all faith should be entitled to education," said Avigdor. "It is truly a great loss."[168]

Perhaps the most touching testimonial was reported by Jonathan Rosenblum in *The Jerusalem Post Magazine*. The day after his funeral, the receptionist "at the Agudat Israel's office whom Rabbi Sherer always made a point of greeting effusively and inquiring after, and the building superintendant whose family had been spared deportation because of Rabbi Sherer's use of his political connections on their behalf, both wept openly."[169]

Rabbi Sherer's treatment of others displayed *chesed* within *tiferet*, making a difference where it counts. Another example of *chesed* within *tiferet* in action is that of Michael Freund and his work on behalf of the Bnei Menashe.

The Bnei Menashe community of northeastern India claims descent from one of the Ten Lost Tribes of Israel that was exiled some 2,700 years ago. Their Jewish ancestry was officially recognized by the Chief Rabbinate of Israel in 2005 and thanks to Michael Freund, founder of the organization, Shavei Israel, nearly 1,750 Bnei Menashe migrated to Israel by 2007.

Then, the Israeli government decided to suspend their *aliyah*. But Freund was undeterred. He and his organization worked tirelessly for five years to turn that decision around. "His efforts bore fruit, and at his urging, the government approved a cabinet decision championed by Absorption Minister Sofa Landver in October 2012, formally resuming the Bnei Menashe *aliyah*."[170]

The goal is to bring the remaining 7,000 Bnei Menashe to Israel. It takes a lot of *chesed* combined with the truth of *tiferet* to devote so much energy to a cause such as this. To simply drop what one is doing and devote one's life efforts to an ideal, because it is the "right thing to do" is a moving display of *chesed* within *tiferet*.

168. *The New York Times*, May 19, 1998.

169. Rosenblum, "My Brothers Do I Seek," *The Jerusalem Post Magazine*.

170. David Parsons, "An End to Exile," *The Jerusalem Post, In Jerusalem*, February 8, 2013, 22–23.

HONEST FEEDBACK REFLECTS *CHESED* WITHIN *TIFERET*

As parents, we sometimes must give *mussar* to our children, trying to communicate with them in a way that they will hear, accept, and apply our instructions, but never in a way that is an assault on their self-esteem. And this is where love combined with truth (*chesed* within *tiferet*) comes in.

Indeed, this applies to all who have to give feedback to those in their charge. For example, as bosses, we must give corrective direction to employees so that they have a better chance of contributing and thus succeeding in their jobs. As teachers, we must "grade" or give feedback to students in a manner that minimizes the possible negative effect on their self-esteem. Every role requires honest feedback, but this should always be given in a constructive way – a difficult balancing act.

Fortunately, the Torah is filled with endless examples of our *Avot* and *Imahot* and other illustrious ancestors displaying *chesed* within *tiferet*.

When Yosef revealed his true identity to his brothers, he said: "I am Yosef. Is my father still alive?" His brothers were literally speechless. Yosef then went on:

> "Come close to me, if you please . . . I am Yosef your brother – it is me, whom you sold into Egypt. And now, be not distressed, nor reproach yourselves for having sold me here, for it was to be a provider that God sent me ahead of you. For this has been two of the hunger years in the midst of the land, and there are yet five years in which there shall be neither plowing nor harvest. Thus God has sent me ahead of you to insure your survival in the land and to sustain you for a momentous deliverance. And now: It was not you who sent me here, but God; He has made me father to Pharaoh, master of his entire household, and ruler throughout the entire land of Egypt. Hurry – go up to my father and say to him: 'So said your son Yosef: God has made me master of all Egypt. Come down to me; do not delay. You will reside in the land of Goshen and you will be near to me – you, your sons, your grandchildren, your flock and your cattle, and all that is yours. And I will provide for you there – for there will be five more years of famine – so you do not become destitute, you, your household, and all that is yours.'"[171]

---

171. *Bereshit* 45:3–11.

One can only imagine what kind of feedback we might have given brothers who sold us into slavery if we were in the same circumstances. One obvious response comes to my mind. It goes like this:

> "I am Yosef, the second most powerful person in Egypt. I have life and death power over your very existence. You thought nothing of me when I pleaded from the pit filled with scorpions and snakes that fateful night twenty-two years ago. Because of your deed I had to be a slave in Egypt and was sent to prison for a crime I didn't commit. Because of you I had to live alone, isolated, with just my wife and two sons, with no family whatsoever. What do you all have to say to me before I mete out your just punishment?!"

This speech may be delivering a truthful message but it displays the opposite of *chesed* within *tiferet*. Yosef chose a different way to respond and, in so doing, he created one of the most moving moments in all of Tanach.

OTHER TORAH EXAMPLES

When the astonishing news reached Yaakov's camp that Yosef was still alive, Serach, the daughter of Asher, made sure he heard the news through the *chesed* of a melodious song to avoid startling him.

As well, Yosef sent wagons with the brothers to give his father a sign that he had not forgotten the last lesson they had studied together twenty-two years prior. This message gave Yaakov immediate relief that despite the debauchery of Egypt he had not lost his son spiritually either.

At the end of his life, when Yaakov blessed Yosef's sons, Menashe and Ephraim, he reversed their order. It may not have been the order that Yosef wanted, but when it came to blessing his two grandchildren, Yaakov knew exactly where to place his hands and which blessing to give them vis-a-vis *tiferet*. His explanation of his actions was filled with consideration (*chesed* within *tiferet*) for both Yosef and the grandsons. When Yosef tried to move Yaakov's right hand to firstborn Menashe, Yaakov responded:

> "I know, my son, I know; he too will become a people, and he too will become great; yet his younger brother shall become greater than he, and [the fame of] his offspring will fill the nations."[172]

---

172. Ibid., 48:19.

THE ULTIMATE MODEL

The *ba'al chesed* – and the ultimate model – is obviously God.

For example, He has consistently and constantly displayed *chesed* within *tiferet* during the forty years that the Jewish people wandered in the desert. First, He took them via a non-direct route so they wouldn't panic and turn back towards Egypt. Then, He provided for their nutrition with miraculous sources of water and the daily manna during their entire sojourn. His Pillar of Fire led the way and His Clouds of Glory protected them from the elements.

Endless *chesed* within *tiferet* flowed to the Jews of the desert so they would learn the truth of Torah, the beauty of a loving relationship with Our Father in Heaven, and so they would understand their national and personal mission in the world.

If we could only learn to consistently emulate God's way in our interactions with others – always displaying *chesed* within *tiferet* – our lives and the world in which we live would be a vastly different place.

It is a tall order, but to succeed, we need only grab His hand as Rabbi Yissocher Frand advises in his teachings concerning Yom Kippur, a day replete with *chesed* within *tiferet*:

> Yom Kippur . . . is the day for peeling away the layers of encrustation from our soul and hearing that *Bas Kol* (Heavenly Voice). "You give Your hand to sinners and Your right hand is extended to receive penitents," we say in *Ne'ilah*, the closing prayer of Yom Kippur, and the *Zohar* comments that Hashem sticks out His hand as if to a man foundering in the dark . . .
>
> Yom Kippur is a vacation for the soul, a day when it escapes the limitations of our physical bodies. Even though we return at nightfall to our daily concerns, we are not the same. By freeing our souls for that one day and sensing our nearness to our Loving Father, Who is patiently awaiting us, we are better able to change. We can reach out for the hand that is extended towards us. Yom Kippur day calls out to us, "Do something different, for God's sake and yours, grab His hand."[173]

Let's not wait for Yom Kippur, let's grab His hand now!

---

173. Frand, *Rabbi Yissocher Frand in Print*, p. 64.

DISCUSSION TOPICS FOR *CHESED* WITHIN *TIFERET*

For adults

1. When I discipline my children or express some dissatisfaction with something they did, do I come across too harshly or do they still feel that I love them deeply?
2. When I give a "performance review" to a student, or a person who works for me, or to anyone who requires my honest feedback, am I comfortable in being completely and fully honest while at the same time finding words that still permit the interaction to be motivational and caring versus critical and crushing?
3. Can I remember a time in my life when someone gave me feedback in a way that was demoralizing or hard to absorb? How did that impact me and my view of that person at the time?

For children

1. When I am upset with members of my family because of a disappointment, are they still able to tell that I love them by the tone of my voice and the words I use?
2. Do I have a tendency to act with more *chesed* or with more *gevurah*? Can I give examples and describe what my parents may think about my reactions? Would it help me to balance this more?
3. Can I recall how I was spoiled by someone in my life? Has that been good for me or not? Why?

היום ששה עשר יום,
שהם שני שבועות ושני ימים, לעומר

(Ha'yom shisha asar yom,
she'hem shnei shavuot u'shnei yamim la'Omer)

"TODAY IS THE SIXTEENTH DAY,
OR TWO WEEKS AND TWO DAYS, OF THE OMER."

DAY 16

Gevurah sh'b'Tiferet
(Strength/Discipline within Harmony/Truth)

Gevurah within *tiferet* involves applying the necessary strength, restraint, and discipline to ensure that truth is properly emphasized. The truth of *tiferet* must sometimes be reinforced with the strength of *gevurah* so that we do not inadvertently feed unacceptable behaviors, or reward poor choices and miscalculate, or fail to see the unvarnished truth.

Just as with the other *sefirot*, for *tiferet* to be successful, it has to be appropriately focused and disciplined. It is so important to make sure that our *chesed* is balanced and honest, and not leading us in the wrong direction.

For example, if a mother shows compassion for her children who just failed a test because they did not study for it, or if she keeps silent while her children complain that the test was unfair or too hard, is she doing a good thing? Or is she just enabling poor study habits in her children who have learned that she will lower her expectations of them and not hold them accountable for their choices. Ultimately, they will pay the price.

It is not being *truly* compassionate to help others hurt themselves.

There are lots of reasons why we want to exercise *gevurah* within *tiferet*. For one thing, we want to make sure we are projecting the right balance of love and strength and not enabling those we love in harmful behaviors. The right balance helps us make sure we don't do too much or too little. Some examples:

- When we visit the sick, we observe the halachic limit (of no more than twenty minutes) to make sure that our visit will bring comfort to the sick person and not impose a burden upon him or her.
- When coping with loved ones who are addicted to alcohol, we do not run to the liquor store to replenish their supply or make excuses to their boss if they are hungover and unable to go to work.
- When observing the mitzvah of making an interest-free loan to a poor person, we use sound judgment what amount is appropriate and how often such a loan should be made. We do not wallow in pity or guilt and make loans to people who cannot make ends meet because they have purchased luxuries they cannot afford. Instead, we try to assess their true needs and help them more constructively by arranging for financial counseling or by finding job leads.

TORAH MODEL: YAAKOV

Perhaps the greatest Torah model of this attribute combination is Yaakov. Let us recall some events in his life, when Yaakov displayed *gevurah* within *tiferet*, restraint balanced with truth.

When Yaakov finally decided to go back to Eretz Yisrael after many years working for his uncle Lavan, he knew that his return would mean confronting his estranged brother Esav who had vowed to kill him twenty-one years prior.

The night when he was to meet Esav after these many years of separation, Yaakov had an encounter with an angel and wrestled with him. Although injured in the battle, Yaakov would not be defeated. Finally, the angel asked Yaakov to let him go because dawn was breaking. To this, Yaakov replied that he would not unless "you bless me." The angel responded: "No longer will it be said that your name is Yaakov, but Israel, for you have striven with the Divine and with man and have overcome."

Afterwards, Yaakov called the place of the encounter Peniel, saying: "For I have seen the Divine face to face, yet my life was spared."[174]

---

174. *Bereshit* 32:25–31.

This encounter took courage, strength, and discipline. It demonstrates that Yaakov knew his mission – to rectify *tiferet* in the world – and he strove to fulfill it.

Later in life, when his children were grown and Yaakov heard the news that his daughter Dina was physically violated by Shechem, the son of Hamor, leader of the region, he stayed silent until his sons formulated a strategy to rescue their sister and exact punishment for the crime committed.[175]

The sons spoke to Hamor, the father of Shechem, who wanted to marry Dina. They pretended to agree to the marriage on the condition that every male in the city be circumcised. Secretly, they planned to kill Shechem and his father, and bring Dina home. Yaakov approved this plan, but when two of his sons, Shimon and Levi, went too far and killed every male on the third day after the mass circumcisions, he rebuked them. Yaakov believed that retribution should only be taken against the perpetrators and not the entire town.[176]

Yaakov understood that the just response to the actions of Hamor was the one advocated by his sons and he allowed them to follow through. But when two of them acted out of line, he demonstrated *gevurah* in chastising them. He further sought to correct their imbalance when he blessed them on his deathbed.[177]

We can learn even more about *gevurah* within *tiferet* from the first meeting of Yaakov and Yosef after more than two decades of separation. These years were torture for Yaakov (not that it was easy for Yosef either). During this time when he believed that Yosef was dead, Yaakov was so despondent that the Divine Presence left him for the entire period.

So when they were finally reunited, what did Yaakov do? Or rather what did he restrain himself from saying and doing that most of us would have blurted out?

Yaakov did not admonish Yosef for not sending word that he was alive. He did not question him. He did not chastise him. He did not make him feel guilty. He did not say, "You couldn't have sent me a message in all this time?" or, "They don't have papyrus in Egypt?" or, "What's with you that you didn't think about your poor old father?"

---

175. Ibid., 34:5–24.
176. Ibid., 34:30.
177. Ibid., 49:5–7.

Instead, Yaakov displayed *gevurah* within *tiferet*. Yaakov had simple, unshakeable faith in God, and he understood that if Yosef was still alive, it was because of direct intervention of Divine Providence. Yaakov knew better than to question. The wagons Yosef had sent were a sign to him that his son was still faithful to God. The fact that he was in Egypt clearly meant that the long-foretold exile was about to begin. And that was all Yaakov needed to know.

Yitzchak is another example of *gevurah* within *tiferet* in the same story. Tradition tells us that Yitzchak was aware that his grandson Yosef was still alive and not killed by an animal as the brothers had claimed, but he chose not to reveal what he knew to his son Yaakov.

Yitzchak understood that for the greater good and harmony in the family – for if he knew that the brothers sold Yosef, Yaakov would surely have become estranged from them – this information should not to be shared. Yitzchak knew full well that when God intended it to be known, it would be known.

Great people display great attributes – among them *gevurah* within *tiferet*, a great *sefirah* combination that the world could use more of.

DISCUSSION TOPICS FOR *GEVURAH* WITHIN *TIFERET*

For adults

1. Describe when you "held your tongue" and not made some curt observation or critical comment because you realized that doing so would hurt the feelings of others and make things worse? How did that feel?
2. If you think back over the past thirty days, how many times did you criticize or correct your child? How many times in the same period did you make a positive comment? Describe the changes you wish to make now?
3. Call a family meeting to discuss worthy topics affecting all members of the family. (Some examples of worthy topics: how all members of the family could pitch in to help take care of an aging grandparent; what the family may want to do during the Sukkot holiday; how dinner-related chores could be more fairly spread around to make it easier on the mother, etc.) Even if you are inclined to be the one who jumps in and offers lots of ideas and solutions, hold back and do the opposite. Practice making sure that every member of the family, including children, has offered ideas, input and solutions. Ensure that every member listens quietly and intently to what every person has to say.

For children

1. When your teacher asks a question, do you ever volunteer an answer, or do you wait to be called upon? Why do you think you have this habit? Would you ever consider doing the opposite?
2. At the dinner table in your home, is there conversation among all the members in the family about what each person did that day? Does one family member do all the talking or does everyone participate? Do you ever ask a follow-up question of the people sharing their day in order to show you are interested, and to learn more?
3. Have you ever felt like making an honest statement but stopped yourself because you knew it would be hurtful to someone?

היום שבעה עשר יום,
שהם שני שבועות ושלושה ימים, לעומר

*(Ha'yom shiva asar yom,
she'hem shnei shavuot u'shlosha yamim la'Omer)*

**"TODAY IS THE SEVENTEENTH DAY,
OR TWO WEEKS AND THREE DAYS, OF THE OMER."**

DAY 17

Tiferet sh'b'Tiferet (Harmony/Truth within Harmony/Truth)

Tiferet **within** ***tiferet*** **accentuates the natural beauty of balance between compassion and truth so that the latter is expressed to another in a healthy manner which produces harmony. This most beautiful display celebrates the just treatment of another with proper** ***derech eretz.*** **In the relationship to God, it is achieved when we choose to serve Him while trusting with complete** ***emunah*** **that everything He does is for the best.**

Achieving mastery of this *sefirah* combination is an important step towards lasting inner balance and self-esteem. A story comes to mind to illustrate it:

It was 6 a.m. in Jerusalem when an American Jewish couple walking to *shul* for *Shacharit* prayers saw at a distance the sight of a woman sitting in the street while a man leaned over her. The couple went over to ensure the woman was safe in all respects.

Approaching closer, they saw that that she was weeping and the man was talking to her very gently, trying to discern if she was hurt. Apparently, the woman fell and either broke or seriously sprained her ankle while on her early morning walk, and the man was trying to help her. Fortunately, they all could speak a common language – English. Unfortunately, none of them had a cell phone.

Together, the couple and the man gently picked up the woman under her arms to get her out of the street so that she did not get hit by a passing car. All the while, the man was soothingly telling her that all would be better soon. And her cries subsided to a whimper.

Once she was safely on the side of the road, a jogger happened by. Miraculously, he spoke fluent English as well as Hebrew, and he had a cell phone. He called an ambulance and instructed the ambulance driver precisely where to come. While the man who first came to this woman's aid waited with her for the ambulance to arrive, the couple went on to *shul* and the jogger proceeded on his way. The woman was grateful to the core.

Let me share some missing details about this early morning Jerusalem story. The five people involved had three different skin colors, were from three different continents and four different nations, were represented by three different religions, and except for the couple, none of them knew the other.

This modern-day incident is a *Kiddush Hashem* – a beautiful and moving balance of harmony and truth on a street corner in the Holy City of Jerusalem. This is the type of behavior that God wants from all of us when He commands us: "You shall love your fellow as yourself, for I am God."[178] This is *tiferet* within *tiferet* in its purity. No politics. No agenda. No crowd watching – only God.

BOAZ AND RUTH

In *Megillat Ruth*, we read about the great judge Boaz who allowed the convert Ruth to glean in his fields, so that she could take home provisions to her mother-in-law, Naomi. He observed Ruth at work, noticed how different she was from the others, and perceived her inner nobility without any external trappings to prove it.

Touched by her, Boaz told his workers: "Let her glean even among the sheaves, do not embarrass her. And even deliberately pull out some for her from the heaps and leave them for her to glean . . ."[179] Thus, he extended his genuine kindness to Ruth and Naomi in a way that preserved their dignity. Such a simple act, yet filled with layers of meaning.

Soon thereafter we learn how God took these two righteous people,

178. *Vayikra* 19:18.

179. *Megillat Ruth* 2:15–16.

exemplars of *tiferet* within *tiferet*, and orchestrated events so that they were married for one night (before the elder Boaz passed away) with their child becoming the grandfather of King David, the progenitor of the Mashiach.

When *chesed* and *gevurah* are in harmony, *tiferet* emerges. The great-grandparents of King David displayed it. Boaz was a great and busy man, but he took the time to instruct workers to ensure that Ruth had sufficient gleanings from the harvest to feed her widowed mother-in-law, Naomi, and herself. Boaz knew that Ruth had given up her life as a princess of Moab to convert and join the now destitute Naomi in returning to Eretz Yisrael. Boaz understood what strength of character it took for her to make that decision, while Ruth displayed pure, simple truth and kindness in her adherence to God's ways. This is precisely why Mashiach will emerge from their union.

Every day, we have opportunities to emulate Ruth and Boaz. Every day, we have opportunities to display loving-kindness (stopping to help) and restraint (putting aside whatever routine we planned). Every day, we can model *tiferet* within *tiferet*.

The five complete strangers in Jerusalem displayed it for those ten minutes or so. Will they continue displaying it when other opportunities present themselves? Will they try to guide their children and grandchildren to understand the importance of *tiferet* within *tiferet*? If they do, they will help to bring Mashiach. What a great contribution to the world!

EMULATING GOD

When we act like the people in the above examples, and do what is right and good in the eyes of God, we emulate Him and as such can hope He will always deal with us in the same way.

Everything God does is right and good. Everything God does is balanced, in harmony, and represents beauty and truth. The tests He sends us may seem painful but, in hindsight, with the passage of time, we are often aware of the perfect harmony in the outcome.

This is the lesson God taught Moshe, when He revealed His "back" for him on Mount Sinai. Moshe asked to see His "face," but God explained that no one can do that and live. God offered Moshe an alternative experience which hints to us of the way things are:

> He [God] said: "You will not be able to see My face, for no human can see My face and live." God said: "Behold! There is a place near

> Me; you may stand on the rock. When My glory passes by, I shall place you in a cleft of the rock; I shall shield you with My hand until I have passed. Then I shall remove My hand and you will see My back, but My face may not be seen."[180]

In other words, it may take a while – even long centuries and millennia – but eventually we will understand why every event occurred exactly the way it did, for us personally and for the world at large. And when we do, we will all understand with complete clarity that it was all done with perfect harmony – *tiferet* within *tiferet*.

DISCUSSION TOPICS FOR *TIFERET* WITHIN *TIFERET*

For adults

1. When I am faced with a complex situation that requires my response, do I consider *all* options before deciding what to think, say, and do?
2. Can I think of a situation when I merely "reacted" without thinking? How did that work out? What was the outcome? How might I have handled the situation and acted with *tiferet* within *tiferet*?
3. Can I think of people with whom I do not have a close relationship? If I am invited to a wedding of one of their children, do I plan to attend? Will I write a loving and caring letter wishing them Mazal Tov?

For children

1. Is there someone at school who is not my friend, whom I could look in the eye, and greet with a smile and a "good morning"?
2. What three things am I good at? How can I apply these strengths in situations that happen around me?
3. Can I name a time in the last year when I went out of my way to help a stranger?

---

180. *Shemot* 33:20–23.

היום שמונה עשר יום,
שהם שני שבועות וארבעה ימים, לעומר

(Ha'yom shemonah asar yom,
she'hem shnei shavuot v'arba'a yamim la'Omer)

"TODAY IS THE EIGHTEENTH DAY,
OR TWO WEEKS AND FOUR DAYS, OF THE OMER."

DAY 18

Netzach sh'b'Tiferet (Endurance within Harmony/Truth)

***Netzach* within *tiferet* helps us to preserve the beautiful harmony of *tiferet.* Commitments, choices, pursuits, relationships, and chosen paths in life can be a rollercoaster ride with their ups and downs, good times and bad. Often harmony needs the element of endurance to weather these difficult periods and reinforce and preserve relationship commitments.**

There are times in each of our lives when we know the truth of the path we embark upon, and we experience the harmony of this truth. One of these moments was the giving of the Torah to the three million men, women, and children who gathered at Mount Sinai. It was a moment – often compared to a wedding – of *tiferet* within *tiferet* when the Jewish people said to God: *Na'aseh v'nishma* ("We will do and we will hear"). But as they learned forty days later when they built the Golden Calf, *tiferet* requires the attribute of *netzach* to achieve the day-in day-out obedience to the will of God.

Similarly, a man and woman who fall in love and marry require endurance to sustain their harmonious commitment to each other throughout their lifetimes. "The only marriages that work are the marriages that husband and wife work at" is an essential insight that Rabbi David Aaron shares in his *shiurim* on relationships. And to this all happily married couples can attest.

In the same vein, good parenting requires a continual and enduring commitment (*netzach*) to raise each child with loving-kindness (*chesed*) and discipline (*gevurah*), so that the proper balance (*tiferet*) between the two can be achieved. Rabbi Twerski reminds us that if we want to create a secure home for our children in this insecure world, then we need to focus on *avodat Hashem* (truly working at service of God) and on *mesirut nefesh* (which he explains is not martyrdom, but rather "expending heroic energy and making sacrifices for the ideas and principles in which we believe").[181]

Netzach within *tiferet* may not always be easy to achieve, but relationships depend upon our successful efforts. We must all keep our sights on "endurance in truth."

RUTH'S LOYALTY

We have previously discussed the story of Ruth – both on Day 4 in the *netzach* within *chesed* section, and on Day 17 in the *tiferet* within *tiferet* section. Her story applies here as well.

When Ruth turned her back on her life as a Moabite princess and accepted the God of Israel as her God despite no apparent reward for doing so, she embraced the truth of knowing that God is One. She never looked back. Her famous words to Naomi ring out until today:

> "Do not urge me to leave you, to turn back and not follow you. For wherever you go, I will go; wherever you lodge, I will lodge; your people are my people and your God is my God; where you die, I will die, and there I will be buried. Thus may Hashem do to me – and more! – if anything but death separates me from you."[182]

This is a profoundly simple display of *netzach* within *tiferet*. And what will one day emerge from this display of enduring harmony and truth is Mashiach, the redeemer of the world.

181. Abraham J. Twerski, "Securing Your Home in an Insecure World," *Jewish Action*, Summer 2011, 37.
182. *Megillat Ruth* 1:16–17.

GOD'S ENDURING PROMISE

God's enduring promise to our forefathers – to give to them the Land of Israel, the Promised Land, the Holy Land – is a quintessential display of *netzach* within *tiferet* that lasts over all time. As Jews, we do a disservice to this primary and indisputable truth if we are not keenly conscious of the many promises made by Our King, Our Shield, Our Master, Our Redeemer. When leaders of other nations ignore and deny these truths, we should take heed. When the media ignores and denies these truths, we should take heed. Further, we must personally obligate ourselves to ensure that we and our family members remain crystal clear about the truth of these promises. Only God can be relied upon to keep His word always.

Avraham was 75 years old when God first spoke to him and made the following promise:

> "Go for yourself from your land, from your relatives, and from your father's house to the land that I will show you. And I will make of you a great nation; I will bless you, and make your name great, and you shall be a blessing."[183]

Upon Avraham's arrival in that land – the Land of Canaan which was then inhabited by extremely barbaric and amoral tribes – God repeated His promise: "To your offspring I will give this land."[184]

When Avraham and his nephew Lot parted ways, God again said to the Patriarch:

> "Raise now your eyes and look out from where you are: northward, southward, eastward and westward. For all the land that you see, to you will I give it, and to your descendants forever. I will make your offspring as the dust of the earth so that if one can count the dust of the earth, then your offspring, too, can be counted. Arise, walk about the land through its length and breadth! For to you will I give it."[185]

183. *Bereshit* 12:1–2.

184. Ibid., 12:7.

185. Ibid., 13:14–18.

After the war between the five kings and the four kings, God came to Avraham in a vision promising him a great reward. When Avraham asked what he could possibly receive when he had no one to inherit it (except his servant, Eliezer), God responded:

> "That one will not inherit you. Only him that shall come forth from within you shall inherit you." And He took him outside and said: "Gaze, now, toward the heavens, and count the stars if you are able to count them . . . so shall your offspring be! . . . [For] I am God Who brought you out of Ur Kasdim to give you this land to inherit it."[186]

To seal the promise, God told Avraham to bring a special sacrifice of three split animals and two split birds. This became known as the "Covenant between the Pieces," and the Torah describes it in vivid detail. Afterwards, God said:

> "To your descendants have I given this land, from the river of Egypt to the great river, the Euphrates River: the Kennite, the Kenizzite, and the Kadmonite; the Hittite, the Perizzite, and the Rephaim; the Amorite, the Cannanite, the Girgashite, and the Jebusite."[187]

This covenant was ratified when Avraham was 99 years old, and God changed his name from the original Avram to Avraham, telling him:

> "As for Me, this is My covenant with you: You shall be a father of a multitude of nations; your name shall no longer be called Avram, but your name shall be Avraham, for I have made you the father of a multitude of nations; I will make you most exceedingly fruitful, and make nations of you; and kings shall descend from you. I will ratify My covenant between Me and you and between your offspring after you, throughout their generations, as an everlasting covenant, to be a God to you and to your offspring after you; and I will give to you and to your offspring after you the land of your sojourns – the whole

186. Ibid., 15:4–7.
187. Ibid., 15:18–21.

> of the land of Canaan – as an everlasting possession; and I shall be a God to them."[188]

Immediately after this, Avraham was commanded to perform a *brit milah* and the birth of Yitzchak was prophesied. And then, God repeated His promise once more:

> "Still, your wife Sarah will bear you a son and you shall call his name Yitzchak; and I will fulfill My covenant with him as an everlasting covenant for his offspring after him. But regarding Ishmael I have heard you: I have blessed him, will make him fruitful, and will increase him most exceedingly; he will beget twelve princes and I will make him into a great nation. But I will maintain My covenant through Yitzchak whom Sarah will bear to you by this time next year."[189]

God's communications with Avraham from the first to the last are testament to His attribute of *netzach* within *tiferet*. Throughout Avraham's life, God's demonstration of enduring truth only increases in terms that can never to be questioned. His words, memorialized for all time, always resonate with truth, harmony, and balance.

GOD'S PROMISES TO YITZCHAK AND YAAKOV

After Avraham died at "a good old age, mature, and content,"[190] Yitzchak took up his mantle. When a famine struck the land of Canaan, Yitzchak considered going to Egypt just as his father had done in a similar situation years earlier. But God told him:

> "Do not descend to Egypt; dwell in the land that I shall indicate to you. Sojourn in this land and I will be with you and bless you; for to you and your offspring will I give all these lands, and establish the oath that I swore to Avraham your father: I will increase your

188. Ibid., 17:4–8.
189. Ibid., 17:19–21.
190. Ibid., 25:8.

> offspring like the stars of the heavens; and will give to your offspring all these lands . . ."[191]

Later, we see how the enduring truth (*netzach* within *tiferet*) passed forward through the generations when the aged Yitzchak blessed his son Yaakov, reminding him of God's promise to the family:

> "May El Shaddai bless you, make you fruitful and make you numerous, and may you be a congregation of peoples. May He grant you the blessing of Avraham to you and to your offspring so that you may possess the land of your sojourns which God gave to Avraham."[192]

Shortly thereafter, Yaakov found himself on Mount Moriah where *Akeidat Yitzchak* had occurred, and where the First and Second Temples would later be built, as well as the third and everlasting Beit HaMikdash. There he fell asleep and had his famous dream:

> And he dreamt, and behold – a ladder was set earthward and its top reached heavenward. And behold – angels of God were ascending and descending on it. And behold! God was standing over him, and He said: "I am Hashem, God of Avraham your father, and God of Yitzchak; the ground upon which you are lying, to you will I give it and to your descendants. Your offspring shall be as the dust of the earth, and you shall spread out powerfully westward, eastward, northward, and southward; and all the families of the earth shall bless themselves by you and by your offspring. Behold, I am with you; I will guard you wherever you go, and I will return you to this land, for I will not forsake you until I will have done what I have spoken about you."[193]

Many decades later, when Yaakov was about to descend to Egypt, having just learned that Yosef was alive and Viceroy of Egypt, God closed the circle on His promises to the *Avot*. The Torah paints the picture:

---

191. Ibid., 26:2–4.
192. Ibid., 28:3–4.
193. Ibid., 28:11–15.

> So Israel set out with all that he had and he came to Beersheva where he slaughtered sacrifices to the God of his father Yitzchak. God spoke to Israel in night visions and He said: "Yaakov, Yaakov." And he said: "Here I am." And He said: "I am God, the God of your father. Have no fear of descending to Egypt, for I shall establish you as a great nation there. I shall descend with you to Egypt, and I shall also surely bring you up . . ."[194]

Note that in this Torah passage, Yaakov is called both by his birth name and also by the name Israel which he received after the battle with the angel. From that point on, whenever Yaakov acts with an eye towards his national role of rearing twelve sons to become a nation of twelve unified tribes, his name is Israel. But when he acts as an individual, he still is referred to by his birth name of Yaakov.

Raising twelve different sons from four mothers into one unified nation was no easy task which required a great deal of endurance. Today, Yaakov's example serves as an encouragement to all parents who are struggling with their challenges. They and all of us can hope to pass our life's tests if we adopt the Torah as our constant guide and if we remember that, in good times and difficult times, God's promises and covenants remain with us. It is through His eternal Torah that we connect to Him, and its words form an everlasting construct of *netzach* within *tiferet* for each one of us and for the Jewish people in this world and the World to Come.

JOHN ADAMS AND THE JEWS

Netzach within *tiferet* is occasionally modeled by certain world leaders, especially as they relate to the State of Israel and the Jews. John Adams was one such leader.

A non-Jew, Adams was brilliant and learned, famous among the "Founding Fathers" of the United States of America, who served in many roles to ensure his country would become independent of British rule in the eighteenth century. He was a signatory of the Declaration of Independence, one of the drafters of the U.S. Constitution, and the second President of the United States. As an elder statesman, he also raised

194. Ibid., 46:1–4.

vital funds for the fight for independence from France and Holland. In 1808 he wrote:

> If I were an atheist and believed in blind eternal fate, I should still believe that fate had ordained the Jews to be the most essential instrument for civilizing the nations . . . They [the Jews] are the most glorious nation that ever inhabited this Earth. The Romans and their Empire were but Bauble in comparison of the Jews. They have given religion to three-quarters of the globe and have influenced the affairs of Mankind more, and more happily, than any other Nation, ancient or modern.[195]

If non-Jews know it, let's be sure that we do too. Let's obligate ourselves to know the facts about the promises God made to our *Avot* and the special role we are meant to play in the world, and let's we must make sure our children know this as well so that they grow up to embody our rich and incomparable heritage.

195. John Adams, a letter from 1808 criticizing the depiction of Jews by the French Enlightenment philosopher Voltaire. Source: American Jewish Historical Society.

DISCUSSION TOPICS FOR *NETZACH* WITHIN *TIFERET*

For adults

1. Have I committed my time and effort to any worthy goal or cause (outside my family) and have I done so on an enduring basis over the years? What was/is that commitment? If I have not made such a commitment, what keeps me from making it?
2. What obstacles are stopping me now from completing a worthy goal I have set for myself? How can I set up reasonable boundaries so I can stay on course?
3. Am I too passive in setting goals and working in a dedicated manner to complete them? What can I do to turn this around?

For children

1. When I start a homework assignment, do I stick with it until the end, or do I need others to push me along?
2. When I do a chore around the house, do I have to be continually reminded to finish, or do I complete it on my own?
3. When I tell someone that I will do something, do I carry through until it is done? Can I give some examples?

היום תשעה עשר יום,
שהם שני שבועות וחמישה ימים, לעומר

*(Ha'yom tisha asar yom, she'hem,
shnei shavuot v'chamisha yamim la'Omer)*

**"TODAY IS THE NINETEENTH DAY,
OR TWO WEEKS AND FIVE DAYS, OF THE OMER."**

DAY 19

Hod sh'b'Tiferet (Humility within Harmony/Truth)

Hod adorns *tiferet* with humility to make it even more beautiful and balanced. When *hod* is coupled with *tiferet,* it manifests itself in quiet consideration and recognition of the other that comes from selflessness and not ego-based self-interest. *Hod* within *tiferet* is righteous truth.

"You shall be holy, for I, Hashem, your God, am holy."[196]

With these words, we are introduced by the Torah to some of the most powerful ethical principles that we are expected to live by.

Prior to this, we read about the dedication of the Mishkan as a dwelling place for the Divine Presence on earth, about the order of sacrifices, about the laws of purity, and how to redress impurity. But now – in *Parshat Kedoshim* – we learn that purity is not the goal. Rather, the goal is to become holy.

Although we will never arrive at God's level of pure holiness, nevertheless, it is our mission to strive to be holy. Indeed, Rashi comments that virtually the entirety of the Torah hinges on what God tells directly to the entire assembly of B'nei Yisrael at this juncture,[197] and Ramban equates

196. *Vayikra* 19:2.
197. Rashi on *Vayikra* 19:2.

Parshat Kedoshim with the Ten Commandments.[198] But while the Ten Commandments were addressed to each and every Jew in the singular, these ethical laws – specifically Chapter 19 of *Sefer Vayikra* – are addressed to the entire Nation of Israel, in the plural. The message here is that to sustain an ethical society, certain principles have to be transmitted to everyone, and everyone must feel responsible for living according to them.

Achieving an ethical society requires *hod* within *tiferet*. First, there must be an acceptance of that which is true, and also a balanced expression of *chesed* and *gevurah*. A society which lacks this balance will not be a healthy society. Too much *chesed* can lead to too much permissiveness and produces a society characterized by sexual promiscuity, debasement, and an attitude of "anything goes." Conversely, too much *gevurah* produces a totalitarian society where the strong and powerful dominate the weak, and where creativity and tolerance are suppressed. Therefore, a dose of humility is essential for an ethical society and that comes from a foundation built on *hod* within *tiferet*.

UNHEALTHY SOCIETIES

When a society is dominated by one group, which believes itself to be wiser, superior, and thus entitled to more rights and privileges, it will be neither balanced nor ethical. And the absence of humility and truth will produce a downward spiral. Indeed, if the group in power couples the absence of *hod* within *tiferet* with the presence of *gevurah* within *gevurah* in its negative manifestation, disaster is inevitable.

Taking it a step further, when one segment of society believes that only it has all the answers and no other group should be entitled to serve in the government, own property, be educated, write books, or be able to teach, then that society is well on the way to becoming radicalized. After a few years, this type of cultural extremism, especially if fueled by the megalomania of its leaders, is likely to spread and negatively impact the entire world.

The prime example is Germany, which began its downward spiral in 1935 when it adopted the Nuremberg Laws just a couple years after electing Adolf Hitler to power. Overnight, these laws of the land, in the

198. Ramban on *Vayikra* 19:4 quoting *Vayikra Rabbah* 24:5.

supposedly "cultured" society, codified widespread racial discrimination against any person of "Jewish blood." Systematically, Jews lost their citizenship, their political rights, and their economic rights.

Did large groups of Germans speak up to point out the sheer immorality and ethical obscenity of such "laws?" No. Instead, these laws were interpreted as license to give free rein to anti-Semitism.

Soon, violence against Jews – such as that unleashed on Kristallnacht (the Night of Broken Glass) in November 1938 – became systematized in what came to be known as the Final Solution. The highly acclaimed Christian historian, Paul Johnson writes in *A History of the Jews*:

> The German people knew about and acquiesced in the genocide. There were 900,000 of them in the SS alone, plus another 1,200,000 involved in the railways. The trains were one giveaway. Most Germans knew the significance of the huge, crowded trains rattling through the hours of darkness . . .
>
> The Germans were beneficiaries of murder. Scores of thousands of men's and women's watches, fountain-pen and propelling pencils, stolen from the victims, were distributed among the armed forces; in one six-week period alone, 222,269 sets of men's suits and underclothes, 192,652 sets of women's clothing, and 99,922 sets of children's clothes, collected from those gassed at Auschwitz, were distributed on Germany's Home Front. The recipients knew roughly where these came from. The Germans did very little to protest about what was being done to the Jews or to help Jews escape . . .[199]

Emboldened by the lack of opposition, Hitler continued with his satanic plan, controlling opinion through his highly-effective propaganda machine. Arrogance, hatred, and anger rode rampant in Nazi society, the flames constantly stoked by its leaders who manufactured their own brand of "truth" to justify their odious and immoral conduct. The end result was the death for twelve million, six million of them Jews.

Only thirteen years passed from the day Hitler was sworn into elected office in Germany. And yet, because no one successfully pointed out that his racist ideology besmirches and tarnishes the image of God within all

199. Paul Johnson, *A History of the Jews* (NY: Harper & Row, 1987), 498–499.

human beings, Hitler was left to virtually destroy the twentieth century world. With *gevurah* run amuck, and a complete absence of *hod* within *tiferet*, Hitler was allowed to suck the life out of individuals, families, and entire nations, leaving a mark of destruction and devastation that shall never be forgotten.

SOCIETIES LACKING *HOD* WITHIN *TIFERET*

Pardon the history lesson, but *hod* within *tiferet* is an essential part of an ethical society. Without it, a "cultured" society like Germany turned "barbarian" in just thirteen years, as was Hitler's stated goal.[200]

Are there any world leaders today whose societies appear to have that fateful combination of *gevurah* within *gevurah* (used negatively) along with a lack of *hod* within *tiferet*? Humankind needs to figure that out before it is too late.

In a must-read essay entitled "The Unlearned Lessons of the Holocaust," Irwin Cotler, former Justice Minister of Canada, warns that history continues to repeat itself:

> As the Canadian Supreme Court recognized, in words echoed by the international criminal tribunals in the former Yugoslavia and Rwanda, the Holocaust did not begin in the gas chambers, it began with words . . . Indeed the genocide of European Jewry succeeded not only because of a culture of hate and an industry of death, but because the crimes of indifference and conspiracies of silence . . . And we have witnessed an appalling indifference and inaction in our own day which took us down the road to the unthinkable, ethnic cleansing in the Balkans, and to the unspeakable, the genocides in Rwanda and Darfur. What makes these genocides so unspeakable is that they were preventable. No one can say that we did not know.

200. Hitler said: "Yes, we are barbarians! We want to be barbarians. It is an honorable title to us . . . Providence has ordained that I should be the greatest liberator of humanity. I free man from . . . the degrading self-mortification of a false vision called conscience and morality . . . Conscience is a Jewish invention." As quoted in: Hermann Rauschning, *Voice of Destruction (Hitler Speaks)* (NY: Putnam, 1940), 87, 220–222.

> We knew, but we did not act in Rwanda, just as we knew and did not act in Darfur, ignoring thereby the lessons of history. . . .[201]

To accurately identify societies that lack *hod* within *tiferet* and pose such a danger today, all we need do is ask a few simple questions:

- How are women treated?
- How are religious minorities treated?
- What laws exist to protect religious minorities and guarantee them freedom to worship?
- Do all citizens benefit from education and health care, regardless of their gender, race, creed, religion, or color?
- How are terrorists and people who murder civilians treated? Are they put in jail and judged as criminals or are they venerated, given financial rewards and Internet fame?
- Does the society condone the use of children as human shields?
- Does it purposely place rocket launchers in residential areas, knowing that any returning fire will likely kill these civilians?

These are clues as to whether or not a society is ethical, or whether it is one dominated by *gevurah* within *gevurah* in its most negative manifestation.

Let us now consider an example of one country during World War II, who got it right – who applied *gevurah* within *gevurah* in its positive manifestation.

In contrast to what happened in Germany and just about everywhere else in Europe, this small country managed to save its Jewish citizens from the Nazi onslaught. When Hitler's troops overran Bulgaria and issued a demand that it turn over its Jews, Bulgaria refused. Although the nearby regions of Thrace and Macedonia did turn over about 10,000 Jews, the 50,000 Jewish citizens of Bulgaria were saved. Why?

Because in Bulgaria, a cross section of leaders – including Christian Orthodox officials, politicians in the Bulgarian governing body, and others in positions of authority – spoke out repeatedly and publicly against the deportation of a single Bulgarian Jew. The result? Not one of Bulgaria's Jews was deported to a camp. None died by Nazi hands. All because the

201. Irwin Cotler, "The Unlearned Lessons of the Holocaust," *The Jerusalem Post Magazine*, February 10, 2012, 13.

society as a whole did not permit it to occur, and showed the world what *hod* within *tiferet* should look like.

A DEFINING *SEFIRAH*

Hod within *tiferet* is a defining *sefirah*. With it, we can all live dignified lives. Without it, we are doomed.

Among the lessons to learn from the Holocaust, Irwin Cotler includes these: the responsibility to remember; the responsibility to prevent state-sanctioned incitement to hatred and genocide; and the duty to act against silence and indifference. These are the responsibilities and duties of every country and every individual – at all times – now and in the future.

The lesson of *Parshat Kedoshim* is that everyone is responsible for the building and maintaining of an ethical society. Simply following the precepts contained in Chapter 19 of *Sefer Vayikra* – and certainly the famous, "You shall love your neighbor as yourself"[202] – is step one in that direction.

So as we ponder *hod* within *tiferet*, and as we build each day toward the pinnacle of *malchut* within *malchut*, let's think about whether or not *we* are striving to live a dignified life, for Ramban's famous insight is that to strive to be holy means to do just that.[203] Do we try to give others the benefit of the doubt and to always look favorably upon them? Do our thoughts elevate us or do they leave us insecure, jealous, or haughty?

Is our speech dignified? Do we use our gift of speech to express gratitude and appreciation and honor to our parents, our spouses, our children, our teachers, our employers, and others? Or, do we use our lips to speak crudely, engage in *lashon hara*, complain, blame, criticize, and judge?

Finally, do we act in a dignified way? Do we eat like animals, quickly stuffing food into our mouths while talking, or do we eat like human beings, carefully and slowly saying the *bracha* both before and after the meal, thus elevating the simple act of eating into something holy? When we drive a car or take a bus, or do an errand, do we display patience and courtesy, or do we impatiently rush through our day oblivious to the needs of those around us – like the older person who may need a seat on the bus, or the pregnant woman who may need some help with her grocery bags? When we give *tzedakah* to others, do we give of ourselves

---

202. *Vayikra* 19:18.

203. Ramban on *Vayikra* 19:2.

quietly and without judgment, or do we somehow believe we are superior to the recipient of the charity?

These are some of many questions we can ask ourselves to determine to what extent we are living up to the attribute of *hod* within *tiferet* and fulfilling the *mitzvot* of *Parshat Kedoshim.*

A TORAH EXAMPLE: SARAH

Let's now look at a more personal example of *hod* within *tiferet* – the best example in the Torah – that of Sarah Imeinu.

There are no words to describe the extraordinary *middah* displayed by Sarah when she gave her maidservant, Hagar, to her husband Avraham.[204] She did this because she was vitally committed to their joint mission of pursuing the truth of God and His word. She acted within that unwavering truth with utter humility.

And what humility! Sarah put God before her, and she put her husband before her. The Torah does not describe her decision to do this as a difficult one – she was not filled with anguish, self-doubt, despair, anger, or resentment. The Torah simply tells us that when Sarah realized she was too old to bear children, she asked her husband to take her maidservant, in the hope that this union would produce a child and fulfill God's promise that Avraham's offspring would be as numerous as the stars in the sky.

I simply do not know any woman who would do this. From this holy sacrifice on the part of Sarah, we come face to face with *hod* within *tiferet.*

Sarah seized the moment and acted. Her personal feelings were sacrificed to her overarching awareness that she had a mission to fulfill, which was to bring the truth of one God into an idol-worshipping world – even if it meant that it would not be her own biological son who would continue this holy mission. Whatever she had to sacrifice to play that vital role so that the world would choose monotheism, she was ready to do.

Aligning oneself with an enduring cause greater than oneself is a selfless display of *hod* within *tiferet* and Sarah did it with a full heart, notwithstanding how difficult it must have been.

How can we emulate her? How can we banish hatred, anger, resentment, and jealousy from our emotional repertoire and elevate ourselves to display *hod* within *tiferet* in our every expression and encounter? How can

204. *Bereshit* 16:1–3.

we reflect truth, harmony, and balance in our personal lives, world views, and actions?

How? By starting now to work on ourselves and by also teaching the ways of God to our children.

DISCUSSION TOPICS FOR *HOD* WITHIN *TIFERET*

For adults

1. The next three times you are upset and feeling the opposite of harmony, identify why you are upset and write it down, so that you can think about it. Are you upset because the outcome was different than you wanted? Is the outcome that occurred something you can live with, even if it wasn't your ideal? Are your expectations so tied into your ego needs that you neglect those that you love and regard?
2. Have you ever sacrificed something you really wanted in the moment for the sake of some higher purpose or goal later on? Do you think that it was the right choice?
3. In a given situation, has arrogance and a lack of flexibility ever prevented you from behaving in a way that required the nuance of truth and harmony?

For children

1. The last time you were upset about something, was it just because you did not get your way? What is a better way that you could express your being upset? What would have been a better way to react?
2. What is *emunah*? How can you show your trust in God when things don't go exactly the way you want?
3. When have you shown that you were flexible about something? Did it turn out okay?

היום עשרים יום,
שהם שני שבועות וששה ימים, לעומר

*(Ha'yom esrim yom,
she'hem shnei shavuot v'shisha yamim la'Omer)*

"TODAY IS THE TWENTIETH DAY,
OR TWO WEEKS AND SIX DAYS, OF THE OMER."

DAY 20

Yesod sh'b'Tiferet (Bonding within Harmony/Truth)

Yesod brings a quality of permanence and reliability to the *sefirah* of *tiferet*. This is the case in all relationships – whether with God, or our parents, spouses, family, friends, community, and in all commitments, whether to projects, objectives, goals, mission or causes. The beautiful balance and truth of *tiferet*, when coupled with *yesod*, allows for a constancy in bonding that creates a fixed cornerstone to life's endeavors.

Many biblical greats achieved this admirable attribute in their relationship with God, and we can be continually inspired by reliving their stories when we – together with our children – learn the *Parashat HaShavuah* each week.

Avraham and Sarah are a beautiful example of people who achieved *yesod* within *tiferet* in their relationship with each other, as well as in their relationship with God. They were lifelong partners who pioneered together, abruptly leaving Mesopotamia simply because God instructed them to. They served God together with a full heart and raised their only son Yitzchak to do the same. Their ethical life choices represented complete departures from the pagan life style of their day. They found the truth and never forgot it. They imparted it to others, most importantly their son who followed suit with his own offspring.

From these two giants we have a core tradition that has lasted for more than 4,000 years. Their adherence to and pursuit of monotheism changed the entire world.

When tested by the bizarre command to sacrifice their only son, Avraham and Sarah demonstrated their bond with God by immediately seeking to fulfill it. They understood that to be faithful servants to the Master involves complete and total bonding with His word.

Of course, God didn't plan for the *Akeidah* to actually take place, but Avraham and Yitzchak demonstrated the completeness of their faith and their total commitment to fulfill His every command. This faith earned for them the privilege of being the progenitors of God's chosen people and the recipients of God's promise that the Jewish nation as a whole would never be destroyed.

AT MOUNT SINAI

Moshe Rabbeinu also achieved this connection with God – and even to a greater degree. Unlike any other prophet, Moshe spoke "face to face" with God.[205] For example, when Moshe returned with the second set of the tablets, his face shone with a radiant light after having basked in the Divine Presence, unlike any other mortal.[206]

We don't need to look much further than Moshe for a vivid model of *yesod* within *tiferet*, one that inspired the entire Nation of Israel when they left Egypt.

Arriving at Mount Sinai, they encamped there, and Moshe ascended to God, as the Torah relates:

> And God called to him from the mountain saying: "So shall you say to the House of Yaakov and relate to the Children of Israel. You have seen what I did to Egypt, and that I have borne you on the wings of eagles and brought you to Me. And now, if you harken well to Me and observe My covenant, you shall be to Me the most beloved treasure of all peoples, for Mine is the entire world. You shall be to Me a kingdom of ministers and a holy nation."[207]

205. *Devarim* 34:10.
206. *Shemot* 34:29–35.
207. Ibid., 19:3–6.

In response to the message from God that Moshe delivered, the entire people said: "Everything that God has spoken we shall do!" Moshe conveyed this response to God, who then instructed him to prepare the people for three days, after which time He would descend in the sight of all on Mount Sinai.[208]

Indeed, this is exactly what happened. The Jewish people responded with *yesod* within *tiferet* to God's display of *yesod* within *tiferet*.

When they responded in this way, they merited an intimate and personal rendezvous with the Creator. They were unified and bonded with each other and with God. But then they fell apart. How can we repair their mistake and return to that state as a nation?

Rav Avraham Yitzchak Kook explains in *Orot HaTeshuvah:*

> The beginning of repentance which immediately illumines the darkness is that man return to himself, the root of his soul, and he will at once return to God, to the soul of all souls. This is true for the individual, the entire nation, for all of humanity, for the perfection of existence as a whole.[209]

When we serve God today, we strive to return to the same level as the Jews at Sinai when they were bonded in truth. When we work to achieve *yesod* within *tiferet* in any relationship in our life, then everything we do is elevated. Our marriage, our parental relationships, our daily *tefillah* and service to God, our learning, our work – everything appears in a new light and with a new truth. Everything is precious. Simply precious.

---

208. Ibid., 19: 7–11.

209. Kook, Avraham Yitzchak, *Orot HaTeshuva*, Chap. 15:10.

DISCUSSION TOPICS FOR *YESOD* WITHIN *TIFERET*

For adults

1. To whom are you bonded in complete harmony and truth such that you can be completely relied upon in both good and bad times to loyally give this other person your very best? Is your bond strong enough that you can convey messages the other may not wish to hear? Is it mutual?
2. How do you show that you are proudly bonded with your Jewish identity? How do you show that you are bonded with other Jews?
3. How do you demonstrate that you are bonded at the deepest level with the truth of Torah?

For children

1. Are you proud to be Jewish? Explain your thoughts and feelings on this subject.
2. What could you and your family do to make Shabbat even more meaningful so that you connect to God? Can you discuss your ideas with your parents?
3. To whom in your life do you feel completely connected? How do you show that connection?

היום אחד ועשרים יום, שהם שלושה שבועות, לעומר

(Ha'yom echad v'esrim yom, she'hem shlosha shavuot la'Omer)

"TODAY IS THE TWENTY-FIRST DAY, OR THREE WEEKS, OF THE OMER."

DAY 21

Malchut sh'b'Tiferet (Leadership/Nobility within Harmony/Truth)

Malchut **within** ***tiferet*** **is the epitome of the** ***sefirah*** **of** ***tiferet.*** **When we independently choose to always act with kingship, dignity, leadership, and nobility in our thoughts, speech, and actions, and in a way that reflects the truth and the beautiful balance that** ***tiferet*** **represents, we have mastered** ***malchut*** **within** ***tiferet.***

Again there are many biblical stories that depict this important *sefirah* combination when truth and harmony are maximized through an individual's choice to "do the right thing." Every time this occurs in the Tanach, we glimpse the real meaning of *malchut* within *tiferet.*

In *Sefer Bereshit,* one of the most inspiring stories is that of Yehuda and Tamar. The Midrash fills in the details about the dramatic conclusion to the story when Tamar stands accused of harlotry, and though innocent, refuses to defend herself and name Yehuda as the father of her unborn child.

According to the Midrash, Yehuda as well as his father, Yaakov, and grandfather, Yitzchak, were in the courtroom along with many others and stood in witness when Tamar displayed her greatness by keeping silent in order not to publicly embarrass Yehuda. Not even when he, not realizing his responsibility, declared: "Take her out and let her be burned."[210] Even then, she left her fate completely to God.

Dealt unfairly by Yehuda's two sons, who then died, Tamar acted. When Yehuda had broken his promise to give her his youngest son in marriage, she chose to become pregnant by subterfuge purely because she wanted to be a part of the lineage of the Jewish people.[211]

Her pregnancy landed her in the courtroom on the accusation of harlotry, and the next stage of the drama unfolded:

In the courtroom scene, as Tamar is being led out to her death, she sends word to Yehuda, along with his signet ring, cloak, and staff, that "by the man to whom these belong I am with child."[212] Realizing he is at fault, Yehuda is then left with the agonizing decision of what course of action to take. Does he let Tamar go to her death, his secret to die with her? No one – except God, Tamar, and he – will know the truth. Does he shield his own responsibility?

Absolutely not. He declares: "She is more righteous than me." Tamar's life is spared and she gives birth to twins, one of whom, Perez, becomes the progenitor of the Davidic line which leads to the future Mashiach.

Can you imagine the embarrassment Yehuda could have avoided? With this noble and dignified act of aligning himself with the truth, despite his own humiliation, Yehuda displayed *malchut* within *tiferet*. With this act, Yehuda merited that the kings of Israel would come from his seed, including the final King Mashiach. As well, we are called "Yehudim" (Jews) after Yehuda (Judah).

Yehuda did the right thing. Tamar did the right thing. They revealed their grasp of nobility within truth, when they took complete responsibility for their own life's choices. Whenever this occurs, Hashem blesses us, and we are blessed. To read about such a display of *malchut* within *tiferet* sends chills up the spine. These are our ancestors who acted in such breathtakingly noble and truthful ways!

---

210. *Bereshit* 38:24.

211. Ibid., 38:6–23.

212. Ibid., 38:25–30.

MALCHUT WITHIN *TIFERET* TODAY

We are each given many chances to do the right thing every day. We are each given a chance to learn what truth is, and express it in harmonious ways throughout the day. We are given a chance to display the wholeness of *malchut* that contains loving-kindness, restraint, balance, endurance, humility, and bonding in the proper amounts, at the right time. The Omer count helps us to learn and practice this skill.

Sometimes we are presented with a life test where we are expected to actually implement this learned ability in a manner that serves as a model and inspiration for others. Some of us will pass this test by choosing to do the right thing. When we do, our lives are forever changed for the better. We achieve the same nobility that Yehuda and Tamar displayed more than 3,000 years ago. This next story is about one of those moments.

I had once met a man I shall call Alan Yitzach through a mutual rabbi friend. His story is remarkable.

When Alan's mother died (a few months prior to our meeting), he was not connected to any Jewish community, nor did he live near any Jewish community. But Alan knew one truth. He knew that he wanted his mother to have a proper Jewish burial, and that he wanted to sit *shiva* for seven days and say *Kaddish* three times a day for the eleven months, as is mandated by Jewish law.

Alan shared that he had done nothing Jewishly since his Bar Mitzvah about forty-five years earlier until this personal decision to keep all the laws of mourning for his mother. He was so alienated Jewishly that the only way he knew to get his mother properly buried was to call the synagogue where he had his Bar Mitzvah nearly half a century earlier. That led him to the rabbi of the *shul*, who happened to be active in outreach to unaffiliated Jews. That rabbi helped Alan to arrange a proper Jewish burial in a Jewish cemetery and a *minyan* of ten men at both the funeral and for each day of the *shiva*. Alan then selected this same synagogue to be the one where he would begin going to daily *minyan*, and he began staying as a guest at the rabbi's home for every Shabbat in order to attend the *minyanim* on Shabbat as well.

"Alan's the Man" in my book. He was given this test. He made a difficult, but right decision out of respect for his mother. When we met, he told me that he felt at peace with himself for his choices and, deservedly, he beamed with a quiet pride. My hat is off to Alan. His mother's *neshamah* will, no doubt, enjoy a higher *aliyah* as a result of her son's profound and far-reaching life choice.

This is a story of *malchut* within *tiferet* but there is more than one hero in it. What about Alan's rabbi? The rabbi of the only *shul* Alan knew about did not know him. This was an Orthodox *shul*, and Alan surely was not Orthodox. And yet this rabbi and his wife reached out to Alan in so many ways over the next year and beyond. They made sure that the funeral and *shiva* were halachic, relevant, and meaningful. They welcomed him into their home to sleep every single Shabbat. And, in the conclusion to the story, they welcomed him to Israel when they made *aliyah*. This is *malchut* within *tiferet* as well.

Wouldn't it be amazing if we woke up one day and everyone acted according to *malchut* within *tiferet*? What a world that would be! It would be the kind of world that would be ready to bring Mashiach – may it happen speedily in our days.

DISCUSSION TOPICS FOR *MALCHUT* WITHIN *TIFERET*

For adults

1. Have I ever chosen to own up to something I did "wrong" even though I knew the outcome would be painful? How do I feel about that decision today?
2. Have I ever chosen to go out of my way to do something that was completely out of character, similar to Alan Yitzach? How did my life change as a result?
3. What is my greatest obstacle to living a life of harmony and truth day-in and day-out? What am I prepared to do about it?

For children

1. Have I ever told the truth to my parents or teacher, even though I knew that in doing so I might get in trouble for what I had done? What happened? How did telling the truth make me feel?
2. When I grow up and become a parent, will I want my kids to tell me the truth even if they have done something "bad?" Why or why not?
3. Have I ever not tattled on someone because I didn't want them to be embarrassed by what they did? How did that make me feel?

WEEK FOUR

Netzach

(Endurance/Eternity)

OVERVIEW

Netzach (Endurance/Eternity)

As we enter the fourth week of the Counting of the Omer, hopefully the attributes of the previous three weeks are still fresh and alive in our makeup. Thus far, we have honed the ability to properly give love, offsetting it with the limits of *gevurah* to achieve the balance, harmony, and truth that *tiferet* brings.

In this Week Four, we begin to add, Kabbalistically speaking, power to our legs, for this week is centered on *netzach* which corresponds to the right leg and which energizes us to act with endurance, drive, and determination, in order to accomplish our objectives and goals with alacrity.

Tiferet (harmony/truth) is essential but, without action, nothing happens. Without action, we cannot complete our mission on earth. And that's where *netzach* (endurance/eternity) comes in. To endure, we must have determination, tenacity, and stamina. *Netzach* is that energy which enables us to hold on until we achieve our goal. *Netzach* is tenacious, determined effort.

As with *gevurah*, pure *netzach*, which is not tempered by any other *sefirah*, can be either positive or harmful.

In *Endless Light*, Rabbi Aaron employed the words "conquest," "victory," and "assertion" in his descriptors of *netzach*. When we energetically pursue our aims in a persistent manner that considers others and is in balance, very positive outcomes can be achieved. However, when we act with an overabundance of *netzach* without restraint, or when we cross the borders of right or wrong, *netzach* can result in broken relationships, corruption, evil, and inhumane acts.

For example: When one country's drive for conquest leads it to invade its peaceful, ethical, and law-abiding neighbor, and in so doing to murder or enslave its inhabitants, then *netzach* feeds evil. But *netzach* is positive when it causes a country to overcome an obstacle or problem that threatens to harm it. It is admirable to "stick with it" until the end and to bring about an outcome that is good for all.

Unfortunately, we have all been witness to the damage that comes from aggressive, uncompromising competition and dominant, aggressive behavior when people disregard working on a team with common goals or the like. It is always impressive when someone like Menachem Begin, who was the leader of the opposition party in Israel at the time, put the good of the country before personal goals during the 1967 Six-Day War, giving full backing to Prime Minister Levi Eshkol. What a difference unity made in that case.

There are times when persistent assertion is acceptable, such as when ethical rights are being advanced for the common good. Used positively, *netzach* can lead the charge, make positive contributions, and win the day.

Some projects or initiatives take many hours, days, months, or even years. For example, it takes nine months to have a baby. It takes years to learn to read and write, to train for many professions, or to wage most wars. It can take decades to build up communities, companies, yeshivas, and armies, or to make headway with major causes such as environmentalism. With the exception of the miraculous development of the State of Israel – which went from an undeveloped to a fully developed country in just sixty years[213] – it generally takes centuries to build nations.

Depending upon the degree of commitment to positive goals, values, and beliefs as shown through a healthy balance of *netzach*, we can either harness its enduring energy to accomplish important changes, plans, and goals, or squander its energy because of our lack of commitment. It is important to recognize that *netzach* must be reined in and allocated in a balanced manner that includes accountability for our actions. These boundaries provide the essential security for ourselves, our families, and other relationships.

213. The International Monetary Fund considers Israel not an undeveloped nation, not a developing nation, but a totally developed nation, ranking its standard of living as the 15th highest in the world, just behind France. See the findings of the International Monetary Fund (Human Development Index) released November 4, 2010.

POSITIVE AND NEGATIVE EXAMPLES OF *NETZACH*

Once again, we need not look far to find amazing stories and examples of the positive application of *netzach*; as well, we need not look far for calamities when *netzach* was used to achieve the wrong ends in the wrong ways. Let's first look at the positives:

In the Torah, Moshe – the fourth of our Seven Shepherds – embodies eternity, which is the epitome of endurance. Why? Because he devoted his entire life to God and His word – the Torah. Earthly possessions are transient, but the Torah alone is of lasting value. During the forty years that he taught the Torah to three million Jews, Moshe constantly displayed *netzach*. This is why he merits being identified with the eternity of Torah, "to become its teacher and to transmit it to all the generations."[214]

In modern-day, we have many examples as well. If you want to encourage your children to develop greater *netzach* – to finish assignments and reach goals – one simple way of accomplishing this is to take them to the library or bookstore and help them select books that feature inspirational stories of *netzach*. While your child reads a given book, show interest by asking him or her to tell you about it over dinner. You can also share inspirational articles that describe the *sefirah* of *netzach* in action.

One such article is "Believing in Willpower," the riveting story of Lt. Colonel Shahar Spada related by Yaakov Lappin in *The Jerusalem Post Magazine*.[215]

In the late 1990s, when Shahar Spada was a young paratrooper on patrol in southern Lebanon, a roadside bomb exploded, wounding him severely. His commanders in the Israeli Army (IDF) thought his military career was over. Spada thought otherwise: "The first time I cried was from the frustration I felt when the IDF called me to say I would be discharged because of my injuries . . . It was like a knife to the heart . . . [But] I believe in willpower. If you want to get it done, nothing can get in your way."

He spent more than two years undergoing rehabilitation – a program of swimming and jogging which he designed himself – refusing to accept the army's decision to discharge him. As Lappin tells it:

---

214. Kitov, *The Book of Our Heritage*, Vol. 2, 684.

215. Yaakov Lappin, "Believing in Willpower," *The Jerusalem Post*, April 20, 2012, 15.

> Spada fought tooth-and-nail against the decision to discharge him, arguing with seven army medical committees before finally being approved for service by an eighth committee, a day he describes as one of the happiest in his life.

When asked about his motivation for fighting so hard to stay in the military, Spada summed it up simply, "We have no other country." Spada continues, "I took no disability benefits, nothing from this country . . . As long as I can stand on my feet, and as long as I have the family God gave me I have everything I need."

The rest of this gripping article describes how, once he was back in the army, Spada quickly rose through the ranks and passed a commanders course. Again, when asked his motivation for becoming a commander, Spada replied that it "was the unparalleled satisfaction of leading soldiers in the defense of their country."

Spada was in the thick of Operation Defensive Shield in 2002 and was part of the team that captured a suicide bomber on route to an Israeli target. Spada went on to marry "the love of his life" and have four daughters. On the night before his first baby daughter's naming ceremony, he was called out with his unit to intercept a terrorist. In the firefight, one of Spada's subordinates was shot in the leg. When Spada saw the wound was not life-threatening, he borrowed the man's bulletproof vest and took his place. "He charged into the battle zone, exchanging fire with the terrorist before shooting him dead."

In 2006, Spada was studying Middle Eastern Affairs at Bar-Ilan University and heard that another war had broken out. He rushed to join the paratroopers, fighting Hezbollah terrorists in southern Lebanon in house-to-house combat.

At the time of this writing, Lt. Colonel Spada is a deputy commander of the Judea Brigade securing Hebron, where our Patriarchs and Matriarchs are buried. Hebron is a complex area "where Israelis and Palestinians live practically on one another's doorsteps." Says Spada, "People come here to Hebron and feel safe . . . That's my mission."

Reading the story of Lt. Colonel Spada lifts me out of my chair. It inspires me to develop a stronger and more focused sense of *netzach* to apply to all my life goals. Frankly, there are no words to adequately capture my emotional state after reading this story. Heroic? Inspirational? These are accurate descriptions, but inadequate to express the impact of this man's story on my life.

And then there is the other side of the coin:

As we have learned, endurance can be used for the good, or for the bad. The negative application of *netzach* can be seen in the Civil War which raged in the United States in the mid-1800s. The Confederate States of the American South were committed to the practice of slavery with such *netzach* and determination that they were prepared to secede from the United States. Eventually, they were defeated and slavery was abolished by an amendment to the U.S. Constitution. The beliefs of the abolitionists who vehemently opposed slavery and the leadership of President Abraham Lincoln prevailed in this cause, displaying positive *netzach* in bringing freedom to all.

During Week Four, we will examine more such examples, as well as our own *netzach* to ensure it is always applied in a productive and healthy manner. And the first place we will begin is the Torah.

The Torah tells us that it was the Jewish women who ensured the survival of the Jewish people during the 210 years of cruel Egyptian slavery. Their husbands, not wanting to bring children into such a harsh world, separated from their wives. The men reasoned that all male newborns would die anyway – they were being killed so that Pharaoh could bathe in their blood or use their bodies as mortar to build the city of Ramses and Pithom.

Miriam, the six-year-old sister of Moshe, implored her father, Amram, a spiritual leader of the Jews at that time, to reunite with Yocheved, her mother. She argued that her parents' decision to separate was worse than Pharaoh's decree since their choice to separate prevented the births of even female babies and not just the male babies that Pharaoh aimed to murder. She further argued that the deeds of her righteous father would win the day, while the decrees of the Pharaoh were doomed. Her argument was persuasive; her parents reunited, and the result was the birth of Moshe, who would lead the entire Jewish nation out of Egypt. Other husbands followed Amram's lead, reuniting with their wives and ensuring the ultimate survival of the Jewish people.[216]

The *netzach* of Miriam became a crucial link in the chain of events that led to our redemption from Egypt.

---

216. *Sotah* 12a.

THE SHOAH

Despite six million unspeakable Jewish deaths – 1.5 million of whom were children – the *netzach* of those on their way to the gas chambers has inspired millions of surviving family members to live, to remember, to be free, and to never again permit a leader or nation to perpetrate another Shoah. Indeed, every Jew, now and ever, should be inspired by their last words and actions.

Every home should have the book *Final Letters: From Victims of the Holocaust*, a collection from the Yad Vashem Archives in Jerusalem. The following is an emotionally searing letter of love from Cilli Dzialowski of Holland who sent this farewell message, with the help of a Dutch woman, to her four children who lived in England during the war:

> *1 April, 1943*
>
> *Beloved, precious children,*
>
> *In these final moments, before I join your dearest father, and will, like him, lose my freedom, there is an urgent compulsion within me to tell you the following . . . I beg each one of you with all my heart to lead honest and straightforward lives always, and to support one another whenever necessary . . . I know what a treasure we have in you, my beloved ones, and that you are committed and firm and of strong character, that – Baruch Hashem – you are all blessed with that essence of personality which makes you liked by your fellow men and will surely find favour in the eyes of the Creator. This knowledge brings me consolation. Never deviate from the path of God-fearing behaviour and always be guided by the example of your beloved father. Our constant thoughts of you have accompanied you so far on your road through life, and our blessings will never leave you! . . . My Precious Children, I bless each one of you from the distance with the traditional blessing, also in Daddy's name: "May you be happy and successful in life; cling one to the other; and never stray even one step from the path, from the precepts of our TORAH." I embrace and kiss you and now feel truly united with you,*
>
> *Always yours,*
> *Mummy*[217]

---

217. Reuven Dafni and Yehudit Kleiman, *Final Letters: From Victims of the Holocaust*, 96–97.

What a legacy Cilli Dzialowski left for her children. Can you imagine her *netzach*? She spent her last moments – knowing she could never write another letter again – to inspire the next generation, and through them, her yet unborn grandchildren and great-grandchildren. There is no confusion in Cilli. She endures through her *netzach*. She endures when anyone reads and is inspired by her advice. She speaks seventy years after her death. The scum who kill her do not endure – only their legacy of guilt and disgrace which they left for their children.

There is another "final letter" which vividly demonstrates the deep meaning of personal endurance and which we must read this week when we study *netzach*.

This letter was penned by Sara and Yechiel Gerlitz of Bedzin, Poland, who had entrusted their only daughter, aged six, to a Polish friend. Believing they would never see their child again, they left her a letter which she was to open when she came of age. Fortunately, the parents survived; they were reunited with their daughter, and together they immigrated to Israel. I quote here their remarkable letter:

> *7 July, 1944*
>
> *My dear, beloved little child,*
>
> *On giving birth to you, my darling, I did not imagine that six and a half years later I would be writing you such a letter . . . I do not know, my dear child, if I will ever see you again. I take with me from home your picture, which I love so much, I am taking along your lovely chatter, the smell of your innocent, little body, the rhythm of your innocent breathing, your smile, and your tears which my heart, the heart of a mother, could not allay . . . That is what will accompany me on my way . . .*
>
> *My sweetheart! I want you to read this, when, by God's will, you are grown up and mature and able to criticize our behaviour toward you. I desire, my dear and beloved child, that you should not condemn us, that you should love our memory and our entire loathed people from which you originate. It is my desire that you should neither be ashamed of your provenance nor deny it. I want you to know that your father was a person of rare qualities – there are not many like him in the world – and that you can be proud of him. He dedicated his whole life to doing good to other people; may God bless every step of his, protect him, and allow him to regain you! My beloved treasure, you are your father's whole*

world, his only ambition, his only satisfaction for all his sufferings and pain. Therefore I wish you to keep a good memory of him, if fate should prove unfavourable to us . . . I want you to remember your grandfathers and grandmothers, your aunts and uncles – people of great value – and the whole family. Remember us and do not blame us! As for me, your mother – forgive me . . . Forgive me, my dear child, for having given birth to you . . . I wanted to bear you for our and your pride and joy, and it is not our fault that things took a different course. Thus, I implore you, my one and only darling, don't blame us. Try to be as good as your father and your ancestors. Love your foster parents and their family, who surely will tell you about us. I ask you to appreciate the self-sacrifice of your foster parents and to be their pride, so that they should never have any reason to regret the commitment which they have taken on voluntarily. There is one thing more I want you to know: that your mother was a proud person, despite our enemies' scorn and mistreatment, and, when she was going to die, she did so without moaning or crying, but with a smile of contempt for the enemy on her lips!

I hug and kiss you affectionately; receive all the blessings of my heart.

Your loving Mother

What can I say to my only child, truly the person dearest to me in the world? One should open one's heart and reveal its inside – no pen is able to describe what goes on in there just now. But I believe firmly that we will all survive and offer our hearts to one another.

Your Father[218]

What could one possibly add to what Sara and Yechiel Gerlitz chose to say to their daughter? *Nothing.* Their words reveal the enduring *netzach* on one cold night in history.

Yechiel Gerlitz captures the essence of a great and decent man and father, thereby creating a living legacy, in the event he does not survive. Sara Gerlitz selflessly hopes for her husband to survive and regain their daughter after the war, being unmindful of what she believes will be her own fate at the hands of the Nazis. She references the legacy of the generations and implores her daughter to be proud of each and every family

218. Ibid., 74–77.

member and of her Jewishness, even while acknowledging that Jews are loathed in their entirety.

Sara Gerlitz defines herself simply through the deepest love a mother could have for her daughter. Finally, she lets her daughter know that, if fate proves unfavorable, her mother will die with a smile of contempt on her lips for the enemy.

This is *netzach* reigning supreme. And yet, thank God, they lived.

EVERYDAY *NETZACH*

It is not easy to be married. It is not easy to be a parent. We have to work hard at these relationships if we want them to be good, healthy, and lasting.

The divorce rate is close to 50 percent in the secular world and climbing in the religious world. Does anyone know of a single family where there is perfect family bliss? Please write me if you do. I would like to know about it.

Remember all the Bible stories about family strife – Kayin and Hevel, Yishmael and Esav, the sale of Yosef by his brothers, the rape of Dina, the immoral action of Zimri who was a prince from the family of Shimon, the conduct of Avshalom, Amnon, and Adoniahu, the three sons of King David, as well as the many sad stories of some of the Jewish kings and their children. As bad as it was then, if we fast forward a couple thousand years, things are even worse.

Adolescent suicide is now the third-leading cause of death in the teen age-group. Eminent psychiatrist and one of the world's leading experts on alcohol and drug rehabilitation, Rabbi Dr. Abraham Twerski hits us between the eyes with today's reality:

> Young people today are exposed to challenges that may exceed their ability to cope. And make no mistake: there is no immunity. These problems are occurring even in the finest and most observant families. "Kids at risk?" *All* kids are at risk . . . We dare not underestimate the gravity of the situation. When weapons were spears and arrows, shields could serve as a defense. When the weapons are grenades and missiles, we need correspondingly greater defenses. The challenges to our youth today are in the category of nuclear weapons . . . Alcohol,

> drugs, promiscuity, and gambling have become rampant, and our youth has become infected with these contagious conditions.[219]

Rebbetzin Tzipporah Heller, in her well-written, practical book, *Let's Face It! The 8 Essential Challenges of Living*, lays it out clearly:

> Relationships are our ultimate challenge for the same reason that they are our ultimate joy. Relationships are about growing, expanding, and giving. This process, when sincerely engaged in, challenges every fiber of our being. That's why the average mother trying to put her young children to bed would gladly trade jobs with a lion tamer, sewer cleaner, or piano mover. And why the same mother, when rocking her baby to sleep or listening to her child perform his first clarinet solo, would not trade jobs with the highest-paying, most prestigious executive.[220]

Even though it might appear harder in today's times, we cannot give up. We must employ *netzach* to keep building positively and constructively. When we refuse to give up on our children, we send them a message of *netzach*. We emulate Our Father in Heaven who never gives up on us and patiently waits for us to do *teshuvah* and return to Him.

NETZACH AND LIFE'S CHALLENGES

How heroic are those people who have been given a challenging diagnosis of their health, who muster all their resources and apply them physically, mentally, emotionally, and spiritually to try and live a noble life with purpose, meaning, and enduring hope.

Dr. Norman Cousins writing in the groundbreaking *Anatomy of an Illness* describes his own journey from discouragement to cure from a "terminal" illness:

> "I was [discouraged] . . . especially at the start when I expected my doctor to fix my body as though it were an automobile engine that needed mechanical repair . . . But then I realized that a human being

219. Twerski, "Securing Your Home in an Insecure World," 36.
220. Heller, *Let's Face It! The 8 Essential Challenges of Living*, 162.

> is not a machine – and only a human being has a built-in mechanism for repairing itself, for ministering to its own needs, and for comprehending what is happening to it. The regenerative and restorative force in human beings is at the core of human uniqueness [although] sometimes this force is blocked or underdeveloped. . . .
>
> I was fortunate . . . in having a doctor who believed that my own will to live would actually set the stage for progress; he encouraged me in everything I did for myself . . .
>
> [That said] not every illness can be overcome. But many people allow illness to disfigure their lives more than it should. They cave in needlessly.[221]

When we choose to apply *netzach* to our own lives at critical times or in critical areas – including when facing the threat of death – we can make a difference because our spirit endures, whether it be in this world or in the next world.

Simply put – no matter what is the issue at hand – we cannot maximize our potential without *netzach*. And when we apply it in the right measure, we transcend whatever ails us, physically or spiritually:

- When we begin each day with an appreciation for our life as a Jew and enter our daily prayers with concentration and focus, we demonstrate to our Father in Heaven that we want to be in an enduring relationship with Him.
- When we choose to continue to fight – despite challenges and tests that seem so numerous and daunting that we truly don't know how we will survive – we send a message to our body, mind, and soul that we want to succeed. Our message is: "I want to endure. I do not want life's tests to defeat me. Rather, I want them to help elevate and purify me. I want to use them as opportunities for growth."
- When we resolve to commit to a course of study that we must complete in order to pursue our professional goals, without succumbing to worldly distractions, or when we relentlessly pursue a job, even after a long period of unemployment, discouraging interviews, and rejections, we display endurance.

221. Norman Cousins, *Anatomy of an Illness* (NY: Bantam Books, 1981), 145–149.

- When we persist with our diet to lose all the weight we need to improve our health, or commit to a regular exercise routine, we demonstrate to ourselves and others that our life is worth living. We do the same every day when we give up smoking, drinking to excess, or whatever else enslaves us.

With *netzach*, we Jews survived Egyptian slavery. We survived the Crusades, the Spanish expulsion, the pogroms in Russia, the brutality of Nazism. We saw the State of Israel established and formally recognized by the United Nations. All this was nothing short of a miracle, and it goes to show how much *netzach* matters.

It matters that we survive. If we have a decent marriage, it matters that we invest in our marriages so that we can grow and expand. If we are parents, it matters that we have a close relationship with our children that endures. If we are grandparents, it matters that our grandchildren know our values and what we stand for, and that, even when we may not be here, our legacy will live on in their hearts, minds and souls. This is how we endure.

When we count the Omer during each night of Week Four and focus on endurance, we tap into eternity. Every one of us must exercise our *netzach* to achieve important life goals, build noble relationships, achieve our life mission, be a light to the nations, bring Mashiach and become part of all eternity in oneness with God. *Netzach* is our strategy – with it we can bring about the Final Redemption.

היום שנים ועשרים יום,
שהם שלושה שבועות ויום אחד, לעומר

*(Ha'yom shnayim v'esrim yom,
she'hem shlosha shavuot v'yom echad la'Omer)*

"TODAY IS THE TWENTY-SECOND DAY, OR THREE WEEKS AND ONE DAY, OF THE OMER."

DAY 22

Chesed sh'b'Netzach (Loving-kindness within Endurance)

The powerful raw force of *netzach* can accomplish important objectives and goals; its impetus can build relationships that endure for a lifetime. But *netzach* must be employed lovingly, and not in a manner that is extreme or harsh which can result in isolation or distortion. When the heart of *chesed* merges with the endurance of *netzach*, it helps to ensure that this attribute will be manifested in a loving, kind and considerate manner – a manner which makes a place for others and does not become severe or destructive to the human spirit.

The Talmud, at the end of Tractate *Megillah*, relates a question posed to seven Sages who had lived in the days of the Mishna period. They were each asked to what they attributed their longevity. Rabbi Nechunya ben Hakana gave three reasons and his answer has always impressed. First, he said, he never permitted himself to enjoy any pleasure at the expense of his friend's embarrassment. Second, he never went to sleep cursing his friend. And third, when it came to money, he was not tightfisted.[222]

He did not qualify his principles with exceptions. He did not act differ-

222. *Megillah* 28a.

ently even if his friend deserved to be embarrassed, or was in the wrong, and he did not withhold money even if a person was unworthy. No, he enduringly displayed *chesed* in every instance.

THE PARENTS OF GILAD SCHALIT

A more recent example is the *chesed* within *netzach* displayed by the parents of kidnapped Israeli soldier, Sgt. Gilad Schalit.

Sgt. Schalit was kidnapped by the terrorist group Hamas in June of 2006 and held for five years before he was finally released in a prisoner exchange. That this eventually happened had a great deal to do with the campaign waged by his parents, Noam and Aviva, who never gave up hope. About the midpoint of his captivity, they moved from northern Israel to Jerusalem, where they peacefully camped out in front of the Prime Minister's residence, vowing never to return to their home without their son. Their actions – a defining example of love and endurance (*chesed* within *netzach*) – stirred the heart of *Klal Yisrael.*

Schalit's parents brought together all kinds of Jews and non-Jews by staging large rallies and organizing marches throughout all parts of Israel. They got the point across that Gilad Schalit was the son of all of us.

When the young soldier was finally released, there were those who argued that the price of releasing 1,000 terrorists from prison was too high to pay, but nonetheless there was not a dry eye in Israel, as the whole country watched this skinny boy finally make it home.

What a display of *chesed* within *netzach* in our time. The parents' outpouring of love coupled with sustained action achieved a goal that many may have thought unlikely, thus displaying the power of this vital attribute.

CHESED WITHIN *NETZACH* IN THE TORAH

As with every other attribute, the Torah is replete with stories that illustrate *chesed* within *netzach*, and many of them center on the person of Moshe Rabbeinu.

Despite all the trials and tribulations his flock put him through, despite their complaining, crying and demanding, and, notwithstanding whether they deserved it or not, Moshe consistently pleaded with God to forgive the Nation of Israel for their transgressions. The most amazing example of this was his defense of the Jewish people following the Sin of the Golden Calf.

While Moshe was on Mount Sinai for forty days and nights receiving the Torah, God informed him that the people were up to no good. Sure enough, some of them had built a statue of an idol and were engaging in promiscuous behavior. God's reaction to this was terrifying:

> Hashem spoke to Moshe: "Go, descend – for your people that you brought up from the land of Egypt have become corrupt. They have strayed quickly from the way that I have commanded them. They have made themselves a molten calf, prostrated themselves to it and sacrificed to it, and they said: "This is your god, O Israel, which brought you up from the land of Egypt."
>
> Hashem said to Moshe: "I have seen this people, and behold, it is a stiff-necked people. And now, desist from Me. Let My anger flare up against them and I shall annihilate them; and I shall make you a great nation."[223]

In response, Moshe forcefully argued with God. In a dramatic display of *chesed* within *netzach*, he pleaded that the Jewish people be forgiven and not destroyed. The Torah recounts:

> Moshe pleaded before Hashem, his God, and said: "Why, Hashem, should Your anger flare up against Your people, whom You have taken out of the land of Egypt, with great power and a strong hand? Why should Egypt say that 'With evil intent did He take them out, to kill them in the mountains and to annihilate them from the face of the earth'? Relent from your flaring anger and reconsider regarding the evil against Your people. Remember for the sake of Avraham, Yitzchak, and Israel, Your servants, to whom You swore by Yourself, and You told them, 'I shall increase your offspring like the stars of heaven, and this entire land of which I spoke, I shall give to your offspring and it shall be their heritage forever.'"[224]

---

223. *Shemot* 32:7–10.

224. Ibid., 32:11–13; here Moshe is quoting *Bereshit* 32:11–13.

Moshe's argument – which prevails – is pure *chesed* within *netzach*, urging God to have mercy because of Avraham, Yitzchak, and Yaakov and to keep His eternal promise to them. Moshe's reasoning with God on behalf of the Jewish people reveals the emergence of Moshe as a true leader of the Nation of Israel. For the first time Moshe not only displays *chesed* within *netzach* but also *malchut*.

The Ultimate Example

Of course, the ultimate example of this attribute – as always – is God.

When He visited the ten plagues upon Egypt in a manner that spared the Jewish people from harm, He manifested *chesed* within *netzach*. God was determined to show the pagan world that He was in charge. Yet, He orchestrated it all with kindness in mind. The devastation of all ten plagues, miraculously, did not harm the Jewish people.[225] For example, if there was darkness throughout the land so thick that Egyptians could not get out of bed, the Jews had light where they lived. If there were frogs jumping out of the ovens and into the mouths of every Egyptian, the Jews were untouched by them. Death of the firstborn? If a Jew spread the blood of the Pascal Lamb on the doorpost of his home, the Angel of Death passed over it, sparing all the Jews within.

He has always looked after the Jews, just as He had promised Avraham, Yitzchak, and Yaakov, and He did so, no matter what they did!

Despite the Sin of the Golden Calf and the Israelites' chronic complaining, God led them through the desert, ensuring all their needs and sustaining them with manna and water which miraculously spouted from rocks. He protected them with His Clouds of Glory and guided them with His Pillar of Fire. And ultimately, He brought them to the Promised Land, just as He had promised the Patriarchs and Matriarchs. He never failed them and He treated them kindly all the way – if that is not *chesed* within *netzach*, I don't know what is.

---

225. Ibid., 8:18–19; *Shemot Rabbah, Va'eira* 9:10; *Bamidbar Rabbah, Naso* 9:14.

DISCUSSION TOPICS FOR *CHESED* WITHIN *NETZACH*

For adults

1. In my family, are there family members who tend to insist on doing things only their way without seeking input from others? What about at work? What efforts could I make to bring about a change?
2. In which areas do I come across as harsh, demanding, stubborn, or uncaring about the views of others? How can I change that insensitivity?
3. With whom do I display the least patience? How can I change this to demonstrate *chesed* within *netzach*?

For children

1. Has anyone ever said I was acting impatiently? If so, how can I learn to develop more patience?
2. When I express what I want, do I sound demanding? How can I change this behavior and modify it in appropriate ways?
3. What must I do to try to be kind and helpful to others over a long period of time and not just when I am asked or just when I feel like it?

היום שלושה ועשרים יום,
שהם שלושה שבועות ושני ימים, לעומר

(Ha'yom shlosha v'esrim yom,
she'hem shlosha shavuot u'shnei yamim la'Omer)

"TODAY IS THE TWENTY-THIRD DAY,
OR THREE WEEKS AND TWO DAYS, OF THE OMER."

DAY 23

Gevurah sh'b'Netzach (Strength/Discipline within Endurance)

Achieving goals and objectives, establishing and building long-term relationships, serving God, accomplishing one's mission in the world – all these require *netzach*. When *gevurah* is combined with *netzach*, there is an added element of strength, discipline, and restraint that can have either a positive or negative effect. The effect is positive when *gevurah* expresses itself as self-control to modulate situations while, at the same time, energetically driving toward results. The effect is negative when the power of *gevurah* is used to achieve immoral, unethical and non-productive ends.

Each of us must always be aware when we're striving to change for the better that our enemy – the *yetzer hara* – is armed with *gevurah* and *netzach*, and thus empowered, it is fighting mightily against us, always intent upon bringing us down. The *yetzer hara* works at creating negativity in our lives, keeping us unhappy, insecure, worried, depressed, angry, fearful, and resentful.

The *yetzer hara* may be powerful, but anyone can learn to cultivate a stronger *yetzer hatov* – also using *gevurah* and *netzach* – and, with God's help, can prevail.

How do you develop this *sefirah* combination? How do you develop the enduring strength to say "no" to unhealthy life choices and how do you resolve to mean it? If you are addicted to anything, you can seek the help you need from former addicts and professionals able to share the techniques that work. And you can enroll in a Twelve Step program.

And more than anything else, you can pray, for prayer is central part of recovering from any state of addiction – whether to drugs, alcohol, or food. Prayer is also an essential part of developing *gevurah* within *netzach* – the will power to win over any weakness – and it can help save your life and that of your loved ones.

GEVURAH WITHIN *NETZAH* AND WEIGHT LOSS

For example, if you have ever tried to lose weight and failed, it is because your *gevurah* within *netzach* is not as strong and pronounced as it needs to be.

The desire to lose weight for health reasons is a chronic battle for many. It is estimated that more than one-third of Americans are suffering from obesity (which is defined by the medical community as weighing 30 pounds, or roughly 15 kilo, more than the desired weight in proportion to height). Childhood obesity is described as an *epidemic* in the United States. Contributing to this health crisis are unnutritious food choices, a lack of portion control, and a tendency toward a sedentary lifestyle.

There may or may not be addictions associated with being overweight – for many, the chief cause may be lack of knowledge about healthy nutrition. Regardless, most people don't want to be fat and they do try to lose weight. The process generally resembles a yo-yo. Up and down, up and down goes the scale and their size. How can they reverse this?

The Rambam (a great doctor and scholar) offers perhaps the simplest rules for healthy eating: don't eat except when hungry, don't drink except when thirsty, and stop eating before your stomach is full. Properly applied, Rambam's wise advice is likely to produce results especially when paired with the right measure of *gevurah* within *netzach*.

TORAH AND *GEVURAH* WITHIN *NETZACH*

As we discussed on Day 22, Moshe applied *chesed* within *netzach* to defend the Jewish people after they sinned with the Golden Calf. Once God agreed not to annihilate the Nation of Israel, Moshe took a different tack.

He determined that, now, a measure of *gevurah* within *netzach* was called for. And he acted with alacrity.

When Moshe descended from the mountain and saw the calf and the debauchery, his anger flared:

> He threw down the tablets from his hands and shattered them at the foot of the mountain. He took the calf that they had made and burned it in fire. He ground it to a fine powder and sprinkled it over the water. He made the Children of Israel drink.[226]

Then he proclaimed: "Whoever is for God, join me!" With the help of the Tribe of Levi, Moshe slaughtered the 3,000 men who were the perpetrators of the debauchery and idolatry.[227] Because of their instinctive ethical response, the Levites merited becoming the teachers of the Jewish people from that point on. Their and Moshe's actions were a demonstration of *gevurah* within *netzach*. The guilty parties were killed for violating fundamental beliefs and truths.

Rabbi Joseph B. Soloveitchik, in a lecture given in June 1974, notes that the main purpose of the Exodus from Egypt was not to attain political freedom, but rather to attain the "conversion of a people into a 'kingdom of priests' and a 'holy nation.'"[228] For this reason, Moshe was selected by God to be the teacher of *Klal Yisrael*. God would take the Jews out of Egypt, but Moshe had to take Egypt out of the Jews. Moshe's role was "that of a spiritual and moral teacher, a pedagogue of *halachah*, to prepare the people to receive and to become committed to the Revelation" that was to take place at Mount Sinai.[229]

Moshe understood and accepted this mandate, which required a great deal of *gevurah* within *netzach*, especially at a time when the Jewish people had fallen into the pit of sin. He demonstrated this attribute when it became apparent that the people would have to wander the wilderness for forty years until their slave mentality died out. During those many

---

226. Ibid., 32:19–20.

227. Ibid., 32:26–28.

228. Joseph B. Soloveitchik, lecture given in June 1974, and reconstructed by Rabbi Avraham R. Besdin. See Hashkafah Unit 7 on Jewish Leadership.

229. Ibid.

years, *gevurah* within *netzach* enabled Moshe to persevere even though his cherished dream of entering the Promised Land would remain unfulfilled.

God's plan had clearly been for the Jewish people to enter the Land within days of building the portable Mishkan. But two events nixed this plan. The first event:

Three million Jews were gathered on the edge of the Promised Land, the Mishkan was packed up, the tribes were in formation with everyone ready to depart. But a tragedy wrecked the would-have-been, should-have-been, could-have-been scenario. We don't have to ask what happened because the Torah tells us:

> The rabble that was among them cultivated a craving, and the Children of Israel also wept once more, and said: "Who will feed us meat? We remember the fish that we ate in Egypt free of charge; the cucumbers, melons, leeks, onions, and garlic. But now, our life is parched, there is nothing; we have nothing to anticipate but the manna!". . . .
>
> Moshe heard the people weeping in their family groups, each one at the entrance of his tent and the wrath of Hashem flared greatly; and in the eyes of Moshe it was bad. Moshe said to Hashem: "Why have You done evil to Your servant; why have I not found favor in Your eyes, that You place the burden of this entire people upon me? Did I conceive this entire people or did I give birth to it, that You say to me 'Carry them in your bosom, as a nurse carrying a suckling, to the Land that You swore to its forefathers?' Where shall I get meat to give to this entire people when they weep to me, saying: 'Give us meat that we may eat'? I alone cannot carry this entire nation, for it is too heavy for me! And if this is how You deal with me, then kill me now, if I have found favor in Your eyes, and let me not see my evil!"
>
> Hashem said to Moshe: "Gather to Me seventy men from the elders of Israel . . . I will descend and speak with you there, and I will increase some of the spirit that is upon you and place it upon them, and they shall bear the burden of the people with you, and you shall not bear it alone. To the people you shall say: 'Prepare yourselves for tomorrow and you shall eat meat, for you have wept in the ears of Hashem, saying: Who will feed us meat? For it was better for us in Egypt! So Hashem will give you meat and you will eat. Not for one day shall you eat, nor two days, nor five days, nor ten

> days, nor twenty days. Until an entire month of days, until it comes out of your nose, and becomes nauseating to you, because you have rejected Hashem Who is in your midst, and you have wept before Him, saying: Why did we leave Egypt?"[230]

Shortly after this:

> A wind went forth from Hashem and blew quail from the sea and spread them over the camp . . . The people rose up all that day and all the night and all the next day and gathered up the quail . . . The meat was still between their teeth, not yet chewed, when the wrath of Hashem flared against the people, and Hashem struck a very mighty blow against the people. He named that place *Kivrot-Hataava*, because there they buried the people who had been craving [meat].[231]

The sin of *Kivrot-Hataava* was a tragic example of unbridled lust. As Rabbi Soloveitchik explains:

> Chazal say that they [the Israelites] turned against the entire philosophy of Sinai which prescribed self-discipline, surrender, and the selective expression of physical indulgence. The Torah precept in contrast to paganism is "do not go after your heart and eyes." The Torah detests paganism even more than idol worship. The latter eventually collapses; one can teach, persuade and enlighten against its validity. But what does one do with paganism which is morally nihilistic; it is not a competing discipline but no discipline. How does one teach the superiority of a restrictive but enhancing system which wants man to identify with God, not to identify with nature . . . To counter paganism, the teacher role is insufficient; Moshe had to become a nursing-father, a role that he bitterly resisted.[232]

Rabbi Soloveitchik points out the dramatic difference between a teacher, which Moshe wanted to be, and a nursing mother/father, which Moshe

---

230. *Bamidbar* 11:1–20.

231. Ibid., 11:31–34.

232. Soloveitchik, lecture given in June 1974, and reconstructed by Rabbi Avraham R. Besdin

did not want to be. While they both instruct a child, only the nursing mother "submerges her identity into that of the child; her own desires become secondary or totally nullified; the needs of the child take precedence over her own life; she becomes one with the child and finds fulfillment through him. There is an emotional fusion of two identities."[233]

At this point in real-time events, truth flashed like lightening and Moshe realized – something which God already knew – that, at this moment, the Children of Israel were not ready to go into the Land. In that moment, Moshe's role changed. He realized that being a teacher was insufficient at this stage, for the Nation of Israel was in its early formative years. Explains Rabbi Soloveitchik:

> They were temperamental, impulsive, restively murmuring – their complaints were primarily pretexts. Moshe doubted his capacity to become an *uman* (a nursing father); he knew that in this new role, he as an individual with a family, personal needs and pleasures, would no longer exist; he would no longer rejoice at his personal good fortune or when his children prospered; he would no longer find happiness like an ordinary human being because he would now lose his family, his wife and children; instead he would become the nursing father of *Klal Yisrael.* That's why the Chazal say that he separated from his husbandly and fatherly roles. He became *Avi-hem Shel-Yisrael*, the father of all Israel . . . This status of Moshe was unique; it wasn't required of later Jewish leaders; he was the *Av Haneviim*, who was literally lifted out of ordinary concerns and attachments, in order to nurture a people in its period of infancy, a people cardinally important to the Almighty's plan for the world.[234]

Just as a nursing mother displays *gevurah* within *netzach*, Moshe had to display this same attribute by powerfully restraining his life dream and, instead, dedicating himself to prepare this young nation for its mission to become a "kingdom of priests and a holy nation."

If this was not enough, the second event, right after the sin of *Kivrot-Hataava* revealed the length of time it would take to complete the education of this infant nation. Tragically, it turned out to be forty years in total.

233. Ibid.
234. Ibid.

Although Moshe never got to step foot in the Land, he died knowing that the Jewish people were ready to enter it and assume their role as a Holy Nation. Moshe's display of *gevurah* within *netzach* saw the Jewish people through years of preparation to finally realize the dream of settling in the Promised Land.

We should remember Moshe's perseverance anytime we are asked to endure in order to complete something important that may not have been our first choice in life. And his greatness in accomplishing so much, notwithstanding his unfulfilled dream, should inspire us and give us strength.

One might think that Moshe's historic display of *gevurah* within *netzach* was unique among our people, but that is not the case. Take for example Yaakov Avinu who worked for seven years for the right to marry his beloved Rachel, suppressing his anger at how he was both tricked and treated by Rachel's father Lavan. We can only conclude from the life of both Moshe and Yaakov that there are times that life unfolds in unexpected ways and that when the unanticipated happens, we must hunker down by displaying *gevurah* within *netzach* and not give up accomplishing our goals and mission in life.

DISCUSSION TOPICS FOR *GEVURAH* WITHIN *NETZACH*

For adults

1. Do I have the enduring strength to break bad habits and form new healthy habits for my life? What three things can I do now that will help form healthier patterns?
2. Have I ever had to sacrifice something I really wanted to do for the sake of another? What was it and how did it feel to do so?
3. Is there a conversation I need to have with someone close to me about our relationship? Am I prepared emotionally and mentally to have the conversation? If not, what do I need to do in order to have it?

For children

1. What bad habits do I have? What is one thing I could do now to stop them?
2. How long am I able to sit and study for a test, to do my homework, or just read a book for pleasure? Why is it important to be able to concentrate for a longer period of time? What messages could I give myself that would help me be able to concentrate for longer periods of time?
3. Was there a time I really wanted to do something, but realized it was not the right time to do it, and so I decided on my own to just give up?

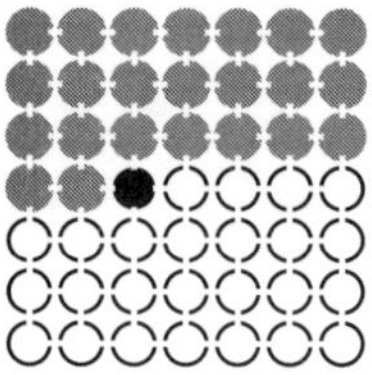

היום ארבעה ועשרים יום,
שהם שלושה שבועות ושלושה ימים, לעומר

(Ha'yom arba'a v'esrim yom,
she'hem shlosha shavuot u'shlosha yamim la'Omer)

"TODAY IS THE TWENTY-FOURTH DAY,
OR THREE WEEKS AND THREE DAYS, OF THE OMER."

DAY 24

Tiferet sh'b'Netzach (Harmony/Truth within Endurance)

Positive applications of *netzach* include tenacious and persistent efforts to achieve worthy goals, build healthy relationships, and serve God. *Netzach* is a concentrated, dedicated momentum that achieves outcomes in every sphere of life. But *netzach* alone can easily become negative. However, when *tiferet* is brought into the picture, the drive and determination of *netzach* is appropriately modulated by the balance and truth of *tiferet,* which respects boundaries and is considerate of multiple priorities, relationships, and responsibilities. The balance of *tiferet* influences *netzach* not to become so extreme that it consumes other life priorities and subtracts from the ability to maintain an integrated balance in all areas of life.

Let's begin with a story told by Rabbi Stewart Weiss, the director of the Jewish Outreach Center of Ra'anana, Israel, who regularly writes inspirational articles for *The Jerusalem Post Magazine*. The one I am about to quote personifies *tiferet* within *netzach*.[235]

As Rabbi Weiss relates it, this particular event took place in Building

235. Stewart Weiss, "The Fifth Candle," *The Jerusalem Post Magazine*, December 23, 2011, 34.

103 at Buchenwald which held mostly religious Jews. The same daily regimen of suffering existed within Building 103 as in the other barracks, but there was a semblance of a religious life there. He writes:

> The residents say prayers each day, using a makeshift *tallit* made from a bed sheet. They learn Torah, maintaining a nightly routine of study with the scholars among them. Together they form a surreal congregation suspended between life and death, Heaven and Hell. Their holy rituals give them a certain inner strength, a higher purpose to life beyond just being fuel for the maniacal Nazi murder machine.

Rabbi Weiss's story continues. Winter has arrived in the camp. The inmates are brought back to Building 103 by dark and have more time to talk among themselves. Hanukkah is coming and they have a bold plan to celebrate this holiday. Although there has never been wine upon which to make *Kiddush* on Shabbat, or matzah for Pesach, or the four species for Sukkot, nevertheless this Hanukkah there is an unreasonable anticipation and excitement. They debate: Should they risk their lives in order to organize a celebration?

They submit the issue to binding arbitration by Reb Herzel, the resident scholar and a Talmudic master who had once headed his own yeshiva:

> He chose to teach his students until the very day the Germans seized him, rather than escape to freedom earlier. His courage and intellect are acknowledged by the entire camp, and they willingly submit the issue to him for judgment. Reb Herzel buries his face in his hands, deep in thought as he ponders the matter. The hungry and hopeful faces of the assembled watch in silence, aware they stand on the precipice of a momentous decision. Finally, he rises and delivers his verdict: "Because this is a life-and-death matter, I find no law absolutely compelling us to observe Hanukkah here. Yet the Hanukkiah [the Hanukkah Menorah] symbolizes our determination that the flame of Judaism within us can never be snuffed out, no matter how powerful the enemy we face. If we were somehow granted the means to observe this holiday, we would recreate the miracle of Hanukkah, and in the merit of this action we might be saved. As no Jew may command another to become a martyr, each of us must choose." The vote is unanimous.

The inmates make the Hanukkiah from iron bars taken from nine beds. A spoon is attached to the end of each bar, which will hold a drop of oil. A shoelace will act as the wick. One of the men who works in the kitchen has stolen some matches at great personal risk:

> The men agree to take the bit of margarine they receive once a week with their bread and hide it in the cold earth beneath the floor. The Hanukkiah is carefully hidden; the inmates count the days until Hanukkah. The first night of the holiday arrives. Roll call comes and goes uneventfully, the inmates retire to their beds and feign sleep as the camp lights are extinguished. At midnight, they gather in the center of the room as a close watch is kept at the window . . . The honor of lighting the first candle is given to the youngest among them, 16-year-old Shmuel, representing all the children unable to celebrate Hanukkah. In hushed tones, the Jews recite the three blessings, and Shmuel lights the lamp. The glow of that fire reflects the faces of men who pray for a miracle, who have somehow reached beyond this place of misery to the homes of their youth, where Hanukkah was synonymous with joy and singing. For just a brief, glowing moment, there is no Buchenwald, no Nazi terror; only faith and the eternity of the Jewish people. The residents go to sleep that night with empty stomachs, but their spirits are satiated.

This joyous scene is repeated on the second, third, and fourth nights. On the fifth night there is a huge snowstorm. The inmates take this as a good omen:

> As they prepare to light the fifth candle, they say the 118th Psalm, "This is the day the Lord has made, let us rejoice and revel in it." Suddenly, without warning, the door bursts open. Several Nazi guards rush into the barracks. They order the Jews to lie face-down on the floor, and seize the Hanukkiah. Several of the men, including Reb Herzel, are taken to the center of the compound and summarily executed, the sounds of the *Shema* prayer mingling with the gunshots. Their bodies are left lying there, a warning to other Jews in the camp . . .
>
> Back in the bunk, no one can speak. Once again, the eyes are hollow and transparent, as if the souls disappeared along with the

> Hanukkiah. At the window, young Shmuel looks out upon the bodies, tears streaming down his face. He shakes his fist with rage and finally screams, "They will not defeat us!" He lets his tears fall upon the fingertips of his right hand, and while they are still wet, he presses them tight upon the icy window. The bitter cold freezes them fast to the glass. With the defiant yell of a Maccabee, Shmuel recites the blessings upon lighting the Hanukkiah. Then, with one final cry, he tears away his fingers from the windowpane, leaving five bits of blood and flesh on the window where his fingers had been. The fifth candle has been kindled.

Would we have felt the same enduring conviction of Reb Herzel, of the inmates with their unanimous vote, and of 16-year-old Shmuel and his fifth candle? I do not know, but I pray that I would have been able to demonstrate this purity of *tiferet* within *netzach*.

If you ask how this story demonstrates this attribute, the simple compelling answer is this:

A group of prisoners celebrated the hope of Hanukkah while living amidst the hellish atrocities of the camps. The *netzach* of the prisoners embodied the *netzach* of the Maccabees of the original Hanukkah story. *Tiferet*, the light of truth and balance was manifested when the prisoners weighed the risks and then chose to observe this mitzvah and merge their lights with God's endless light.

Their menorah of *tiferet* within *netzach* still burns today and will continue to burn until the Mashiach comes.

THE QUEST FOR BALANCE

The above is a stellar example of endurance in the face of all odds. But there can be such a thing as *too much* endurance.

Historically, on a macro level, many tyrants have displayed massive amounts of endurance in their quest for whatever their evil hearts and minds desired. Every infamous despot and dictator has displayed a horrific capacity for *netzach*. But *netzach* without *tiferet*, especially when employed for a wrong motive, will result in horror – and indeed has resulted in the most egregious atrocities in history.

Eventually, of course, the tyrant's life (or time in office) comes to an end, but not until hundreds of thousands or many millions of people have been massacred. Sadly, we know the names well: Haman. Hitler. Stalin. Hussein. Qadaffi. Assad. Ahmadinejad.

On the other hand, balanced with *tiferet*, *netzach* can move mountains especially when it is directed towards worthy and healthy purposes.

When we help another person grow and develop, and brave it out with them even during more difficult times, we are employing *netzach* for a positive end. What emerges in the end is truth. It is not just stubborn determination in doing what we want or need. Rather, it is a determined effort to achieve what is best for everyone – for the *other* person, for the community, the nation, and the world.

TIFERET WITHIN *NETZACH* IN THE TORAH

Oftentimes it is about displaying endurance in performing the will of God as described in the Torah. For example:

After interpreting Pharaoh's dream, Yosef played a critical and enduring role as the chief commander in Egypt during the seven years of plenty and the seven years of famine, in order to save Egypt and the neighboring nations from starvation.

It was Yosef's destiny to display *tiferet* within *netzach* to save Egypt while, simultaneously, implementing God's plan of bringing his entire family there to begin the prophetic first exile which would build them into a nation.

On another, personal level, Yosef displayed *tiferet* within *netzach* by adhering to Jewish tradition and practice, raising his sons as Jews despite his family being the only Jewish family in Egypt. And for this reason we bless our sons to this day to be like Josef's Menashe and Ephraim.

DISCUSSION TOPICS FOR *TIFERET* WITHIN *NETZACH*

For adults

1. Is there a lack of balance in my priorities? Do I spend less time with my children than they need me to? Do I rush through my prayers, or omit them altogether? Do I set aside regular time for Torah study? Do I schedule time to visit with my parents? Do I act in a way that puts my spouse in the place of importance that he or she deserves?
2. Has my health suffered because of an imbalance in my life? What can I do to change this?
3. How persistent am I in reaching my goals and not giving up until they are achieved? Are my goals worthy ones?

For children

1. Can I describe something I did that made me feel proud? How long did it take me to do it? What is another project that I would like to complete?
2. Have I ever given up or quit a project because I was frustrated? Thinking back, did I ever wish it could have ended up differently?
3. What activities do I spend too much time on? Should I, instead, do something more worthwhile?

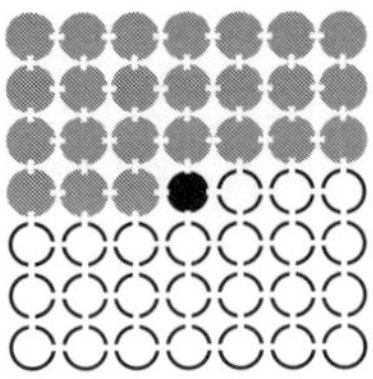

היום חמישה ועשרים יום,
שהם שלושה שבועות וארבעה ימים, לעומר

(Ha'yom chamisha v'esrim yom,
she'hem shlosha shavuot v'arba'a yamim la'Omer)

"TODAY IS THE TWENTY-FIFTH DAY, OR THREE WEEKS AND FOUR DAYS, OF THE OMER."

DAY 25

Netzach sh'b'Netzach (Endurance within Endurance)

Netzach is the ability to steadfastly adhere to a path, whether positive or negative, to accomplish plans and goals, and to adhere to values and commitments. One who has *netzach* is able to stay focused on a course of action and be faithful to commitments whether in the physical, mental, emotional, or spiritual realm over extended periods of time. *Netzach* within *netzach* is the extra power to reinforce pure *netzach* to produce an even more intensified drive and focused discipline to complete plans or goals. It is a booster that empowers endurance to stick to a path, objective or plan, whether good or bad, and to achieve its end.

As with other *sefirah* combinations which we have examined earlier, *netzach* within *netzach* has a negative side. It can become overly severe, critical, or even obsessive, possibly affecting relationships and displacing other life responsibilities or relationships by sacrificing them for a perceived higher purpose. Either great outcomes or very destructive results can emerge from *netzach* within *netzach*.

One such negative example of *netzach* within *netzach* is the Nazi plot to accomplish their diabolical ethnic cleansing of all Jews in Europe and the world – a plot better known as the Final Solution. Not only did the Nazis rigidly adhere to the execution of their depraved plan, but they celebrated their successes as well. And in the end, despite knowing that they had virtually lost the war to the Allies, the evil Nazi killing machine kept on its murderous course. This is an example of the ugly and destructive face of *netzach* within *netzach* when it is totally divorced from *tiferet.*

And then we have the opposite side of *netzach* within *netzach* in the same situation.

It is a little known fact is that, on October 7, 1944, one of the four crematoria that was used to burn Jewish corpses that had been gassed was blown up by a group of Jewish prisoners at the Auschwitz-Birkenau concentration camp in Poland.

Two of the women who helped smuggle raw materials that were used for the explosion were captured and tortured mercilessly to pressure them to reveal the names of the Jewish SonderKommander members that hatched the plot and placed the bomb. Despite the inhuman horrific torture, and in a heroic display of *netzach* within *netzach* neither Roza Robata nor her co-conspirators – Ala Gertner, Estusia Wajcblum, and Regina Safirsztajn – ever revealed the names of any surviving Jewish plot members.

We should never have to suffer the agonies that Roza and her colleagues willingly took upon themselves so that the Nazi capacity to burn Jews daily was reduced by one-fourth.

We are, to this day, eternally grateful to these brave souls who gave their lives to fight an evil enemy.[236]

THE *NETZACH* WITHIN *NETZACH* OF ISRAELIS

I have earlier referred to the *Jerusalem Post* columnist, Barbara Sofer, who writes a weekly feature called "The Human Spirit." On the occasion of the State of Israel's 64th Anniversary, she compiled 64 reasons why she loves Israel. This list reveals numerous displays of *netzach* within *netzach.* Consider some of her 64 reasons:

- Reason 12: The winner of the "A Star is Born" singing contest comes from a town under fire, Sderot, and from a family that crossed Sudan on foot.

236. http://en.wikipedia.org/wiki/Roza_Robota.

- Reason 13: So did the family of Eli Mantson, a seventh grade school dropout who sold lentils in an open-air market. Today, he's a lawyer, one of several law graduates from Ethiopia.
- Reason 28: Dan Schectman, a Technion professor who won the Nobel Prize for Chemistry. He showed that atoms in quasicrystals were packed together in well-defined patterns, but that they were unique and non-repeating . . . [He] was born in Tel Aviv in pre-state Israel. He was inspired by a book he read as a boy, Jules Verne's *Mysterious Island*, in which an engineer changes uninhabited territory into a lush garden.
- Reason 29: Yad Vashem, Israel's Holocaust Museum, recently uploaded thousands of stories of rescues by righteous gentiles to show that "even in times of war and tyranny, women and men retain the innate right and ability to act upon moral precepts."
- Reason 57: One Jerusalem runner [in the Jerusalem Marathon] was Richard Bernstein, a blind man from Michigan. He was guided through the streets by Major Shaked, an Israeli fighter pilot. Said Bernstein: "This marathon has a profoundly beautiful and wonderful meaning."
- Reason 64: The country held its breath as Gilad Schalit emerged to freedom. Was there a dry eye? Gilad Schalit celebrated Pesach, the holiday of freedom, at home with his family.[237]

THE ANGEL OF DEATH AND *NETZACH* WITHIN *NETZACH*

The Reishit Chochmah quotes our Sages that, when we die, we will see the Angel of Death with a sword drawn. The Angel will ask us four questions and depending upon our answers, we will either face a peaceful and serene death or a terrifying one:

- Did we learn Torah (if a man) or (if a woman) help our husband learn Torah?
- Did we do acts of kindness to others?

237. Barbara Sofer, "The Human Spirit: Top 63 + 1 Reasons I Love Israel," *The Jerusalem Post Magazine*, April 29, 2011.

- Did we recite the *Shema* in the morning and evening?
- Did we treat our fellow Jews like kings?

It may be that these four questions direct us to display *netzach* within *netzach* in this world.[238] Let's all be able to answer these four questions in the affirmative when our time comes.

But beware: answering these seemingly simple questions takes more hard work and dedication than any of us might think and the answers require *netzach* within *netzach*.

DISCUSSION TOPICS FOR *NETZACH* WITHIN *NETZACH*

For adults

1. What viewpoints am I stubbornly clinging to that perhaps I should reconsider?
2. What is the greatest challenge I am facing now? Am I committed to passing this test and come out of it a better person, or does the challenge get the better of me on some days?
3. Do I display enduring commitment to my family, and they to me?

For children

1. Is there any time that I have been stubborn about something? Should I have been more flexible?
2. What is something I really believe in? Have I ever worked hard and consistently to demonstrate my commitment to that topic, cause or relationship?
3. Can I be counted on to finish an important assignment or request?

238. Frand, *Rabbi Yissocher Frand in Print*, 153.

היום ששה ועשרים יום,
שהם שלושה שבועות וחמישה ימים, לעומר

(Ha'yom shisha v'esrim yom,
she'hem shlosha shavuoat v'chamisha yamim la'Omer)

"Today is the twenty-sixth day,
or three weeks and five days, of the Omer."

Day 26

Hod sh'b'Netzach (Humility within Endurance)

Hod within *netzach* introduces the ability to modify endurance with humility. *Hod* within *netzach* makes it possible to restrain egotistical or extreme drives in order to achieve a desired goal, plan, or outcome. *Hod* influences *netzach* with the neutralizing factor of humility to keep it from becoming extreme in its intensity and thus harming our lives and others. It also helps us recognize that everything comes from God, who alone is in control, not us, and that the ultimate outcomes, whatever they may be, are for our own good.

The words to the popular Kenny Rogers song, "The Gambler," metaphorically sum up this attribute combination:

> You gotta know when to hold 'em and when to fold 'em,
> Know when to walk away, know when to run . . .[239]

True endurance sometimes requires the ability to yield or compromise appropriately rather than steadfastly clinging to a position once it becomes clear another course of action is necessary. Individuals have to learn this.

239. "The Gambler," written by Don Schlitz, recorded by Kenny Rogers in 1978.

Families have to learn this. Business leaders have to learn this. Teachers have to learn this. Nations have to learn this. The wisdom to know when to yield and when to stand firm takes insight, understanding, experience, strategy, and most of all, humility.

Sometimes, even though one strategy has worked well, another strategy must be employed when the facts on the ground have changed. The flexibility to tailor our actions according to the situation at hand is a skill that each of us must have and be able to put to use at the appropriate time in the appropriate situation. We must not just stubbornly adhere to a wrong-headed approach; our thoughts, speech, and actions must adjust and change to avoid these pitfalls and thus enable us to achieve a positive outcome.

We all must learn the wisdom of routinely turning to God to ask His help to properly align our thoughts, speech, and actions with what He knows is best given the circumstances. After decades of seeing results, I believe that daily personal prayers of asking God to help is the best way of employing *hod* within *netzach* to find balance in even the most complex and difficult crises.

THE CEDAR AND THE REED

There is a fascinating discussion in *Shnei Luchot HaBrit* by Kabbalist Rabbi Isaiah Horowitz, also known as the Shlah, regarding *Parshat Balak*, which describes how the evil sorcerer Bi'laam had blessed the people of Israel by comparing them to a tall cedar.[240] Citing the Talmud,[241] the Shlah notes that the curse of Achiyah HaShiloni, referring to the people of Israel as "reed in water"[242] was actually more beneficial to them than all the supposed blessings given by Bi'laam, and then he elaborates:

> Just as such a reed can stand in water, its stem can grow back [if cut] and develop many roots, so that all the winds of the world will not uproot it, but it will bend in the direction the wind blows until the wind has stopped blowing and resume its original posture, so Israel will recover from such storms.

240. *Bamidbar* 24:6.
241. *Taanit* 20.
242. I *Melachim* 14:15.

> [However Bi'laam's comparison of Israel to a cedar is really a curse because] a cedar cannot survive in water, its roots are few, its trunk does not grow back once it has been cut. Even though it is strong enough to resist all the storms of the world, a south wind will dislocate it immediately . . . [Also,] one can make a quill from the reed to write a *Sefer Torah*, which cannot be done with the remains of a cedar.[243]

Have you ever seen photo images of the regal, massive King palms which routinely snap in two during a hurricane, while the less grand-looking plants and reeds are able to survive the storm?

This is the quality of *hod*. Humility allows us to bend under the right circumstances and withstand life's challenges. That is what *hod* within *netzach* is all about.

MEASURE FOR MEASURE

In our discussion on Day 22, we mentioned that the Talmud, at the end of Tractate *Megillah*, relates a question posed to seven Sages as to what they attributed their longevity. We cited three responses from Rabbi Nechunya ben Hakana that demonstrated *chesed* within *netzach*. In addition, Rabbi Nechunya – focusing on *hod* within *netzach* – said that he never insisted on being properly respected for whatever he had achieved, and that he never stood on principle.[244]

I found this intriguing. I, too, have principles I live by, but what if someone violates a principle I hold dear? For example, what if someone lies to me?

Although I may have a responsibility to confront the person about it, I am not allowed to hold a grudge. The person who lied should do *teshuvah*, of course, but I am supposed to let it go. Why? Because that is a commandment of the Torah,[245] and because we believe that if we let it pass once they have done *teshuvah*, God will treat us measure for measure

243. Isaiah Horowitz, *Shney Luchot Habrit*, Volume III (translated by Eliyahu Munk [Jerusalem: 1992]).

244. *Megillah* 28a.

245. *Vayikra* 19:18.

– *middah k'neged middah* – and will also let our sin pass, after we have done *teshuvah* for it.

Hod within *netzach* is the ability to overlook offenses and thus retain relationships and maintain the peace.

This idea is reiterated elsewhere in the Talmud – in the context of a story about two Sages who prayed for rain. One prayed but rain did not come. Then Rabbi Akiva began to pray addressing God as *Avinu Malkeinu* and the heavens opened.[246] Why? Because Rabbi Akiva also never stood on principle. Once a dispute was over, he was able to forget about it and go on with his life. That is why God answered his prayer.

Holding enduring principles, and living by them in a way that allows room for others to be what they are, displays *hod* within *netzach*.

AARON'S REACTION

The Torah relates that on the eighth day of the ceremonies surrounding the inauguration of the Mishkan, a terrible tragedy happened.

Nadav and Avihu, two of Aaron's four sons, died when they brought a strange fire, without God's permission.[247] And yet we do not hear a word from Aaron about it. He humbly accepted the events as God's will and proceeded to perform the duties of the *Kohen Gadol* as taught to him by his brother, Moshe, over the preceding seven days.

Thus Aaron modeled for us the degree of acceptance that is ultimately asked of every mourner.

When a Jewish mourner recites *Kaddish* during the prescribed period, the mourner displays humility in accepting the loss of a loved one, yet at the same time praising God and acknowledging the enduring healing capacity of faith.

In a thought-provoking essay, "On Sitting Shiva & Its Aftermath: Some Reflections," Rabbi Jeffrey Bienenfeld writes:

> Against this backdrop of death and mortality, an amazing realization soon dawns upon us. All the trivialities and irrelevancies of life are seen as just that. Our priorities realign and that which is truly important emerges with compelling freshness and renewed vitality. The

246. *Taanit* 25b.

247. *Vayikra* 10:1–3.

> dross settles and a new commanding sense of mission rises to the fore. Emboldened by these inspirations, the *Kaddish* takes on new meaning.[248]

We pray that we will not be tested with the loss of a loved one, but were it to ever happen, God forbid, we can be elevated from our grief through the help of *hod* within *netzach*.

MODERN LEADERSHIP

One of the best-selling business books ever written is *GOOD TO GREAT: Why Some Companies Make the Leap and Others Don't* by Jim C. Collins.[249] The author formerly taught at Stanford University's Graduate School of Business and subsequently formed a management research laboratory where he and teams of researchers examined a variety of relevant business strategies and practices. This book was a product of that research.

Collins and his research team studied the characteristics and qualities of leaders of those companies defined as "great" based on specific criteria. They created a five-level hierarchy of leadership capabilities, with Level 5 being the top. They found that every company that made a transition from "good" to "great" had Level 5 leadership during the pivotal years when the company was making that transition.

What does Level 5 leadership look like?

Collins concludes that these leaders "embody a paradoxical mix of personal humility and professional will." He goes on:

> They are ambitious . . . first and foremost for the company, not themselves . . . Level 5 leaders display a compelling modesty, are self-effacing and understated. In contrast, two thirds of the comparison companies had leaders with gargantuan personal egos that contributed to the demise or continued mediocrity of the company.

---

248. Jeffrey Bienenfeld, "On Sitting Shiva & Its Aftermath: Some Reflections" *Ben Yerucham* (Jerusalem: 2012), 66.

249. *GOOD TO GREAT: Why Some Companies Make the Leap and Others Don't* attained long-running positions on *The New York Times*, *Wall Street Journal*, and *Business Week* best-seller lists, has sold 3 million hardcover copies since publication, and has been translated into 35 languages, including Latvian, Mongolian, and Vietnamese.

> Level 5 leaders are fanatically driven, infected with an incurable need to produce sustained *results.* They are resolved to do whatever it takes to make the company great, no matter how big or hard the decisions. Level 5 leaders display a workmanlike diligence – more plow horse than show horse. Level 5 leaders look out the window to attribute success to factors other than themselves. When things go poorly, however, they look in the mirror and blame themselves, taking full responsibility . . . One of the most damaging trends in recent history is the tendency (especially by boards of directors) to select dazzling, celebrity leaders and to de-select potential Level 5 leaders.[250]

Interestingly, Collins shares that he believes "potential Level 5 leaders exist all around us, if we just know what to look for, and that many people have the potential to evolve into Level 5" leadership.

The qualities enumerated by Collins sound a lot like *hod* within *netzach*, but they actually can go beyond *hod* within *netzach*. For example, some leaders may achieve the attribute of pure *malchut*, which we will address shortly. Regardless, *hod* within *netzach* is an important trait to develop during the Omer count. Little wonder that it also appears to hold the key to stellar success in business.

250. Jim Collins, *GOOD TO GREAT: Why Some Companies Make the Leap and Others Don't* (NY: HarperCollins, 2001), 39.

DISCUSSION TOPICS FOR *HOD* WITHIN *NETZACH*

For adults

1. Do I yield to the needs, requests, or demands of others too much or too little? What would it take for me to get it right?
2. Can I recall a situation from my life that I thought was going to defeat me? How did I end up passing this test?
3. Are any situations facing me right now that demand my humbly recognizing that everything is from God, and that I should try to figure out what God is trying to teach me with this current challenge?

For children

1. Do others try to pressure me to give in and do things I really don't want to do? What can I do about this?
2. Do I tend to always want things to go my way? What happens if I don't get my way? How can I handle this differently?
3. When things happen during the day that frustrate me, do I realize that God loves me and is giving me these experiences in order to learn from them and grow up to be an even better person?

היום שבעה ועשרים יום,
שהם שלושה שבועות וששה ימים, לעומר

*(Ha'yom shiva v'esrim yom,
she'hem shlosha shavuot v'shisha yamim la'Omer)*

"TODAY IS THE TWENTY-SEVENTH DAY, OR THREE WEEKS, AND SIX DAYS, OF THE OMER."

DAY 27

Yesod sh'b'Netzach (Bonding within Endurance)

Netzach can be a determined and steady force to accomplish goals, to establish, build, and maintain relationships, to build character and values, and to integrate new experiences, extracting from them meaning and fulfillment. When _netzach_ is coupled with _yesod_, endurance becomes grounded so that, while being resolute, we do not lose sight of the critical importance of maintaining strong relationships and worthy values. _Yesod_ within _netzach_ ensures that we not only focus on our goals, but that we achieve them within the context of bonding with people, so that there is a "win win" for everyone involved.

With a divorce rate today at 50 percent, it is little wonder that relationships appear more fragile than ever before. Up until 100 years ago, it was common for three generations to live under one roof. Today, it is the rare exception.

Whereas two hundred years ago, most Jews considered themselves religious on some spectrum of observance, certain other influences in the last century – including but not limited to communist ideology and "modern" industrialism – have had an adverse impact on the time spent on religious observance (and this is true not only for Jews).

So what has happened to the attribute of *yesod* within *netzach* in all this?

It has atrophied – it has become like a muscle that has not been exercised enough. But maybe the downward slide is reversing itself. According to a recent survey, a majority of Israel's Jews described themselves as religious (*dati*, *charedi*, or *mesorti*) as opposed to secular (*chiloni*).[251]

Frankly, if we want God to stick with us and shield us from harm, we must at least recognize how very much we need Him. We must want to connect with Him by inviting Him into our lives, and we must act in ways that will keep Him actively involved with us, so that He doesn't just withdraw from us, leaving us vulnerable to the turbulent, treacherous dangers of our times.

A FAMILY TORN

Have you ever had the experience of being part of a close family that drifted apart? Perhaps family members moved too far from each other, physically. No longer do family members daven at the same synagogue. The family Shabbat table has shrunk. After the distance of so many miles or kilometers, comes the absence of heartfelt communications about life experiences. After the passage of even more time, the holidays spent together become a rare event. As the years fly by, no one quite remembers how or when it all happened, but the close bonds that formerly existed are gone. Everyone's life migrated in opposite directions.

Even worse than this scenario are families torn apart by strife, jealousy, anger, insecurities, and resentment, all of which have the tendency, if unchecked, to breed like a cancer into the next generation. No one puts forth the requisite efforts to surgically remove the tumor, and indeed, after even one generation, no one knows what the feud was about in the first place. But no one is willing to bury the hatchet. Instead they all bury the exquisite memories and wonderful dreams of family unity and loyalty. Everything that was once precious can be torn asunder.

Without a strong manifestation of enduring bonding, it may be virtually impossible for the families of the twenty-first century to survive the brutal effects of torn and absent families. And this is why yeshivas, seminaries, pulpit rabbis, teachers, parents, and others need to inculcate and teach an awareness of the importance of *yesod* within *netzach*, in order to

251. Rabbi Nachman Kahana, in his commentary on *Parshat Beshalach* and *Yitro* 5773/2013.

reintroduce this important *sefirah* combination into their curricula, their daily discussions, and their *shiurim*. Otherwise, the plague that is killing families will go unchecked.

To have unity and togetherness, each of us must pursue *yesod* within *netzach* relentlessly. This requires strategies and discipline to come together and stay together.

TORAH EXAMPLES

The best example we have of steadfast bonding is that of Moshe, Aaron, and Miriam – the three siblings who bonded with each other to play out their quintessential roles in carrying out God's assignment to take the people out of Egypt, and to then teach and inspire them for the next forty years.

While playing their distinctive roles, they each displayed *yesod* within *netzach* in all their interactions – with their siblings, with God, and with the Jewish people. However, as a singular example, Moshe surpassed all mortals.

Moshe bonded completely and enduringly with God and with the Jewish people. And there was only one like him, which is why the Torah states: "In Israel none like Moshe arose again who knew God face to face."[252] And which is why Rambam makes belief in Moshe's prophecy one of his "Thirteen Principles of Faith."

Moshe merited standing before God and speaking to Him in conversation while he was awake, versus the trance or sleep-state of all other prophets. Yet despite his elevated status, he steadfastly displayed *yesod* within *netzach*. He bonded deeply with the Jewish people and defended them throughout his life.

Raised in Pharaoh's household and trained as an Egyptian general, he nevertheless risked his position and life to come to the aid of a Jewish slave who was being beaten. Later, for forty years, he taught and served the Jewish people even though his role of a "nursing father" was not his definition of leadership. Despite all this, Moshe steadfastly bonded with his people until the end of his life when he gave them both direction and comfort so that they could face life without him in the Promised Land.

Moshe was so great that, at 120 when he was to die, his *neshamah* did

252. *Devarim* 34:10.

not want to leave his body to return to *Shamayim.* God had to come and kiss Moshe on the lips so that his *neshamah* would depart and return to its divine source.[253] With such complete bonding, God displayed the pinnacle of *yesod* within *netzach*.

DISCUSSION TOPICS FOR *YESOD* WITHIN *NETZACH*

For adults

1. Is there a long simmering dispute within my family that cannot be resolved without outside help? What am I going to do about it?
2. Is there a group of people or family members about whom I am highly judgmental? Do I consider myself superior to them? Is it time to silence my judgments and determine if I can attempt to resolve our differences or at least to take a neutral stand?
3. What are three things I have done in the last year to further the unity among all Jews?

For children

1. Is there anyone I am fighting with right now who is a good person? Can I sit down with this person and try to resolve our problem?
2. What causes do I consider important enough to give of my time? Would I be willing to work as part of a group in order to accomplish a good outcome?
3. If one of my friends said something bad about my sister or brother, what would I do?

---

253. Numerous sources for this Midrash, including *Bava Batra* 17a; *Yalkut Shimoni Va'Etchanan* 247:821; *Tanchuma, Va'Etchanan* 6.

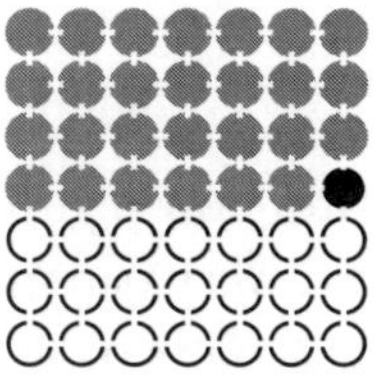

היום שמונה ועשרים יום, שהם ארבעה שבועות, לעומר

(Ha'yom shemonah v'esrim yom, she'hem arba'a shavuot la'Omer)

"TODAY IS THE TWENTY-EIGHTH DAY, OR FOUR WEEKS, OF THE OMER."

DAY 28

Malchut sh'b'Netzach (Leadership/Nobility within Endurance)

***Malchut* within *netzach* allows all the *sefirot* to come together in a holistic, comprehensive way to ensure that our endurance is balanced and not distorted by extremes in our drive to actualize and achieve results. *Malchut* within *netzach* is a steady course that incorporates a mature state of being that can overcome challenges and obstacles over time, while working towards a worthy outcome with dignity, sovereignty, leadership, and vision.**

The leader and teacher who embarked on a mission from God to bring three million Jews out of Egypt, receive the Torah, teach a people how to transform themselves into servants of God, and survive through forty years in the desert was none other than Moshe Rabbeinu. With the completion of this task, Moshe rectified the *sefirot* that had been imbalanced since the sin of Adam and Eve.

We must do the same in our own lives by displaying *malchut* within *netzach* – sovereignty and leadership in achieving, through hard work and determination, worthy life goals and ultimately our mission. Let's look at a couple of people who succeeded at this.

TOVAH'S STORY

I am deeply inspired by the following story that demonstrates how a girl, with the help of her family, achieved *malchut* within *netzach*. Every parent should read and try to apply the message of "Tovah's Story," which appeared in *Jewish Action*, the magazine of the Orthodox Union.[254]

The entire issue of *Jewish Action* in which Tovah's story appeared was entitled, "Getting Their Attention," and it underlined the pressing problem of Jewish identity. Excerpts follow. Don't skip a word. I don't doubt you know other children who feel like Tovah:

> "I come from a religious family. I was always a good kid, but I never did well in school . . . My teachers said I was lazy and didn't care, which made me feel frustrated. I didn't feel accepted in school or at home; I became kind of a loner. Eventually, I found friends who felt the same way I did and began hanging out with them. I started not keeping Shabbos and rebelled against everything . . . One of the friends I hung out with told me about NCSY's *Latte and Learning* . . . [I went.] It was really cool. It was a very open atmosphere; I didn't feel stressed out because I wasn't wearing a skirt. Eventually, I decided to go to a NCSY Shabbaton . . .
>
> "At my first NCSY regional Shabbaton, before Shabbos started, the regional director told us we are all keeping Shabbos together – no phones, no Internet, no straightening your hair. I kept Shabbos for the first time in a long while. I loved it. Once I got back home, I felt a spiritual high from the fun I had while doing things that were religious. It made me feel happy to be Jewish. I had found a way to connect with God and thought: Why not try this? I decided to drop my old friends and made new ones who were more open to accepting me as a religious person. I wanted to keep Shabbos and wear skirts. I started learning Torah. I let people into my life who wanted to help me. I am now an observant Jew and feel Hashem is my best friend.
>
> "But it was very hard for me after all the negative things I had done. Sometimes, I would sit down, think about them and cry. An

254. Bayla Sheva Brenner, "Reaching the iPod Generation," *Jewish Action*, Summer 2011, 28.

NCSY advisor told me a great *mashal* (parable) to explain the relationship between a person and God. There is a rope. Sometimes God is pulling the rope closer to Him and sometimes you're pulling the rope. When you do something really bad, the rope gets cut. Then you do *teshuvah* and say you're sorry, and tie both ends and the rope gets shorter. Every time you do something where the rope gets cut and you tie it back together, you get closer and closer to Hashem. When I heard this *mashal*, I felt so much better. I've tied the knot to that rope so many times that I'm practically touching Hashem.

"A lot of parents just don't know what to do when their kids go off, so they give up. My parents were never embarrassed by me and stuck with me the whole way. We got into a lot of fights, but at the end of the day, they truly love me. As much as I didn't see it before, I see it now."

As a result of Tovah's parents standing by her – a display of *malchut* within *netzach* – Tovah was able to wander and then return and get back in touch with her true love. Today, she is "happy to be Jewish" and feels that God is her "best friend" and that she is "practically touching Hashem."

Netzach can be a bridge which allows us to reach the other side because, without endurance, we cannot change. *Malchut* within *netzach* then harmonizes all the seven *sefirot* in our lives as in Tovah's story. There, we see all seven attributes playing themselves out, back and forth over a number of years, but ultimately arriving at a positive outcome for Tovah, her parents, her mentors, and God. At the end, the *sefirot* and all players in this story unify in perfect harmony through *malchut* within *netzach*. Let's examine how:

Tovah's parents demonstrated endurance (*netzach*) combined with restraint (*gevurah*) and humility (*hod*) in their approach to their daughter. They understood that there is not only one path for each child, certainly not one to be forced onto their daughter. We see the enduring love (*chesed*) inherent within God's system of *teshuvah* that permitted Tovah to return at any time. Returning required the attributes of strength/restraint (*gevurah*) and truth (*tiferet*) from Tovah. She also had to choose to persevere and discover who she wanted to become. She successfully navigated through some rough patches and experienced *yesod* (bonding/foundation) with all the worthy people in her life, in alignment with God's *malchut*. Tovah had also achieved mastery (*malchut*) over her own life, as can be seen in her summary of her experiences and her plans for the future.

Her story perfectly captures the interplay of the seven attributes and what it takes for all players in a life script to act together in order to enrich their shared journey. Tovah's story is a microcosm of how all seven *sefirot* work together, with a goal toward harmony and self-actualization that is "Balanced to Win."

Tovah inspires me. And here is another story that not only inspires me but brings tears to my eyes:

"TRUE SUPER HEROES"

You may recall her face and name when all of Israel mourned the loss of her courageous son, Nachshon, brutally murdered by terrorists in October 1994 and her response then: "Hashem answers all our prayers, but sometimes His answer is no."

But few know that Esther Wachsman has another courageous son, Raphael, who has Down syndrome. In a moving article in *The Jerusalem Post*, Esther describes how society has scorned Raphael and how his four-year-old twin brother has tried to defend him against the cruelty of other children by saying: "My brother has a soul from God, and you should just thank God that he made you normal." Relating this incident, Esther writes:

> My hands shake and I burst with pride, knowing that my husband and I were instrumental in enabling Raphael's brothers to love him, care for him, and protect him just a little more than anyone else. My wish is for all of you readers, all of society to treat those among us who are slower, less sophisticated (and thus less cynical), as the beautiful and pure souls they are. Accept them, embrace them, love them, for they are your brothers and sisters. Please show them the empathy and caring, the concern that you showed my family in our darkest days, while praying for and mourning my son Nachshon. I have made it my mission to be both of these sons' voices, for they have no voice.[255]

255. Esther Wachsman, "True Super Heroes," *The Jerusalem Post*, October 26, 2012, 21.

In the quest to give both her sons voice, she has created a project called "True Super Heroes" that is designed "to promote tolerance and combat prejudice against challenged individuals . . . [for] these heroes and their Herculean struggles to overcome their God-given disabilities do not always make headlines, but True Super Heroes they remain."

Esther Wachsman has had to endure the unspeakable murder of her son Nachshon, may God avenge his blood, as well as to find the strength to face the challenge of raising a child that society labels as inferior. She has gathered her love for her children and then deployed its power to focus and worked tirelessly along with Shalva, the Association for Mentally & Physically Challenged Children in Israel. In this she has created a lasting legacy while bonding with God and her family.

Esther is a true Super Hero.

DISCUSSION TOPICS FOR *MALCHUT* WITHIN *NETZACH*

For adults

1. Among the goals which I have set for myself – in all areas, whether physical, mental, emotional, or spiritual – which have I been able to reach?
2. Recalling the largest project or effort I have ever undertaken, how was I able to wade through the labyrinth of the accompanying challenges? What did I learn from the experience?
3. When I suffer a setback, does it leave me defeated, or am I able to pull myself up and start over again? Can I give examples?

For children

1. Can I remember something that was not easy for me to do but I did it? What could I do to consistently cross the finish line?
2. How did I feel about myself when I have finished a big project?
3. Am I aware that God is my best friend? How can I show God my loyalty and gratitude in return for His faithfulness?

WEEK FIVE

Hod
(Humility)

OVERVIEW

Hod (Humility)

Hod (humility) is an umbrella under which its opposite on the *sefirot* tree – *netzach* (endurance) – is protected from harshness. *Hod* can be defined poetically as a glorious sky with wispy clouds floating over a calm sea that is lapping upon a pristine sandy beach. More concretely, humility is experienced in that moment of connection with God's light, when we become receptive to the flow of His wisdom, allowing it to guide our thoughts, speech, and actions. It is a state of being that is marked by a serenity and consideration of others. *Hod* is the opposite of ego, arrogance, anger, jealousy, enmity, hatred, and drive to win at all costs. *Hod* is the avenue to peace and tempered outcomes. *Hod* is reflected by our shepherd, Aaron, who in his humility, always pursued peace.

Instead of looking inward to control, direct, or take for oneself, *hod* looks outward to listen and respond to others – including God. *Hod* is inviting, compassionate, approving, and relatively silent.

Hod does not take, but rather quietly receives and contemplates the worthy positives of all. However, make no mistake, when behaviors or actions are unworthy, *hod* is not a "pushover" or "milquetoast." Rather, *hod* responds appropriately so as not to be mistakenly seen as endorsing negative opinions or actions through silence or inappropriate humbleness. The *Ways of the Righteous* (*Orchot Tzaddikim*) is quite clear on this matter when it admonishes its readers to never be humble or self-effacing before evil:

> If one has the power, he must take revenge on the wicked for the sake of God (*Berachot* 7b) and adamantly oppose them and stand up against them as a roaring lion to rescue the robbed from the robber

> . . . He must exhort to good and against evil with mouth and tongue according to his ability.[256]

In Week Four, we learned that *netzach* is a trait that can be used for the good or bad. But when it is balanced with *hod*, it cannot be used for a bad purpose.

When there is a display of arrogance and ego, it is highly likely that *netzach* may cross borders and be used for the bad, contributing to destructive world events and egregious societal phenomena. For example, on the global level, it is unbounded arrogance that permits some people to believe that they are a superior race and that they can enslave other human beings, whom they deem inferior. On the personal level, it is unbounded arrogance that permits one family member to think that only his or her views should prevail because he or she is smarter, better, and knows all the answers.

Hod is the antithesis of arrogance and can be its antidote if we truly access its ways.

HOD AS COUNTERBALANCE TO *NETZACH*

As we begin Week Five of the Omer count with its focus on *hod*, the reader may be moved to ask: Why is *hod* being introduced now?

The reason is that *netzach* needs to be counterbalanced, and *hod* is a state of being that precludes, by its very definition, extreme acts of *netzach* that display exaggerated ego and self-centeredness. Unbridled endurance must be tempered with humility in order to be healthy. Without *hod*, self-interests and unfettered desires can employ *netzach* to control every outcome and persist in pursuing distorted, selfish, unhealthy aims that adversely affect relationships and life in general.

It is simply essential to cultivate humility, and to emulate God in doing so.

This may surprise some. It seems more obvious that we can learn *chesed*, *gevurah*, *tiferet*, and *netzach* from God, but *hod*? Can God who is the Omnipotent and Omniscient, who is the Creator, the Sustainer, the *Almighty*, also be humble?

Yes.

256. *Ways of the Righteous* (*Orchot Tzaddikim*), 75–77.

The Talmud says: "Wherever you find God's greatness, you also find His humility."[257] Talmudic sages also teach us that God cannot abide in the same world with a haughty man.[258] And the Prophet Isaiah relays God's message to us: "I dwell in a high and holy place, but I am with the broken-hearted and humble. I revive the humble spirit and give new life to the broken heart."[259]

Rabbi Aryeh Kaplan, a brilliant Kabbalist of the twentieth century, puts it well:

> We know God for His mighty deeds, but also from his small miracles. God fashioned the stars, but He also listens to the cry of a small child . . . We know God as the Highest, and yet, we seek Him with humility. As long as one is filled with his own egotism, he has no room for God . . .[260]

So if God, demonstrates *hod* in His actions in dealing with humankind, we can clearly understand that *hod* is an essential *middah*.

THE BENEFITS OF HUMILITY

None other than the Rambam writes: "There is no ornament as attractive as humility." And none other than King Shlomo writes: "Every haughty heart is an abomination to God."[261]

King Shlomo also advises: "If [one is drawn] to the scoffers, he will scoff; but [if one is drawn] to the humble, he will find favor."[262] And in the *Ways of the Righteous*, we read:

> Humility is a noble trait and a good quality . . . One who possesses this trait has already spared his soul many kinds of evils . . . For

257. *Megillah* 31a.
258. *Sotah* 5a.
259. *Yeshayahu* 57:15. See also *Tehillim* 68:5–6: "He rides upon the skies, His name is God . . . the Father of orphans, the Judge of widows, He is God in His holy place. God gives the friendless a home, and frees the captive, bringing him to safety."
260. Aryeh Kaplan, *The Infinite Light: A Book about God* (NY: National Council of Synagogue Youth, 1981), 22.
261. *Mishlei* 16:5.
262. Ibid., 3:34.

> humility is the root of divine service, and a small deed of the humble man is a thousand times more acceptable to the Blessed One than a great deed of the proud man.[263]

Ramban, writing in the 13th century to his son in Spain – in the famous *Iggeret HaRamban* – proposes a path toward humility, the benefits of which he praises to the skies:

> Once you have distanced yourself from anger, the quality of humility will enter your heart. This sterling quality is the finest of all admirable traits . . . When your actions display genuine humility – when you stand meekly before man, and fearfully before God; when you stand wary of sin – then the spirit of God's Presence will rest upon you, as will the splendor of His Glory; you will live the life of the World to Come . . .
>
> All men stand as equals before their Creator. In His fury, He casts down the lofty; in His goodwill, He elevates the downtrodden. Therefore, humble yourself, for God will lift you.[264]

The Ramban goes on to explain how to habituate oneself in the quality of humility, "to walk with it always." This is part of his advice:

> In all your words, actions, and thoughts – at all times – imagine in your heart that you are standing in the presence of the Holy One, Blessed be He, and that His Presence rests upon you. Indeed, the glory of God fills the universe. Speak with reverence and awe, like a servant who stands in the presence of his master. Act with restraint in the company of others: if one should call out to you, do not answer with a loud voice, but respond gently – in low tones, as one who stands before his mentor . . . Review you actions every morning and evening, and in this way live all your days in repentance. . . .[265]

---

263. *Ways of the Righteous*, (*Orchot Tzaddikim*), 57.
264. Avrohom Chaim Feuer, *Iggeres HaRamban, Ramban: A Letter for the Ages* (Brooklyn, NY: Mesorah Publications, 1989), 17–19.
265. Ibid., 19–21.

When we are humble, we interact with anyone without creating resistance. We acquire the ability to listen and reason where appropriate and to always act with respect towards others. We are not so invested in ourselves and our own views that we must control situations and outcomes. Humility is not about winning, but rather about walking gently on this earth.

Many benefits derive from this attribute. A humble person is more patient. Patience, in turn, leads to peace as King Shlomo writes: "A gentle reply turns away wrath, but a galling word incites anger."[266]

Peace in one's life is a huge benefit. In addition, the humble person is doing what God asks, as the Prophet Micah preached: "He has told you, O man, what is good! What does Hashem require of you but to do justice, to love kindness and to walk humbly with your God?"[267]

AARON, THE FIFTH SHEPHERD

As noted at the outset, *hod* is reflected by Aaron, the fifth of our Seven Shepherds, who in his humility, always pursued peace. The older brother of Moshe and the first *Kohen Gadol*, Aaron was a model of enduring humility in all spheres of his life.

Although Moshe is identified as the most humble person who ever lived, Moshe could not be the shepherd whose assignment it was to repair this attribute following the sin of Adam and Eve, as humility came naturally to him. Moshe's mission was to repair *netzach*, as he is the one whose mission it was to teach Torah, the gift for all eternity. Thus the task fell to Aaron.

Although he was the oldest brother, and therefore the one who inherited the birthright, Aaron never expressed or sought any desire for the leadership role that Moshe Rabbeinu held. He was completely satisfied helping his younger brother.

In addition to assisting Moshe in speaking to Pharaoh to let the Jews leave Egypt, Aaron served as *Kohen Gadol* for forty years while the people wandered in the wilderness, performing his prescribed duties in the Mishkan. In so doing, Aaron was always in the presence of God, a distinctly humbling experience. We know that the *Shechina* cannot dwell where there is arrogance or anger or depression, and so the role that Aaron

266. *Mishlei* 15:1.
267. *Michah* 6:8.

filled as a peaceful, humble servant of God was of paramount importance to the Jewish people.

In addition to his absolutely demanding full-time job as *Kohen Gadol*, Aaron worked tirelessly and continually to bring peace between quarrelling friends and spouses. It is famously said in *Pirkei Avot* that we should be like Aaron "who loved peace and pursued it."[268] It is also written that anyone who saw the holiness of Aaron was immediately drawn to be like him.[269]

It takes huge amounts of humility to effect serene, respectful family dynamics. To bring peace between two people each of whom believes he is "right" is an art. Aaron achieved this, by building others up, and not tearing them down. If we could emulate Aaron and discipline our children without diminishing who they are, what a difference that would make in cultivating peace within the home and upon every family member's self-esteem.

THE TRUE MEANING OF HUMILITY

Hod shares its Hebrew root with *hoda'ah* which means thankfulness. *Hod* is gratitude. It is modesty. It is the recognition that everything comes from God, even our talents and traits. Everything – and certainly any honor that comes our way.[270]

But lest there be any misunderstanding, humility is not self-negation. Just the opposite – humility builds self-esteem.

Although Moshe Rabbeinu is described by the Torah as exceedingly humble, it is clear that Moshe was aware of his incomparable strengths and many achievements (after all, he was granted the privilege of speaking to God directly in an awakened state). This awareness, however, did not interfere with his humility. Why not?

I think Rabbi Dr. Abraham Twerski captures the reason in his priceless *Generation to Generation*:

> If one stands before the vastness of the Pacific Ocean, the disparity between a teaspoonful and a gallon of water is grossly diminished.

268. *Pirkei Avot* 1:12.
269. Kitov, *The Book of Our Heritage*, Vol. 2, 684.
270. "Wealth and honor come from Hashem" (I *Divrei HaYamim* 29:12).

> In the awareness of the ever-presence of the Infinite, self-effacement is inevitable. Indeed, the greater one's grasp of Infinity, the more complete is the self-effacement. But it doesn't stop there. For humility and greatness are not disparate. They are one and the same . . . [as are] the apparent divergent feelings of self-esteem and humility.
>
> A person must never delude himself as to his capabilities and personality endowments. Falsehood is falsehood, and a delusion of worthlessness is as fallacious and pathological as a delusion of grandiosity . . . As a psychiatrist, I have advocated the need for a positive self-image as a vital ingredient for mental health, pointing out that people with poor self-esteem, who see themselves negatively, are apt to have many psychological and emotional problems.[271]

In the twenty-first century where so much of the focus is on the "me, me, me," we tend not to like words like "humility," or the other words associated with *hod*: "submission" or "retreat" or "surrender." But rather than focus on the "me," which distorts the meaning of these words, it is more useful to focus on the Great "I" – that is, God – and on building a relationship with Him, so that we might discover the purpose for which we were uniquely created. This discovery will then become a self-esteem builder and a giant step towards the humble acceptance of our individual worth and greatness.

HUMILITY AND DESTINY

The more we think we control our destiny, the farther away we are from living a life filled with both *hod* and *emunah*.

This is a basic, fundamental principle. To live a life of *emunah* requires an absolute awareness that we control absolutely nothing except our God-given power of free will to choose to (or not to) live by the guidelines that God gave us in the Torah. This is also a fundamental principle of living a life filled with *hod*.

It seems counterintuitive, but once we humbly accept the absolute sovereignty of God over our individual life, as well as the entire world,

271. Abraham J. Twerski, *Generation to Generation*, (Brooklyn, NY: Traditional Press, 1987), 81–84.

we actually access the highest form of power and strength, because we become aligned with Him.

To encapsulate this in the best way, I draw from one of my favorite books by Rabbi David Aaron, *The Secret Life of God:*

> We imperfect human beings are in this imperfect world to do a divine mission. The Torah and the commandments define that mission. Without that divine mission, we are insecure and feel like nothing. We find inner peace and security when we choose to do what we must do for the One who must be, because in this way we express and experience our true self – the soul, a spark of the Absolute. The commandments enable us to become the living reflection of God, so to speak, a mirror for God. Our ultimate goal and only true accomplishment is to serve God in His process of self-reflection and knowledge of His oneness. Then we will achieve the joyous experience of love. We are secret agents in the secret life of God. God lives His secret life on earth through you and me – if we let Him in. Our mission is to serve, grow, love, and know. This is our ultimate purpose, power, passion, and pleasure.[272]

Hod compels us to realize that without a divine soul inside of us, we are nothing but a body that will deteriorate and die. But when we choose to be a secret agent in God's divine mission, we become something of worth, connected to the oneness of God. This mission "to serve, grow, love, and know" is "our ultimate purpose, power, passion, and pleasure" (to repeat Rabbi Aaron's words).

So the path to living a powerfully meaningful life is *hod.* When we surrender our "me, me, me" to God, who is the Great "I," then we can live a truly powerful and meaningful life.

HOD AND PHYSICALITY

On the physical level, humility is identified with the left side of the body (specifically, with the left leg) – the same side of the body as *gevurah.* This is because it takes more strength and power to have humility, than to

272. David Aaron, *The Secret Life of God: Discovering the Divine Within You* (Boston: Shambhala Publications, 2004), 184–185.

endure. Humility channels what we endure to levels beyond what is even humanly possible.

When we humbly surrender to God and ask Him to help us fight our battles – when we ask God to help us run our businesses, our classrooms, our families, our nation – we become capable of achieving so much more. Why? Because we are humble and are open to feeling His influence. It is delusional to think that somehow it is we who create the strength, the brilliance, and the success of our lives, but when we acknowledge that God enabled us to achieve these things, we have then combined the astonishing power of both humility and endurance. We learn this from two of our illustrious ancestors: Queen Esther and Rabbi Yehuda HaNasi.

As we have already learned, humility is a strong character trait, not a weak one. *Hod* is a regal state of being that allows us to align with God's light. One of our greatest heroines, Queen Esther, teaches us this every year on Purim when we read *Megillat Esther*. There we learn that Esther prayed for herself and taught the value of prayer to all the Jews in the capital of Persia. Notwithstanding her royal stature, Esther understood that God is the only source of salvation, and thus her faith and humility guided her every action. We should remember Esther when we are faced with a grave challenge and strive to emulate what she did.

Rabbi Yehuda HaNasi taught a similar lesson, and people who want to master *hod* in thought, speech, and action in relation to self, others, and God will follow the principles he outlined in *Pirkei Avot*:

> What is the proper path that a person should choose for himself? Consider three things, and you will not come into the grip of sin . . . Know what is above you – a watchful Eye and attentive Ear – and that all your deeds are recorded in a Book.[273]

Commenting on this teaching, Rabbi Samson Raphael Hirsch poetically captures its essence:

> Never forget that the consequences and repercussions of everything you do reach far beyond the fleeting time span in which your act occurred. God is mindful even of the least conspicuous of your actions, and all will be recalled when your life will pass in review at the end

273. *Pirkei Avot* 2:1.

> of your days; this should be sufficient reason for you to do nothing of which you might have to be ashamed in the presence of God and of your own self-respect; it should be sufficient reason to be careful, with all your deeds, to plant nothing but the seed of goodness into the soil of the future yet unborn.[274]

Rabbi Yehuda HaNasi's wise-three step method to refrain from sin's grasp is all the more remarkable because of who he was – first and foremost the redactor of the Mishnah, the basis of Jewish law. He was considered to be a "phenomenon" in his generation (around second century CE), possessing "noble character traits and superior talents." And he was "the universally loved and acknowledged spiritual and temporal leader of Israel."[275]

The Talmud[276] records that "from Moshe until Rabbi [Yehuda], we do not find anyone with such a combination of wisdom and wealth." Called HaNasi, "the Prince," he had a warm and respectful relationship with the Roman Emperor Antonius (Marcus Aurelius) which "assured a tranquil existence" for the Jews in Eretz Yisrael during his lifetime. But despite his prestige and power, he was so humble, according to the Talmud,[277] that "with his death, real humility and fear of sin ceased to exist."

As from the example of Queen Esther, we see also from the example of Rabbi Yehuda HaNasi that the cultivation of *hod* at the highest level comes from following the fundamental principle of living each day with the full knowledge that God is watching and ever-mindful of our actions.

And if that is true, then He is certainly always there when we ask for His help. Our tradition teaches that God will assist the humble to achieve great spiritual heights.[278] All we need do is make it our goal and turn to Him for guidance. This will be our first step in Week Five, as we peel away layers of arrogance and begin applying some of the principles taught to us by our illustrious ancestors.

Among them is Eliyahu HaKohen, the eighteenth century author of

274. Moshe Lieber, *The Pirkei Avos Treasury* (Brooklyn, NY: Mesorah Publications, 1995), 66.
275. Ibid., 60.
276. *Gittin* 59a.
277. *Sotah* 49b.
278. *Tehillim* 25:9.

the *Shevet Mussar*[279] which lists six behavior patterns that identify genuine humility:

- Speaking gently to all
- Accepting only deserved praise, while realizing whatever one has accomplished is only a fraction of one's full potential
- If blessed with success, increasing one's devotion to God and helping others in need
- In times of argument, making quick amends
- Avoiding revenge
- Accepting suffering without breaking down, for a humble person's intense love for God is a bulwark in times of harsh life challenges

In doing your own personal accounting of your mastery of the *sefirah* of *hod* thus far, how do you rate in each of the above six areas?

This is the week you will discover where you measure up and where you are deficient, and you will acquire the tools to grow in this vital *sefirah*.

279. Among the most popular works of Mussar literature produced in Ottoman society was Elijah HaKohen's *Shevet Mussar*, first published in Ladino in 1748. See specifically Chap. 17.

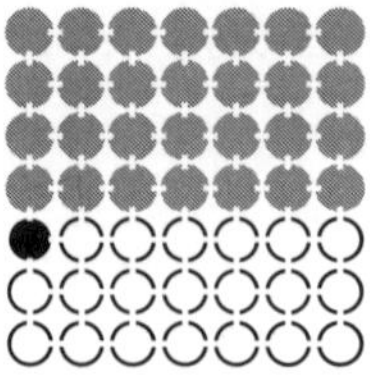

היום תשעה ועשרים יום,
שהם ארבעה שבועות ויום אחד, לעומר

(Ha'yom tisha v'esrim yom,
she'hem arba'a shavuot v'yom echad la'Omer)

"TODAY IS THE TWENTY-NINTH DAY,
OR FOUR WEEKS AND ONE DAY, OF THE OMER."

DAY 29

Chesed sh'b'Hod (Loving-kindness within Humility)

Hod is a magnificent *sefirah* which, in its pure form, is free of any element of anger or arrogance. *Hod* reflects an outward versus an inward, self-centered focus. *Hod* does not manifest itself in weakness, but rather emanates from serene strength that seeks truth and understanding, and fosters harmony and peace. When *chesed* combines with *hod*, humility is further accentuated with love and an even greater sensitivity and caring toward others.

The Talmud[280] teaches that anyone who wants to be devout and pious should fulfill the teachings of the Mishnah in *Avot*, more commonly known as *Pirkei Avot*. I do not think the custom of learning *Pirkei Avot* during Shabbat afternoons between Pesach and Shavuot (when the Omer is being counted) is coincidental.[281]

What do we learn when we study *Avot*, each year?

We learn the moral and ethical teachings of more than sixty of our greatest Sages who lived over a span of 500 years, and whose traditions

280. *Bava Kamma* 30a.

281. Although more recently, the practice has been expanded to continue until Rosh Hashanah, many retain the custom of doing it just during the Omer count.

emanate from Sinai. Their teachings cover the gamut of *mussar* from the profound to the mundane – for example, the simple act of greeting one another, which they view as a sign of empathy. Let's look at what they say about it:

Shammai says, "Receive everyone with a cheerful face."[282] Later, Rabbi Yishmael echoes this advice, "Receive every person cheerfully."[283] And Rabbi Akiva says, "The world is judged with goodness, and everything depends on the abundance of good deeds."[284]

If you want to cultivate healthy displays of loving-kindness within humility in yourself and your children, then try to habituate yourself and them to think, speak, and act with empathy toward others. You and they will benefit, but more importantly you will be emulating God's ways.

DERECH ERETZ

The statement of the sages, *Derech eretz kadma laTorah* (meaning, "the treatment accorded others precedes the Torah") is often quoted, but what does it mean exactly?

Rabbi Elchanan Adler, Rosh Yeshiva of RIETS, explains[285] that this expression originates in the Torah's description of the divine gatekeepers of the Garden of Eden whose purpose – as stated in *Sefer Bereshit* – is "to guard the way to the Tree of Life."[286] He cites the Midrash[287] which notes that in that verse the word *derech* precedes the words *eitz hachayim*, which is "a symbolic reference to Torah." Accordingly, Rabbi Adler concludes that "societal norms were enshrined in human consciousness from time immemorial while Torah was presented to the Jewish People via Moshe, who numbered the 26th generation to Adam."

Rabbi Adler also describes the juxtaposition of *Parshat Yitro*, which records the Revelation at Mount Sinai, and *Parshat Beshalach*, the Torah portion that precedes *Yitro* and which epitomizes *derech eretz*. That Torah portion recounts how, upon leaving Egypt, Moshe took with him the

282. *Pirkei Avot* 1:15.

283. Ibid., 3:17.

284. Ibid., 3:19.

285. Elchanan Adler, "*Derech Eretz Kadma LaTorah*: A Multi-faceted Perspective," Shavuot Bulletin of Yeshiva University's Center for the Jewish Future, 5772/2012, 5–12.

286. *Bereshit* 3:24.

287. In *Vayikra Rabba*, Chap. 9.

bones of Yosef for burial in Eretz Yisrael – this is, says Rabbi Adler, "an aspect of *derech eretz* for it [means] honoring another's request, and extending a gesture of gratitude." *Parshat Beshalach* also recounts the gift of the daily manna, "the archetype of *parnasa*," which is also an aspect of *derech eretz*. But the most compelling reason that this Torah portion epitomizes *derech eretz* is the account of the events at Mara, an early stop in the desert shortly after the Jewish nation crossed the Red/Reed Sea:

After three days of traveling without water, the Jews complained bitterly to Moshe who asked God for help. God then told Moshe how to sweeten the water miraculously. The Torah concludes with: "There he established for [the nation] a decree and an ordinance, and there He tested it."[288]

Rabbi Adler asks what is meant by "decree and law," and cites Ramban's explanation on this verse:

> When they began to enter the great and awesome desert, and thirst where there was no water, He established for them practices concerning their livelihood and their necessities, that they should follow until their arrival in an inhabited land . . . Alternatively, He disciplined them with the rules of the desert, i.e. to endure hunger and thirst, and to call out regarding them to God, but not in a manner of a complaint. And laws, for life, to love each man his fellow, to act upon the elders' advice, to be modest in their tents regarding women and children . . . these are not Torah decrees and laws, but rather standard practices and bylaws for regulating a civilized society.[289]

Rabbi Adler concludes:

> In other words, the laws of Mara were not Torah laws; they were norms of *derech eretz*. They were a regimen for life, for getting along, a code of living. And, as noted by the Alter of Slabodka, *derech eretz* norms are "a comprehensive system which encompasses the entire human being" . . . Because the Jews exhibited a failing in *derech eretz* by demanding water in an unrefined manner, it became necessary to

288. *Shemot* 15:25.
289. Ramban on *Shemot*, 15:25.

present them with a series of *mitzvot* which encapsulate the spirit of *derech eretz kadma laTorah*.[290]

Giving us these special *mitzvot* was a huge gift of *chesed* within *hod* from Hashem.

It is a magnificent display of *chesed* within *hod* when Hashem shines His kindness on us even though we may not deserve it. As part of that *chesed*, He also gives us tests to help us realize our lack of God awareness. Passing these tests from Hashem, and being willing to receive and obey His decrees and laws, fosters our *hod*.

We are noble leaders of our own worthy life when we learn how to consistently display *derech eretz*, regardless of the "thirst" or the "desert-like" conditions we are facing. When we learn from our errors and display a willingness to serve God through His decrees and laws, we mirror the *chesed* within *hod* that God has directed our way.

HONORING OUR PARENTS

While the Talmud has many stories about how our Sages fulfilled the Fifth Commandment by honoring their parents, the most often cited example is the story about a non-Jew, Dama Ben Natina.[291]

Dama Ben Natina's mother was apparently insane. Once, when he was dressed in all his finery and meeting with Roman leaders, his mother burst into the room, tore his clothes, attacked him and spit in his face. Dama Ben Natina kept silent and did not shame his mother. Certainly his was an awesome expression of loving-kindness within humility.

On another occasion, Dama had a valuable precious stone that was needed for the service of the *Kohen Gadol* in the Beit HaMikdash. He was offered a huge amount of money for the stone, but because his father was sleeping on the pillow under which lay the key to the safe where the stone was located, he would not awaken his father even though so much money was at stake. Again, Dama Ben Natina put his parent before himself. This was another act of loving-kindness within humility.

A question: Why does the Talmud hold up a non-Jew as the model for honoring our parents? An answer: Possibly, to teach us that the honoring

290. Adler, "*Derech Eretz Kadma LaTorah*, 11–12.

291. *Kiddushin* 31a.

of parents is a universal norm and should come completely naturally to every child.

And yet despite the fact that it would seem to be ingrained deep inside our hearts and inside our very essence to honor our parents, how many of us have not done so as well as we could have? How many of us have put spending time with our friends ahead of spending time with our parents? How many of us have held onto some anger, resentment, or bitterness towards one or both parents for some past omission or commission rather than just letting it go?

It is an important act of honest introspection to assess the quality of our *kibbud u'mora av v'aim.*

CHESED WITHIN *HOD* AND TORAH MODELS

Moshe displayed a high degree of *hod* in the manner in which he treated his father-in-law, Yitro, as the Torah tells us:

> Moshe went out to meet his father-in-law, and he prostrated himself and kissed him, and each inquired about the other's well-being.[292]

Moshe was the leader of the Jewish people. He had accomplished the superhuman task of taking them out of Egyptian slavery. He was the only living person before or since who had received instruction – in the form of the Written Torah and the Oral Torah – from God Himself, and the only person who conversed with God "face to face." And yet, Moshe humbled himself before his father-in-law. Moshe displayed *chesed* within *hod* toward Yitro.

Moshe also displayed *chesed* within *hod* to his brother Aaron and vice versa.

Aaron was never jealous of Moshe's leadership role, nor did he ever seek any personal glory. Rather, Aaron loved the Jewish people and tried, because of his intense love for them, to bring those who were quarrelling back together, and to promote unity among them during their forty years in the wilderness. No easy task, but Aaron was devoted to it. This is why Aaron personifies *hod.* He simply loved every person just as much as Moshe loved the nation.

292. *Shemot* 18:7.

Another example of Moshe's *chesed* within *hod* is contained in the story of the daughters of Zelophehad. He listened carefully to their request after their father had passed away. They wished to have an inheritance "among our father's brothers" in the Land of Israel. It was an unprecedented inquiry, but Moshe respectfully and caringly brought their claim *directly* to God, who responded:

> "The daughters of Zelophehad speak properly. You shall surely give them a possession of inheritance among the brothers of their father, and you shall cause the inheritance of their father to pass over to them."[293]

Moshe implemented the decision immediately, creating a new law in the process.

Have you ever stopped to think about how absolutely astonishing this Torah narrative is? Give inheritance of land to daughters? Do you think that was occurring in other lands or codes of law in 1300 BCE? Of course it wasn't! There are countries *today* in the world that do not permit females to own land in their own right.

Some would have considered the request of the daughters of Zelophehad outrageous. But Moshe listened with respect, and then, recognizing that he didn't have a ready answer to their request, he immediately brought it before God. That is an awesome display of *chesed* within *hod*.[294]

---

293. *Bamidbar* 27:4–7.

294. What an awesome religion Judaism is! More advanced by many millennia in the treatment of women. In stark contrast, just contemplate the horrific truth that in 2012, Taliban members in Pakistan shot a 14-year-old girl in the face because she was an advocate for education for girls in her hometown.

DISCUSSION TOPICS FOR *CHESED* WITHIN *HOD*

For adults

1. When people disagree with me or offend me, am I able to display humility by not reacting or getting into a disagreement? Can I give examples?
2. When I'm teaching someone how to do something, or to do it better, do I display patience, never becoming critical or judgmental? If not, how can I work on that?
3. Do I take credit for all the small and large accomplishments I achieve in my life, or do I give credit to others? Regarding others, do I not only give them credit, but also express my gratitude to them? Do I show my genuine appreciation to my spouse, my parents, my children, my boss, my co-workers, my neighbors, to other relatives, to public service employees, to waiters, to strangers, to my rabbi, to God?

For children

1. Can I give examples of times that my interaction with people whom I find it hard to get along with resulted in angry disagreement? Instead of reacting the way I did, how could I have reacted using *chesed* within *hod*?
2. Are there times when I have to have the last word on a topic? Are these expressions of arrogance or of *chesed* within *hod*?
3. When is the last time I expressed gratitude to my parents, to my brothers and sisters, to my teacher, to my rabbi, to God?

היום שלושים יום,
שהם ארבעה שבועות ושני ימים, לעומר

(Ha'yom shloshim yom,
she'hem arba'a shavuot u'shnei yamim la'Omer)

"TODAY IS THIRTIETH DAY,
OR FOUR WEEKS AND TWO DAYS, OF THE OMER."

DAY 30

Gevurah sh'b'Hod (Strength/Discipline within Humility)

Hod is looking outside of one's self and one's ego to understand another's perspective or position without becoming embroiled in unsettling conflict. *Hod* is devoid of jealousy, enmity, hatred, anger, arrogance, and other negative emotions. The orientation of *gevurah* within *hod* is one of inner silence and the ability to intuit other people's viewpoints, and then responding to them in a disciplined, humble manner that makes a space for their convictions.

The negative side of *hod* is that the people with whom we are interacting can interpret our silence or restraint as acceptance or recognition of their positions, opinions, or actions, even if these are immoral or unethical or even evil. And this is where *gevurah* comes in. *Gevurah* within *hod* recognizes where we must assert ourselves in an appropriate, delicate manner, in order to clarify a position that could otherwise be taken as approval of an improper behavior. *Gevurah* within *hod* introduces the element of "backbone" so that *hod* is not misinterpreted as weakness or a willingness to bend in any direction and go along with anything, no matter how deplorable it is. *Gevurah* puts a balanced amount of discipline, strength, or restraint into *hod* when needed.

IN THE FACE OF EVIL

This is a fundamental question: When faced with evil, what should we do?

Sometimes, in the name of humility, we may compromise when we should have expressed a different viewpoint. On a person-to-person level, we always have to listen and decide if, when, and how to respond with *hod*, and yet in a manner that does not mislead others into thinking that we affirm or support improper behavior. For example, if an addicted person is confused by our humility and concludes that we affirm their addictive behavior, this is neither helpful nor constructive. In fact, we have committed an injustice.

Gevurah of *hod* properly assesses our interpersonal interactions and applies the strength of restraint to help us respond in a careful manner that does not mislead.

Whether we are struggling with this issue on a person-to-person level, or on a national level, a visit to Yad Vashem (or another Holocaust museum) should clarify our thinking. For nothing sends a stronger wake-up call than the tragic examples of both individuals and countries who remained silent and "neutral" in the face of a greatest act of inhumanity in the twentieth century. Although some of the silence was motivated by anti-Semitism, some of it may have been the helpless/hopeless attitude of "I am just one person, what can I do?" This is not humility – this is apathy.

In stark contrast, others – for example, Oskar Schindler or Raoul Wallenberg – risked life and limb in order to save Jewish lives. Their actions exemplify empathy, humanity, self-sacrifice, discipline, focus, and strength – all components of *gevurah* within *hod*.

Another inspirational example of this attribute is Naphtali Lau-Lavie, the brother of the former Chief Rabbi of Israel, HaRav Israel Meir Lau. As noted in our discussion for Day 7, Rabbi Lau's life during the Holocaust was saved by the incredible sacrifice of his mother and the brave actions of his brother, only eighteen years old at the time. In order to insure that six-year-old Israel would survive the transport to and internment in Buchenwald, Naphtali had to execute many tactical strategies including hiding him in a sack, posing as Israel's father, and on more than one occasion having to negotiate and redeem the life of Israel Meir – once with their father's gold watch and another time with a diamond that had been hidden in one of his teeth as a result of the foresight of their mother, who anticipated the need for just such a bribe.[295]

An important take-away of the Naphtali story is to always try to discipline ourselves to think, speak, and act as a servant of God who is guided by the Torah – this is the best way to know what to do when faced with a situation that calls for *gevurah* within *hod*.

On the national level, Israel displayed tremendous *gevurah* within *hod*, during the first Persian Gulf War when thirty-nine Scud missiles were launched by Iraq towards cities within Israel. At that time, President Bush asked Prime Minister Yitzhak Shamir that Israel "stand down" and not retaliate against these onslaughts. Shamir and the cabinet elected to do so. The nation was unified in prayer and in helping each other. The outcome? God ensured that despite thirty-nine Scud missiles that fell, only one casualty occurred, and the Iraq war was over in short order. Israel benefitted in numerous ways from its decision to exercise restraint and by its display of humility in trusting God, who responded with His miraculous protection during that war.

GOD'S LOVING COMMITMENT TO US

In the introduction to *hod*, we learned an important truism about *hod* and *emunah* –specifically that, when we experience trials and tribulations, it is a sign of God's love for us. Through the prism of *emunah* we sense that everything He does is for our ultimate benefit, even if we do not understand how that can be.

It is *gevurah* within *hod* that underlies God's decision to give us freedom – we are free to "choose life" and blessing and not their opposites. God alone is perfect, and yet He refrained from completing creation and permitted an imperfect mortal, whom He endowed with His divine image (*tzelem Elokim*), to freely choose to finish the job. This takes humility of the highest order.

On the receiving side of this equation, it takes *gevurah* within *hod* on the part of all of us to freely choose to submit ourselves to a system of *mitzvot* which provides a pathway toward a relationship with God. This requires restraint of our physical desires and selfish inclinations, and the

295. Lau, *Out of the Depths*, 32–34, 42, 44.

humble realization that we are only flesh and blood, destined to live for only a short time.

Just as God displays *gevurah* within *hod*, so too, we can choose to display this awesome attribute and, in so doing, experience His presence always.

The Ramchal, Rabbi Moshe Chayim Luzzatto, elaborates on an important principle:

> It is indeed fitting that [one's] every inclination be towards the Creator, may His Name be blessed, and that his every action, great or small, be motivated by no purpose other than that of drawing near to the Blessed One and breaking all the barriers . . . that stand between him and his Possessor, until he is pulled towards the Blessed One just as iron to a magnet. Anything that might possibly be a means to acquiring this closeness, he should pursue and clutch, and not let go of; and anything which might be considered a deterrent to it, he should flee as from a fire.[296]

The Ramchal begins with the trait of "watchfulness" as the necessary first step to begin the process of developing closeness with the Blessed One, and he offers this advice:

> The idea of watchfulness is for a man to exercise caution in his actions and his undertakings: that is, to deliberate and watch over his actions and his accustomed ways to determine whether or not they are good, so as not to abandon his soul to the danger of destruction, God forbid, and not to walk according to the promptings of habit as a blind man in pitch darkness . . . One who walks this world without considering whether his way of life is good or bad is like a blind man walking along the seashore, who is in very great danger, and whose chances of being lost are far greater than those of his being saved. For there is no difference between natural blindness and self-inflicted blindness, the shutting of one's eyes as an act of will and desire.[297]

The Ramchal adds that it takes humility to engage in a daily practice of setting aside time to carefully "observe all of [one's] actions and watch over

296. Luzzatto, *The Path of the Just* (*Mesillat Yesharim*), 27.
297. Ibid., p. 29.

all of his ways so as not to leave himself with a bad habit or a bad trait, let alone a sin or a crime."[298]

Inherent in this outstanding sage advice is the development of the trait *gevurah* within *hod* so that we will come to think of God as our "best friend," and, so that – as in everything – we would emulate His ways.

GOD'S WAYS

We see God's display of restraint and gentleness with the Nation of Israel, even in response to their erroneous judgments.

While standing at the threshold of the Promised Land, certain leaders informed Moshe they wanted a small group to spy out the land prior to *Klal Yisrael* entering. Why did they want to do this? Why didn't everyone just accept, with *emunah*, that God had promised them a land flowing with milk and honey and that He would take care of them there, just as He had in Egypt and in the desert since their exodus?

All good questions, but there is a more important question: When Moshe shared their plan with God, why did God permit them to go forward? God's response to Moshe was: "Send forth men, *if you please*."[299] Why didn't God just say, "No, you ungrateful people, don't you trust Me?"

The answer: Because God was modeling *gevurah* within *hod*. Whenever God, who can do anything He wishes, anytime He wishes, in any way He wishes, restrains Himself from determining the events in the world and in our lives, that is a display of *gevurah* within *hod*, and it obligates us to do the same.

THE TRAGIC MISTAKE OF NADAV AND AVIHU

Lest we underestimate the value of this important attribute, the tragic mistake of the two sons of Aaron, who failed to display *gevurah* within *hod*, serves as an important warning.

We know the story well. On the day that was to mark the dedication of the Mishkan in the wilderness, Nadav and Avihu, "brought before God an alien fire that He had not commanded them."[300] They immediately

298. Ibid., p. 37.
299. *Bamidbar* 13: 2.
300. *Vayikra* 10:1–2.

lost their lives, and Torah commentators struggle to explain this shocking turn of events.

Some say the mistake of the two sons of Aaron was that they failed to consult with either their uncle Moshe or their father who was the *Kohen Gadol*. Others opine that they drank alcohol before bringing the incense into the Mishkan. Ramban says that whatever they did, they did not do it for sake of God. But, perhaps the mistake made by Nadav and Avihu could have been avoided had they restrained their own motivations and desires and acted only in accordance with God's word. This is what *gevurah* within *hod* is all about.

When our mission is to serve God, we must do it on His terms, not ours. Service is an act of humility. It is arrogance to think that we can serve God in the way we determine is acceptable to us.

Imagine being an older adult with grown children who have moved out of the family home. If they visit you only when they "feel like it," and when it happens not to interfere with anything else they have planned, without regard to your preferences, how do you feel? Do you feel they appreciate the years of sacrifice you gave them, trying to address their every need? Do you feel that they love you? Do you feel that you are a priority in their lives? Hardly.

It is the same when it comes to our relationship with our Father in Heaven. Why should God tolerate neglectful behavior from any of His children? True, He may hold off for awhile to see if we will change our errant ways after experiencing a few tests and travails. But eventually, *we* are the ones who arrogantly cut the cord with our actions. And *only we* can repair what we have done. And that will take *gevurah* within *hod* – restraint/strength and humility, which translates into an ability to acknowledge when we have made a mistake, to correct our error, and to resolve not to repeat it.

DISCUSSION TOPICS FOR *GEVURAH* WITHIN *HOD*

For adults

1. When others are speaking *lashon hara* what is my response? How do I plan to respond in the future?
2. Have I ever witnessed an instance of injustice? What did I think, say, or do to stop it?
3. How aware am I of the times I need to do *teshuvah*? Do I have the habit of a nightly *cheshbon hanefesh*? Having realized my mistakes, do I try to correct them? If not, what keeps me from doing this? Is it a deficiency of *hod*?

For children

1. Have other kids ever talked about me and made me feel bad? Do I talk about other kids? What can I do differently?
2. Have I ever been around someone who was telling a joke that made fun of another group of people, but I just kept quiet and didn't tell him or her to stop? What could I do next time?
3. When I have misbehaved, am I pretty quick to realize it and genuinely ask forgiveness from the person I have hurt?

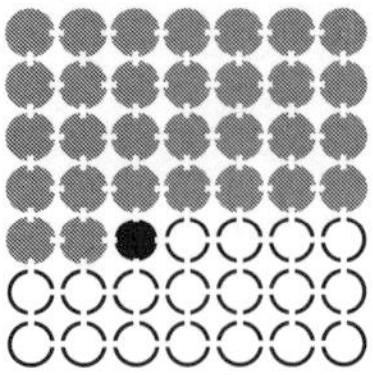

היום אחד ושלושים יום,
שהם ארבעה שבועות ושלושה ימים, לעומר

(Ha'yom echad u'sheloshim yom,
she'hem arba'a shavuot u'shlosha yamim la'Omer)

"TODAY IS THE THIRTY-FIRST DAY,
OR FOUR WEEKS AND THREE DAYS, OF THE OMER."

DAY 31

Tiferet sh'b'Hod
(Harmony/Truth within Humility)

As we learned over the previous days, *hod* can be motivated by either an appropriate level or an overabundance of *chesed* or *gevurah.* But when *hod* is influenced by *tiferet, hod* achieves the proper delicate balance necessary. It does not provide undeserved approval, nor is it overly critical or silent. *Hod,* when influenced by *tiferet,* emphasizes truth and balance and is not misguided, weak, or inappropriate, but rather a beautiful and balanced reaction to every relationship or situation.

The Zohar, the mystical interpretation of the Torah by Rabbi Shimon Bar Yochai, dating from the second century CE, says humans were created by God for the purpose of using their free will to come close to Him by serving, loving, and knowing Him. This is a deep, but simple truth. We serve God by humbly choosing to love and know Him, and we grow by doing so.

If for some reason, we instead arrogantly choose to ignore this truth, what happens? Warns Rabbi Arush in *The Garden of Emuna* that "those who fail to get to know God in good times" risk having to get to know

Him in bad times, when "the only remaining alternative is to cry out to God."[301] The Zohar says the same thing:

> How beloved are the children of Israel before the Holy One, blessed by He! He desires to reprove them and to lead them on the straight path, like a loving father who wields a rod in hand in order to lead the son on the straight path, so that the son shall not stray to the right or to the left.[302]

So, why don't we simply accept the glorious harmony and truth that comes from a life of serving God. To do so is to acquire *tiferet* within *hod.*

ALIGNING WITH THE "GREAT ESSENTIAL I"

Tiferet within *hod* puts us on a path of aligning with the greater truth of our existence, as taught by Kabbalah and our Sages, as well as more contemporary scholars.

If you are ever fortunate enough to attend any of the seminars offered at the Isralight Institute, you will be exposed to the writings of Rav Avraham Isaac Kook, Rabbi Joseph B. Soloveitchik, Rabbi Aryeh Kaplan, and other great teachers. The founder of Isralight, Rabbi David Aaron attempts to simplify, for the participants' sake, some deep mystical concepts. He teaches that, in sum, we share an "inner essential I" with every person and the entire community. That "I" is God. We experienced it at Mount Sinai where we met our entire collective self, revealed in all its holiness and singularity. As Rabbi Aaron summarizes:

> That moment at Mount Sinai rectified the sin of Adam who lost his true "I-ness" because he thought he could decide for himself what he thought was good and bad and rebel against the mistaken notion that somehow God was trying to control him. *Chet* (a Hebrew word poorly translated as "sin") really means to be cut off, to lose and betray your true self. The sin is being estranged from your essence.

---

301. Shalom Arush, *The Garden of Emuna* (Jerusalem: Chut Shel Chessed Institutions, 2008), 22.
302. Zohar commentary on *Bechukotai*, 114.

> When Adam was asked by God after the sin, "Where are you?" he should have responded, "I am in You" because by ourselves we are nothing, but in and of God, we are a part of the Essential Self. But Adam had already committed the sin of being "estranged from his essence, when he heeded the snake and lost himself," as Rav Avraham Yitzchak Kook describes.[303]

It is clear from the language in the Torah text how estranged Adam and Eve had become after their sin:

> They heard the sound of Hashem God manifesting itself in the garden toward evening; and the man and his wife hid from Hashem God among the trees of the garden. Hashem God called out to the man and said to him, "Where are you?" He said, "I heard the sound of You in the garden, and I was afraid because I am naked, so I hid." And He (Hashem God) said, "Who told you that you are naked? Have you eaten of the tree from which I commanded you not to eat?" The man said, "The woman whom You gave to be with me – she gave me of the tree, and I ate." And Hashem God said to the woman, "What is this that you have done!" The woman said, "The serpent deceived me, and I ate."[304]

A tragic story. Jewish tradition teaches that this event occurred on the sixth day, Friday, just as the first Shabbat was approaching. Had the sin not occurred, after the first Shabbat, Adam would have ushered in the Messianic Era.[305] This was to have been Plan A. But that's just one part of the tragedy.

When we analyze God's questions and the response of Adam and Eve, we come face to face with how dreadful their sin was. Why, then, did God ask all His questions? He knew where they were, just as He knew how they violated the one commandment they were given not to eat from the Tree of Knowledge of Good and Evil. But it appears from His questions that He wanted to know whether or not *they* were aware that they had cut

---

303. Rabbi David Aaron *shiur*, July 2012, referring to teachings of Rav Avraham Yitzchak Kook.

304. *Bereshit* 3:8–12.

305. Siftei Kohen, *Bereshit* 22.

themselves off from themselves, and therefore also from God, "the Great Essential I."

Adam and Eve tried to hide from God. When asked what they did, first Adam blamed Eve and then Eve blamed the snake. No one accepted responsibility. No one did *teshuvah* and said, "I am so sorry. Forgive me. I momentarily lost myself and thought I could be the one to determine what is good and bad, but I was wrong, wrong, wrong to do so. I will never do it again. I am completely aware once again that I am part of You, and I do not ever want to be estranged from the Great Essential I." But that is not what they did, because that is not what they believed. They did not understand that they had separated themselves from their own "inner essential I" that only has relevance as part of the "Great Essential I," the One God.

We, too, become cut off from ourselves and the "Great Essential I" when we sin.[306] And, therefore, *hod* becomes a critical *middah* to develop if we want to recognize our essential connection with God. When we focus on "me, me, me" we are estranged from our source in the "Great Essential I." But *hod* seems to be a way to begin the way back by helping us re-align our true self with the "Essential Self."

How fortunate are the people who know that they are part of something bigger and who behave accordingly. How fortunate are the people who align themselves with *tiferet* within *hod*, accepting the truth of being an integrated ray of the "Great Essential I."

TIFERET WITHIN *HOD* IN EVERYDAY LIFE

Let us now consider how *tiferet* within *hod* displays itself in everyday life.

The primary example is through simple *derech eretz*, such as greeting others or responding to their greetings.

In the last twenty years – and accelerating at epidemic proportions – we have seen an erosion of basic manners. The simple greeting of another person has been completely neglected, with some parents no longer even attempting to convey to their own children the need to show this most basic level of politeness.

Imagine observing or experiencing the following: A child under the age

306. The Sin of the Golden Calf nullified the rectification of the first sin that occurred at Sinai and so our struggle continues.

of ten is greeted by a parent, grandparent, other family member, rabbi, teacher, *shul* member, or guest, and the child does not even respond to their greeting with "Hello." The child may not even stop what he or she is doing to stand up and shake hands or hug the person who has entered the room. What would you conclude from this scene? How would you feel if this happened to you?

Conversely, have you ever ignored someone who entered the room or your home? It takes a sense of harmony and humility to realize that every person you encounter during a day deserves a cheerful smile, and if you, yourself, are greeted, even by a stranger, that a simple "hello" in return is required and is proper *derech eretz*.

Some people may try to excuse themselves by saying it is hard for them to speak to others, particularly strangers, because they are shy. They might even think that their shyness is actually an expression of humility. And it is true that shyness is often confused with humility, but a shy person may or may not be humble. Sometimes a person's shyness is so acute that he or she acts in a manner that is consistently self-contained or anti-social without displaying empathy for others. If so, then that is not real humility. Such behavior lacks the needed balancing component of *tiferet*.

Without *tiferet*, shyness that is self-contained and anti-social is self-centered. If left unaddressed, such shyness may push the people who suffer from this condition to withdraw and choose to turn their natural introversion into a shield behind which to hide, in order not to engage in human contact except on their terms. This is not *tiferet* within *hod* – this is not harmony within humility.

One way to break out of this mold is to volunteer in a venue like a hospital, food kitchen, or *gemach*. In these settings, when the shy person forces himself or herself to think about and speak to complete strangers – to bring harmony to others – he or she becomes more aware of the needs of others and begins to place them above the needs of self.

MIRIAM AND *LASHON HARA*

The Torah is filled with stories illustrating an excellent balance of *tiferet* within *hod*, thanks to the amazing *middot* of our ancestors.

For example, there is the incident involving Miriam, who was punished for speaking *lashon hara* about her brother Moshe to her elder brother Aaron. Even though her comments were not public and were also undoubtedly well-intentioned, she was punished with *tzaraat*, her skin turning white, and she had to be quarantined outside of the camp.

How did Miriam respond? First, we see that Miriam endured her punishment with complete and humble acceptance of the truth of God's judgment. She did not protest. She did not blame others. She did not hold a grudge. Miriam, a very righteous person, had made a mistake and she realized it.

While Miriam was quarantined, the Jewish people waited patiently for her for seven days and welcomed her back into the camp as soon as her period of seclusion was over, also displaying *tiferet* within *hod*.[307]

DISCUSSION TOPICS FOR TIFERET WITHIN HOD

For adults

1. Do I socialize in a balanced way? If not, what will I do about it?
2. Do I know when to be flexible and give in, and when to set limits for my children if a given situation would be harmful to them or inappropriate in the eyes of God?
3. Do I display balanced empathy for others and an interest in their thoughts, words, and actions?

For children

1. Do other kids take advantage of me? How can I change that?
2. Am I overly shy? How might that work against me as I continue to grow up?
3. What issues are so important that I should hold my ground and not let my peers influence my thoughts, speech, and actions?

307. *Bamidbar* 12:11–16.

היום שנים ושלושים יום,
שהם ארבעה שבועות וארבעה ימים, לעומר

(Ha'yom shnayim u'shloshim yom,
she'hem arba'a shavuot v'arba'a yamim la'Omer)

"TODAY IS THE THIRTY-SECOND DAY,
OR FOUR WEEKS AND FOUR DAYS, OF THE OMER."

DAY 32

Netzach sh'b'Hod (Endurance within Humility)

When *netzach* modifies *hod*, the appropriate expression of *hod* is both accentuated and extended. If we master this *middah*, we are able to remain positively humble and modestly appropriate when asserting our position in a clear, grounded manner, even in the face of arrogant behavior. In such a case, *netzach* imbues *hod* with endurance so that it is able to stand its ground in a respectful manner.

When we steadfastly choose to think, speak, and act with humility in all situations, we have achieved *netzach* within *hod*. We accustom ourselves to listen carefully to all, thinking quietly about the person and the topic, and determining if and how we should react. We do not need to take center stage or bask in the limelight, because we put others before ourselves. Most importantly, we realize that in every event of our lives, God is in control. Our repose and comfort is staying aligned with God's will.

SHLOMO NATIV AND HIS EXCEPTIONAL FAMILY

As noted earlier, humility does not mean being insecure or weak. True humility imbues us with strength and helps us to withstand life's tests and challenges. Acknowledging that we do not run the world or even control many of the events in our lives should give us the wisdom to realize that when something happens, our only choice is going to be deciding how to bounce back from an apparent setback: Will we play the role of victim, blaming others, or will we grow through this experience? Will we demonstrate that we fully believe the words of prayer we recite each morning:

> My God, the soul You placed within me is pure. You created it, You fashioned it, You breathed it into me, You safeguard it within me, and eventually You will take it from me, and restore it to me in the Time to Come. As long as the soul is within me, I gratefully thank you, Hashem, my God and the God of my forefathers, Master of all Works, Lord of all Souls. Blessed are You, Hashem, Who restores souls to dead bodies.

It was this prayer, sang to a melody, which accompanied a moving video released on the 8th of Nissan in 2012 by *The Jewish Press.*[308] The video shares the special life and tragic death of a sensitive and loving 13-year-old boy, Shlomo Nativ, who died at the hands of a terrorist right outside his home in the Gush Etzion area of Israel. Shlomo's parents and siblings – remarkable for their honesty, their unity, their dedication to living a worthy life of service to God and many other qualities – are interviewed against a backdrop of flashbacks interwoven with the joyous celebration of a Torah scroll dedication in Shlomo's memory.

If you want to learn about modern-day *netzach* within *hod* at the highest of levels, watch this video. The Nativ family has sacrificed in ways that words can never describe, and yet what they reveal about enduring belief and service to God serves as an inspiration for all of us.

Do we think for a moment that the terrorist who axed this pure, innocent boy prevailed? Or that this terrorist will escape his punishment on Judgment Day? Conversely, how many hundreds of thousands will be inspired by Shlomo's short life and how his family found deep meaning and purpose in the face of this tragedy?

---

308. The video is accessible at http://www.youtube.com/watch?v=8lWd1VTE540.

THE EXAMPLE OF YAAKOV AVINU

Two striking examples reveal the *netzach* within *hod* of Yaakov Avinu, at two very different points in his life.

First, Yaakov had applied this *sefirah* combination over and over in dealing with his deceitful father-in-law, Lavan. Enduring what he did for two decades, Yaakov had to bite his tongue while his father-in-law tried to cheat him at every turn. But he did what was required of him, without compromising his values, and he was able to extract himself from the situation. With the help of God, he left Lavan and returned to Eretz Yisrael with his family intact and with great wealth as well.

Many years later, Yaakov experienced another life test requiring this *sefirah* combination. Yaakov knew from his parents that the Jewish people were destined to live in exile (*galut*) for 400 years. Because it was the will of God, Yaakov worked with full understanding and acceptance of that destiny that lead him and his family to leave Israel and "descend" into the furnace of Egypt. When, on his last night in Israel, he received the message and promise from God that his future generations would return to the Land, he entered the *galut* armed with *netzach* within *hod*, in humble, calm acceptance of the events that were about to unfold.[309]

Yaakov embodied *netzach* within *hod* consistently – day in and day out – recognizing that everything is from God and that God controls everything. He had enduring *emunah* and became a vessel for God's will. Thus he served as a conduit between God and man, revealing God's will to others.

When we embody *netzach* within *hod*, we virtually suspend our ego so as to receive the goodness and wisdom of the situation confronting us or the person before us, and, most imperatively, we receive the goodness and wisdom flowing down to us from Hashem.

THE EXAMPLE OF AARON

Another Torah example of *netzach* within *hod* is the reaction of Aaron following the death of his two oldest sons, Nadav and Avihu (which we already described on Day 30). Let us recall what the Torah tells us about this incident:

---

309. *Bereshit* 46:1–7.

> A fire came forth from before Hashem and consumed them, and they died before Hashem. Moshe said to Aaron: "Of this did Hashem speak, saying: 'I will be sanctified through those who are nearest Me, thus I will be honored before the entire people'"; and Aaron was silent.[310]

We can only imagine his trauma. But he did not waver in his *emunah*. He simply went on to perform his critical mission – to be the *Kohen Gadol* of the Jewish people.

In his commentary on this event, Ramban says that, upon the death of Nadav and Avihu, Aaron cried and then he held his peace. This is *netzach* within *hod*. He did not quit his job, resign from being the High Priest, or try to challenge God. Rather, he submitted humbly to God's inscrutable will.

In one of his insightful drashas on *Parshat Shemini* – which describes both the episode of the unfortunate deaths of Aaron's sons on the same day as the dedication of the Mishkan, as well as the laws of *kashrut* – Rabbi Jeffrey Bienenfeld notes: "When I ask what God wants, that's the beginning of genuine spirituality."[311] It is also the beginning of *netzach* with *hod*.

---

310. *Vayikra* 10:3.

311. Rabbi Jeffrey Bienenfeld shiur on *Parshat Shemini*, March 22, 2011.

DISCUSSION TOPICS FOR *NETZACH* WITHIN *HOD*

For adults

1. Have I established enduring, reasonable personal boundaries for the sake of my physical, emotional, and spiritual well-being in order to ensure that neither I, nor others violate those boundaries? If not, will I do so now?
2. In any of my relationships, is there some improper behavior about which I've been silent? What stops me from expressing my views?
3. What have I done to consistently attempt to bring out the "inner voice" of someone around me who may lack the confidence or ability to express himself or herself?

For children

1. Is there someone who takes advantage of me? What am I going to do about it?
2. Am I being pressured to do something that I really do not want to do? How can I say "no" and mean it?
3. Am I willing to share my inner thoughts about personal matters with my parents? Can I try doing so?

היום שלושה ושלושים יום,
שהם ארבעה שבועות וחמישה ימים, לעומר

(Ha'yom shlosha u'sholshim yom,
she'hem arba'a shavuot v'chamisha yamim la'Omer)

"TODAY IS THE THIRTY-THIRD DAY, OR FOUR WEEKS AND FIVE DAYS, OF THE OMER."

DAY 33

Hod sh'b'Hod (Humility within Humility)

***Hod* within *hod* is humility in its purest form. When we demonstrate complete respect for ourselves, others, and God in our thought, speech, and action, and in all situations, no matter how stressful, we have mastered *hod* within *hod*.**

This means that we not only refrain from judging or criticizing others, but we also do not view ourselves as superior to them, no matter how unlearned or how crude they appear to be. We recognize that every person we encounter is put there by God for an explicit purpose. This recognition challenges us to respectfully respond to perplexing situations with enlightened humility that exudes serenity, gratitude, and appreciation for the variety of life experiences. We learn through the lens of *hod* within *hod* how to modestly and appropriately respond with grace to whatever situation we find ourselves in.

When we have mastered *hod* within *hod*, we are always empathetic and interested in the thoughts, well-being, and condition of others, seeking out ways to help, without ever seeking honor or public credit for our acts of giving. We share our thoughts or make gentle suggestions without ever lording over any other human being. Or, our *hod* can take the form of silence so that we can better absorb the essence of a person or situation, and understand the will of God for us.

Hod within *hod* manifests as a greater receptivity to do God's will and its acceptance with humility and modesty. It is an elevated recognition that everything comes from God, is for the "good," and all we have to do is connect, be patient, and allow oneself to be uplifted.

THE LESSON OF LAG BAOMER

The 33rd day of the Omer count is one of tremendous significance in terms of our *middah* development, for this is the day when the plague afflicting the students of Rabbi Akiva ended.

The famed Rabbi Akiva lived at the time of the Roman persecution. He had 24,000 students who were going to be the bearers of the tradition during these difficult times. Sadly, while they knew Torah, they did not display considerate *derech eretz* to each other.

What did they do wrong? They did not share their learning. They engaged in "one-ups-manship." They were concerned with their own honor, not the honor of their fellow students. And then, suddenly, a plague hit with deaths occurring daily. It was only on the 33rd day of the Omer count, the day which corresponds to *hod* within *hod*, that the plague stopped, but by then 24,000 of the best and brightest had perished. Rabbi Akiva started over, teaching Torah to only five students, including Rabbi Shimon Bar Yochai (to whom the revelation of the Zohar, the deeply mystical Jewish tradition, is attributed and whose *yahrzeit* we celebrate on Lag BaOmer).

In a profound lesson of humility, Rabbi Akiva instructed his five students not to make the same mistake as the other 24,000. It is significant that Rabbi Akiva is noted in the Talmud[312] for stating that the most essential principle of the Torah is: "Love your neighbor as yourself."

Loving your neighbor leads to unity. And unity among human beings emulates the oneness of God.

When the Jewish people left Egypt, all three million of them, making up the Twelve Tribes, were unified. When they received the Torah at Mount Sinai, they were unified. But since then, the Jewish nation has been marred by discord and division. The worst of it came just before the Second Temple was destroyed, but disunity continues to this day. So

312. Sifra, *Kedoshim* 2:4.

much of it appears to relate to not judging others favorably, a lack of tolerance, a lack of respect, and a violation of the principle of treating others as one would wish to be treated. Will there be leaders from the various segments of Jewish society who step forth, as Rabbi Aryeh Levin did in his generation, and conduct their lives in a manner that displays a love and regard for all Jews? We can only pray for that to happen.

There is no question that – if we can cultivate genuine *hod* within *hod*, pure humility, and express it in refined ways – this *sefirah* combination will help unify us. We will always have our differences, but we will treat each other with dignity. This requires the kind of humility that God wants us to display.

THE MOSHE MODEL

No one models this trait better than Moshe Rebbeinu.

As we have previously noted, Moshe reluctantly accepted the leadership role that God hand-picked for him. He led the Jews out of Egypt, prepared them to receive the Torah, and ultimately became both their teacher and nurturer for the entire forty-year period that they wandered in the desert. The dutiful acceptance of this role did not make Moshe arrogant. Just the opposite – it increased his humility.

Rebbetzin Tzipporah Heller conveys a keen understanding of Moshe Rebbeinu and his mindset in her wonderful book, *Let's Face It! The 8 Essential Challenges of Living*. She writes:

> The Torah states: "You are children to the Lord your God."[313] So, it is true that one person [say Moshe] may have a more important function than another person, but it is blatantly false that any person is more or less a part of God than any other person. This is the spirituality of the human race. . . .
>
> Moshe understood that he had a specific, important function, while Betzalel, the artist who crafted the vessels for the Tabernacle, had a different function, and an ordinary Israelite whose name is not even mentioned in the Torah had yet a different function. Yet Moshe was not self-important. He understood the difference between function and essence. He knew that, while his function was more

313. *Devarim* 14:1.

important, his essence was equally a part of God as the multitude he led.[314]

HOD WITHIN *HOD* OF THE TEN MARTYRS

Fortunately, the Sages of Israel who came after Moshe, imitated this wonderful quality. They serve as an example for us today, and none more so than the Ten Martyrs whose heroic stories constitute one of the most gripping portions of the Yom Kippur liturgy. I cannot recall a Yom Kippur when reading these stories did not move me to tears.[315]

First, let us recall the setting: The Roman ruler asks the fateful question of members of the Sanhedrin, "[What is the law] if a man is found to have kidnapped a member of his Jewish brethren, enslaved him, and sold him?" They answer, "That kidnapper is to die."

This "set up" results in the edict demanding that the Sages must now pay for the sin of the brothers of Yosef, who kidnapped and sold him centuries ago. Says the Roman ruler: "Now you must accept the heavenly judgment upon yourselves, for since your forefathers' time there have been none like you. Were they alive I would have prosecuted them before you, so you must bear the sin of your ancestors." The members of the Sanhedrin ask for three days time to determine whether the decree is from God. To make this determination, Rabbi Yishmael utters the Divine Name, ascends to heaven, asks the Angel Gabriel and gets this answer, "Accept it upon yourselves, O righteous and beloved ones, that you have been destined for this."

From this point forward, we read of the brutal and barbaric methods employed to kill these Sages. Each one was brave, loyal, and fully accepting of the Divine decree. Let's elaborate on the death of Rabbi Akiva:

> [He] was taken out to be murdered publicly. During his frightful ordeal, he accepted God's sovereignty upon himself by reciting the *Shema* joyously, and oblivious to the pain . . . Even Rabbi Akiva's own students wondered, "Our teacher, even to this extent?" The dying Sage explained, "All my life I was concerned over a phrase in the Torah that we should accept God's sovereignty and decrees upon

314. Heller, *Let's Face It! The 8 Essential Challenges of Living*, 106–107.
315. We also read about them during the *Kinnot* of the Tisha B'Av service.

> ourselves *with all your soul*.[316] This implies that one must serve God even if it means forfeiting one's life. I used to wonder if I would ever have the privilege of serving God to such a degree. Now that the chance has come to me, shall I not grasp it with joy?"
>
> He then repeated the first verse of the *Shema* – "Hear O Israel, Hashem is our God, Hashem is One" – and he drew out the word *One*, until his soul left him. A heavenly voice was then heard saying, "You are praiseworthy, Rabbi Akiva, for your soul left you as you proclaimed God's Oneness! . . . You are praiseworthy, Rabbi Akiva, for you are ready to enter the life of the World to Come."[317]

What is there to say? Absolutely nothing. This is *hod* within *hod*. Just as Rabbi Akiva accepted the tragedy of losing 24,000 of his students, at this terrible moment, he never forgot the importance of accepting God's will and, until his last dying breath, he sanctified God's oneness.

In addition to the martyrdom of each Sage, there is a remarkable story in the commentary to the ArtScroll Yom Kippur Machzor that also captures pure *hod* within *hod*:

> When the Romans were murdering Rabbi Chananya for teaching Torah publicly, they soaked a Torah scroll and wrapped him in it before setting him on fire. Out of cruelty, they placed water-soaked wool on his chest to prolong his agonizing death. To his horrified daughter and students, Rabbi Chananya said, "The parchment is consumed, but the letters fly up in the air."
>
> The Roman executioner was deeply moved by Rabbi Chananya's holiness and asked, "If I remove the wool from your heart, will I have a share in the World to Come?" Rabbi Chananya promised that he would, whereupon the Roman removed the wet wool and put more wood on the fire, so that the agony would end as soon as possible. Then, the Roman threw himself into the fire and died. A heavenly voice proclaimed, "Rabbi Chananya and the executioner are about to enter the World to Come."[318]

---

316. *Devarim* 6:5.

317. *Berachot* 61b; *Yehushalmi Berachot* 9:5. See also ArtScroll Yom Kippur Machzor, 590–591.

318. ArtScroll Yom Kippur Machzor, 591.

Hod within *hod* can be elusive. We can work at it our entire lives, only to understand its purity in the flash of a moment on our dying day, and finally be able to embrace it as an ennobling attribute. But once we do so and it enters us, we will reflect God's glorious light.

DISCUSSION TOPICS FOR *HOD* WITHIN *HOD*

For adults

1. Do I display sufficient *emunah* to make it through the challenges I face?
2. When I do something special, how important is it to me that my deed be recognized and honored?
3. How do I demonstrate an interest in the lives of those around me?

For children

1. Do I realize that what God does for me is for the best, even if I don't understand it completely at this time?
2. Do any of my friends put other people or groups of people down? What can I do to discourage them from doing so?
3. Can I try to do something nice for someone without telling others (except maybe my parents)?

היום ארבעה ושלושים יום,
שהם ארבעה שבועות וששה ימים, לעומר

(Ha'yom arba'a u'shloshim yom,
she'hem arba'a shavuot v'shisha yamim la'Omer)

"TODAY IS THE THIRTY-FOURTH DAY,
OR FOUR WEEKS AND SIX DAYS, OF THE OMER."

DAY 34

Yesod sh'b'Hod (Bonding within Humility)

Yesod within *hod* is the ability to perceive the essence of another person or situation. *Hod* in its purest form is the polar opposite of jealousy, enmity, anger, hatred, resentment, and arrogance, all of which are rooted in self-centeredness. *Yesod* coupled with *hod* brings an increased emphasis to permanence and bonding with others. When *yesod* within *hod* is added to the mix, relationships are a balanced by a give-and-take dynamic which, in turn, leads to harmonious acceptance. Once *yesod* within *hod* is achieved, satisfaction and contentment abound.

When we have truly established a connection with something outside of ourselves, and when we display genuine humility, we are fully aware at our core that we could never abuse or otherwise harm another person, animal, or object. Humility includes bonding and having respect for other living creatures, as well as for the environment.

The miraculousness of our earthly environment is indescribable: breathable air; water on three-fourths of the earth's surface, providing a natural habitat for enough marine life to feed the entire world's population; land that permits a safe and easier habitat for human and animal life; diverse vegetation that provides sustenance, a means to create more food, as well as astonishing beauty all at the same time; the heavens that provide a sun for warmth and growth, the moon to brighten the darkness; rain for the vegetation; the wonderment of thunder, lightening; and, finally, constellations that are so distant and mysterious that they remind us just how small and dependent we are on the Creator of it all.

As we develop the attribute of *yesod* within *hod*, we begin to perceive a bond with the infinite gifts and all aspects of creation that connect us even more closely to God. Consequently, we become acutely aware of and appreciative of all the gifts that flow to us constantly from the world He created for us. We feel a part of it all, not distinct or distant from it. Because of this appreciation, we are not able to waste, pollute, damage, or harm it. We see God in all of nature, and of course beyond nature, and therefore, we do not want to misuse anything that is His.

So when we recycle, use water carefully, and *never ever* litter the roads, beaches, city parks, sidewalks, or anyplace at all, we demonstrate a heightened sense of *yesod* within *hod*. We want to be humble stewards of the earth and all its precious natural resources. We do not take them for granted. They do not belong to us. The entire world and everything in it belong to God. They are only on loan to us. God watches how we relate to nature. When we respect our natural resources, we demonstrate *yesod* within *hod* in our connection and bonding with the Creator, according to whose will the axis of the world continues to turn. We know that all of God's gifts can be taken from us at any time, and that realization ought to humble us.

THE MALE/FEMALE LANDSCAPE

If you are not married but want to be, or if you are a parent of someone who is not married but wants to be, you may want to read *The Magic Touch* by Gila Manolson, an Accredited Life Coach. The opening tells it all:

> Superglue can join two pieces of a broken plate – or two of your fingers. Similarly, touch – and particularly the "more than casual" kind – will make you feel closer to someone, irrespective of who he or she is and whether a real bond is ever likely to develop between you.
>
> If touch were commercially produced and packaged, the following would be printed on the tube in bold red: "WARNING: Use with extreme caution. Bonds instantly and indiscriminately." The instructions would be equally unequivocal: "Use only after marriage.

> Touch will then express and cement your genuine connection. If used any earlier, touch will generate feelings of closeness with no basis in reality." And that is playing with fire."[319]

Manolson delivers her message with a practical, humorous punch, and her point is that observing the Jewish laws regarding touch between a man and woman (*shomer negiah*) works. We believe that observing *shomer negiah* before marriage and the laws of family purity (*niddah*) after marriage have a huge beneficial by-product. First and foremost, we are listening to and being obedient to God's will. In addition, we believe that doing so increases our ability to display and develop *yesod* within *hod*, a critical attribute for a successful and happy married life.

When a man insists on getting his way on a date, or even in marriage, without any restraint on his libido, that signifies the opposite of *hod*. Why? Because he is doing what he wants, not what God wants. God knows what men and women truly need, which is a deeply significant love and life with their *ezer kinnegdo* – their specially chosen soulmate (*zivug*). God knows that this won't happen if the man is able to demand and expect sexual pleasure anytime he wishes. Hence, the various laws concerning relationship. If these are followed, the outcome is heightened bonding between husband and wife – but it is bonding within humility; it is bonding that shows humble deference to God's will and His wisdom in designing the Jewish way of touch.

A wonderful example of how it is meant to work can be seen in the kind of extraordinary deep relationship, love, and lasting bonding that existed between two of the greatest life partners in the history of humankind: Avraham and Sarah. Their relationship serves as a model for the proper physical, emotional, and spiritual bonding that ought to inspire and guide every couple. How meaningful and beautiful when we recognize *yesod* within *hod* in our relationships with the opposite sex.

UNITY: THE ESSENCE OF *YESOD* WITHIN *HOD*

Marital relationships are all about unity, and unity is the essence of *yesod* within *hod*. Since lack of unity has plagued the Jewish people for centuries

319. Gila Manolson, *The Magic Touch* (Southfield, MI: Targum/Feldheim, 2005), 26.

and led to the destruction of the Temple 2,000 years ago, we should pay extra special attention to this *middah*.

In a quintessential example of disunity among Jews, Yosef was sold into slavery by ten of his brothers. Despite this act, once Yosef became the Viceroy of Egypt, he set up a system to track his brothers – not because he was plotting vengeance, not at all. He realized that God influences every event involving the Jewish people and that the mission assigned to him by God was to insure the survival of his father, brothers, and their families.

Note carefully that Yosef had every justification to disown his brothers. After all, they sold him into slavery, and just prior to that, they wanted to kill him. He could have said, "Siblings like these? Who needs them? Unity?! How can I help contribute to unity after what they did to me? It's all their fault!" But, of course, this is not what he said.

No. Yosef understood that everything is directly from God: his multiple dreams, his brothers' jealousy; his sale into slavery and imprisonment; the dreams of the wine steward and baker; the dreams of the Pharaoh; and his own subsequent meteoric rise within the Egypt government. He also understood with crystal clear vision that God wanted the family of Yaakov to unite. So Yosef humbled himself and received the wisdom and goodness that only God could offer. He realized, looking at the seemingly irrational events of the last twenty-two years, that he was meant to be a conduit for God's will, even if he lacked total clarity about how the specifics would play out. During this period in Egypt, Yosef displayed patience and remained connected to God and his father's teachings at all times.

As a result, Yosef's *emunah* was on the highest of levels, having developed immensely from the time he cried while alone and afraid in a pit full of scorpions and snakes.[320] So Yosef did not need to hold onto any grudges when he confronted his brothers. Yosef had become a vessel for God's will. He did not need to push his own agenda. He merely had to discern if the brothers had done *teshuvah* for the deplorable enmity they displayed towards him. So Yosef set up a situation that would reveal if that had happened. The brothers passed the test. The rest is history – our history.

Yosef displayed *yesod* within *hod*. His bonding with his brothers was a *tikkun*, a restoration of the foundation that would be needed to solve the problem of senseless hatred between Jews.

---

320. *Bereshit* 37:24.

This was the type of foundation and unity that was lacking in the Jewish community during the time of the Second Temple. Therefore, God elected to use the Romans as His "messengers" when He chose to destroy the Temple yet again. This has lead to the current exile, which will continue until we can all do the *tikkun* that will return unity to the Jewish people.

WHERE WE STAND TODAY

Long before the Temple's destruction, the prophets warned us of this calamity. But the people at the time lacked *yesod* within *hod* to take this warning seriously.

What about today? Is it any better? Are the divisions between Jews polarizing us even more? What about us personally? Do we sincerely try to bond with Jews who are different than we are? Can we attempt to cultivate and reveal a sense of belonging to each other, knowing that our common enemies think of us all as the same, despite our own habit of labeling each other?

For the sake of unity, can we focus on our common challenges and goals and on God's plan for us, rather than on our own need to preserve our selfish differences?

Tough questions. A pathway to an answer lies in the cultivation of *yesod* within *hod* – in our relationships with each other and with God.

One of the most important points that Rabbi Arush makes in *The Garden of Emuna* is this:

> *Emuna* isn't activated in its entirety until a person begins a daily personal dialog with Hashem . . . With true *emuna*, any person – by means of simple personal prayer and dialog with Hashem – can transcend any natural limitation and work wonders! . . . Once we become accustomed to praying in every situation, we develop a spiritual sensitivity that is conducive to feeling Hashem's constant presence. When we feel Hashem's presence, we willfully and happily thank Him, speak to Him, and pray to Him all the time. When we're constantly seeing Hashem, He doesn't need to send us wake-up calls of troubles, trials, and tribulations.[321]

---

321. Arush, *The Garden of Emuna*, 32–36.

I cannot underscore the immediate change that can occur in one's life, if one strives each day to achieve this state of relationship with God. When we are bonded with God, and He is the firm foundation of our existence, then our service to Him is elevated, and we along with it.

DISCUSSION TOPICS FOR *YESOD* OF *HOD*

For adults

1. When I pray in synagogue on Shabbat, am I trying to connect to God, or do I mainly go in order to be seen by others or talk to my friends?
2. How do I show that I am genuinely interested in the thoughts and opinions of others?
3. Have I succeeded in bonding with humility to my spouse, my children, and my parents?

For children

1. Am I afraid to express my thoughts or opinions at home or school? What stops me? Do I realize that if I don't express them, then others will find it hard to get to know me better?
2. Do I pray to God in a way that shows that I love Him and that I also want to listen to Him and obey Him?
3. From the way I talk and act, can God see that I listen and obey Him, or might He think I just do what I want to do?

היום חמישה ושלושים יום,
שהם חמישה שבועות, לעומר

(Ha'yom chamisha u'shloshim yom,
she'hem chamisha shavuot la'Omer)

"TODAY IS THE THIRTY-FIFTH DAY, OR FIVE WEEKS, OF THE OMER."

DAY 35

Malchut sh'b'Hod (Leadership/Nobility within Humility)

As we have defined it previously, *hod* is the ability to suspend our own needs and desires in order to focus on receiving the holy lights that exist around us. It is a combination of patience and faith, which enables us to see the beauty and positive aspects of every person and situation despite life's interfering static. When *malchut* combines with *hod*, we are able to uplift relationships and situations to a higher level because *malchut* adds a noble presence – not through a display of ego, arrogance, or superiority, but rather through the very absence of these self-absorbed traits. This *sefirah* combination teaches us how to become vessels to receive the goodness of others, thus revealing God's majestic oneness in the world.

On this day, let us examine the attribute of *malchut* within *hod* as it made itself manifest in the Purim story, with both Mordechai and Queen Esther optimizing their roles as "secret agents" of God.

QUEEN ESTHER AND HER STORY

Megillat Esther recounts the heroic actions of a young queen who personified nobility within humility at the highest levels, and whom God selected to save the Jewish people from annihilation.

Finding herself unwillingly thrust in the role of queen by events orchestrated by Divine Providence, this strikingly beautiful but modest young woman did not reveal who she was and seemingly sought to downplay her role in the palace court. However, Esther (a name which the Talmud[322] says comes from the Hebrew word, *hester*, meaning "to hide") was called into action by her uncle Mordechai, the spiritual leader of the Jews of Persia. He asked her to act boldly to save the lives of all the Persian Jews who had been condemned to death by a royal decree, instigated by the evil minister, Haman.

At first, Esther demurred, pointing out that she could be killed for approaching the king without being summoned (after all, she was one of many wives in his palace). But Mordechai said:

> "Do not imagine in your soul that you will be able to escape in the king's palace any more than the rest of the Jews. For if you persist in keeping silent at a time like this, relief and deliverance will come to the Jews from another place, while you and your father's house will perish. And who knows whether it was just for such a time as this that you attained the royal position!"[323]

Now Esther had to decide – would she play the role she was destined to play, or step aside, with God selecting another to save the Jews?

As we know, God keeps all His promises and He had clearly guaranteed the survival of the Nation of Israel, but at that moment the stakes were high. Haman was bent on nothing short of genocide, and he would not be easily stopped. Esther understood this.

So how did she respond? *Megillat Esther* tells us:

> Then Esther said in reply to Mordechai: "Go, assemble all the Jews that are to be found in Shushan, and fast for me; do not eat or drink

322. *Chullin* 139b.
323. *Megillat Esther* 4:13–14.

> for three days, night or day; And I, with my maids, will fast also. Thus I will come to the king though it is unlawful; and if I perish, I perish."[324]

That was the *one* matter she had control over. She could choose to turn to God and pour out her heart, begging God to save her people.

Did Esther rise to the occasion? Yes, she did. Did she willingly and humbly risk her life and take immediate action? Yes, she did.

Esther recognized and accepted that it is God who determines all outcomes. She knew that God constantly intervenes in world history as well as in our personal lives. We need only make ourselves a vessel by humbly acknowledging God's presence in everything, even though He may appear hidden. This was the mindset that Esther modeled with her request that all Jews fast and beseech God, just as she would.

ESTHER'S ACTIONS AND *HOD*

Esther fasted and prayed and asked all the Jews of Persia to do the same. By these actions, she acknowledged that she, even as a queen, could do nothing. But as a vessel playing a role chosen for her by God, she could ask God to change the outcome.

Let's look at her carefully chosen words as she approached the king to learn the outcome of her humble prayers. *Megillat Esther* reports:

> When the king noticed Queen Esther standing in the courtyard, she found favor in his eyes. The king extended to Esther the gold scepter that was in his hand, and Esther approached and touched the top of the scepter. The king said to her, "What is it for you, O Queen Esther? And what is your petition? [Even if it be] until half the kingdom, it shall be granted you."[325]

Upon hearing this shockingly generous offer, Esther realized that the collective fasting and prayers of the Jews of Shushan and her own had been answered by God. She was acutely aware that she had found such favor in the eyes of King Ahasuerus only as a result of Divine intervention.

---

324. Ibid., 4:15–16.
325. Ibid., 5:2–3.

But Esther spoke humbly before the mortal king, "If it please the king, let the king and Haman come today to the banquet that I have prepared for him."[326]

This was a simple, modest request and the king seemed happy to comply. During the wine feast, the king again asked, "What is your request? It shall be granted you. And what is your petition? [Even if it be] until half the kingdom, it shall be fulfilled."[327]

Again she humbly responded, "My request and my petition: If I have found favor in the king's eyes, and if it pleases the king to grant my request and to fulfill my petition, let the king and Haman come to the banquet that I shall prepare for them, and tomorrow I shall fulfill the king's word."[328] Another simple request, though by now the king may have been wondering why Haman was also getting invited to these social events.

The next twenty-four hours saw a sequence of astonishing events orchestrated by none other than God (whose name never appears in the entire *Megillah*). And the outcome upended Haman's plot, bringing salvation for the Jews.

This teaches us that God can do anything, and the worst calamities can be reversed in the blink of an eye. The Exodus from Egypt is the prime example – after stubbornly holding onto the Jewish slaves through nine plagues, the Pharaoh could not wait to get rid of all them overnight when all the firstborn of Egypt died and he sent them out laden with gold and valuables. So, too, many years later in Persia:

King Ahasuerus suddenly developed insomnia and asked for the royal book of chronicles to be read to him. He was thus reminded that Mordechai the Jew helped to save his life much earlier and received no honors for his deed. At this exact moment, Haman arrived to ask the king for permission to hang Mordechai, but before he could get his request out, the king posed this question, "What should be done for the man whom the king desires to honor?" Because of his complete *lack of humility*, Haman thought that the king was referring to him, and he proposed a grand scheme – the honoree riding in royal attire through adoring crowds.

326. Ibid., 5:4.
327. Ibid., 5:6.
328. Ibid., 5:7–8.

The king approved but Haman was appalled to learn that the intended honoree was none other than his archenemy Mordechai, the Jew.[329]

After these unexpected events, Haman found himself at the second feast arranged by Queen Esther, where the king again asked her to make a request and again affirmed that she can have up to half of the entire kingdom. Finally, Queen Esther got to the crux of the matter. She had obviously heard about Haman's recent embarrassment in having to lead a horse carrying Mordechai in royal garb throughout the town, and she realized these events could only have come from God answering her prayers.

She now went for the close, but again, listen to her humble language:

> "If I have found favor in your eyes, O king, and if it pleases the king, let my life be granted to me as my request and my people as my petition. For we have been sold, I and my people, to be destroyed, to be slain and to be exterminated . . ."[330]

The king reacted with rage; he demanded to know who would plot against his queen. And to this Esther responded: "A man who is an adversary and an enemy! This wicked Haman!"[331]

The king was so furious he stomped out of the room, and God again manipulated the situation. While trying to beg Queen Esther to spare his life, Haman stumbled and fell on her couch, which appeared to the king as an attack upon her.

At that exact moment one of the chamberlains suggested, "Furthermore, the gallows which Haman made for Mordechai – who spoke good for the king – is standing at Haman's house; it is fifty cubits high." The king's immediate reaction was: "Hang him on it." The very next verse declares: "So they hanged Haman on the gallows that he had prepared for Mordechai, and the king's anger abated."[332]

Hollywood could never come up with drama like this. And yet it is recorded history! Quite a turn of events in just twenty-four hours.

---

329. Ibid., 6:1–14.
330. Ibid., 7:3–4.
331. Ibid., 7:6.
332. Ibid., 7:9–10.

ESTHER VS. HAMAN

Esther the Queen displayed *malchut* within *hod* at the highest of levels. *Malchut* is the natural outcome when one has mastered the previous six *sefirot*. Esther displayed love (*chesed*) to Mordechai, and even to the king. She showed strength and restraint (*gevurah*) in all her actions. She did not demand half the kingdom. She simply stayed focused on saving the Jewish people from annihilation. She balanced (*tiferet*) her love of the Jewish people and her bonding (*yesod*) with them against her need to respect the king, her husband. She demonstrated endurance (*netzach*) in her efforts to save the Jews and merited that her son Darius would become king and permit the rebuilding of the Second Temple.

Esther believed with a complete heart that her fasts and prayers would reach God, who could change any factor He desired. Instead of Mordechai being hanged on the gallows Haman built, Haman was hanged by permission of the very king who had formerly permitted Haman to draw the "lots" to determine the day when all the Jews in 127 provinces would be annihilated. Months later, his sons shared that fate.

In stark contrast to Esther, Haman displayed arrogance and complete lack of any form of humility. This ultimately did him in. His ego drove his need for power, approval, and adoration, and his megalomaniacal Jew-hatred drove him to try to destroy all the Jews in Persia. Queen Esther's call to all Jews for three days of fasting and prayer was the turning point. God heard and responded. Salvation came within twenty-four hours.

Ever since then, the Book of Esther in which all these events are recorded has been read on Purim by Jews the world over. Each year we fast for a half-day to remember the original fast of Esther and the Persian Jews. Each year we give money to the poor. Each year we deliver gifts of food to our friends to emphasize the unity of our people and our responsibility one for another. Each year we hide our faces behind "masks" to remind ourselves that while God may appear "hidden" to us, He is always there, and that sometimes evil is "masked" as goodness, but we must always remember to see through these masks to discover the truth.[333]

---

333. Another great commentary on the use of masks on Purim is that we should always remember not to "mask" or hide from our true inner self.

HAMAN AND HITLER

Like Haman, Hitler was megalomaniacal. His delusions of grandeur included world domination by the Nazis and the German master race. Believing to the core that "the bigger the lie the better," Hitler projected his own demonic plans for world domination onto the Jews. He publicized fraudulent, Jew-bashing accusations again and again through a fiercely controlled Nazi propaganda machine. His efforts stopped at nothing, including a reliance on "The Protocols of the Elders of Zion" – a mendacious document of Russian origin which the Nazis propagated as fact.[334] And like Haman, Hitler was dedicated to the total annihilation of the Jews.

Apparently, these similarities were not lost on the Nazis themselves. After the Nuremberg Trials, several high-ranking Nazis were sentenced to death by hanging. As *Newsweek* magazine reported, moments before Nazi Julius Streicher was hanged on October 16, 1946, "He stared at the witnesses facing the gallows and shouted 'Purimfest, 1946!'"

Why would a high-ranking Nazi mention Purim moments before he was hanged on the gallows, just as Haman was hanged on the gallows 2,300 of years earlier? And how do all these events relate to the *sefirah* of *hod* and our need to live a life of faith and humility?

Rabbi Warren Goldstein, the chief rabbi of South Africa, answers this question with an astonishing insight in a *Jerusalem Post* article:[335]

After the Nuremberg Trials, eleven Nazis were sentenced to death, but Hermann Goering committed suicide in jail. Therefore, ten Nazis, including Streicher, were hanged, just like Haman's ten sons were hanged at the end of *Megillat Esther*. Rabbi Goldstein writes: "Amazingly, Streicher saw the historic link between the Nazi genocide and Haman, who, like the Nazis, also intended to wipe out every Jew – man, woman, and child." But that's only the beginning of the irony.

Rabbi Goldstein goes on to reveal "an even deeper irony, which

334. Despite our hope that the world would learn the lessons of the Holocaust, there are still avowed Jew-haters in the 21st century who still today insist that these fraudulent pages are factual in order to "mask" their own virulent anti-Semitism, and the world as a whole has yet to denounce it.

335. Warren Goldstein, "Purimshpiel, 1946: The Purim Link between Nazi Germany and a Nuclear Iran," *The Jerusalem Post*, March 2, 2011, 23.

Streicher was certainly not aware of." When *Megillat Esther* lists the names of Haman's ten sons, three of the letters in these names are written in smaller font than the rest of the text – *tav*, *shin*, and *zayin* – and one letter is written in larger font – *vav*. What do these unusually-sized letters signify? Rabbi Goldstein explains:

> The large *vav* is numerically 6, corresponding to the sixth millennium; the small *tav*, *shin* and *zayin* are numerically 707; together, these numbers refer to the 707th year of the sixth millennium – in other words, the Jewish year 5707, which corresponds to 1946, the year in which these ten high-ranking Nazis were hanged. Thus, the unusually sized letters – *vav*, *tav*, *shin*, and *zayin* – found in the names of Haman's ten sons allude to the year of the execution of these 10 Nazi war criminals . . . What is further fascinating is that they were sentenced on the 1st of October, in the days between Rosh Hashana and Yom Kippur of 1946, and hanged on the 16th of October, which that year came out on Hoshana Rabba, which, according to the *Zohar*, is the day that judgment of the world is finalized.

GOD'S PRESENCE IN HISTORY

Rabbi Goldstein then asks, "What does all this mean?" And he answers:

> Through her bold and dramatic life, Queen Esther showed us that God's presence permeates our history. She understood that her fate and destiny – and that of her people – were in God's hands. Esther taught us that sometimes God interacts with the world through open miracles as we experienced with the ten plagues and the splitting of the sea during the Exodus from Egypt. But mostly He does so in a hidden way, as happened during the time of Purim, when the miraculous salvation of the Jewish people was just as great as the open miracles, and yet occurred in a way that was hidden from view and seemingly "natural" . . . [But] Queen Esther's message is that we must not relate to these events in natural terms alone; we need to see God's presence in everything, even though He is hidden. Esther's message applies to us as individuals in our day-to-day lives, where, as Judaism teaches, God is involved and interested in every aspect of life; and it also applies to Jewish destiny and history at large, which

> powerfully demonstrate God's involvement in the affairs of people and the direction of civilizations. The supernatural miracles of the establishment of the State of Israel and the rebirth of Torah learning throughout the world following the devastation of the Holocaust are but two examples of many which show God's power and presence in everything.[336]

Rabbi Goldstein says it so well. We know that God has worked miracles for us throughout our history. But our transgressions have cost us. We no longer merit prophets who communicate with God on our behalf, and we no longer have the Temple (due to a lack of *hod*). But, if we choose to do so, we still are able to sense God's Presence even when it is hidden from view.

Revealing what is hidden is part of our mission in the world. And that also means our own hidden side where lies our potential to achieve *malchut* (kingship, leadership, sovereignty, dignity, nobility). For some of us, our own potential for leadership is hidden even from us. We need to uncover it, and the Omer count is an excellent way to begin. For some of us, our potential leadership is hidden from others. We may be hiding it purposefully for a variety of complex reasons. But certainly it exists. A good opportunity to assess where and how we display dignity and personal sovereignty is to look at those areas in which God tests us.

Queen Esther passed her test and met her destiny. What about us? Let's reflect on all the areas we have explored in the seven *sefirah* combinations within *hod*. Have we been able to display *derech eretz* in passing our tests? Was our *emunah* elevated and strengthened by the "bitter waters" of Mara that we were given to drink, or was our *emunah* shaken? Did our life tests bring us closer to our true self and to the realization that we are part of God, or did they distance us further? It is clear that our answers to these questions matter to God, and that He wishes us to master *malchut* within *hod* and display it as consistently as possible.

---

336. Goldstein, Ibid.

DISCUSSION TOPICS FOR *MALCHUT* WITHIN *HOD*

For adults

1. Do others consider me humble?
2. What does my spouse think of my *derech eretz*?
3. Can I name two actions I took in the last two months to demonstrate to my children that *derech eretz* is a highly important value?

For children

1. Did I treat everyone I met today with *derech eretz*? If not, what can I do differently tomorrow?
2. What is the best example of a high level of *derech eretz* that I saw in the actions of one of my parents this week?
3. What does it mean that God has a "Watchful Eye and Attentive Ear," and that all deeds are recorded in His book?

WEEK SIX

Yesod

(Bonding)

OVERVIEW

Yesod (Bonding)

Yesod is the healthy facility to bond with others, but it is even more than that. It is also peace and grounding. These are very important outgrowths of healthy bonding and solid foundation.

As noted previously, in his book *Endless Light*, Rabbi Aaron provides a useful summary of the first six *sefirot*, including *yesod*. There he points out that the triad of *chesed*, *gevurah*, and *tiferet* are attributes that direct our behavior after consideration of *our own* needs and interests. But the triad of *netzach*, *hod*, and *yesod* is vital for modifying our behavior to meet the needs and interests of *others* whom we love. Rabbi Aaron writes:

> *Netzach* means "victory" or "conquest." It's associated with assertion, dominion, endurance. It's the drive to overcome obstacles and make things happen. *Hod*, on the other hand, is the ability to submit, retreat, let go, and surrender. *Yesod* means "foundation." This principle ensures that what you do is grounded in reality, like the foundation of a building, which anchors it into the ground.

Expanding on *yesod* – our work for this Week Six – Rabbi Aaron adds:

> *Yesod* is identified also with peace, because it negotiates a peaceful relationship between your ideals and what is practical and possible. It integrates assertion with surrender so you will move forward with both confidence and caution, knowing how much you can stretch borders without breaking them . . . In terms of relationships, *netzach*,

> *hod*, and *yesod* guide you in considering how much of your giving your partner can take.[337]

Rabbi Aaron reminds us that the two balancing principles are *tiferet* and *yesod*. They create harmony in living and in loving, for "when you live and love in accordance with *tiferet*, you are true to yourself, when you live and love in accordance with *yesod*, you enjoy peace with others."

THE SIX-PLY CORD

The "foundation" and grounding aspect of *yesod* occurs when one weaves all six of the *sefirot* into a six-ply cord that creates the potential for honest, mutual, mature, and grounded bonding in all types of relationships. *Yesod* is a cornerstone that produces balance of mutuality and respect, both essential to the forming of long-term, enduring relationships, whether with family members, friends, or others.

With proper respect, communication, love and care, such relationships can change and grow as each person matures in life. Whether between self and God, self and other, or self and self, such bonding is more precious than any material possession.

It is a foundation that firmly stands – *yesod* is intended to be eternal – because bonding, integration, and loyalty have been achieved. With *yesod*, one is attached to the other in total devotion and peace.

Every person needs bonding to grow. The first bonding we know is between mother and child. Later, additional bonds are added between father and child, brothers and sisters, husband and wife, between close friends, between army buddies in wartime, between relatives, and most importantly, between us and God. Each of these bonds provides "generativity," the transference to the next generation of important social values and way of life. A breach in these bonds disrupts peace and shatters relationships.

We are counseled, "So great is peace that God's Name is Peace . . . God found no vessel to hold blessing for Israel other than peace."[338] It behooves us, then, to understand this important *sefirah* of *yesod* which is so essential to peace.

Yesod connects the deeply rooted feelings of one to another in a manner

---

337. Aaron, *Endless Light*, 65–67.

338. Derech Eretz, *Perek HaShalom* 11 and *Uktzin* 3:12.

that creates commitment, permanence, loyalty, and devotion that deepen and grow stronger over time. *Yesod* forms a physical, emotional, mental, and spiritual channel between people (and between ourselves and God) through which each becomes a permanent part of the other.

Without the proper proportions of each *sefirah*, the cord that bonds one *sefirah* to the other may lack permanence and may snap after a time. Rabbi Yaakov Haber writes in his booklet, *Sefiros*, that *yesod* is the channel through which all the higher *middot* interact with the world:

> Therefore, *yesod* is the means of embedding *kedushah* in the world . . . *yesod* creates a relationship between God and His world. It is *yesod* which allows each individual to change the world and make it a better place.[339]

Acting with *yesod* builds a foundation upon which we grow in an increasingly more expansive, permanent, integrated, and connected manner. When achieved, we have a sense of completeness, balance, trust, security, and a kindred feeling that defines all our interactions in life. From such bonding comes the harmony that brings people together in oneness with God and filters down to all our relationships, as well as clarifying our mission in life.

This is especially true for us Jews as we struggle to maintain our nation in this ongoing exile. And for this we have special advice from nature.

In Chapter Four of *Perek Shirah*, the daily song of none other than the bat is this verse from the Prophet Isaiah, "Comfort, comfort My people says your God."[340] What do we learn from the bat? How to act in *galut*:

> Unlike other birds, the bat does not fly to warmer climates in winter. It hibernates and huddles with others to share body warmth. Such behavior comforts the Jewish people in the winter of exile. We do not flee from our heritage, nor do we isolate ourselves from our fellow Jews. Our Torah goes with us wherever we are, and we derive comfort from our unity with our brethren who remain loyal to the word of God.[341]

---

339. Yaakov Haber and David Sedley, *Sefiros* (Israel: TorahLab, 2009), 110.

340. *Yeshayahu* 40:1.

341. Scherman, *Perek Shirah: The Song of the Universe*, 76.

Yesod shows us that with the right foundation and bonding, we can endure and survive even 2,000 years of exile and countless efforts to eradicate every last living Jew. Why? Because we are connected as one with the Creator of the Universe. We are fused. All we need do is choose to be bonded to God and our Jewish brethren.

It is up to us. God gives us that free choice. When we choose to bond with the Creator of the Universe and follow the *mitzvot* He gave us in the Torah, we then "choose life" and survive against immense odds. All we need to do is follow His clear and simple instructions: "You shall observe the words of this covenant, so that you will succeed in all that you do."[342]

YOSEF, THE SIXTH SHEPHERD

Yosef, the sixth of our Seven Shepherds, is called "*HaTzaddik*" because he lived for twenty-two years as the only Jew in Egypt, amid all types of idolatry, temptation, and moral debauchery, and yet he remained totally committed and loyal to the teachings of his father, Yaakov. Yosef represents the foundation aspect of *yesod*, due to his unswerving devotion to our traditions.

Rather than participate in an immoral act with the wife of his master, Potiphar, he ran away, provoked her ire and was thrown into prison as a result. After his release and elevation to the second highest position in Egypt, he raised his two sons, Ephraim and Menashe, according to the teachings of his father Yaakov. This was a mammoth achievement – not to become assimilated despite being alone in an alien and dominant culture.

When Yosef was again reunited with his father, he displayed the bonding aspect of *yesod* by not sharing the story of his disappearance. He understood that to "tattle" on his brothers would have killed Yaakov and harmed the unity of the family. Yosef acted with *yesod* to protect the only Jewish family in the world at that time.

We constantly revisit Yosef's story to reinforce the important lessons of survival in exile, especially resisting assimilation and preserving the Jewish family.[343]

The most vulnerable are our youth. How to keep our children bonded to the foundation of Torah Judaism is such a critical issue that *Jewish*

342. *Devarim* 29: 8.

343. Kitov, *The Book of Our Heritage*, Vol. 2, 684.

Action devoted an entire edition to the topic in Summer 2011. The cover story, "Getting Their Attention: Keeping Our Kids on the Derech" was written by Rabbi Steven Burg, the international director of NCSY, who has worked with youth for more than twenty years. I quote his words here because his advice for bringing greater peace, grounding, and bonding into every family is priceless:

- *Reintroduce God into our schools, homes, and relationships*: Some people lead ostensibly Torah-observant lives . . . But they are not motivated by the desire to lead a spiritually rich and meaningful life . . . Judaism is first and foremost about one's relationship with the Almighty, not about fitting into a social group . . . The concept of God's existence is neglected, barely even mentioned in our day schools and *yeshivot*. While we spend much time teaching Jewish texts, we spend way too little time emphasizing *emunah* and *bitachon* – the very foundations upon which Judaism is built . . . A rabbi I know recently wrote about this very problem [noting that] while his Bubbie never studied the commentaries on *Tehillim*, which his daughters all currently learn and know, his daughters cannot cry over *Tehillim* the way his Bubbie did.
- *Learn Torah with your teens*: As teenagers are keen social observers, they need to see that their parents value Torah learning. Parents should take time to learn with their children. By studying together, children absorb their parents' passion and love for Torah . . . The trick may be in finding the aspect of Torah that speaks to your child at this particular stage of his or her life.
- *Invest religious life with joy*: Is going to *shul* a chore? Is Shabbat all about what we can't do rather than about what it gives us? . . . If we recognize the *mitzvot* as gifts and opportunities, and encourage our children to have a more profound understanding of them, they will be transformed from rote motions to precious opportunities to help us connect with God.
- *Make holidays and Jewish rituals relevant, meaningful and exciting*: Even with off-tune voices, *zemirot* bring life and beauty to Shabbat tables. At our Shabbat table, my wife and I give each child (and guest) a choice to either present a *devar Torah*, sing a Jewish song, tell a Jewish story, or discuss a mitzvah he or she plans to focus on during the upcoming week . . .

- *Teach the value of genuine prayer*: Our *yeshivot* teach young children about the mechanics of and basic meaning behind *tefillah*. However, as children grow and mature, the topic of *tefillah* is rarely revisited. The result is that oftentimes a 15-year-old retains a third grader's understanding of the concept of prayer. This imbalance causes many teens to regard prayer as a burdensome obligation instead of a unique opportunity to develop an ongoing dialogue with God . . . It is important for every Jew to develop his own personal relationship with God. Even the *Kohen Gadol* . . . had to offer daily personal sacrifices in addition to the communal sacrifices he offered on behalf of the entire Jewish people. This continuous personal interaction ensured that the *Kohen Gadol* maintained his own ongoing relationship with God. If the *Kohen Gadol*, who spent every day in the Temple had to constantly renew his relationship with God, shouldn't we, who are daily occupied with mundane things, recharge our spiritual batteries?
- *Embrace unconditional love*: [When] the path a child chooses does not fit the dreams and plans that his or her parents had hoped for . . . it is critical that parents refrain from judging their child and continue to demonstrate their unconditional love. During a recent visit to Israel, I met with an influential rabbi who told me about his child who was struggling religiously. Consequently, this rav traveled to the *kever* of a *tzaddik* where he fervently recited *Tehillim* for two days. The rabbi looked me squarely in the eye and said, "You probably assume I went to the *kever* to *daven* for my son. Really, I was davening to the Almighty for myself, to give me the strength and patience to continue to love and support my son." We may not always agree with the choices our children may make, but we must remember that they will always be our children. Furthermore, we must ensure that they know we are always there for them, even when we disagree with their life choices.[344]

344. Steven Burg, "Getting Their Attention: Keeping Our Kids on the Derech," *Jewish Action*, Summer 2011, 22–24.

RAISING CHILDREN IN THE TWENTY-FIRST CENTURY

"Difficult" is a mild word to describe what it is to be a parent today. Raising children in the twenty-first century with the easy access and availability of today's technological advancements at the fingertips of most youth is a challenge not faced by prior generations. The report card of the impact is mixed.

I observed this during a lunchtime scene at a restaurant, where two adolescent girls were eating with their parents. For 90 percent of the meal, the girls were texting on their cell phones. Not a word was uttered about it by the parents. The girls only spoke to each other, but not very often, as most of the time they spent glued to their respective phones. It occurred to me that perhaps the girls were modeling behavior they saw at home, with their parents sending emails from their "smart phones" at dinnertime.

The current unprecedented explosion of new technological means of communication affects all ages, genders, and religious orientations: whether it is television (invented only sixty years ago), or movies (now able to be downloaded and played on a computer or phone so one doesn't even need to leave his or her home to go to a theater), or computers (now totally portable and featherweight), or electronic e-books that are read on especially designed tablets (which don't permit the reader to write in the margins to record a thought or reaction, or fold a page of a message that is especially relevant for one's life), or digital cameras that store the images on a disc (from which they are seldom printed, put in a frame, and placed on a bookshelf to help us relive the moment), or mobile phones with capabilities to compute as well as speak and text. This list continues to grow at an accelerating rate each week, suggesting that it is only the beginning. More is coming, but where is it taking us?

These technological innovations, when applied without boundaries, seem to be taking us away from a psychological principle of huge significance – that of being "here and now" as opposed to being "over there" or "all over." As noted by family counseling expert D.C. Briggs, whenever we are overly busy, it cancels our presence in the here and now. Every day this happens in our homes is a lost opportunity for developing meaningful bonding (*yesod*) within our family.

Consider this fictional, but unfortunately typical, home scene:

There is no doubt that Racheli loves her children very much, but where is her focus at breakfast? While braiding little Sarah's hair, she absentmindedly says "Uh-huh" to the story little David is telling, as she stops to take a few gulps of coffee, pour cereal for young Benny when he joins the table, and then start to make the sandwiches the kids will take to school. When husband Sam, who also no doubt loves his family, walks in, he checks his emails on his "smart phone" and returns a few phone calls. At one point, Racheli and Sam do sit down at the table with the kids, and little Sarah starts to tell her family a story about her baby doll, but Racheli interrupts with: "Oh really, Sarah'le? David, please lean over your bowl when you eat, and Benny you are getting crumbs all over the place. Sam did you remember to call the plumber and is he coming today? Oh no, you spilled, now you have to change your shirt and hurry so you are not late for the bus." Sound familiar?

I cherish the wisdom in Briggs's conclusion:

> Unintentionally, not realizing the importance of encounter, we buzz, buzz, buzz. Deep involvement in "all-*thereness*" cancels our "all-*hereness*." Few of us live in the present with focused attention. Locked in the past or concentrating on the future, we are not in the present, which is, after all, the only time we actually have. We try to be everywhere at once. Then, in a sense, we are nowhere.[345]

Every distraction we remove gives us time for our children, for our spouses, for our aging parents, for God. And, therefore, each of us needs to ask, "Does my behavior give priority to things and schedules, or to human beings?"

The good news is that, according to our Sages, technological advancements will accelerate prior to the coming of Mashiach.[346] The bad news is that, until the Mashiach comes, these technological advancements appear to be wreaking havoc with the development and maintenance of interpersonal bonding.

Further, the reality that many people are "plugged in" all day long and much of the night has had the undesirable effect of interfering with their daily quiet time where they might listen to their inner voice. Perhaps there is a need to be "unplugged" for at least some reasonable amount of time

---

345. Briggs, p. 64.
346. Zohar 1:116b–118b.

each day. The twenty-first century lifestyle seldom carves out spaces for reflection, contemplation, and assimilation of an ever-increasing amount of information.

Can any of us remember lying on the grass as children and looking up at the clouds passing by ever so slowly for what seemed like an hour? We imagined shapes. We breathed in fresh air. We thought. We dreamed. We shared our thoughts with a brother or sister or the neighbor next door. Does anyone do this anymore?

It is almost unthinkable for most people to have their mobile phones turned off. Almost everyone checks the email or voice mail at least twice a day; some check it every ten minutes or even more frequently. There are homes where the parents are on the Internet almost twenty-four hours a day. There are homes where every member of the family has an individual television and/or own computer – in his or her room.

At the present time, the influx of all of these stimuli does not seem to be conducive to greater bonding between self and other, self and self, or self and God. While many sources of Torah learning are more broadly available than ever before, it is unclear whether this has resulted in a heightened ability to bond with the Creator of the world. Things might change, but, at the present time, the trend does not seem to be towards increased *yesod* in fundamentally important relationships and precepts. So what is the antidote?

Rabbi Israel Lashak, regional director of Southwest NCSY, reminds both parents and teachers:

> The personal relationship counts. Young people today live in a world of texting and Facebook, where a boyfriend can drop a girlfriend via a text. They've become used to virtual relationships. We have to give them genuine, real-life relationships – take them out and play soccer and basketball, make a bonfire, tell stories. Instead of talking, let them talk. Teens don't often get to talk about the issues that matter to them the most. They want and often need to discuss their feelings, hopes, and fears.[347]

347. Brenner, Bayla Sheva, "Reaching the iPod Generation," *Jewish Action*, Summer 2011, p. 32.

Rabbi Lashak continues:

> Shabbat in a faraway place is very powerful . . . Lighting Shabbat candles, singing *zemirot*, and learning Torah in a foreign environment allows these kids to get off the treadmill of the daily grind and appreciate more deeply that we are unique among the nations and have a wonderful moral mission to mankind . . . [For example] a day school teen who had become disillusioned with Judaism attended NCSY's Eurotrip under a lot of parental pressure. The trip included visits to Spain, Portugal, Gibraltar, Italy, and Israel. During Tishah B'Av, we actually sat right near the Arch of Titus in Rome. We followed the Rambam's life path from Cordoba all the way to Tiberias. This was an incredible experience for him. He had found religion boring and suffocating; the trip made it relevant and alive. At the close of the trip, this boy, who had before stopped keeping Shabbat and *kashrut*, told me he wants to learn in a yeshivah in Israel. It's been four years and he's still learning there.[348]

The bottom line: The rich garden of face-to-face interpersonal relationships must be replanted, watered, weeded, cultivated, and continually maintained if we want to harvest *yesod* in our lifetimes. We must set borders on the disruptions and distraction of today's technology, so that we can plant deep roots in the garden of *yesod* that will bring meaning and fulfillment in our relationships and promise of opportunities for peace that lasts.

SPECIAL TEEN ISSUES

From the alarming statistics that we referenced on Day 2, when we discussed *gevurah* within *chesed*, it is clear that many of today's adolescents and teens constantly struggle with "substance" abuse (whether of drugs, alcohol, nicotine, food, games, gambling, or electronic devices) as they try to assert their strong, sometimes misplaced, drive for independence from their parents. They continually experience the crushing pressure of peers which they are too weak to withstand, especially in light of their own need for acceptance and self-definition that every youth struggles to attain.

348. Ibid.

When adolescents and teens face these temptations, peer pressure is a pervasive influence on the outcome of their individual choices of "yes, I will" or "no, I won't," especially when faced with enticements that carry the potential for harmful outcomes. *Yesod* – bonding with a solid ethical and moral foundation in alignment with God's will and light, and bonding with parents whose feet are solidly and lovingly planted on the ground – provides the lifeboat with which to traverse these sometime rough waters.

The incursion of technology into the lives of many families is a relatively new phenomenon. And it is up to the parents not to allow this invasion to take over and conquer family bonds. If parents are inaccessible and not truly "present" for their children (because they are multitasking or on the cell phone or checking emails themselves), they diminish opportunities to intervene and positively help their children. This kind of intervention requires daily guidance in order to sustain moral values, a strong connection to God and primary and secondary relationships – all that makes up the interconnectivity of *yesod* within all aspects of life.

Technology can kidnap our children by keeping them hypnotized and "linked in" with local peers and strangers a world away. If our children are "tweeting" and "texting" and linked at all times with their Facebook "friends," the opportunities for parents to substantively influence and nourish them is significantly undermined. Children can be lost to a hi-tech addiction and consequently ignorant of the moral, ethical, and spiritual paths of "right" and "wrong." They can become like a horse wearing blinders for the rest of their lives.

Inherently, there is nothing wrong with technology. Everything is from God. He gave the talent to technological geniuses who came up with these inventions and applications. But the use of this technology must be controlled, monitored, and evaluated for the "good" and "bad." And every parent must engage in this evaluation and wisely define the borders for their children and every member of their family, including themselves. Remember, there is only a small window of opportunity to influence children – and it is while they're young.

To look on the positive side, technology makes learning more accessible if we make the right choices. With technological advances, no matter where we live, there are opportunities to see and hear live motivational and educational events. For example: the celebration of the completion of the Daf Yomi cycle; the transmission of a variety of *shiurim* and interviews with knowledgeable and wise rabbis on a variety of topics; historical educational videos about Holocaust Remembrance Day, Yom HaZikaron, Yom HaAtzma'ut and others; moving messages on various topics such as Jewish unity, the threat of Iran and the efforts to delegitimize Israel, and the like. Needless to say, such positives can be harvested from technology if we know how to be selective and how to safeguard against its negative effects.

Indeed, it is hard to imagine that a concentration camp could be built in the twenty-first century and not be filmed on someone's cell phone and shared around the world within days with millions of viewers, as opposed to the hush-hush environment that permitted the perpetration of these atrocities only seventy-five years ago.

If technology were to be bounded within appropriate time restraints and regulated by the right use of balance of *chesed*, *gevurah*, *tiferet*, *netzach* and *hod* in a manner uniquely tailored for each person's makeup, it could lead to greater Jewish unity. It could also lead to greater Jewish identification through vehicles such as Jerusalem On Line University, which reaches students all over world via an on-line curriculum. Yes, if properly channeled, it could contribute to the spread of Torah learning at lightning speed and in monumental proportions. It could also make it easier to expose anti-Semitism for what it is.

But – and it's a big but – it is up to each of us to determine what direction the technological revolution is going to take and how it is going to affect our families, our schools, our communities and our nation. If we aren't proactive, technology can lead to the depletion of our collective strength through the weakening of our bonds with each other as Jews and concomitantly create a greater pull towards assimilation and identification with the dominant cultures that encroach on our lives so easily. Ultimately, this will lead to a weakening of our bond with God, the one relationship we most need.

Technology can be likened to the staff which turned into a snake and then back into a staff. God instructed Moshe to throw his staff down and it turned into a snake, but then He instructed Moshe to pick up the snake "by its tail" and it once again turned back into a staff.[349] That is the image today's technology brings to mind – if properly handled by us, it need not be harmful.

We know that increasingly rapid technological advancements are the

349. *Shemot* 4:1–5.

precursor to the Mashiach. We know the Mashiach will come soon. We know that the Jewish people, as a whole, will make it. But we do not know whether or not, we, as individual Jews, will make it. Our ability to do so will be facilitated by our dexterity to grasp something potentially harmful by its tail, and not its head, and turn it back into a staff of *yesod* – the foundation of who we are and what we stand for.

OUR FOUNDATION

What is the source of our foundation? What binds us together?

Is it the hundreds of daily text messages we send to our "friends?" Is it the cell phone glued to our ear while we simultaneously feed our child? Is it our favorite, just-can't-miss-it, TV show? Is it the five hours or more a day attached to our computers, responding instantly to each email that compels us to respond? Is it a job that consumes the vast majority of our resources? Is it the need to be seen and heard, be popular and accepted?

Or, is it, perhaps, some other, more worthy endeavors and relationships? Is it the moments free of hi-tech we have carved out to take care of our spiritual and physical health? Is it the fixed schedule for learning Torah? Is it the time we have dedicated to be with God (our Lord, Master, King, and Savior) whom we invite into our thoughts, speech, and actions every day? Is it the talks we regularly have with our spouses about meaningful topics? Is it the quality and quantity of time we spend with our children on a regular and consistent basis? Is it the work we put into having meaningful relationships with our parents? Is it the daily reality check (*cheshbon hanefesh*) we do to assess our behavior and the health of our souls?

During this week of *yesod*, let's evaluate how we spend the increments of time that compose our day, and let's honestly answer these questions. I know that most all of us "say" that the most important things are our family, our health, and God, or some variation of that order. But do we really "walk the talk?"

Consider this wise adage: "Genuine encounter is simply focused attention,"[350] and put it to use. Practice focusing your attention onto whatever you are doing at the moment, right now, and make certain it's worthwhile. If you are praying, turn off all electronic devices and focus on establishing a relationship with God. If you are eating dinner with your family, do not

350. Briggs, *Your Child's Self-Esteem*, 64.

answer any phone calls and do not multitask while eating, but rather focus your attention on this dinner "encounter." If you are working out, do that one thing and enjoy the boost of health you are giving yourself.

Take this week of *yesod* to apply this across the board, since bonding and healthy encounters with all that is truly important is one of the most important keys to living a life of fulfillment. In so doing, draw upon the inspiration of the exceptional role models in the Jewish tradition who have mastered *yesod* in their relationship with God, with their spouses, with others in their immediate family, and with themselves:

- Avraham and Sarah were joint partners in their work to preach to a pagan world about one God. They were so much in love with each other and at one with God. They spoke to God and were loved by Him. They were grounded in the *yesod* of their mission, both in their life's work and in their faithful service to God.
- Yaakov and Rachel had an immediate and lifelong bond. Not even Rachel's untimely death could affect it. Later when Yaakov and Esav met, it is the children he had with Rachel that he put last in the event Esav was planning to kill his family upon their meeting. Yes, Yaakov and Rachel plumbed the depth of *yesod* with each other, with their family, and with the family of *Bnei Yisrael*.
- Yehuda, the fourth of the sons of Leah, aligned with and defended Binyamin, the youngest son of Rachel, and assumed responsibility for protecting his life. This foundational bonding was a *tikkun* and contributed to bringing about ultimate family unity in the house of Yaakov.
- *Bnei Yisrael* expressed *yesod* between themselves and God when they said, *na'aseh v' nishma* ("we will do and we will hear"). In other words, they said that we will fulfill all the *miztvot* even while we strive to find the deepest meaning contained within each mitzvah. This was the ultimate expression of *yesod* between God and humankind, then and now.

We have been in exile for nearly 2,000 years since the Romans destroyed the Second Temple in 70 CE. That exile will end with the coming of the Mashiach, the ingathering of the exiles to the Land of Israel, the rebuilding of the Temple in Jerusalem, and the ushering in of 1,000 years of utopia when the world will act as God had hoped we would act from the creation of man.

How can we help bring the Mashiach? We can master *yesod* in our lives. Bonding in loving and lasting relationships is the rock foundation and it expresses, in a concrete way, our attempt to emulate God's oneness. Let us choose a meaning life. Let us help our children to do the same. Let's make it a top priority. That is how we will become part of bringing about the Final Redemption speedily in our days.

היום ששה ושלושים יום,
שהם חמישה שבועות ויום אחד, לעומר

*(Ha'yom shisha u'shloshim yom,
she'hem chamisha shavuot v'yom echad la'Omer)*

**"TODAY IS THE THIRTY-SIXTH DAY,
OR FIVE WEEKS AND ONE DAY, OF THE OMER."**

DAY 36

Chesed sh'b'Yesod (Loving-kindness within Bonding)

Chesed within *yesod* strengthens and augments bonding with the added dimension of love and kindness. Bonding without love lacks the emotional glue and security that the *sefirah* of *chesed* brings to the building of foundational relationships, whether between self and God, self and other, or self and self. *Chesed* is a living life force that sustains, nourishes, and grows as it deepens the bonding within enduring relationships. It is an essential component which germinates within *yesod* to help create and maintain committed and devoted bonding on the physical and spiritual level.

Have you ever experienced the breakdown of relationship within your family? If so, you know that such a thing happens for many reasons. Perhaps the root was jealousy, ill chosen words carelessly spoken, or a perception of prejudice or injustice. Sometimes the reason for the breakdown is forgotten, and no one can name the original cause. But if one or both parties are unwilling or unable to resolve the breach, it continues to fester. Such a breach can even infect the next generation. The result is a catastrophic disunity within the family – a tragic state of affairs with persisting repercussions.

YOSEF AND FAMILY UNITY

Although it isn't likely that any of us were sold into slavery by our siblings like Yosef was, his story reveals how we should work to repair breaches in our family. Despite having narrowly escaped death at his brothers' hands, he did not bear a grudge; indeed, he assumed they did *teshuvah*. Then, he not only forgave them, but he also extended himself to support and protect them, because he still loved them! He demonstrated *chesed* within *yesod* – the foundation of unity within each and every family.

We each have a lot to learn from the story of Yosef and how he forgave his brothers. Strict justice would have required that the brothers be punished for the huge sin they committed. But *chesed* within *yesod* ensured that strict justice was not applied. Once Yosef saw that his brothers did *teshuvah*, he felt free to forgo the demands of justice and treat his brothers according to *chesed* within *yesod*. The reward was restored unity within the family of Yaakov.

In our own families, if there are unresolved splits in some relationships, it is incumbent upon us to use the model of Yosef and his brothers to seek peace, do *teshuvah* and heal the wounds, by applying *chesed* within *yesod* in order to restore what is broken.

It is fundamental to our system of belief that God treats us according to the principle of *middah k'neged middah* – therefore, how we forgive others for their transgressions against us is how God will forgive us for our sins.

We have to ask ourselves: What is the gain in having the unity in a family torn asunder? Is it worth our being judged more harshly by God because we harshly judged others and would not forgive? Important questions to answer.

It is through *chesed* within *yesod* that the roots of relationship can be nurtured so that the bond of interactions between family members can grow to withstand life's challenges and temptations. Having our family stand on a foundation of *chesed* within *yesod* allows generational continuity to flourish with each of us watching out and caring for the other personally and as part of the Nation of Israel as a whole.

BONDING WITH A CAUSE

Almost everyone knows that within days after May 14, 1948 when the State of Israel was declared, armies from six surrounding Arab nations invaded the Land with the goal of pushing every living Jew into the sea. We had to fight for our lives and for the survival of our newly reconstituted nation.

Few know the role that the Mahalniks, the overseas volunteers, played in the early years of the history of the state. In order to help Israel in the War of Independence, these Mahalniks developed key infrastructures for the fledgling state. Harry "Smoky" Simon, chairman of the World Mahal organization, conservatively estimates that there were 4,500 such volunteers from 58 countries. During the War for Independence, 95 percent of Israel's pilots were Mahalniks. Each had served in World War II and had the experience necessary to launch airstrikes.

Simon, who served in the South African Air Force and the Royal Air Force, came to the new Israel Air Force as a navigator-bombardier and chief of Air Operations, rising to the rank of major. In an inspiring article entitled "The First Volunteers,"[351] Simon points out that there were 426 Mahalnik air crew members, 92 of whom were not Jewish. Notable Mahalniks included octogenarian Zippora Porath. A New Yorker, she was on a one-year scholarship program at Hebrew University when the War of Independence began. Zippora joined the Haganah, serving as a medic during the siege of Jerusalem when the Arab armies surrounded Jerusalem to choke all food, water, and supplies to its Jewish residents. Later, Zippora served in the intelligence division of the Israeli Air Force and helped to set up nursing services across northern Israel. She is rightfully proud of what she and other Mahalniks accomplished: "Our attitude was, do what you can, when you can, while you can, and give it your best . . . That's how it was for all of us." What a great motto.[352]

Her story and the stories of others demonstrate the *chesed* within *yesod*, the loving bonding of Jews of the Diaspora (as well as non-Jews) with the Jews of Israel, and with the supremely worthy cause of helping the nascent State of Israel survive. All their stories are so inspirational that you get goosebumps reading about them.

The message of another Mahalnik, Murray Greenfield captures *chesed* within *yesod* perfectly. But first his story:

Greenfield was an American who served on some of the ships (a project called *Aliyah Bet*) that attempted to bring Jewish immigrants to Palestine

351. Barry Davis, "The First Volunteers," *The Jerusalem Post Magazine*, June 29, 2012, 13–15.

352. Read her book *Letters from Jerusalem 1947–1948* for more.

between 1939 and 1948, despite British efforts to prevent them from doing so. (He has since written a book about this called *The Jews' Secret Fleet.*) As he tells it and as history testifies, urgent efforts had to be made to get as many Jews as possible out of Nazi clutches, but there was no country willing to allow them in. The volunteers started looking for ships in America, and they needed experienced hands to move the boats from America to wherever the Jews were. Greenfield had been in the merchant marines during World War II and he went to synagogue one day where a fellow pointed in his direction. Greenfield remembers:

> "The guy who spoke to me said it could be dangerous, and I could go to prison, and there was no pay in it for me . . . I was 20 years old and I went for it . . . There were 250 young Americans like me who also joined in." Greenfield says it was on the boats that he first learned about the horrors of the Holocaust . . . he soon received first hand testimony about the concentration camps. "I knew Yiddish and every single Jew on the ship had a whole Holocaust story to tell. It was terrible . . . When the British caught us and stopped us from reaching Palestine, they beat us up and fired tear gas at us, and then they sent us all to Cyprus . . . [But] we couldn't abandon our passengers . . . [We tried again.] When the British caught us, we started singing 'Hatikva' . . . at night outside Haifa Port. That was very moving. I don't think Israel would have survived without *Aliya Bet.*"[353]

This wonderful article concludes:

> At the end of the day, Greenfield says it is about continuing to contribute: "All the Mahalniks are heroes, they all did wonderful things. But the real story is about the ones who stayed here, or went back and then came back on *aliya*, and had children and grandchildren. That's the real legacy."

This is the most amazing flourishing of *chesed* within *yesod* in our history, and it formed the grass roots of modern-day Israel. Murray Greenfield's message captures it all: Bonding with a cause. Volunteering out of pure

353. Davis, "The First Volunteers," 15.

love. Contributing to the survival of the State of Israel. Each Mahalnik could have met with death, and some did. But the legacy of the Mahalniks was a bonding that passed through them down to their children, grandchildren, and on till today.

BEING A STEP-PARENT IS *CHESED* WITHIN *YESOD*

Anyone who has ever played the role of step-parent or step-child knows that sometimes these relationships are fraught with their own challenges. And most of us know the story of Cinderella, the fictional step-child whose travails we all remember.

So whenever step-parents regard their step-child as "their own," it is a pure example of *chesed* within *yesod*. So difficult is this task that there is a special supplication (*techina*) for a step-mother. It goes like this:

> "Kind Father: Your Holy Torah tells us that our mother Rachel was jealous of her sister Leah because she had children and she, Rachel, had none. You gave Rachel the inspiration to give her maidservant, Bilha, to her husband, Yaakov, in order that she could raise the children of Bilha as her own. In the merit that she brought up her husband's children whom he had from another woman, Rachel was answered with having her own children.
>
> With this, You showed us how great is the merit to bring up step-children and to treat them kindly. This merit is much greater than that of bringing up your own children, because the attachment that you have for your own children is natural; all animals have it. The hen raises her own chicks, but she has no instinct to care for strange chicks, so she pecks at the stranger and chases it away.
>
> Raising stepchildren is a holy task. It shows a higher human feeling, one that is higher than that of any other living creature. The step-mother is likened to the ministering angels and that is why her reward is so great. Therefore, You repay her with two great gifts. To Rachel you gave two righteous children, Yosef the Righteous who sustained the Tribes in Egypt, and Binyamin the Righteous in whose portion was built the *Bais Hamikdash* in the Land of Israel. She had *nachas*, joy, without boundary in this world and in the eternal world.
>
> So, Kindhearted Father, purify my heart from all bad traits, especially anger and hatred, and plant in me good-heartedness and

> nobility. If my lot is to be that of a step-mother, at least let me be one of the good step-mothers that are a blessing to the world. Let me treat my step-children as my own children. Let me merit to see from them and my own children much *nachas*, joy. Amen.[354]

Extending loving-kindness in a consistently reliable way that another can depend upon through both joyous and challenging times is most naturally found in the unconditional love (*chesed* within *chesed*) that flows from a parent to their own child, raised since birth. However, when this is displayed by a step-parent towards a step-child, or vice versa, the "step" relation embodies *chesed* within *yesod*. One has the opportunity to demonstrate the selfless sacrifices of giving and loving, oftentimes without reward or genuine love in return, until one day a miracle and reciprocal love or gratitude blossoms as fruit on the tree of *chesed* within *yesod*.

354. Rivka Zakutinsky, *Techinas: A Voice from the Heart* (Brooklyn, NY: Aura Press, 1992), 401–405.

DISCUSSION TOPICS FOR *CHESED* WITHIN *YESOD*

For adults

1. What actions might I take to restore a breach of relationship or remove the distance that has grown between two members of my family?
2. How have I reached out first and forgiven someone who was once very close to me, even if he or she has not reached out or done *teshuvah*?
3. Have I ever extended myself and given to another person whom I did not know? Why did I do it and how did it feel?

For children

1. When I am angry with someone in my family, is it hard for me to forgive him or her? Why? How can I do it anyway? Has someone ever been mad at me for a very long time for something I did? How did that make me feel?
2. What *mitzvot* do I do simply because I am sure God wants me to do them, and I want to show that I love Him?
3. Do I volunteer for anything at this time? If so, how does that make me feel? If not, is there something I would be willing to volunteer for?

היום שבעה ושלושים יום,
שהם חמישה שבועות ושני ימים, לעומר

(Ha'yom shiva u'shloshim yom,
she'hem chamisha shavuot u'shnei yamim la'Omer)

"TODAY IS THE THIRTY-SEVENTH DAY,
OR FIVE WEEKS AND TWO DAYS, OF THE OMER."

DAY 37

Gevurah sh'b'Yesod (Strength/Discipline within Bonding)

Gevurah **within** ***yesod*** **is displayed when strength, restraint, and/or discipline assist bonding in difficult times that can put stress upon relationships. Drawing upon** ***gevurah,*** **we can carefully respond, or even remain silent, in order to facilitate the delicate balance required to preserve relationships, so that breaches don't occur. How we sensitively respond to another is paramount in keeping relationships healthy and uplifted.** ***Gevurah*** **helps to maintain already existing** ***yesod*** **through restraint, thoughtfulness, wisdom, and understanding.**

During extremely difficult times, acts of solidarity can wax or wane. At such times, some people want to only look after themselves or their families. Others are driven to help their fellows as well as themselves, often at great risk to their own lives.

An interesting article entitled "The Complexities of Jewish Solidarity in the Holocaust," by Robert Rozett, the Director of the Yad Vashem Libraries, addresses the topic of strength and bonding among Jews during World War II. Rozett describes Jewish partisan groups, for example the Belski brothers, who created large family camps and protected some 1,200 Jews. He points out that they "could have concentrated exclusively on fighting and their own survival, but instead focused on rescuing Jews and taking care of them . . . The fact that some Jewish partisan leaders made rescuing whomever they could their main priority says much about their dedication to traditional Jewish values."[355] Rozett adds that there were Jewish underground units totally focused on the rescue of fellow Jews in many countries occupied by the Nazis, including France, Hungary, Belgium, and the Netherlands. They are all examples of one kind of *gevurah* within *yesod*.

Rozett also cites many illustrations of the other kind – the kind that requires even greater self-sacrifice. As we discussed in Week Two when we covered *gevurah*, it also takes strength – sometimes even more strength – to restrain or discipline oneself from taking action. From this perspective, Rozett sheds light on another way that Jews displayed solidarity during the Holocaust – a way which came with a price:

> Many young people refused to consider flight or armed resistance, because they would not leave their families in dire circumstances. Repeatedly, young Jews accompanied their families to concentration camps because of family bonds. One could say that a similar sense of solidarity drove other parents to encourage their older children to strike out on their own, or place younger children with non-Jewish strangers, hoping they might survive to continue the family.[356]

The Holocaust is replete with examples of *gevurah* within *yesod*. Some displayed the aspect of *gevurah* that involved action and attempted to do battle with weapons. Others displayed *gevurah* just as strongly though they didn't use weapons, but they still fought this vile evil on a highly moral and spiritual level using the *gevurah* aspect of restraint. However, on all rungs of the continuum, we are deeply indebted to our Jewish brothers and sisters who had to confront the basest of evils with heroic displays of *gevurah* within *yesod*, regardless of the way it was manifested.

---

355. Robert Rozett, "The Complexities of Jewish Solidarity in the Holocaust," *The Jerusalem Post Magazine*, April 20, 2012, 35.
356. Ibid.

YOSEF IN EGYPT

Since Yosef is the shepherd who rectified the attribute of *yesod* in a world that was imbalanced since the sin of Adam and Chava, his life obviously provides many examples of *yesod* with each *sefirah* combination. For example, Yosef had to muster tremendous amounts of *gevurah* to restrain himself from bonding with the Pharaoh who was his "boss" and ally for the many years before his family resurfaced on the scene. Yosef also used *gevurah* to restrain himself from bonding with the Egyptian society during the time he was Grand Vizier and wielded huge amounts of power and authority over the Egyptian economy and laws of the land.

Imagine the position that Yosef was in – all he knew was that his brothers sold him as a slave. He undoubtedly also knew that some of them actually wanted to kill him. He did not know that Reuven planned an escape for him. He simply believed that every single brother present, when they threw him in the pit, wanted to get rid of him in one way or another. Further, no one searched after him for all of these years, not even his father. So he must have felt totally abandoned by his family. In contrast, he was treated well in Egypt, first by his master Potiphar, and then by the prison warden who put him in charge of the jail. After his interpretations of the Pharaoh's dreams, he was promoted to be the second in command of the most powerful civilization in the entire world at that time. And, still, no word from home.

Wouldn't it have been the easiest thing in the world for Yosef to just blend in with the Egyptian culture and people? But that's not what he did. Yosef demonstrated, in test after test, that he was permanently bonded to the God of his father and to the moral principles he was taught by his parents. Yosef demonstrated a perfect mastery of *gevurah* within *yesod* which, as we noted in the overview for this week, is a model for us living in the *galut.*

The moment his brothers arrived in Egypt to purchase food because of the worsening famine at home, and Yosef learned that his father was still alive, his whole aim became to reunify the family.

Once Yosef determined that the brothers had done *teshuvah* for their misdeeds, he revealed himself to them and set in motion the necessary steps to ensure his entire family would come to live in Goshen, apart from the Egyptian society. Yosef knew that it takes great amount of restraint to remain bonded to the right path when one is surrounded by other alluring ideologies, and he minimized this threat not only for himself but for his extended family as well. He had vision and strength, and he became an embodiment of *gevurah* within *yesod.*

GEVURAH WITHIN *YESOD* AND ANGER

Now let us examine how *gevurah* within *yesod* plays out in our everyday lives. On the simplest level, it means holding back angry words we might wish to yell at our child, spouse, or friend for the sake of preserving the bond between us.

In his cogent and impactful *Words that Hurt, Words that Heal: How to Choose Words Wisely and Well,* Rabbi Joseph Telushkin writes about the lifelong rifts that have occurred between people over a few poorly-chosen words spoken in anger. Before turning to practical advice for dealing with this issue, Rabbi Telushkin describes the break-up of King David's marriage to Michal.

As we know from the First Book of Samuel, Michal and David were very much in love with each other. David risked his life battling 200 Philistines to win her hand in marriage and, later, Michal helped David escape the wrath of her father, King Saul, who sought to kill him, mistakenly believing that David was trying to usurp his throne. While David spent years in hiding, King Saul married off Michal (who was still David's wife) to another man. Although many husbands would have cast aside a wife who went along with such an arrangement, when David became king, he restored Michal as his queen. However, their marriage unraveled. How did this happen? Rabbi Telushkin explains:

> David and Michal both suffered from the same character flaw – a sharp tongue, which they refused to control when angry. The Bible describes the incident that triggered the end of their love. Ironically, it was a celebration: King David was supervising the return to Jerusalem of the Ark [of the Covenant] . . . In an outburst of joy, he danced passionately, even wildly, in front of thousands of his subjects. Watching the whole scene from a palace window, Michal was disgusted by the spectacle . . . And so when David returned to the place, she greeted him with cold sarcasm: "Didn't the king of Israel

> do himself honor today – exposing himself . . . as one of the riffraff might expose himself?"[357]
>
> Michal's attack, however, was only the first factor in the tragedy that ensued. In the face of his wife's scorn, David did not remain silent, walk away until the tension eased, or even try to defend his behavior. Instead, he responded with the cruelest attack he could muster: "It was before the Lord who chose me instead of your father and all his family [that I danced]. . . ."
>
> In the very next verse, the Bible records: "So to her dying day Michal, daughter of Saul, had no children."[358]

Rabbi Telushkin points out what went wrong: She criticized him tactlessly on what may have been the greatest day of his life. In retort, he did what many people do when they are denigrated – he went straight for the jugular, attacking the most painful event in Michal's life: God's rejection of her father, and his subsequent death, along with three of Michal's brothers, at the hands of the Philistines.

Why does the Prophet Shmuel mention Michal's childlessness at this juncture? To tell us that, after this exchange, they were never again intimate.

The most important warning from this example for modern-day couples and friends, says Rabbi Telushkin, is that if people "do not restrain their words when they are angry, love is unlikely to survive, no matter how deeply the two people once cared for each other. The ability to control what we say when we're angry is a prerequisite for a lasting relationship."[359]

The bottom line: if we want to have lasting relationships, we must demonstrate restraint in what we say, how we say it, when we say it, to whom we say it. This is *gevurah* within *yesod.*

357. II *Shmuel* 6:20.

358. Ibid., 6:23.

359. Joseph Telushkin, *Words That Hurt, Words That Heal* (NY: William Morrow, 1996), 70–71.

DISCUSSION TOPICS FOR *GEVURAH* WITHIN *YESOD*

For adults

1. What tempts me now in a way that distances me from God? How will I try to demonstrate the restraint I need in order to close this gap?
2. Do I overly depend on members of my family or do they overly depend upon me? How can I change this so that our relationship is healthier?
3. How well do I control what I say to my spouse during an argument? How can I do better?

For children

1. Who, of my friends, has a really good influence on me? Who, of my friends, doesn't? And why?
2. When I am in a bad mood or am upset at someone in my family, do I say things that hurt them? How can I stop that behavior?
3. Have I ever talked about a friend to another friend, or about my sibling to my parents in a way that has triggered a quarrel? What did I learn from that experience?

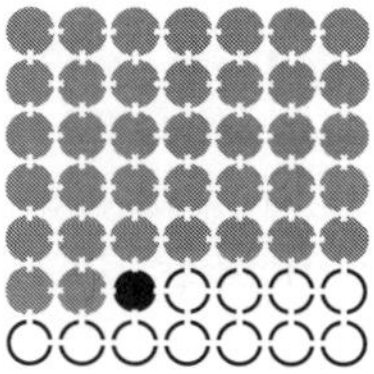

היום שמונה ושלושים יום,
שהם חמישה שבועות ושלושה ימים, לעומר

(Ha'yom shemonah u'shloshim yom,
she'hem chamisha shavuot u'shlosha yamim la'Omer)

"TODAY IS THE THIRTY-EIGHTH DAY,
OR FIVE WEEKS AND THREE DAYS, OF THE OMER."

DAY 38

Tiferet sh'b'Yesod (Harmony/Truth within Bonding)

Yesod is the bedrock of all relationships. And when we master *tiferet* within *yesod,* we can make sure that all our relationships are built on a foundation of trust, loyalty, and truth. Aided by *tiferet* within *yesod,* a proportionately balanced and mature equilibrium of bonding becomes harmonious and beautiful in its expression.

Thanks to *tiferet* within *yesod,* our relationships and contributions to the world can flourish. This is because a balance is achieved by this *sefirah* combination, where the nature of giving and receiving between two parties does not make either one feel selfishly exploited, or overburdened, or desperately needy.

RELATIONSHIPS BETWEEN PARENTS AND CHILDREN

Rebbetzin Esther Jungreis, in her book *The Committed Life,* addresses the commandment to honor our parents:

> The Fifth Commandment is one of two places in the Torah where "the reward of a good, long life [which is not necessarily measured

> in years] is promised for its observance . . . If we have descendants who will cherish our names, who will continue our lives, then our *families* will live on. In families in which parents are honored, families endure and have "length of days." Where there is disrespect, there is also dysfunction, and such families disintegrate and disappear.[360]

If a family has ever achieved a lasting resolution to a dispute that results in a deeper level of bonding and respect for one another, then those involved can experience the resurrection of *tiferet* within *yesod* in their lives, the feeling of a meaningful "length of days."

Tiferet within *yesod* comes alive when two (or more) people decide that for a higher purpose (such as the well-being of the immediate family, or the unity of the extended family, or the legacy for generations, or other reasons) "bygones should be bygones." *Tiferet* within *yesod* also comes into play when a previously lopsided relationship (where one party did far more giving than the other) is adjusted to become more equitable and balanced in mutual giving and receiving. These examples illustrate a lasting, positive outcome for all.

In contrast, to pinpoint what it feels like to fail to achieve *tiferet* within *yesod* in our most important parent/child relationship, just read the following:

The late Lewis Grizzard, an American humorist and writer, shares a story involving his father and himself in his book, *My Daddy was a Pistol, and I'm a Son of a Gun*. Grizzard talks about going through his father's meager possessions at the hospital where he died. In his father's coat, he found a weathered and tethered letter that his father had been carrying for some time:

> It was a letter from me. I had written it six months before. It was short, maybe a page, typewritten. Down at the end, I had given him some grief about straightening out his life . . . I'd just signed my name. I didn't say "love" or anything . . . I still wonder why he carried such a letter around with him for so long. Maybe he kept it to remind himself that his only son was turning on him. Whatever, I

360. Esther Jungreis, *The Committed Life* (NY: Cliff Street Books, 1998), 304.

> never forgave myself for that letter. I can't get it out of my head that he died not knowing how much I loved him.[361]

Lewis Gizzard might not have written that letter, or written a different letter altogether, had he been able to apply *tiferet* within *yesod* and figure out how to balance his love for his father with his need to privately rebuke him (if the latter was indeed, necessary). Thus he might have been able to achieve his ends and yet not hurt his father.

It is through training ourselves to display honor and respect for our parents that we learn to show the same for God.[362] Our Sages teach that one who denies or fails to recognize the good others do for him will also deny the good God does for him.[363]

Indeed, who does more good for us than our parents? To whom should we be more grateful? Our parents have given us everything!

YOSEF'S TOTAL COMMITMENT TO GOD

As previously noted (on Day 37), Yosef lived for more than two decades without father or family, simply by clinging to God. God was Yosef's only "family" in Egypt. And his bonding to God was complete. His devotion to God and to Judaism reflected pure *tiferet* within *yesod*. He married a Jewish woman (the daughter of Dena, his half-sister). He had two sons, Ephraim and Menashe, and raised them strictly to behave as Jews. They did not eat the food of the Egyptians in their home. Yosef ate separately from the Egyptians at work. In our language of today, they kept *kosher* and remained *kosher* despite being the only Jewish family in Egypt!

We also learned on Day 37 that Yosef applied *gevurah* within *yesod* to bring about the reconciliation with his brothers despite the tragic lack of unity they had displayed while growing up. He also worked hard to ensure their collective survival and continuity during the family's years of Egyptian exile. Yosef not only succeeded in this mission, but created true harmony as a result.

When Yosef's father, Yaakov, was on his deathbed many years later, he

361. Lewis Grizzard, *My Daddy was a Pistol and I'm a Son of a Gun* (NY: Dell Paperback, 1986), 11.

362. *Kiddushin* 30b.

363. *Chayei Adam Klal* 67.

was surrounded by all of his twelve sons – united as they should be. And 210 years later, when the Jewish people left Egypt on the night of the first Pesach, their descendants, the Twelve Tribes, were still in complete unity, displaying *tiferet* within *yesod*, marching with common purpose to serve God together and in truth.

When there is harmony and balance within bonding, the jealousies and rifts that plague many families do not rear their ugly heads. The nascent Jewish nation had achieved *tiferet* within *yesod* in exile, thanks to the extraordinary efforts of Yosef.

THE SLIPPERY SLOPE

How many times have you heard someone living in the Diaspora say, "It's so hard to be a Jew." And because it is hard, how often does Jewish practice in *galut* suffer?

An early first warning sign down this slippery slope is the slow weakening of halachic observance in one's life. For example one might rationalize, "Well, it's hard to keep kosher in this city; there are so few kosher restaurants, so I will just eat fish or dairy when I eat out at a non-kosher restaurant." Or, "I am a business person and I have to set an example for my employees, so I have to work on Shabbat." Or, "I am permitted to not wear a *kippah* if I might engender anti-Semitism, so I won't wear one at work, so as not to stick out."

How many times have we heard business topics being discussed by "observant" Jews on Shabbat? How many times do we speak *lashon hara*? How many times do we race through *tefillah* in order to get on with our day? How many of us sacrifice our Jewish identity so that we can fit in and be more accepted by our non-Jewish (or non-observant Jewish) friends?

Thinking we can get away with such halachic infractions without paying a high price is a terrible mistake for all. With each deviation, we start down a very slippery slope into a less religious and a more secular lifestyle, foregoing *tiferet* within *yesod*, and allowing ourselves and our children to drift away from a deep and binding alignment with God and the truth of Torah.

DISCUSSION TOPICS FOR *TIFERET* WITHIN *YESOD*

For adults

1. Name any of your relationships that you know are unbalanced and where you do more of the giving than the other person. Discuss your views and how to make them better balanced from this day forward.
2. Think of a relationship that you have where you feel you have achieved a fair, consistent, and satisfying level of giving and receiving. Talk to the other person and ask if he or she feels the same way about it.
3. What is a dominant trait that you have to balance better so that your relationships can improve?

For children

1. What can you do to repay your parents for all they have and continue to do for you?
2. What can you do to repay God for all He does for you?
3. Do you say "please" when you ask for something or say "thank you" after someone does something for you? Do you help with the chores around the house? Do you say "I'm sorry" after you have made a mistake or hurt someone's feelings? Do you listen to your parents the first time they ask you to do something?
4. Can you make a gift for your mother or father? Can you tell them something you have learned at school to give them *nachat*? Can you offer to help your parents with your younger siblings so they know you are trying to be there for them?

היום תשעה ושלושים יום,
שהם חמישה שבועות וארבעה ימים, לעומר

Ha'yom tisha u'shloshim yom,
she'hem chamisha shavuot v'arba'a yamim la'Omer

"TODAY IS THE THIRTY-NINTH DAY,
OR FIVE WEEKS AND FOUR DAYS, OF THE OMER."

DAY 39

Netzach sh'b'Yesod (Endurance within Bonding)

Netzach within *yesod* translates into consistent and enduring effort to both establish and maintain the foundation of relationships and keep them healthy and everlasting. *Netzach* is a driving quality that must always be applied carefully and in the right amounts to preserve bonding without smothering the independence of another. Healthy bonding, reinforced by *netzach*, is essential because, without it, relationships are shallow, lack substance, permanence, and trust.

Over the past twelve years, terrorists have infiltrated the Israeli settlement of Itamar a number of times resulting in the murder of twenty-two of its residents. On March 11, 2011, in an attack shocking for its brutality, five members of the same family were murdered by two Arab teenagers from a nearby village. The victims included Rabbi Ehud and Ruth Fogel and three of their children, Yoav age 11, Elad age 4, and Hadas age three months. Three of the other Fogel children survived: Ro'ee age 9, and Yishai age 3, who slept through the attack and were not detected by the terrorists, and Tamar age 13, who was away at a youth group activity.

The Fogel family moved to Itamar after their forced evacuation from their home in Gush Katif, Gaza Strip, in 2005, when then Prime Minister Ariel Sharon voluntarily withdrew from the area as a peace gesture to the Palestinians. The Gaza Strip has since become a hotbed for violence, terrorism, and is Hamas-controlled.

The 220 Itamar families were very traumatized by this attack on a family who had touched their lives so deeply. In a touching example of *netzach* within *yesod*, the residents renamed the Beit Midrash where Rabbi Ehud once taught, Mishkan Ehud. The goal of all the residents is to keep the memory of the Fogels alive, as they continue to build their community.

Yeshar Koach to the people of Itamar who continue to display *netzach* within *yesod* in memorializing the Fogel victims, as well as standing their ground and continuing to build their community in the face of such despicable inhumanity. Indeed, this is truly endurance and perseverance in bonding, and commitment to an important cause.

Other examples of Jewish commitment abound in Eretz Yisrael. In 2012, on the occasion of Israel's Yom HaZikaron – when we remember those who died in various wars defending the state, as well as the victims of terror – a poll was released showing that:

- 82.7 percent plan to fly an Israeli flag at their home or car on Israel Independence Day
- 81.9 percent feel a connection to the Jews in the Diaspora
- 74.3 percent believe that the State of Israel is a good country to live in
- 80.1 percent would prefer to live in Israel than overseas
- when asked what is "most Israeli," 30 percent responded "helping others"[364]

Frankly, these are extraordinarily high results for a full-fledged democratic state where one is free to express honest views and opinions. These results display an enduring bond of Jews to one another and an enduring bond of Jews to the Land of Israel. *Baruch Hashem*! But we must remember that while all this is positive, it doesn't obfuscate the biggest problem we're facing – the hemorrhaging of our people through intermarriage and the slippery slope to secularism and lost identity.

---

364. Dr. A. Lerner, IMRA (Independent Media Review & Analysis), see: http://www.imra.org.il, April 25, 2012.

CRUMBLING *NETZACH* WITHIN *YESOD*

Outside of the Land of Israel, especially in America, one cannot pick up a magazine today without being alarmed by the reality of today's Jewish teenagers being disconnected from their Jewish identity.

A survey of 1,200 teenagers in Modern Orthodox institutions in the Diaspora revealed that the number who use their cellphones and text on Shabbat is approaching 20 percent. Jonathan Rosenblum, in a penetrating article for *Jewish Action* observes:

> Texting is just the most open expression of a much more general problem – a lack of idealism, enthusiasm, and connection to Torah on the part of many Orthodox teenagers . . . "Addicted" and "bored" are the two most common explanations offered by teenagers for texting on Shabbos. Both [reasons] should scare us.[365]

The experts all rightly question how this spiritual apathy in our teenagers began? Is it possible that when our kids see their parents ignore *tefillah*, or attend a *minyan* that races through the prayers as if it were an Indianapolis 500 time trial, they are being given a mixed message about the importance of daily communion with the Master of the Universe? When we discuss our business, talk about sport scores or other non-Torah related topics on Shabbat, what message do we send to our teenagers about the sanctity of this day? No wonder they text!

We need to set a good example for our kids. Let's do the right thing by God. Yosef did both in Egypt, virtually without any support, and continued to do so until his death at 110. His last instruction was to have his body buried in the Land of Israel, so important it was for him to enduringly identify with being a Jew.

If we want our children to have enduring bonding with *Yiddishkeit* and all our Jewish traditions so that they keep the Torah, act with proper *derech eretz*, and serve God, then we have to be a model of *netzach* within *yesod*. We must consistently demonstrate how we want them to act. No double standards. No passing the buck to schools or others to be the role models for our children.

---

365. Jonathan Rosenblum, "Half Shabbos is No Shabbos," *Jewish Action*, Spring 2012, 12.

It is true that these are trying times. The Talmud says that in the period just prior to the coming of the Mashiach, the young will humiliate their elders and the elders will rise before the young.[366] This is precisely the period we are living in. Rabbi Frand summarizes this sorry state of affairs:

> "The world owes me" is the national anthem of the yuppie generation . . . [But] the truth is we are partly to blame for the situation. We simply do not teach our children how to respect a parent, and then we are surprised when they do not show any respect. The *halachah* is that a child should stand when his parents enter the room, but how many of us insist on that? We are so eager to show that we are regular guys that our children would be amazed to learn such a mitzvah even exists. They would be equally amazed to learn that one is not supposed to interrupt his parents, even to agree with them . . . We teach our children Torah and *chesed*, but we do not teach them how to respect their parents.[367]

Exacerbating the sense of entitlement among many is the fast pace of living – instant gratification, instant interaction, instant response in "real time." No more long distance letters that take months to arrive by sea or over land or via horse or camel. The immediacy of all communication, the availability of streaming information 24/7 has contributed to an even more heightened need to get what we want without waiting. We have come to expect that all of our demands will be fulfilled instantaneously.

Few children wait for their parent to come home from work to ask them a question. Rather, the children, who may be at school or home, calls their parent on their cell phone to discuss the most minute issue or detail, and the child expects an instant answer. But it is not just the children. Spouses call each other, often numerous times per day, without apparent regard for what important matter the other may be involved in. Parents call or text children on their cell phones all day long.

Not that long ago there was a slower response time – but that was before telephones were invented. Then, there was a time when not every home had a phone. After came a time when phones were only available as "land lines." It is a relatively recent invention that people can walk around

366. *Sotah* 49b.

367. Frand, *Rabbi Yissocher Frand in Print*, 106–108.

carrying a cell phone enabling them to speak, text, or email any person anywhere in the world. Just this one phenomenon has revolutionized – both for good and bad – family communication patterns, priorities, and the insistence on immediately getting an audience with whomever one is calling.

Netzach within *yesod* is being inappropriately applied when an exaggerated sense of urgency creates an expectation of instant response. So what are we going to do with this latest challenge as it affects raising a family?

WHO IS WISE?

All members of a family can follow the advice of the Sages: "Who is wise? One who foresees the future consequences of his actions."[368] It seems that this simple precept could help each family achieve *netzach* within *yesod* by examining the future effects of the unbridled use of technology.

For children, this means implementing the fifth of the Ten Commandments, "Honor your father and mother," an issue we also discussed under *tiferet* within *yesod*.

Rabbi Joseph Telushkin points out that the Torah does not command the love of parents, but it does demand a measure of respect:

> It means that even when a child is furious at her parents, she doesn't cut them out of her life (except perhaps in rare instances of when a child suffers real physical or sexual abuse at a parent's hands), and when she expresses anger, she suppresses saying, "I hate you, " or "I wish I had had decent parents, not you."[369]

For parents, this means adhering to several important principles:

First, if you want to have an enduring bond with your children, it is wise to continually reflect and make every effort to achieve the proper balance of whatever *sefirot* are called for in a given situation. As Rabbi Samson Raphael Hirsch advises:

> An excitable parent will not be able to teach his child patience; a hot-tempered parent will not be able to teach his child to keep his

368. *Tamid* 32a; *Pirkei Avot* 2:9.

369. Telushkin, *Words That Hurt, Words That Heal,* 116.

> composure; a frivolous parent will not be able to teach his child to be serious; a parent who is rude will not be able to teach his child good manners; a parent who is devious will not be able to teach his child to be sincere; a spendthrift will not be able to teach his child moderation; a parent who is vulgar in his own thoughts, words, and actions will not be able to teach his child how to be noble-minded, and so forth . . .[370]

Second, do not compare any of your children to their siblings, cousins, or other children. Again, Rabbi Telushkin describes the importance of ensuring that "all their children feel equally loved and appreciated." He offers that:

> Comparing children undermines family unity. Instead of making them feel that they are part of one united family . . . children come to see themselves as competitors for a finite amount of parental love and approval. This type of competition rarely brings out the best in anyone, and increases the likelihood that such children will not be close to each other when they grow up.[371]

Yosef, the shepherd who was assigned the mission of rectifying the deficiency in *yesod* created by the sin of Adam and Chava, was the victim of just such a situation in his youth – sibling jealousy caused his brothers to sell him into slavery. The Sages of the Talmud conclude from this tragic episode that "a man should never single out one of his children for favorable treatment for, because of the two extra coins' worth of silk, Yosef's brothers became jealous of him, and one thing led to another until our ancestors became slaves in Egypt."[372]

Third, the message for both parents and children of all ages is to look ahead and imagine the future consequences of today's thoughts, words and actions as they relate to the fundamental parent/child bond. It takes both parties to build an enduring connection that is profoundly meaningful to both. There is no question that working diligently to cultivate and

370. Hirsch, "On the Role of Education in the First Years of a Child's Life," included in: *Collected Writings of Rabbi Samson Raphael Hirsch*, p. 134.
371. Telushkin, *Words That Hurt, Words That Heal*, 115–116.
372. *Shabbat* 10b.

preserve *netzach* within *yesod* between parents and children of all ages is an investment that pays meaningful returns.

If we make such an investment, we will reap the reward of having reared grounded children who act with *derech eretz*, are well adjusted, are part of a Jewish community, are a source of joy and *nachat*, are happy, self-fulfilled, and productive – if we follow these simple rules. How can we go wrong in diligently applying *netzach* within *yesod* to achieve these life benefits that, with God's help, will pass on to the next generation and beyond?

DISCUSSION TOPICS FOR *NETZACH* WITHIN *YESOD*

For adults

1. Do I compare my children to other children? Should I stop this practice?
2. Am I setting a good example for my children on Shabbat regarding the topics we discuss? Do I set a good example for them in how I recite my daily prayers?
3. Can I name three deep, healthy, and enduring relationships I have at this time? How do I display loyalty, devotion, love, and trust to others?

For children

1. Has anyone ever criticized me by comparing me to another kid? How did that make me feel?
2. Have I shown that I am a good, loyal friend to another person? What did I do to show it?
3. How can God know I love Him if I don't say my daily prayers and act accordingly?

היום ארבעים יום,
שהם חמישה שבועות וחמישה ימים, לעומר

Ha'yom arba'im yom,
she'hem chamisha shavuot v'chamisha yamim la'Omer

**"TODAY IS THE FORTIETH DAY,
OR FIVE WEEKS AND FIVE DAYS, OF THE OMER."**

DAY 40

Hod sh'b'Yesod (Humility within Bonding)

Hod (humility) enhances _yesod_ (bonding) with sincere, appropriate, and considerate expression of gratitude and appreciation of the give-and-take between self and God, self and other, and self and self. The presence of _hod_ within _yesod_ keeps all relationships fresh; it helps us to always express our thoughts, speech, and actions in a manner that does not take another person for granted but rather demonstrates our desire to keep every relationship alive and thriving.

As we learned in *tiferet* within *yesod*, ideally, there should be some form of balance between giving and receiving in a relationship. If either is lopsided for an extended period of a time and real correction is not forthcoming, discord and strain will result within the bond. Generally, the one doing most of the giving will feel that he or she is being used or taken advantage of. If the one doing the taking is tuned in, he or she will have to apply heartfelt humility to solve the problem.

Humility allows the taker/receiver to become aware of what is happening and begin to express the deep gratitude, appreciation for all that he or she has been given. With humility, feelings of entitlement on the part of the taker disappear. With humility, the habitual taker begins to initiate thoughts, speech, and actions that put the needs of the other before his or her needs, for a change. Without humility, patterns of lopsided giving may eventually create a wider and wider chasm between two people, threatening to sever the bonds of *yesod* that once existed.

Parent-child relationships are by their very nature lopsided. They start out that way, and typically never change. The reason one has the status of a mourner for one's parent for a year, saying *Kaddish* for eleven months of that time, is in partial recognition of the lopsided nature of most parent-child relationships. The gratitude goes in one direction from child to parent for, in general, parents never stop giving to their children. It is the fortunate parent who has a child that recognizes that he or she can and ought to give something back to the parent.

I know one very busy Rosh Yeshiva who used to stop by his widowed mother's apartment every single morning on his way home from morning prayers (before beginning his very demanding job) in order to have breakfast with her. I also know a very busy business executive who has invited his father for lunch at his office every Friday for more than a decade, and who has arranged to go on multiple vacations with his father, especially planning activities that his father would enjoy. It takes thought, care, time, and energy for adult children to make a loving place for their parents in their daily lives. It takes humility for the children to recognize the importance of taking the time to honor their parents. This is *hod* within *yesod*, humility within bonding.

Hod within *yesod*, when properly displayed, results in the deepest, most mutually fulfilling relationships we can imagine.

A SPECTACULAR DISPLAY OF *HOD* WITHIN *YESOD*

The story of David Feiglin, a brave young man, and his courageous parents demonstrates so many *sefirah* combinations – including *gevurah*, *chesed* and *netzach* – but the combination I want to focus on is their beautiful display of *hod* within *yesod*.

In June 2010, an auto accident left David in a coma for three months. During this time, most of David's doctors lost hope. However, his parents, Tzippy and Moshe Feiglin refused to give up. With unending *chesed* within *netzach*, Tzippy, despite her own battle with Parkinson's, stayed in David's hospital room 24 hours a day, communicating with her son continuously. On the second day of Rosh Hashana in 2010, Moshe (a public figure in Israeli politics) was called to the Torah in the synagogue at the

Sheba Medical Center in Tel Hashomer where David was being treated. For the occasion, Tzippy arranged that comatose David to be rolled in on a gurney so that he could hear the *shofar*. The Torah portion being read was that of *Akeidat Yitzchak*, as Moshe relates:

> There I stood, with my son tied in a gurney, struggling between life and death. I felt as if it was my son bound next to me, and I had no way of helping him. I could not control myself; the tears streamed straight onto the Torah scroll. I shed so many tears that I moved my head because I was afraid that my tears would render the Torah scroll unfit for use. On the way back to the room, following the most powerful Rosh Hashana prayers I had ever had, I felt a strange sensation of relief, a type of acceptance. I said to God, "I have done all that I can. Now it is in Your hands." Our Sages say that the repentance of the completely righteous is accepted immediately, while the repentance of people neither completely righteous nor completely wicked waits until Yom Kippur for resolution. On Yom Kippur Eve, David said his first word.[373]

This is what happened: On the eve of Yom Kippur, Tzippy asked David if he wanted something to eat, and he responded that "It's a fast day!" After that, David did not speak again for three months. Doctors thought that he had to relearn his entire vocabulary as his injuries were so severe, but speak he did.

Prior to the accident, David's attitude had been filled with *netzach*, "I can do everything – if it's hard, so what?" Once he began to recover, he focused only on *hod* within *yesod*:

"Once, I didn't believe in finishing all the matriculation exams," he admits. "I hated studying. Now that it has suddenly become difficult, I want it, I appreciate it. I hope I manage to finish everything by the time I'm 21. All of my friends are in pre-military academies, some are already serving in the army. It is very difficult for me to be left behind."[374]

Asked if he is angry at God, David responds:

---

373. Racheli Melech-Sodah, "A Miracle Recovery," *The Jerusalem Post Magazine*, January 13, 2012, 19–20.
374. Ibid.

> "I am angry at the idiot who ruined my life, not at God. God has a plan for every person in the world. His plan for me was to have an accident, to be critically injured, and maybe to live afterward . . . I want people to read this interview and say, God is great, God is tremendous. He took my life and then He said, 'You are still young, we will let you go, take your life back.'"[375]

What a display of humility and gratitude and well-established bonding with the Creator of the world.

David's parents have maintained an album filled with letters that poured in from all over at the time of his accident while he was in the coma:

> "To our David," writes a non-observant relative from his father's side. "You know? We were never good at praying but you managed to rectify us a bit. Now we pray every day, every hour, with every improvement in your condition, with each of your responses that bring us joy."[376]

David Feiglin, you inspire me. Tzippy and Moshe Feiglin, God should bless your son, and each of you, with a long and meaningful life until 120. You have bonded with God and with each other. You have passed an ordeal and taught us what *hod* within *yesod* means.

ESTHER DRUCK SCHLISSER AND HER *TEHILLIM*

We have all felt overwhelmed by life's events, but *hod* within *yesod* gives us the ability to live for yet another day.

For more than two thousand of years, hundreds of millions have turned to King David's *Tehillim* at such times, for almost every one of his psalms is infused with the attitude of *hod* within *yesod*, the humble acceptance of whatever has happened, and the restatement that God is with us and we are not alone.

I cannot think of the timeless wisdom of the *Tehillim* without thinking of Esther Druck Schlisser, who read *Tehillim* cover to cover from her tattered purse-size book on a daily basis. Esther was, and shall always

375. Ibid.

376. Ibid.

remain, one of the most remarkable people I have had the privilege to meet and count as a dear friend. Widowed in her 40s, raising three sons alone, Esther returned to her native Israel to forge on for almost three decades before her own untimely death from cancer. For any who was blessed to know her, Esther combined zest, brilliance, Torah knowledge, deep affection for God and the Beit HaMikdash (about which she was an expert), and also a passionate love for and acceptance of all Jews. When she experienced loss after loss, she turned to her *Tehillim* and God with an attitude of *hod* within *yesod*.

What did King David write that comforted her so deeply?

- "In my distress I would call unto Hashem, and to my God I would cry [for salvation]. From His abode He would hear my voice, my cry to Him would reach His ears."[377]
- "Hashem is my shepherd, I shall not lack."[378]
- "Make Your ways known to me, Hashem; teach me Your paths. Lead me in Your truth and teach me, for You are the God of my salvation, to You I have hoped all the day."[379]
- "Why are you downcast, my soul, and why are you disturbed on my account? Hope to God! For I shall yet thank Him for the salvations of my countenance and because He is my God."[380]
- "Hashem, incline your ear, answer me, for I am poor and destitute. Guard my soul, for I am devout; save Your servant who trusts You, O You, my God."[381]
- "I love [Him], for Hashem hears my voice, my supplications. As He has inclined His ear to me, so in my days shall I call."[382]

It is from *Tehillim* that we learn *hod* within *yesod*, and how to be comforted despite the greatest of life's disappointments. Writes Rabbi Avrohom Feuer in his masterful *Tehillim Treasury*:

---

377. *Tehillim* 18:7.
378. Ibid., 23:1.
379. Ibid., 25:4–5.
380. Ibid., 42:12.
381. Ibid., 86:1–2.
382. Ibid., 116:1–2.

> *Tehillim* penetrates into the innermost recesses of the heart and brings forth the purest pristine feelings of faith and devotion to God. Therefore, *Tehillim* forge a bond with God in a way that nothing else can. Embrace *Tehillim* and you embrace God – constantly, consistently, confidently . . .[383]

Every home should have Rabbi Feuer's book to refer to weekly. A great family project is to assign each member to pick a favorite psalm and present it on Shabbat, rotating the responsibility each week. Children love this activity, and it will reaps many rewards, not the least of which is enhancing the *hod* within *yesod* of every family.

Esther Druck Schlisser leaves a living legacy of outreach and spiritual passion to thousands of the students she taught, as well as thousands of people she guided through the Kotel Tunnels – people whose lives have never been the same since their encounter with her.

In her merit and memory, let's try to tap into the timeless treasure that the *Sefer Tehillim* represents and learn the attribute of *hod* within *yesod* from the effort.

MODERN SOCIETAL ONSLAUGHT

Previously, we referred to Rabbi Twerski's article "Securing Your Home in an Insecure World" in which he says:

> Young people today are exposed to challenges that may exceed their ability to cope. And make no mistake; there is no immunity. These problems are occurring even in the finest and most observant families. "Kids at risk?" *All* kids are at risk.[384]

This eminent rabbi and psychiatrist provides parents with essential guidance. His guidance requires the development of all the *sefirah* combinations, and especially *hod* within *yesod*. Why? Because his advice is that we need to expend tons of energy and make sacrifices for principles that are

383. Avrohom Chaim Feuer, *Tehillim Treasury* (Brooklyn: Mesorah Publications, 1993), 26.

384. Twerski, "Securing Your Home in an Insecure World," *Jewish Action*, Summer 2011, 36.

worthy if we want to help our own children. The sacrifices he names do not require that parents start working at more jobs to buy their children more "things." He says something so fundamentally simple, yet difficult to attain without *hod* of *yesod*. Here it is:

> To provide security for a child, the most important element is true *shalom bayit*. But this requires that parents make sacrifices, yielding one's wants and even one's needs in consideration of one's spouse. As long as a husband or wife is self-centered, insisting on things being the way he or she wants them to be and disregarding the wants of the other spouse, there is no *shalom bayit*. When there is true love and mutual respect between the husband and wife, the *Shechinah* (Divine spirit) is present, and that brings in an element of *kedushah* (holiness) into the home that can help counteract the toxicity of the surrounding environment. *Kedushah* in the home, with a child feeling that he or she is holy, can provide resistance to negative environmental influences.[385]

To protect our kids who are "all at risk" in this modern world with its influences, we need to ensure there is true love and mutual respect between the husband and wife. This means many things. First, we need to be careful to marry the right person for the right reasons. Second, both husband and wife must work each day to achieve this lofty goal, so that the *Shechinah* can dwell in their home, adding yet another layer of protection against the harmful influences on our children.

Both require *hod* within *yesod*. They require a demeanor of humility and acquiescence to the other in caring and considerate ways, without any trait of arrogance or self-centeredness. It also requires the relationship to be deeply rooted in the garden of *yesod*, forever bonding in loving gratitude and appreciation for what was surely born in heaven and in oneness with God.

385. Ibid., 37.

DISCUSSION TOPICS FOR *HOD* WITHIN *YESOD*

For adults

1. In my relationship with my spouse, is there a lopsided nature to the level of giving and receiving? What am I going to do to balance it?
2. Have I expressed adequate gratitude and appreciation verbally and in writing to someone in my life who has been generous to me? Do my children do so? What can I do to improve this?
3. In daily prayers, do I remember to thank God for specific gifts with which I have been blessed?

For children

1. What are the three most special things that my parents have done for me? Even if I think I've thanked them before, I should take the time today to tell them about these three things and how much I appreciate all they have done (and continue to do) for me.
2. Can I name something kind and considerate that I can do for my parents, my siblings, or my teachers to show I can give to them also?
3. Do I spend too much time thinking about what I want and what I need, and then begin pressuring my parents to get/do it for me? How can I change this?

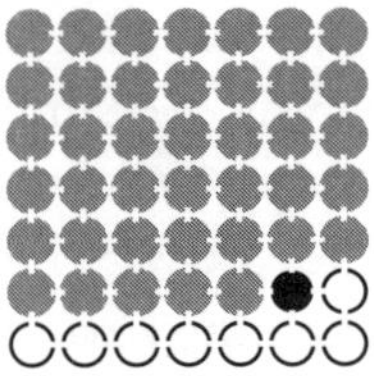

היום אחד וארבעים יום,
שהם חמישה שבועות וששה ימים, לעומר

Ha'yom echad v'arbaim yom,
she'hem chamisha shavuot v'shisha yamim la'Omer

**"TODAY IS THE FORTY-FIRST DAY,
OR FIVE WEEKS AND SIX DAYS, OF THE OMER."**

DAY 41

Yesod sh'b'Yesod (Bonding within Bonding)

***Yesod* within *yesod* helps us to exercise the utmost sensitivity, personal wisdom, and understanding in approaching matters or relationships. The goal is to always connect to the common ground that will both preserve and strengthen bonding, while addressing life's demands and challenges to bring mutually beneficial, positive outcomes in all spheres. *Yesod* within *yesod* is the apex of bonding and actualizing relationships and life experiences.**

"Being *shomer negiah* protects a woman's heart – and a man's sensitivity." With this statement, Gila Manolson describes simply how a man and woman should handle physical contact outside of marriage. And her message captures *yesod* within *yesod*. If you want to be privileged to experience and then master the most intimate bonding that you will ever have with another human being – which is that of a husband and wife – then I strongly suggest heeding her guidance.

In *The Magic Touch*, in the chapter entitled "We Women are from Venus," Gila Manolson writes the following:

> We women never learn. Somewhere in our brains, we've stored the information that men aren't like us, but we often fail to access it . . .

We so want to believe that men relate to us exactly as we relate to them – or at least that "this one's different." Either way, we suffer from recurrent amnesia . . . The fact is, in relationships, males are wired to be focused more on the physical. And females are wired to forget this. Furthermore, "scoring" usually means something beyond whatever a girl has in mind. The well-known Rabbi Dovid Orlofsky puts it this way:

"No guy," he'll tell a group of skeptical young women, "has ever walked down the street holding a girl's hand, thinking, 'Ahh. Completion. I feel so satisfied and content just holding her hand!' And no guy has ever seen a beautiful woman walk by and said to himself, 'Wow, I'd sure like to hold her hand!' Get this through your heads!!" . . .

Needless to say, this is nothing new. Fifteen hundred years ago, the Talmud,[386] in its typically straightforward style, described the difference between male and female sexuality in the following statement: "Go out and learn from the prostitutes' marketplace. Who's hiring whom?" In other words, men have historically paid for an experience that, for most women, wouldn't be worth it. But there's more. The Talmud then sums it up: "His drive comes from the outside, hers from the inside." Both men and women have hormones. But the average woman can't relate to a man totally externally. To become physically involved, she has to feel something more. He doesn't . . .

In addition to forgetting how men work, women are blessed with fertile and eager imaginations. Consequently, as long as an attractive guy isn't saying stupid things, a woman will invest him with all sorts of imaginary virtues so she can feel better about where her hormones are taking her . . . The upshot is that women are more prone to this type of self-delusion than men, and inevitably suffer the consequences. If you're a woman, you will be more likely to want to see something, believe you see it, and, based on this illusion, devote yourself physically and emotionally to someone about as appropriate for you as King Kong. And in the end, when it doesn't work out, and he says, "Thanks, it's been fun, and I hope you didn't take things too seriously," you're the one who gets hurt . . .

---

386. *Ketubbot* 64b.

> [Speaking to the man:] Though you may not be intentionally "leading her on" or "using her," that is what's happening. The cost to you is diminished sensitivity to other people's feelings and realities – a trait likely to manifest itself in other areas of life and keep you from becoming as caring a person as you could be.
>
> So I want to conclude with a plea to both sexes: Be careful. Women, realize that you're more vulnerable than you think. And men, realize that women suffer tremendously by being unable to sideline their emotions. The safest route is to keep a relationship non-physical. Without physicality, a woman will have less reason to delude herself, and a man will have less reason to let her. Being *shomer negiah* protects a woman's heart – and a man's sensitivity.[387]

Manolson brings her logic home in a later chapter entitled "In Defense of Not Knowing What You're Missing":

> The truth is, once they find their soulmate, most people don't exactly relish their memories of past involvements . . . The mistake in thinking you're "missing out" should be clear. You're not missing out by not doing something now if later you'll be relieved you didn't do it. When you're happily settled down with your partner for life, you won't regret all those experiences you've "missed." You'll know, with a certainty you've never had, that the only thing you've missed is what lies ahead.[388]

If you are a person who has "happily settled down with your partner for life," then you've achieved *yesod* within *yesod* at the highest levels with your spouse. It is unlikely that any barrage of life's tests will be able to shake the foundation that you have built with each other. *Kol ha-kavod* to you both. You have reached the serene truth that you and your soulmate are forever meant to be with each other in oneness with Hashem. How beautiful is this foundation of *yesod* within *yesod* in your life and love!

Each of us knows at least one married couple that feels this way. It is such a privilege to be around them. In the public sphere, it seems that the relationship between Menachem Begin and his beloved wife, Aliza, falls

387. Manolson, *The Magic Touch*, 53–55.

388. Ibid., 64–65.

into this category. Having met in Poland when Aliza was only 17, they married in 1939 wearing their brown Betar Zionist youth movement uniforms, shortly before Begin was imprisoned in Siberia and Aliza elected to make *aliyah* to "Palestine." There Begin joined her when released from prison. One of Aliza's rare press interviews provides a privileged peek into their deep bond and synchronicity from the beginning of their love: "All he [Begin] could promise me was that there was not much likelihood we would have any money, but on the other hand, there was every likelihood that we would have to spend a lot of years in jail."[389] In forty-three years of marriage, they were partners in their courage, strength, beliefs, and devotion to their family, to each other and Israel, remaining deeply in love until her untimely death at age 62.

Also consider the marriage of Rabbi Aryeh Levin and Hannah previously described on Day 6, and of course, that of Avraham and Sarah, Yaakov and Rachel, and Rabbi Akiva and his beloved wife Rachel, who gave up everything in order to support his spiritual path leading to greatness and to whom he credited all of the Torah he learned.

Yesod within *yesod* is within our grasp, if we simply open our eyes, honor one another and strive to enhance each other.

EMUNAH AS A SOURCE OF PURE BONDING

A litmus test of the genuineness and depth of relationship we have with God is the level of *emunah* we display in our everyday life. As noted previously, a "must read" book on this topic is *The Garden of Emuna*, where Rabbi Shalom Arush describes faith as an essential aspect of bonding with God:

> The key to inner peace is the internalization of the fact that Hashem is righteous and that His decisions are just. We achieve this by constantly reviewing the principles of *emuna*, namely, that Hashem runs the world, does everything for the best, and has a specific purpose for everything He does. Just as one believes that everything comes from Hashem, one must believe that all of Hashem's judgments are not only righteous, but merciful and compassionate as well. Since

389. "Aliza Begin Shared the Danger but Not the Spotlight," by the Associated Press, *Gainsville Sun*, November 15, 1982, 14a.

> Hashem's judgments are merciful and compassionate – even though they might not seem that way sometimes – they are always for our ultimate personal benefit. The trials and tribulations that Hashem sends us are designed to bring us closer to Him.[390]

There are certain foundational understandings that represent the underpinnings of our belief system and understanding of God *vis-a-vis* the world and *vis-a-vis* ourselves. The most fundamental is that God is only good, that He can do whatever He wishes, and that He completely controls and runs the world He created. God, however, desires that we establish a relationship with Him since He is a loving God and all of humankind matters to Him. God gave us humans free will, and He hopes that we will use it to establish a true bond with Him, based on the ethical principles of Torah He gave to Jews at Sinai and the Seven Noahide Laws He gave to the rest of the world. For whatever imperfections we have, He has also given us a system of *teshuvah*, so that we can make changes in our life and ask forgiveness for our misdeeds. While no human will ever be perfect, we are meant to strive to become the best we can be by emulating God's ways. He has endowed us with a *tzelem Elokim*, enabling us to strive towards the holiness that is His.

The principles of *emunah* described above provide a simple path of achieving a permanent bond with God, notwithstanding all our struggles, tests, and trials in life. This is how we can establish *yesod* within *yesod* in the most important relationship we will ever have – our relationship with God.

When we are aligned with God's will, and we communicate with Him daily, both as prescribed by our tradition as well as in personal meditations/contemplations, we have a direct connection to the "Hot Line of Hot Lines."

Problems with our spouse and children? We can talk to God and ask for guidance. Problems at work? We can vent to God. Problems with our health? We can ask God to reveal to us what areas He wants us to improve. ("Cast your burden upon Hashem and He will sustain you,"[391] says King David in the *Tehillim*.)

Whatever the problem, God is the "only address." And, for this, the

390. Arush, *The Garden of Emuna*, 237.

391. *Tehillim* 55:23.

cultivation and development of a high level of *emunah* that demonstrates *yesod* within *yesod* in a complete and profound way is essential.

THE EXAMPLE OF TWO BROTHERS

The description in the Torah of the relationship between two brothers – Moshe and Aaron – demonstrates, from beginning to end, a mastery of *yesod* within *yesod.* Just read the respectful interaction between them at the inauguration of the Mishkan, when Aaron was worried that his service would not be accepted by God because of the sin of the Golden Calf:

> Moshe said to Aaron: "Come near to the Altar and perform the service of your sin-offering and your elevation-offering and provide atonement for yourself and for the people." . . . Aaron raised his hands toward the people and blessed them . . . Moshe and Aaron came to the Tent of Meeting, and they went out and they blessed the people – and the glory of Hashem appeared to the entire people!"[392]

Read how seamlessly Moshe gave over the role of the priesthood to Aaron and his family. Look at their skillful partnership and division of labor – whether it was in communicating with Pharaoh or in the service of the Mishkan. Take note of how lovingly Moshe addressed Aaron after the tragic loss of two of his sons, Nadav and Avihu.

There was no comparison or jealousy over who was getting the most honor. This was truly *hinayh mah tov u'mah na'im, shevat achim gam yachad* ("how good and pleasant it is when brothers live together in harmony").[393]

Yesod within *yesod* can be between brothers, siblings, husband and wife, parents and children, very close friends, and us and God. This *sefirah* combination is absolutely essential to experience if we want to reach *malchut.*

---

392. *Vayikra* 9:7, 22–23.

393. *Tehillim* 133:1.

DISCUSSION TOPICS FOR *YESOD* WITHIN *YESOD*

For adults

1. Have you ever been tempted to do something "wrong," but visualized how either God or your family would be hurt by your doing so and this gave you the strength not to succumb to the temptation?
2. Have you and your spouse achieved, in your eyes, a mastery of *yesod* within *yesod*? What could you do so it can become a reality?
3. What is your level of *emunah*? How can you improve it?

For children

1. Who are you the closest to? How do you show it?
2. How close do you feel to God? How do you show it?
3. Have you ever been tempted to do something wrong, but stopped yourself? What caused you to do that?

היום שנים וארבעים יום,
שהם ששה שבועות, לעומר

Ha'yom shnayim v'arbaim yom,
she'hem shisha shavuot la'Omer

"TODAY IS THE FORTY-SECOND DAY,
OR SIX WEEKS, OF THE OMER."

DAY 42

Malchut sh'b'Yesod (Leadership/Nobility within Bonding)

Malchut coupled with *yesod* brings to bear a breadth and depth of personal development, experience, and actualization in building and maintaining highly effective relationships and fulfilling life goals. *Malchut* within *yesod* can be characterized as a trait that is steady, mature, serene, deliberative, loving, kind, considerate, and restrained, and that has enduring energy focused on achieving goals and maintaining bonds in a balanced, truthful, and responsible manner. Relationships which are augmented by *malchut* within *yesod* don't end when faced with obstacles, rather they grow stronger and closer. *Malchut* within *yesod* provides us with all the tools to organize, plan, execute, and accomplish challenging goals and missions, while helping us bond with people in all areas and walks of life.

Rabbi Jeffrey Bienenfeld shares an insight on the *Shema*, specifically the verse that reads: "Do not follow after your hearts and after your eyes." Rabbi Bienenfeld contrasts Lot's decision to move to Sodom, "And Lot *lifted his eyes* and saw the valley of the Jordan . . . well-watered everywhere . . . like the land of Egypt,"[394] with Avraham's journey to Mount Moriah,

394. *Bereshit* 13:10–11.

in describing which the Torah uses the exact same expression, "And on the third day, Avraham *lifted up his eyes* and saw the place from afar." Rabbi Bienenfeld writes:

> After decades upon decades of cultivating a heart suffused with a God-intoxicated awareness, Avraham had no trouble seeing what his heart knew to be true. Avraham was about to have a rendezvous with God, an encounter that would forever inspire all future generations of man . . .
>
> The lesson here is clear. Two people can perceive the same reality and yet see totally different things. Why? Because in each case, the heart is different.
>
> Here in Jerusalem, I travel by bus quite frequently and see many things. I see young people who jump to help the elderly and disabled, and I see others – just as close – who do nothing. I see people who somehow are able to sense when a total stranger is lost and immediately offer to help, and there are others totally oblivious to the plight of such a person. In a word, certain individuals see things that others don't. They have hearts with acute sensitivities for those in need, for those for whom a smile, a good word, a generous deed can make all the difference in the world . . .
>
> Hearts like these are not gifts. They are born of much effort and discipline. Over years and years, they are filled with elevating teachings, exposed to models of great religious passion and rectitude, and taught the sacred traditions and wisdom of the past. No wonder the eyes of such hearts see things differently, act differently, and display an ethical heroism of great spiritual significance.
>
> It's the difference between an Avraham and a Lot. And when we choose to be a true descendant of Avraham, his rewards are ours. And in that realization lies our *chizuk*.[395]

When we are able to feel a bond strong enough to aide a stranger, a passer-by, a hard-to-get-along-with family member or someone with whom we have nothing in common except that we both belong to the human race, we display a measure of *malchut* within *yesod*, and we stake our membership in the "Family of Man."

395. Jeffrey Bienenfeld, *Chizuk*, November 4, 2011.

GOD'S BOND WITH US

God always demonstrates *malchut* – whether within *chesed*, *gevurah*, *tiferet*, *hod*, or *yesod* – because He is perfection. By illustration, He created and sustains the world from a state of *malchut* within *chesed* because He needs nothing. He doesn't need a world inhabited by "other" than God.

However, it appears that God demonstrates the other *sefirot* combined with *malchut* through His "operating" systems of the *middat ha-din* and the *middat ha-rachamim*. For example, God operates in the *sefirah* combination of *malchut* within *gevurah* and *malchut* within *tiferet* in whatever He does, or restrains Himself from doing. This is because he has our ultimate good in mind.

Continuing through the *sefirot*, His love for us and desire to have an enduring relationship and dwell with us is an eternal demonstration of *malchut* within *netzach*, *malchut* within *hod*, and *malchut* within *yesod*. After all, He does not need anything, but He chose to create us in His image and He gave us free choice. He asks that we use that free choice to recognize that we are part of Him. When God chose to have a relationship with us, He revealed His attribute of *malchut* within *yesod*, encompassing all the previous *sefirah* combinations in that choice.

Beyond creating us and choosing to have a relationship with us, God gathered the Jewish people of three million around Mount Sinai, and addressed every man, woman and child who heard His voice.

Many commentators, from the Ramban to Ibn Ezra to the Kuzari, ask why the first commandment is "I am Hashem, your God, Who has taken you out of the land of Egypt, from the house of slavery,"[396] instead of "I am Hashem, your God, Creator of the universe." Rabbi Aryeh Kaplan summarizes their answers:

> They answer that this is because the latter statement would allow us to make a serious mistake. We could erroneously think of God as Creator, and yet believe that He has no interest in the affairs of man. In the opening words of the Ten Commandments, God was telling us that He is involved in the affairs of man, and has a profound interest in everything we do. God gave the Exodus as an example, for it was here that the entire Jewish people experienced Him . . . We believe in

396. *Shemot* 20:2.

> God, both as the God of creation and as the God of history. Judaism totally rejects the deistic concept of a God who created a world and then abandoned it with neither ruler, guide nor judge.[397]

God's *malchut* within *yesod* reveals His kingship and sovereignty in both creating us human beings and bonding with us through His gift of the Torah and its *mitzvot*, which allows us to structure our individual lives for the good.

YOSEF AND DIGNITY IN BONDING

All the *sefirah* combinations that make up *malchut* within *yesod* are revealed in Yosef's actions. The following describe some of these events that relate to each of the previous six *sefirot*, all of which are included in *malchut*:

- First, Yosef demonstrated his mastery of *chesed* within *yesod* when he forgave his brothers for selling him into slavery after they demonstrated they had done genuine *teshuvah*. This was clear to him when they showed their willingness to become slaves, in order to ensure that their brother Binyamin was freed and brought back to their father.
- Second, we see the *sefirah* of *gevurah* within *yesod* displayed when Yosef refused to acquiesce to Egyptian culture and engage in idolatry despite being the "only Jew on the block."
- Third, Yosef orchestrated *tiferet* within *yesod*, the harmony of the twelve brothers at the deathbed of their father, because Yosef completely forgave his siblings.
- The fourth *sefirah*, *netzach* within *yesod*, was displayed by Yosef in the twenty-two years when he lived in Egypt – he never assimilated, and raised his sons to honor the teachings of God and his father.
- In the fifth *sefirah*, *hod* within *yesod*, we see Yosef's humble and respectful reaction to his father's decision to give the mantle of leadership – that Yosef may have felt was his – to Yehuda instead.
- In the sixth *sefirah*, *yesod* within *yesod*, we see how Yosef resisted seductions of Potiphar's wife and instead clung to the image of his father in this moment of great vulnerability.

---

397. Kaplan, *The Infinite Light*, 14–16.

- With the achievement of each of the six *sefirah* combinations of *yesod*, Yosef elevated himself to the seventh *sefirah*, *malchut* within *yesod* in bonding with his family and the Jewish people.

The fact that three million Jews left Egypt, chose to receive the Torah and serve God is due in no small part to the unification and integration of the seven attributes that Yosef displayed in Egyptian *galut*.

TODAY'S PLAGUE OF JEWISH DISUNITY

That was then; this is now. Unfortunately, today there is widespread disunity among Jews. While so much of the world appears to be joined in delegitimizing Israel, denying the Holocaust and participating in unbridled "Jew hatred," it would seem nonsensical for Jews to waste a minute putting down their brethren, but this kind of behavior goes on nonetheless.

Let's look at the bigger picture. Surrounded on all sides by enemies and with only God to rely upon to protect us, is it really wise to label, attack, and put down our fellow Jews who are a bit different than us? God has made it crystal clear with the destruction of the Second Temple that baseless hatred of each other is something He will not tolerate. It is counterproductive and destructive. It goes against our collective Jewish mission. Who among us doesn't see this fact?

And yet, today, people still will label each other to set themselves apart and to criticize other groups that are not like them. The "religious" don't like the "secular"; the "*haredim*" don't like the "national religious"; the "Orthodox" don't like the "Conservative and "Reform" and vice versa. And there is lots more where that came from.

Aren't we all supposed to be working together to bring the Mashiach and restore the Divine Presence on earth so that the Third Temple can be built? Perhaps the more cogent question to be asked of every single Jew, without labeling, is suggested by Rabbi Arush in *The Garden of Wisdom*: "Are we living our lives with Hashem or not?"[398]

Living with God means learning to live with all other Jews. If that is not what we are doing, then we should realize that we have a choice to

398. Shalom Arush, *The Garden of Wisdom* (Jerusalem: Chut Shel Chessed Institutions, 2012), 151.

make, and God will one day hold us accountable for this choice. So, will we try to establish a relationship with Him by doing what is right and good in His eyes?

On this very topic, Rabbi Bienenfeld provides eloquent insight, in an article written just prior to Shavuot:

> When studying the history of the Second Temple and its destruction, I was always amazed – quite naively so – in learning how with the Roman armies besieging the city, the Jews inside fought with one another as if the enemy was non-existent . . . [But] had the Jewish people not managed to put aside their differences and merge together as one at the foot of Mount Sinai, the revelation of God's word would never have taken place. The message here is rather straightforward. Even if we cannot find common ground with everyone, there is enough good in most people to forge bonds of fellowship. And even if the differences can never be reconciled, the [sustained] efforts to create such concord are to be treasured . . . The mandate of forging a common cause inspired a once slave people to rise and be worthy of hearing the Divine Voice. Today, we must do no less.[399]

I am sure most of us agree that *malchut* within *yesod* must be manifest between the various groups making up our people, and between our people and God. We can all imagine – yes, we can! – gazing at a finished masterpiece whose central theme is bonding with each other with deep respect, forbearance, humility, peace, and unity.

Let's start by genuinely praying for this daily, and then let each of us do our part so that we can get on with the show of bringing Mashiach in our day.

PASSING JUDGMENT

So great is the issue of Jewish unity that *Jewish Action* devoted an entire issue to the topic in Summer 2012, entitled "Jewish Unity: It Starts with You." One of the contributors, Chief Rabbi Lord Jonathan Sacks of England, offers both an insight and a suggestion:

---

399. Jeffrey Bienenfeld, *Chizuk*, May 24, 2012.

> The beauty of creation, as we believe and as science ever more wondrously shows, is that unity above creates diversity below, and the more complex the life form, the greater the diversity . . . the Netziv writes in his commentary on the Tower of Babel, uniformity of thought is not a sign of freedom, but its opposite . . .
>
> Judaism is the only religion I know all of whose canonical texts are anthologies of arguments: arguments between God and humans, humans and God, humans and one another . . . Differences, arguments, clashes of style and substance, are signs not of unhealthy division but of health. The Judaism of Torah, *emunah* and *halachah* continues to do what it has done for so long – to defeat the law of entropy that states all systems lose energy over time. Not Judaism. Where you find argument, there you will find passion.

That's the good news from Rabbi Sacks. He goes on to suggest more proper responses to address this diversity in a manner that is not destructive. First he recalls the dying words of Rabbi Yochanan ben Zakkai who said: "Would that you worried about what God thinks instead of worrying about what another person thinks." Second, he notes that it is possible "to maintain your own position without criticizing others":

> One who passes judgment on his fellow is judged first. It is not necessary to negate in order to affirm. All that is necessary to achieve *ahavat Yisrael* is to remember daily that Hashem loves us – all of us – despite our differences, failings and disagreements. Hashem loves and forgives. Let us love and forgive.[400]

God's promise to us is that He will ensure the survival of the Nation of Israel as a whole. But that does not mean that each individual Jew will survive. To the extent we affirm and conform to the principle of Jewish togetherness, our fate and destiny will be assured. But, right now, we need to ask ourselves what we plan to do about Jewish disunity. It should bother us to the point that we are moved to work on it – first within our families, then within our communities and then within our entire nation.

---

400. Jonathan Sacks, "Jewish Unity. It Starts With . . . You," *Jewish Action*, Summer 2012, 44.

DISCUSSION TOPICS FOR *MALCHUT* WITHIN *YESOD*

For adults

1. Have I cut myself off from other Jews different than me by judgmental thoughts, speech, and actions?
2. When is the last time I provided some form of assistance to a complete stranger? What keeps me from doing it?
3. Am I living my life with God?

For children

1. Have I ever helped carry something for someone I don't even know? What about smiling at others and greeting them warmly?
2. Have I ever treated someone in a way that I would not have liked if it had been done to me?
3. How do I show every day that I live my life with God?

WEEK SEVEN

Malchut
(Leadership/Nobility)

OVERVIEW

Malchut (Leadership/Nobility)

God is King. And the world is His kingdom.

When His will is manifest in all the details of the world in which we live, this is God's *malchut* (kingship). When all the details of the kingdom manifest God's will, then His kingship is fully realized, then "His Name is One."

Each of us was created in the image of God. We each have some area for which only we are responsible. In assuming that responsibility, we are meant to attend to every detail, just as Hashem attends to every detail of the world. How well we fulfill the obligations we have been uniquely charged with indicates the strength of our *malchut* (sovereignty).

Our realm of responsibility and sovereignty may be small or large. It may be highly evident or hidden to us for most or all of our lives. Whatever our responsibility or our mission, it can only be carried out by us. If we do not do it; it will not get done, and we will not do our part to fix the world.

Because God chose to partner with us humans in the perfection of creation, when we play our part in completing our mission, we help to bring Mashiach and the ultimate *tikkun ha-olam*.

In this context, the simple way of defining our *malchut* is as the measured, insightful, and perceptive way of formulating thoughts and acting upon them through speech and deeds that display our mature wisdom, leadership, dignity, and nobility in any situation that we face.

LIVING IN HARMONY

By now, after all that we have learned in the past six weeks, we hopefully appreciate that we are meant to engage in a *process* of harmonizing our various personality traits to create a beautiful symphony that is unique to us. In this process of growth and development, we discover both our uniqueness, as well as recognize deep within our soul that we want to live a life in harmony with the "Great Essential I," God, and all of His creation.

In the last chapter, we quoted Rabbi Sacks: "The beauty of creation . . . is that unity above creates diversity below." And diverse is what we want it to be. We do not want to be like everyone else because we are not. Not only do we have a unique and singular destiny but, as a people, we have a similar uniqueness. Both matter.

Shalom, meaning "peace," shares its Hebrew root with *shaleim*, meaning "completeness." True peace is completeness in our personal and national "tent" with all that is good and whole. Our goal is not homogeny. Our goal is harmony within diversity. Each of the Twelve Tribes that left Egypt had their unique natural attributes and talents, their distinctive flags and location in the camp, their own blessing from their forefather Yaakov, and their own mission. All these missions, of course, shared a common source in God. Similarly, within each tribe, each individual member reflected the same dynamic – each was different but each shared a common goal with the others of achieving a relationship with God. And, as their descendants, we share this goal as well.

Beyond the mission that we have as individuals and as members of the Nation of Israel, we are also part of a larger world of humankind, which also has a mission. What is that mission? We find the answer in the words of the *Aleinu* prayer which we recite three times a day:

> It is our duty to praise the Master of all, to ascribe greatness to the Molder of primeval creation . . . we bend our knees, bow, and acknowledge our thanks before the King who reigns over kings, the Holy One, Blessed be He. He stretches out heaven and establishes the earth's foundation, the seat of His homage is in the heavens above and His powerful Presence is in the loftiest heights. He is our God and there is none other. True is our King, there is nothing beside Him . . .
>
> Therefore, we put our hope in You, Hashem our God, that we may soon see Your mighty splendor, to remove detestable idolatry from the earth, and false gods will be utterly cut off, to perfect the universe through the Almighty's sovereignty. Then all humanity will call upon Your Name, to turn all the earth's wicked toward You . . . they will all accept upon themselves the yoke of Your kingship that

> You may reign over them soon and eternally. For the kingdom is Yours and You will reign for all eternity in glory. . . .
>
> And it is said, "God will be King over all the world – on that day God will be One and His Name will be One."

That world of Final Redemption, of utopia, will be a world of *malchut*, when all the inhabitants of the Planet Earth finally realize that each of us matters, that each of us was created to make a positive difference in the world, and that each of us is a part of something greater, the "Great Essential I." Rabbi Aaron summarizes it succinctly:

> Our mission is to realize that we are, in essence, one with each other and one with God. This is what it really means to serve God – to be God's agent and work on His behalf to facilitate this divine process, whereby the One becomes conscious through free choice. This is why the significance of our choices is measured not by how we affect what is going on around us, but by what happens within us. The focus of our choices is about how to change ourselves, become living reflections of God, and achieve a higher awareness of God's oneness.[401]

This, then, is our vision and our goal for Week Seven of the Omer count when we focus on *malchut*.

NOBILITY OF EACH HUMAN BEING

When the first six *sefirot* of *chesed*, *gevurah*, *tiferet*, *netzach*, *hod*, and *yesod* are properly channeled in our thoughts, words, and deeds, the outcome is *malchut*. Because then the nobility within each human being, as a *tzelem Elokim*, surfaces.

My husband shared a wonderful analogy on this point, juxtaposing the six days of creation with the six *sefirot* and the seventh day, Shabbat, with the *sefirah* of *malchut*. To explain:

God created the world in six days and, then, came the seventh day – Shabbat. On Shabbat, God refrained from further creative acts, just as we are to refrain from creating on Shabbat. We call this day the "Shabbos

---

401. Aaron, *The Secret Life of God*, 182–183.

Queen," we wear our finest clothes, and we fill our homes with light as we usher in this day of heightened spiritual awareness. On this day we do not make individual requests of God, for Shabbat is *shaleim*, complete and in need of nothing. It is a day of *malchut*.

Shabbat, the seventh day, is the completion of our work for the preceding six days when we were hopefully engaged in successful acts of *chesed*, *gevurah*, *tiferet*, *netzach*, *hod*, and *yesod* – the other six attributes. But now comes *malchut*, the seventh. Now that we have devoted 42 days immersed in the six *sefirot*, we are ready to "take in *malchut*," much like after working wisely for six days we are ready to "take in Shabbat."

What does it mean to "take in *malchut*"?

It is to live in a state of dignity, self-respect, nobility, completion. Let's look at what that means in practice:

Most psychologists acknowledge the importance of high self-esteem. And it's logical – when we have a strong personal sense of dignity and worth, we are likely to rate high in the four areas of physical, emotional, mental, and spiritual health. Therefore, as we examine *malchut*, we will need to accurately assess our balance in all of these areas.

Rabbi Dr. Abraham Twerski writes:

> One does not really have an option whether or not to have a self-image. All humans have a self-concept. The only option is whether to have one that is accurate or one that is distorted . . . Thinking poorly of oneself is not a virtue. Virtue is truth, and there is no virtue in denying the reality or the truth about oneself . . . A proper adjustment to reality can only be achieved when reality is correctly perceived . . . Just as one must have a valid concept of one's external reality, so one must have a valid concept of one's internal reality. One must know what one's positive components are in order to cultivate them and develop them to their fullest, and one must know one's weaknesses in order to correct them and improve upon them . . .[402]

Making a common sense analogy, Twerski points out that just as one is typically not aware of one's throat until it is sore or infected, one is not aware of "the self" unless it, too, is ill:

402. Twerski, *I'd Like to Call for Help, but I Don't Know the Number*, 29–30.

> Ideally, a healthy person is not self-conscious. A true self-awareness will result in neither vanity nor self-centeredness, but to the contrary, is necessary to avoid and overcome vanity and self-centeredness. It is also essential for the self-fulfillment requisite for spiritual growth . . . The unique features that constitute our humanity require no less effort in bringing them to their fullest potential than do our artistic, mechanical, or intellectual talents. The ennobling process of character development comprises spiritual growth.[403]

I would say that this process of character development, engaging in self-improvement, and achieving a healthy self-concept that flows from living a life of worth and fulfillment, is the process of mastering *malchut.*

MALCHUT AND HAPPINESS

In addition to impacting our self-esteem, *malchut* plays a key role in our happiness.

Because anti-depressants are among the biggest selling drugs in the world, it is essential that people begin to understand more deeply what true joy is. Dr. Tal Ben-Shahar, a former researcher/professor at Harvard and author of *Happier*, developed a "happiness model" that he has chosen to call the "hamburger model." He named it such after a personal experience involving healthy foods and hamburgers.

While preparing for a squash tournament, Dr. Ben-Shahar spent one month eating only lean fish and chicken, whole-grain carbs, fruits and vegetables. His plan was to reward himself with a junk-food hamburger binge after the squash tournament was over. Indeed, after the tournament, he went to a fast-food joint and ordered four hamburgers, but when they came he had an epiphany. He realized that in the month he had been eaten well, his body felt cleansed and full of energy. While he would enjoy eating the burgers, he knew that afterwards he would feel tired and stuffed. "Staring at my untouched meal, I thought of four kinds of hamburgers, each representing a distinct archetype, with each archetype describing a distinct pattern of attitudes and behaviors."[404]

---

403. Ibid., 30–31.

404. Tal Ben-Shahar, *Happier* (NY: McGraw Hill, 2007), this and subsequent quotations are from pp. 14–26.

In his book, he identifies these archetypes and correlates them with the kind of benefits and detriments each brings to life:

- The first hamburger/archetype he calls "the *hedonism* archetype" for hedonists focus on "enjoying the present while ignoring the potential negative consequences of their actions," just as he knew that eating the junk burger would "yield *present benefit*, in that I would enjoy it, and *future detriment*, in that I would subsequently not feel well."
- The second hamburger type he thought of was a tasteless vegan burger which "would afford me *future benefit*, in that I would subsequently feel good and healthy, and *present detriment*, in that I would not enjoy eating it. The corresponding archetype is that of the *rat race*. The rat racer, subordinating the present to the future, suffers now for the purpose of some anticipated gain."
- The worst hamburger of all both tastes bad and is unhealthy, "eating it, I would experience *present detriment*, in that it tastes bad, and suffer *future detriment*, in that it is unhealthful. The parallel to this burger is the *nihilism* archetype . . . [which] describes the person who has lost the lust for life; someone who neither enjoys the moment nor has a sense of future purpose."
- Finally, Dr. Ben-Shahar asks, "What about a hamburger that would be as tasty as the one I had turned down and as healthy as the vegetarian burger? A burger that would constitute a complete experience with both present and future benefit? This hamburger exemplifies the *happiness* archetype. Happy people live secure in the knowledge that the activities that bring them enjoyment in the present will also lead to a fulfilling future."

Each of us has characteristics identified by Dr. Ben-Shahar – those of the rat racer, hedonist, nihilist, and the one who is happy. Now let's look at how these four archetypes relate to the *sefirah* at hand – *malchut.*

THE RAT RACER

When we raise our children to believe that they are going to school – whether it is a university or yeshiva – *only* to get good grades so they can later get a good job, then we are instilling traits of a "rat racer" in our children.

Instead, we should be teaching our children that learning is fun. And we should be modeling this attitude by our own joy in reading, learning, and sharing what we have learned.

There is nothing negative in setting high expectations for our children or encouraging hard work. If working hard will provide both present and future benefits – if we work hard because we like our work in the present and it will also profit in the future – then great. But what distinguishes those who are rat racers "is their inability to enjoy what they are doing, and their persistent belief that once they reach a certain destination, they will be happy." Dr. Ben-Shahar notes that our culture reinforces this belief system:

> We learn to focus on the next goal rather than on our present experience and chase the ever-elusive future our entire lives. We are not rewarded for enjoying the journey itself but for the successful completion of a journey. Society rewards results, not processes; arrivals, not journeys. . . .
>
> Once we arrive at our destination, once we attain our goal, we mistake the relief that we feel for happiness . . . When we mistake these moments of relief for happiness, we reinforce the *illusion* that simply reaching goals will make us happy . . . We can consider the experience of relief to be *negative happiness* as it stems from the negation of stress or anxiety. By its very nature, relief presupposes an unpleasant experience and cannot, therefore, yield lasting happiness.

The rat racer, in the parlance of Judaism, is a slave stuck in Egypt. When we model this archetype for our children much of the time, they may well learn to imitate it, failing to learn how to achieve lasting joy. Rat racers cannot achieve *malchut*, because they don't value the process, only the product.

I have a friend who creates a wonderful Shabbat environment for many guests – including soldiers, students, and those from all walks of life. She once shared with me that she tries hard to make sure that she is smiling and happy when she is preparing the Shabbat chicken, and that she is thinking thoughts of harmony and peace when she is making her challah. She inspired me to adopt a version of this practice – as I cook, I put on wonderful instrumental guitar music of Jewish tunes that both touch something deep inside of me as well as bring out something higher in me.

I must confess that this is not what I did for most of life, when I would rip myself away from house and work responsibilities minutes before candle-lighting time. Yes, I was a rat racer and not a very good model to others. But I changed, and I believe any rat racer can.

In the language of our Omer count, when we appreciate the sweetness of the tree (i.e., the process of growth) as much as the sweetness of the fruit (the product), we have mastered an important component of *malchut*.

THE HEDONIST AND THE NIHILIST

Unlike the rat racer, the hedonist "seeks pleasure and avoids pain." He or she satisfies desires with no thought to future consequences. Friendships and relationships are entered with enthusiasm but when the newness disappears, the hedonist moves on. If a hedonist finds work hard, he or she avoids it. Writes Dr. Ben-Shahar:

> Without a long-term purpose, devoid of challenge, life ceases to feel meaningful to us; we cannot find happiness if we exclusively seek pleasure and avoid pain . . . The hedonist suffers from the "floating moment fallacy" – the false belief that happiness can be sustained by an ongoing experience of momentary pleasures that are detached from a future purpose.

Nothing could be further from *malchut*. In the language of the Omer count, the very feeling that we need a life of meaning – now and in the future – is an awareness of *malchut*.

And what about the nihilist archetype?

Writes Dr. Ben Shahar: "If the rat-race archetype describes the state of living for the future and the hedonism archetype the state of living for the present, then the nihilism archetype captures the state of being chained to the past." The nihilist has resigned himself to his present unhappiness and expects more of the same in the future. His "Egypt" is that he is enslaved by his past failures and has developed a "learned helplessness" – an attitude that he has no control over his life. This kind of thinking leads to despair.

When I think about the problem of the nihilist, I think about the words of Dr. Viktor Frankl – an Austrian-born neurologist, psychiatrist, and Holocaust survivor – in his extraordinary book, *Man's Search for*

Meaning, a book that the Library of Congress has called one of the ten most influential books of the twentieth century, he writes:

> I had wanted simply to convey to the reader by way of concrete example that life holds a potential meaning under any conditions, even the most miserable ones. And I thought that if the point were demonstrated in a situation as extreme as that in a concentration camp, my book might gain a hearing. I, therefore, felt responsible for writing down what I had gone through, for I thought it might be helpful to people who are prone to despair.[405]

Dr. Frankl noted from observing others in the four camps he inhabited, including Auschwitz, that those who survived the longest were those who perceived they had something to live for. Following the Holocaust, those most able to move on and lead worthy and productive lives were those who also believed they had something to live for. This realization led him later to develop his famous and revolutionary model of psychotherapy called "logotherapy" which holds that the "search for meaning" is the most primary motivational force for all of humanity.

In one searing example, he writes about being marched to forced labor and gleaning what gave his own life meaning:

> . . . the man marching next to me whispered suddenly: "If our wives could see us now! I do hope they are better off in their camps and don't know what is happening to us." That brought thoughts of my own wife to mind . . . nothing was said, but we both knew: each of us was thinking of his wife. Occasionally, I looked at the sky, where the stars were fading and the pink light of the morning was beginning to spread behind a dark bank of clouds. But my mind clung to my wife's image, imagining it with an uncanny acuteness. I heard her answering me, saw her smile, her frank and encouraging look. Real or not, her look then was more luminous than the sun which was beginning to rise. A thought transfixed me: for the first time in my life I saw the truth . . . The truth – that love is the ultimate and the highest goal to which man can aspire. Then I grasped the meaning

405. Frankl, Viktor, *Man's Search for Meaning* (NY: Washington Square Press, 1985), 16.

> of the greatest secret that human poetry and human thought and belief have to impart: *The salvation of man is through love and in love.* I understood how a man who has nothing left in this world may still know bliss, be it only for a brief moment, in the contemplation of his beloved. In a position of utter desolation, when a man cannot express himself in positive action, when his only achievement may consist in enduring his sufferings in the right way – an honorable way – in such a position man can, through loving contemplation of the image he carries of his beloved, achieve fulfillment. For the first time in my life, I was able to understand the words, "The angels are lost in perpetual contemplation of an infinite glory."[406]

No one should ever have to experience what Dr. Viktor Frankl experienced, or what all of the victims and survivors of the Holocaust or of the many acts of terror experienced. And yet in being exposed to their stories, we are witnesses to *malchut,* the polar opposite of hedonism and nihilism.

THE SECRET TO HAPPINESS

Dr. Ben-Shahar concludes that not everything we do can provide both present and future benefit. Expecting constant happiness is setting ourselves up for disappointment and failure:

> The key is to keep in mind, even as one forgoes some present gain for the sake of a larger future gain, that the objective is to spend as much time as possible engaged in activities that provide both present *and* future benefit.[407]

In every life there is some mundane work. Sometimes it is worth it to give up a present benefit for a future gain, such as studying for a test necessary for us to achieve a goal we truly desire, or saving money for some future objective. At such times, a brief focus on the present can revitalize us if done in moderation – a walk on the beach, an ice cream cone, reading a good book for pleasure can all bring momentary happiness. But Dr.

406. Ibid., 56–57.
407. Ben-Shahar, *Happier,* 26.

Ben-Shahar's potent message is that "happiness is not about making it to the peak of the mountain nor is it about climbing aimlessly around the mountain; happiness is the experience of climbing toward the peak."

We have been climbing toward Mount Sinai for 42 days and we are about to make a sprint for the top. For the duration of the 49-day Omer count, we have been preparing ourselves to receive the Torah anew, to repeat the most important event to ever occur in Jewish – and I dare say – human history. This process is part of a journey towards *malchut*. True inner joy and a sense of being *shaleim* is the outcome of participating in this process.

Malchut has many faces. Our task is to discover our uniqueness and, in so doing, give expression to a beautiful, sacred nobility that resides within us. How we demonstrate this nobility will not be how others demonstrate it – nor how our mothers, father, siblings, or best friends demonstrate it. Each person's mission is distinctive and singular, each person's mission is unique and their expression of *malchut* is also unique.

ARI WEISS AND OTHER FALLEN SOLDIERS

In a moving article in *The Jerusalem Post Magazine*, entitled "Between Two Sirens," Rabbi Stewart Weiss writes of the "emotional roller coaster" that he experiences each year between the "thrilling heights" of the Pesach Seder and Israel's Yom Ha'atzmaut. One celebrates the day when the Nation of Israel was born, the other when the State of Israel was born. But, he writes, "sandwiched in between these glorious events are intense moments of sadness and solemnity."

These sad moments include the last day of Pesach when we recite *Yizkor* for loved ones no longer living, "whose seats remain empty at our Seder table," Holocaust Remembrance Day a week later, and then another week later, Remembrance Day for those killed in Israel's wars. He adds his perspective on these events:

> I was born after the last death camp had been liberated, but made *aliya* too late to personally experience army boot camp. And so I live between two sirens: the one that sounds on Holocaust Remembrance Day for my many relatives who perished in Poland, and for my mother-in-law who spent her 16th birthday in Auschwitz; and the

> one that wails on Remembrance Day in a cry of commemoration for our son who fell in battle 10 years ago, as well as for all the heroic men and women of our holy armed forces.[408]

I have heard Rabbi Weiss speak about his son Ari, who was 21 when he was killed. There are no words to describe the lingering effect his remarks about Ari have on an audience. Years later, I can still recall what he said, and his message helps me form my own impressions of what living a meaningful life – a life of *malchut* – truly means. In his article, he explains how he feels:

> The same ill wind that blew over Europe, as the Germans emptied the continent of Jews in a brash and brutal blitzkrieg, is polluting our air once again . . . Anti-Semitism is rampant, whether poorly disguised as anti-Zionism or unabashedly flaunted as pure, unadulterated Jew-hatred . . . It is not a good feeling . . . But then I remind myself that, despite all the signs of danger around us, there is a pronounced and powerful difference between Then and Now.[409]

Before and during the Holocaust, the world was largely divided between those countries in which Jews were not allowed to live and those countries which they could not enter, Chaim Weizmann has noted. Jews around the world waited for "some knight in shining armor to come and rescue us and he never appeared." The rail lines leading to Auschwitz were not bombed and Jews seeking asylum were turned away repeatedly by democracies all over the world.

That was then. And now? Rabbi Weiss paints the picture:

> Now we have an army. And a navy. And the best air force in the world. God has blessed us with the finest soldiers ever to put on a uniform, and they are sworn to our protection. They will not let us ever again be attacked with impunity . . . They live on the front, but they have our backs. *They are the definition of everything good that*

408. Stewart Weiss, "Between Two Sirens," *The Jerusalem Post Magazine*, April 27, 2012, 34.
409. Ibid.

> *derives from sovereignty*, and the antidote to all the deadly ills that flow from statelessness.[410]

He is right. And he adds a moving postscript to the death of his son: During *shiva*, a crying woman appeared at the door of his home; she related that she was born, raised, and married in Israel but when her son turned 16, she and her family decided to leave the country, because "we could not bear the thought of him standing in harm's way," and he very much wanted to join a combat unit. They moved to California. When he turned 18, her son still wanted to serve in the IDF. She and her husband decided to buy him a car, hoping that this would make him happy. He loved his car, said the mother, breaking down: "Three months ago, just after his 21st birthday – the same age as your son – he was killed in a car accident. I came here to tell you what a fool I was for taking my child away from Israel. If he was destined to die young, he should have died in an IDF uniform, not in a car in California. He should have been a hero, like your boy, and not just another statistic."[411]

KING DAVID, THE SEVENTH SHEPHERD

It is only fitting that David – the warrior, the king – is the shepherd who personifies this seventh and final attribute of *malchut*. Look at his life. Such highs and lows. Such adversity and glory. Such pain. And yet he glorified God through his timeless *Tehillim* that bring solace to billions of people of all faiths who, for more than two thousand years, have read them to attain the comfort that only these verses seem to bring to the broken heart.

Treated as an outcast by his father and brothers as a youth, David nurtured a love and devotion to God that was so complete that it truly lacked nothing. He was a boy who lived alone in the hills tending sheep and, there, God tested him and found him worthy. God saw that David took the little sheep out first to eat the new tender grass. Then he took the older sheep to chew the somewhat tougher shoots. Only then did he take the young adult sheep to consume the rough fodder. He also grazed his sheep only in the wilderness so they would not steal from people's fields. Such

410. Ibid.
411. Ibid.

instinctive, natural care, consideration, and wisdom applied to sheep! Seeing this, God said: "You have been found faithful with sheep. Now come and tend My flock[412] . . . You shall shepherd My people Israel."[413]

What does the story of David's young life teach us? Many lessons. For example, that only God knows the outcome of a series of inexplicable events. God knew what David's mission was supposed to be, even if his own family was late in seeing it, but they did come to eventually understand David's role in the history of Israel.

But while he played out that role, he also dealt with innumerable problems. For forty years of his seventy-year lifespan, he was the king of Israel, and for thirty-three years of that time, he was plagued with sickness.[414] Two of his sons aligned themselves with efforts to dethrone him.[415] One of his daughters was raped by his son.[416] Trusted advisors aggressively plotted to block Shlomo, David's choice for his successor, from becoming the king of Israel. Despite these travails, it is said that later in life the *yetzer hara* had no power over him.[417] He could not abide the evil inclination and killed it in his heart, forcing it to comply with the will of God.[418] He was humble and knew that everything came from God, as he said:

> "Yours, God, is the greatness, the strength, the splendor, the triumph and the glory, even everything in heaven and earth. Yours, God, is the kingdom, and the sovereignty over every leader. Wealth and honor come from You and You rule everything – in Your hand is power and strength and it is in Your hand to make anyone great or strong. So now, our God, we thank You and praise Your splendorous Name."[419]

He also said to God: "Although I was king, I made you King over me." When he went to war, he said: "I did not win because of my might; [Hashem] helped me and granted me victory."[420]

---

412. *Shemot Rabbah* 2:2.
413. II *Shmuel* 5:2.
414. *Sanhedrin* 107a, b.
415. I *Melachim*, Chap. 1, and II *Shmuel*, Chap. 15.
416. II *Shmuel*, Chap. 13.
417. *Bava Batra* 17a.
418. *Yerushalmi Berachot* 9:5.
419. I *Divrei HaYamim* 29:11–13.
420. *Shocher Tov* 16:2 and 144:1.

From David's example, we clearly see that sovereignty, nobility, and leadership come from bonding first and foremost with God. We should also cleave to God when alone – as he did. As well, like King David, we should make sure that day-by-day we are living a life in accordance with the will of God. A great tool for this is a nightly personal introspection, better known as *cheshbon hanefesh*. This tool will help us do *teshuvah* the moment we realize our actions were not aligned with God's will. And finally, we should long to do the will of God and discover what is our special mission, so that we can carry it out in a manner that pleases Him.

Though he was the great and powerful king of a mighty nation, when he was admonished by the Prophet Natan for his involvement with Batsheva, David's instant response was: "I have sinned before God."[421] Then he donned sackcloth and ashes, fasted, and lay on the floor. He accepted full responsibility for his actions and begged for forgiveness from God, his Father in Heaven. No excuses. No blaming of others.

David taught all of humanity for all time. He taught us how to live a life totally interwoven with God and how, in the event we transgress and disappoint our Father in Heaven, we can restore that relationship. Can you imagine a twenty-first century world leader behaving in such a manner?

We each *can* be in charge of our lives instead of our lives being in charge of us. In whatever amount of time we are given to live in this lifetime, we each *can* make noble choices that define our lives as meaningful and not meaningless. From David, we learn everything we need to know about achieving sovereignty – *malchut* – over our lives.

While David personified the attribute of sovereignty, he did not become king through his own wisdom or might. He was not king because he inherited the throne from his father. Rather, he became king and received the kingdom from the King of Kings, who lifted him from tending sheep to become His faithful shepherd of the flocks of *Bnei Yisrael.*

Why do we think God chose David? Rabbi Kitov answers:

> God chose David because He knew that even if he were granted the ability to rise to the greatest of heights, he would forever remain a servant in his own eyes. David remained humble – when he tended the sheep and when the kings from west and east came to his court

421. II *Shmuel* 12:1–13.

> to pay him homage. It was David who made God sovereign among mankind. It was he who provided humanity with the means to sing God's praises. He rejoiced in the greatness of others and combined that greatness with his own to pay tribute to the One to Whom greatness belongs.[422]

Recalling David's example, in our daily morning prayers we repeat his words:

> "Blessed are you, God . . . Yours is greatness, strength, glory, eternity, and splendor . . . Yours is sovereignty and You are uplifted above all . . . Who am I and who is My nation that we might have the strength to volunteer for this . . . for all is from You and that which we give You is from Your hand."[423]

This prayer reinforces for us what we have already learned in the Omer count, which is that when we cleave to God (*yesod*), as King David did throughout his life, there is an outpouring of greatness (*chesed*), strength (*gevurah*), glory (*tiferet*), eternity (*netzach*), and splendor (*hod*). And we, ourselves, become great. We fulfill our mission. We achieve a sense of *malchut* – that is, sovereignty over our own lives, and we enjoy the satisfaction that comes from a balanced physical, emotional, mental, and spiritual health.

Sometimes, others help us to recognize what our mission is. Sometimes we don't realize it until later adulthood. The point is this: we have a role to play in our own lives and that of our family members – to help us and them to achieve their own unique greatness.

RACHEL, THE WIFE OF RABBI AKIVA

The great Rabbi Akiva was the child of a shepherd who was a convert to Judaism. He, himself, was a shepherd in his youth. He was illiterate and only began his Torah studies when he was forty years old. Despite this ignoble beginning, Rabbi Akiva rose to become one of the leading sages of all time, as notes Rabbi Chaim Kolitz in his outstanding and well-sourced

---

422. Kitov, *The Book of Our Heritage*, Vol. 2, 685.

423. I *Divrei HaYamim* 29:10–14.

biography, *Rabbi Akiva: Sage of All Sages*, "No sage of his stature has arisen in all the generations."[424]

How did this transformation occur?

Rabbi Akiva's second wife, Rachel was the daughter of a wealthy man from Jerusalem; she lacked no material comforts, and yet she was attracted to this humble shepherd, seeing him as "the most humble of all her father's herders." And she decided to bring out his hidden potential. She urged him to study. When she said she would marry him, her father disowned her. She did it anyway.

In the beginning, they lived in complete poverty. She cut her hair and sold it so that he could continue studying. He chopped wood, sold half and used the other half to heat the house and study by the fire. After abandoning shepherding, he worked as an agricultural laborer for three years for the father of Rabbi Eliezer, who later became his main teacher. It was said, "Here is Rabbi Akiva, whose poverty is unequalled – and whose studying also is unequalled."[425]

When Rabbi Akiva realized that he had reached a plateau in his studies and knowledge, he went to learn Torah from Rabbi Eliezer ben Hyrcanus and Rabbi Yehoshua for a period of twelve years, during which time he and Rachel did not see each other. He mastered the complete Torah, including the esoteric wisdom.

> [Meanwhile,] Rachel went to live with Rabbi Akiva's mother and hired herself out to work for other women. Half of her wages were sent to her husband so he could continue to learn. Years later, Rabbi Akiva returned along with his many students after he had learned the entire Torah. Rachel came before her husband wearing rags. After she fell upon his feet and kissed him, his students rebuked her. Rabbi Akiva silenced them and said, "Leave her be – my and your Torah is hers."[426]

Rachel personified *malchut*. She sacrificed for the greater good, so that all of Israel would be blessed with a Sage of this magnitude. She perceived

424. Chaim Kolitz, *Rabbi Akiva: Sage of All Sages*, this and subsequent quotations from pp. 3–28.
425. Ibid., 28.
426. Ibid.

the greatness of Rabbi Akiva when, by all external trappings, his greatness was not at all evident.

Can you imagine how Rabbi Akiva would be judged today?

But not by Rachel. She accurately perceived the great potential within her husband and helped him achieve the apex – *malchut* – no matter what it cost her.

NO MATTER THE COST: *MALCHUT* IN ADVERSITY

To examine this aspect of *malchut*, we turn again to the final letters sent by Holocaust victims to their loved ones. To read their letters is to glimpse the astonishing sense of nobility of those confronting the most horrific challenge of our time.

Here is a letter written by Pinchas Eisner, age 17, to his older brother, Mordechai, just when he knew his life was over. On November 3, 1944, Pinchas and seventy other Jews from Budapest were led to a forest nearby Csomad. They were forced to dig a huge pit, ordered to take off their clothes and, then, they were all machine-gunned into their self-made grave.

When Pinchas wrote his letter to Mordechai, his older brother was in a labor camp. After Budapest was liberated from the Nazis, Mordechai returned home and found this letter:

16 October, 1944 6:15 p.m.

My Dear Brother,

Goodbye! Think of our talk that night. I felt as one with you. I knew that, if it were you whose life would end, I would go on living as if I had lost half my body and soul. You said that, if I die, you will kill yourself. Think of what I told you, that if you stay alive I will live on within you. I would have liked to continue my life, with you and with our family. Plans, desires, hopes were before me . . . But now it is all over. In the city, Jews were exterminated from entire streets. There is no escape . . . At seventeen I have to face certain death . . .

Farewell and forgive me if ever I have offended you. (For the first time my eyes begin to fill with tears. I am careful not to cry as there are others present.) Because I loved you . . . I feel great tenderness, great love and my eyes are filled with tears. Farewell. Live happily, all the best to you my dear brother, lots of success, much love and happiness, don't weep,

> *don't cry. (I felt so bad hearing you cry that night.) Think of me lovingly. Remember me with a good heart and, if there is another world . . . then I will pray to God to help you in whatever you do. Farewell, my dear only brother!*
>
> *Farewell! Remember me. I hope that I, too, will be able to think of you even from over there. I would like to hug and kiss you once more. But who knows to whom I write these lines? Are you alive?! Farewell, my dear brother, my sweet Mordechle, live happily. Kissing you for the last time – till we meet again.*
>
> *Your Loving Brother*[427]

Pinchas Eisner, age 17 – five days prior to being gunned to death by Nazis – is giving final strength to his brother. Calmly and bravely facing death. Taking care of business. Asking forgiveness for anything he may ever have done to offend his brother. Setting things in order. Knowing that they will "meet again" only in *Olam Haba*. Who is more powerful – Pinchas Eisner or Adolf Hitler, *Yimach Shemo*? Who chose to lead a God-powered life? The answer is so very clear for all of us, as we witness *malchut* in a 17-year-old boy, so similar to King David in his youth and life.

MALCHUT AND SPIRITUALITY

A key feature of *malchut* is spirituality, which can be achieved in a variety of ways, not all necessarily involving religious practice. This is how the eminent psychiatrist Rabbi Dr. Abraham Twerski defines spirituality which, he says, plays a key role in attaining balanced emotional health:

> All the unique features of a human being *in their totality* are what constitute the *spirit* of man. When man exercises these unique features, he is being *spiritual*. Thus, *spirituality* is simply the implementation of those distinctive features that separate man from animal.[428]

In his book, *I'd Like to Call for Help, But I Don't Know the Number*, which he subtitled *The Search for Spirituality in Everyday Life*, Rabbi Twerski

427. Dafni and Kleiman, *Final Letters*, 44–47.
428. Twerski, *I'd Like to Call for Help, but I Don't Know the Number*. See pp. 10–67 for the list of twelve distinctive features of spirituality and their descriptions.

goes on to enumerate twelve such distinctive features. Considered in total, they describe a person who has achieved *malchut,* as well as balanced the previous six *sefirot*:

1. *Only humans have freedom of free moral choice – making this choice is being spiritual.*

Both humans and animals "have biological drives such as hunger, thirst, sex, desire for comfort, avoidance of pain, etc. Animals are at the mercy of their biological drives and cannot resist them." In contrast, "our entire concept of human responsibility, with our elaborate system of positive and negative sanctions, is based on the assumption that man is not at the mercy of his impulses . . . Man functions in his unique human capacity when he chooses to deny an urge when there is no possibility of any unpleasant consequences. When his decision to deny his biological drive is based only on his principles of right and wrong, man rises to a supra-animal level. That is when man makes a free moral choice, something which is uniquely human . . ."

Indeed, when a person makes a free moral choice and restrains behavior that would be harmful physically, emotionally, mentally or spiritually, we consider this a display of both *gevurah* and *malchut.*

2. *Spiritual people are willing to sacrifice physical comfort for an external goal.*

When one sacrifices comfort or contentment to achieve an external goal, one is acting spiritually. Rabbi Twerski cites the example of a person who sets an alarm in the morning in order to get to work on time, so that he can hold onto a job and support his family. In this scenario, the external goal overrides a natural tendency to stay in bed and sleep. "This is a prototype of accepting a degree of discomfort or making a sacrifice for the sake of an ultimate goal."

Unlike animals who are largely driven by instinct, humans may select from among endless worthy goals – to be an outstanding teacher, artist, musician, Torah scholar, soldier, speech therapist, an elected official who will bring honesty and integrity to political office, computer programmer, doctor, lawyer, scribe, rabbi, farmer, bus driver, and on and on. Perhaps a person wants to invent something useful to improve irrigation for use in famine stricken countries, design furniture that is ergonomically correct, engage in Jewish outreach, start a company, volunteer for the fire brigade or in a hospital, or be a Scout leader. In addition, one may also have a goal to become a good parent and have children who will later work towards their own worthy goals.

When we dedicate ourselves to any of such cause, we are displaying *tiferet* and *netzach*.

3. *Only humans engage in a conscious self-reflection, which is a spiritual action.*

When we engage in this effort, we are striding toward *malchut* – nobility and dignity within life. Rabbi Twerski advises that we should be "fearless" in making moral inventory of ourselves. In the language of Omer count, this is called *tiferet*, *hod* and *malchut*.

4. *Humans bear responsibility for who they become, and spirituality ensures continual self-improvement.*

Constant self-improvement and continual spiritual growth are the distinctive features of a spiritual person. Correcting a common misperception, Rabbi Dr. Twerski points out that, "amassing wealth is not a uniquely human trait, since squirrels hoard more nuts than they can consume . . . The human uniqueness is not in acquiring from without, but in maximizing that which is within. This is an essential of spirituality." In the parlance of the *sefirot*, "maximizing that which is within" translates into *malchut*.

5. *Spiritual people are aware of and learn from their mistakes.*

Sometimes our ego prevents us from learning from our past experiences and mistakes that may have proven to be self-destructive. We may delude ourselves into thinking that this time around will be different. When we want something badly enough, many of us will come up with any reason to justify it as a wise choice. A safeguard against our duping ourselves with rationalizations is to seek advice and guidance from others whom "we trust and whose opinion we respect."

I would suggest that it requires both *tiferet* (truth) and *hod* (humility) to be willing to let go of one's ego and face cold facts without rationalization.

6. *Spiritual people think about and search for the purpose of existence.*

The search for meaning is unique to humans. Spiritual people will embark on a quest to discover the purpose of life; they will think about "why we are here" even if they never discover an answer that totally satisfies them. Finding the answer is not all important however. "What is important," says Rabbi Twerski, "is that one thinks about it and searches for it. The search is what is uniquely human, and the finding is incidental." He goes on to elaborate: "An ultimate purpose presumes a reason for living. It triggers action in life to make it all worthwhile. If we have a reason for living, we are of value and hence our ultimate purpose is to live a life of value which will affirm that we are here for a reason. Such is the basic tenet of human spirituality." He makes an important observation that spirituality and comfort are generally on opposite poles: "If the way to spirituality were comfortable, most of mankind might have chosen it. It is, however, a long and arduous path, often requiring a basic reorientation of one's character and patience, perseverance, and preparedness for whatever comes." In the language of the Omer count, we would call this perseverance *netzach*.

Rabbi Twerski makes an additional observation, which is both ironic and insightful. When traveling by a field of cows in the countryside, he opines on how completely tranquil they seem. But if tranquility and contentment were the goals of life, then humans would not need to possess a mental capacity that is so much greater than that of these cows. If the purpose of life was to work all day, then come home and either sit in front of a television or computer screen or sit in a bar for hours, then the human capacity "for abstract thinking, meditation, and philosophizing [would be] a complete waste."

7. *Spiritual people will respect the rights and freedoms of others.*

A frequent source of interpersonal problems is controlling, or attempting to control others. Rabbi Twerski describes that, as people grow in spirituality, their self-concept improves and they have less need to control another. This is *tiferet*, *hod*, *yesod*, and *malchut*.

8. Spiritual people will practice what they preach, living according to spiritual values.

While none of us is perfect, it is an ideal to strive to live a spiritual life and apply spiritual values to all that we do – at home, at work, or at play – and to all our social interactions.

In Heaven we will be asked if we enjoyed all the beauty and blessings that God bestowed upon us. So enjoy them we should. But if our enjoyment crosses a boundary into hedonism and overindulgence, then our spiritual life is compromised and corrupted. Bill Wilson in *Twelve Steps and Twelve Traditions* puts it so succinctly: ". . . character-building and spiritual values [have] to come first . . . material satisfactions [are] not the purpose of living."

Wilson calls the completion of all the twelve steps a "spiritual awakening." The message as it relates to *malchut* is important. When we apply spiritual values to all endeavors, we experience an awakening that leads to sovereignty/control over our lives. Rabbi Twerski shows us what this looks like and feels like:

"Spirituality [i.e., *malchut*] is not a 'thing,' not an object that can be identified as something one possesses. It is a *process*, a growth experience. Ironically, when someone thinks he has achieved spirituality, he has probably lost it. One has it only as long as one is striving for it. Because we can never quite achieve perfection, we are always capable of improving ourselves. As long as we continue to improve ourselves . . . we are *spiritual* [we have achieved *malchut*]. If we lose the momentum for growth and become stagnant, baser human inclinations toward gratification and comfort are certain to arise and work against the spiritual life. In spirituality, the searching is the finding, and the pursuit is the achievement."

We can all do it; it is not beyond us.

9. In a spiritual life, time is recognized as an irreplaceable gift.

In pursuing our goals, time should be used carefully. Laziness is a defect in character and should be eliminated. We should be in charge of time, but not slaves to it. This requires *gevurah*.

10. A prominent aspect of spirituality is honesty.

Rabbi Twerski observes that we have become accustomed to rationalizing lying, which is only permissible in extremely rare circumstances. Therefore, we need to break the habit of lying so that telling the truth is a "reflex." He suggests a technique of committing ourselves to "respond truthfully to every question without giving any thought to our answer for a period of thirty days. A spiritual life cannot coexist with falsehood." Remember that *tiferet* is truth.

11. A life of spirituality translates into considerate behavior and accountability.

Rabbi Twerski stresses that a spiritual life does not require that we repress or deny our anger, since denial is a falsehood and a spiritual life is based on truth. However, he strongly suggests that we make ourselves aware of issues that provoke our anger and then choose to exert appropriate control. Anger is not an impulse that cannot be controlled. And "how one reacts to [and with] anger is an issue of spirituality."

Rabbi Twerski calls on us to exhibit sensitive behavior that subjects every deed to a high level of ethical accountability. This consideration "constitutes the highest level of responsibility, giving utmost thought not only to the immediate effects of our behavior, but to the long-range effects."

This approach, when applied to all of life's events, displays *gevurah*, *tiferet*, *hod*, *yesod*, and most of all *malchut* (dignity and sovereignty) in living a worthy life.

12. Spiritual people do not believe they control or run the world.

Spiritual people do not think they are omnipotent. Rather, they have made a decision to turn their lives over to the care of God, however He is understood by them. They seek through both structured and personal prayer to improve contact with God, praying that He give them the ability to know His will and the power to live accordingly. They choose to believe. They choose to do the will of God.

If we examine and analyze Rabbi Twerski's twelve unique spiritual features of human beings, we can conclude that they clearly emanate from the *sefirot* of *chesed, gevurah, tiferet, netzach, hod, yesod,* and merge into *malchut. Malchut,* then, is grounded in the spiritual foundation of God's attributes that are the key features of spirituality.

A TWENTY-FIRST CENTURY EXAMPLE

There are many ways that each of us will elect to display our spirituality throughout our lives. And, if we act in accordance with the Torah, we will be guided onto varied paths toward independence, dignity, and nobility.

I would like to share a twenty-first century example to demonstrate the diversity of such paths – this example comes from an article in *The Jerusalem Post Magazine* entitled, "The New Palmach" by Josh Hasten.[429]

Hasten describes a center, Shomrei Ha'am, established in 2010 by Rabbi Avi Schwartz. Located in Brooklyn's Flatbush section, this center aims to reach teenagers and college students from "all streams of Judaism, [and] teach them the values that made those who fought for the establishment of the State [of Israel] exemplary role models of the Jewish people." Rabbi Schwartz knows something about this as the son of Mordechai Schwartz, a legendary Palmach commander during the War for Independence in 1948. He explains that Shomrei Ha'am, "emphasizes four pillars embodied by the original Palmach fighters, which we want to transmit to today's youth in order to create extraordinary Jewish leaders . . . Those [pillars] include the Torah, Jewish history, recognizing and combating persecution, and the overall spirit of 1948."

Rabbi Schwartz points out that "every Jew has 4,000 years of history in his or her family" but right now "there are too many divisions between the Right and Left and the religious and non-religious." He states that "all sides need to recognize the contributions made by the other." A simple illustration is that certain ostensibly "secular" leaders, including Theodor Herzl and other early Zionists, did their own part to save Judaism by checking the assimilation so rampant in their time. Addressing a present-day issue of lethargy, Rabbi Schwartz notes the great contributions and sacrifices made by Jewish youth during the fighting for the Land of Israel. He contrasts this passion with his observation that "the sense of selflessness amongst Jews both in Israel and the Diaspora has diminished."

---

429. Josh Hasten, "The New Palmach," *The Jerusalem Post Magazine*, June 29, 2012, this and subsequent quotations from pp. 20–21.

In 2012, thirty Shomrei Ha'am youth traveled to Israel for a two-week leadership program learning about Israel and also attending workshops on conflict resolution, time management, self-awareness, and martial arts. They came home energized and dedicated to the Jewish nation.

Rabbi Schwartz sums up his mission: "We as a Jewish people need to focus on our commonalities and not on our differences . . . The story and the spirit of 1948, must continue to be taught because it is still relevant today, and can be the ultimate hook which connects the Jewish people, and readies the next generation to serve as committed Jewish leaders, in all fields of endeavors."

Rabbi Schwartz believes that he is pursuing the path that God has laid out for him – working with youth and teaching them the importance of Jewish unity.

We each have our path. What should our path be? What does God want from us?

We have some clues in Tanach – for example in the Book of Micah, where the prophet says: "What is it that God asks of you, but to do justice, love acts of benevolence, and walk humbly with your God."[430] Also in *Devarim*, we read:

> For this commandment that I command you today – it is not hidden from you and it is not distant . . . See, I have placed before you today the life and the good, and the death and the evil, that which I command you today, to love Hashem, your God, to walk in His ways, to observe His commandments, His decrees, and His ordinances; then you will live and you will multiply, and Hashem, your God, will bless you in the Land to which you come to posses it . . .
>
> I call heaven and earth today to bear witness against you: I have placed life and death before you, blessing and curse; and you shall choose life, so that you will live, you and your offspring – to love Hashem, your God, to listen to His voice and to cleave to Him, for He is your life and the length of your days, to dwell upon the Land that Hashem swore to your forefathers, to Avraham, to Yitzchak, and to Yaakov to give them.[431]

430. *Micah* 6:8.

431. *Devarim* 30:11–20.

This is not so complex, but it will involve a struggle with our *yetzer hara* to fulfill God's will, which is that we learn to master our drives.

We all have different strengths and different combinations of character traits – illustrated by the many *sefirot* combinations we have been examining during the Omer count. While it may be easier for me to control my love of good food which could lead me to overindulge, it may be a much greater struggle for my sister, or my neighbor, or my child. While my best friend seems to control her anger in all circumstances, I may find that far more difficult when others "push my buttons." Suffice it to say that each of us is unique.

God's will for us is that we master our drives, improve our traits and make choices to live a life of purpose and worth, always aware that we are a ray of His Infinite Light. Each of us is capable of engaging in the *process* toward mastery while conducting a meaningful Omer count.

Thus far, we have completed six weeks of this work to hone all the *sefirot* within us with the goal of achieving wholeness in all our endeavors – in our relationships, in our roles and responsibilities, and most of all in our service to God.

Let's complete this process during the final week of *malchut*.

היום שלושה וארבעים יום,
שהם ששה שבועות ויום אחד, לעומר

(Ha'yom shlosha v'arbaim yom,
she'hem shisha shavuot v'yom echad la'Omer)

**"TODAY IS THE FORTY-THIRD DAY,
OR SIX WEEKS AND ONE DAY, OF THE OMER."**

DAY 43

Chesed sh'b'Malchut
(Loving-kindness within Leadership/Nobility)

Malchut contains within itself a composite of the six prior *sefirot* of *chesed, gevurah, tiferet, netzach, hod,* and *yesod.* Accordingly, *malchut* represents wholeness, completeness, sovereignty, leadership, kingship, dignity, and nobility. The emphasis on *chesed* in the *sefirah* combination of *chesed* within *malchut* floods *malchut* with beneficent kindness, goodness, and the nourishing light and love of God. *Chesed* within *malchut* influences and guides all relationships and interactions with acute sensitivity, care and love for ourselves, others, and God.

When God took the Jews out of Egypt after only 210 years of enslavement, instead of the 400 years that He had earlier decreed, He modeled for us the attribute of *chesed* within *malchut.* God recognized that the Jewish people were down to the forty-ninth level of impurity and could not have survived any additional servitude.

Once freed, they went out into the wilderness, where God provided manna daily and took care of all their needs for forty years. Their clothes did not wear out, and the manna miraculously tasted like whatever they wanted it to taste. This was another display of *chesed* within *malchut* – God nourishing the bodies and souls of the Jewish people and protecting them in a multiplicity of ways, like a mother unconditionally caring for her child.

Then God instructed the Jews to build the Mishkan which would become a Tent of Meeting for His Divine Presence and the Nation of Israel. He provided detailed instructions about the design, the vessels, the clothing and roles of the *Kohanim*, along with all the details relating to the performance of the sacrificial offerings, so that the Jewish people could serve Him and receive His blessings. Through His attribute of *chesed* within *malchut*, God lovingly created a special place for the Jewish people to bond with Him and elevate themselves through their divine service.

AN UNLIKELY SOURCE OF *CHESED*

The Torah is replete with examples of *chesed* within *malchut*, but at this stage I would like to present one unlikely source – Lot.

Previously, we have addressed some of Lot's less stellar traits. However, now is the time to describe a couple of incidents in Lot's life that won him the merit of being the progenitor of the Mashiach.

We know that Lot left Avraham's side to pursue his own not so spiritual path in Sodom. Despite this lapse of judgment, Lot nevertheless still demonstrated some worthy traits of *chesed* which he acquired from his famous uncle. Even though the people of Sodom would kill a person who welcomed strangers, Lot chose to show hospitality to the three guests (angels) who visited him just before the city's destruction. And he protected them from the mobs who wanted to persecute them.

In addition to this act of *chesed*, there was another act of *chesed* for which Lot was rewarded. Much earlier, when Avraham and Sarah were going into Egypt because of a famine in Canaan, an incident occurred in which Lot saved Avraham's life. Knowing that the Pharaoh would be attracted by Sarah's beauty and would likely order her husband killed, Avraham asked her: "Please say that you are my sister, that it may go well with me for your sake, and that I may live on account of you."[432] Although Lot knew that this was not true, he did not give Avraham away and thus he saved his life.

This teaches us that even though a person's whole life may not represent a consistent and complete characterization of a *sefirah* combination like

432. *Bereshit* 12:13.

chesed within *malchut*, there can be single moments when one's actions are commendable and worthy. Such was the case with Lot. For these reasons, as poor as many of his life choices were, Lot was rewarded with becoming the progenitor of the Mashiach – through his son Moab, the founder of the Moabite nation from which Ruth, the convert and the great-grandmother of King David, came.

RAV NOSSON TZVI FINKEL

Jumping ahead to modern-day, we have another example of *chesed* within *malchut* in the person of Rav Nosson Tzvi Finkel.

From 1990 until his untimely death in 2011, Rav Nosson Tzvi was the Rosh Yeshiva of the Mir in Jerusalem. He was already suffering from Parkinson's disease, when in his late forties, he took over the reins of this famous 1,000-student yeshiva. His untiring efforts, despite this debilitating illness, resulted in the growth of the Mir to nearly 7,000 students, housed in nine buildings. How did he do it? Part of it had to do with his down-to-earth approach which attracted even the most unlikely students, as related in *Jewish Action*:

A number of years back when addressing the boys of the NCSY summer learning program, he asked if any were from Chicago and had any attended the co-ed Ida Crown Jewish Academy as he had. When hands went up, he then asked, "Who's on the basketball team?" and a few hands were raised. Rav Finkel surprised the entire group by responding, "So was I." Thus he demonstrated that "our *gedolim* do not materialize fully formed. They come from among us, drawing upon the strengths and potential that God has placed in each one of us."[433]

In touching words about his brother-in-law, Rabbi Ahron Lopiansky writes:

> His days were a nonstop whirl of *shiurim*, *shmuessen*, personal meetings with students and endless fundraising . . . the fire of *hasmadah* was so hot, the enthusiasm so infectious and Rav Nosson's smile and embrace so beckoning that *bochurim* were simply swept into the maelstrom of Torah that raged all around.

---

433. Ahron Lopiansky, "Remembering Rabbi Nosson Tzvi Finkel," *Jewish Action*, Summer 2012, this and subsequent quotations from pp. 20–25.

On visits over the last decade of his life, Rabbi Lopiansky would sometimes ask him:

> "So much sacrifice? Must every minute of your ferociously long day be spent teaching and comforting others? Do you not leave a second of your time for yourself?" . . . . [In response] Rav Nosson Tzvi's eyes would dance, and his beatific smile would radiate and, in a silent whisper, he would reply in amazement, "Who is sacrificing? I have taken the ephemeral days of a human, the dignity of a mere flesh and blood, and a disease-racked body, and I have converted them into millions of hours of Torah study . . . thousands of uplifted spirits and tens of thousands of *neshamos* burning with *ahavas* Torah. What a deal!"[434]

Writing in *The Jerusalem Post Magazine*, Jonathan Rosenblum relates a special story about Rav Nosson Tzvi which is touching on so many levels:

A religious family had decided to pay for fertility treatment expenses for a non-religious couple. This family determined the couple should go to Israel for blessings from *tzaddikim*, including Rav Nosson Tzvi Finkel. Upon arrival at his home wearing summer clothing not typically seen in Mea She'arim, Rebbetzin Finkel greeted the wife with a hug and words of encouragement, "You are both Jewish. It is such a big thing to marry Jewish today." To avoid embarrassing her visitor, the Rebbetzin explained that her husband was such a holy man that out of respect she herself donned a shawl when she went in to speak to him, and offered her guest another shawl and a piece of matching jewelry [to fasten it]. When the couple entered, Reb Nosson Tzvi looked at them in silence. The person who escorted them in started to explain their situation, but the Rosh Yeshiva stopped him short: "Of course I know who they are, I'm thinking of their pain." Then he turned to the husband and asked, "Do you ever feel people are staring at you?" The husband nodded. Reb Nosson Tzvi added, "I often feel that way and that people cannot understand what I'm saying [on account of the loss of muscular control from debilitating Parkinson's disease]. Let's cry together." And that's what the Mirrer Rosh Yeshiva and the childless couple did.[435]

Rav Nosson Tzvi mastered *chesed* within a life of *malchut*, showing how

434. Ibid.

435. Rosenblum, "My Brothers Do I Seek," 25.

one can maximize potential, without excuses for any limitations placed on us by health, or any other life circumstance. Rav Nosson Tzvi led with resolute love for Torah and a devoted love for his Mir students. At the same time, he tried to cultivate the fire of *gevurah* (both strength and restraint) in the *bochurim* so that they would always love the learning of Torah. He displayed *netzach* (endurance) despite a physical condition that required miraculous levels of strength to overcome. He personified *hod* and *yesod*, trying to bond with others in any way possible, as we see in the example of his treatment of both the NCSY students and the childless couple. Ultimately, he helped to lead tens of thousands of Mir students who learned under his tutelage.

EVERYDAY ACTS OF KINDNESS

I once knew a Chief Executive Officer of a busy, fast-growing company who personified *chesed* within *malchut*. As his business grew, he made it a company goal to maintain an atmosphere of "family" and caring, such as it had when it was small. He directed the personnel department to keep abreast of any tragedy that happened in the lives of the employees, and to inform him as well.

Over the years there were many tragedies – people were diagnosed with cancer, a hurricane hit, a fire destroyed a home, a child committed suicide. Every employee received a personal letter expressing sympathy, and some an invitation to lunch for a one-to-one talk with the CEO, when he would let them know he cared deeply about them. In other cases, he directed the company to provide financial assistance, and he made sure that the company carried outstanding medical coverage so all employees were spared the worry that a major illness might impoverish them. All this caring and reaching out to help and comfort others represents *chesed* within *malchut*.

To get a better idea of the reach of this *sefirah* combination, let us examine three separate acts of *chesed* within *malchut* by this CEO and how various employees responded.

One woman, a secretary of one division of the company, was diagnosed with cancer. After a lunch with the CEO, she wrote this note, demonstrating how his caring helped her gain a new perspective on her problem:

> Your prayers and thoughts are really valuable for me and my family . . . Some times when we least expect it, a door closes in our lives.

> Circumstances may change, dreams may get shattered, and plans for tomorrow may have to wait. But when one door closes, God always opens another.

Another letter came from a factory level employee whose husband needed a liver transplant to save his life. She wrote:

> The transplant organization would not put [my husband] on the transplant list because the Union Insurance would only pay $50,000 towards the transplant . . . I was told $50,000 was a life-time benefit. This meant, only paid once per patient . . . To make a long story short, [our company] allowed me to go from Union to company insurance in April. [My husband] was put on the liver transplant list less than a week later. He got his new liver on July 16, 2006. All told, our bills would be well over $900,000. I haven't had to pay one penny. I promise I'm not lying. The only thing we had to pay for was the co-pay on his prescriptions . . . Sadly we are again living with cancer. This is his second big crisis. We more than met our lifetime max with the first one. Again, the company insurance is coming through. . . .

Having already written a letter to an employee who had lost a child to suicide, the CEO later invited the employee and spouse to a private dinner at his home. The thank you note sent from the employee:

> [My spouse] and I will never be able to express how grateful we are to you. The evening we had together was just the perfect thing for us . . . The wonderful note you wrote us was read and re-read by everyone in our family. It propped us up when we most needed support. We still read it, but not every day now . . . We promise you that we will put our lives back together. We will have a different way of perceiving what is truly important, but we will be OK . . .

Unfortunately, such CEOs are not as common as one would hope. Do you know of any head of a large company who makes the effort to extend him/herself in these ways? It is rare and represents a very special application of the *sefirot* combination of *chesed* within *malchut.*

DISCUSSION TOPICS FOR *CHESED* WITHIN *MALCHUT*

For adults

1. Am I satisfied with the level of *chesed* within *malchut* I consistently display, or do I waver in this attribute when pressures in my life take me off-track?
2. Do I display consideration and kindness to strangers?
3. Do I remember to display *chesed* within *malchut* to my children? How about to my spouse? If not, what can I change beginning today?

For children

1. When I hear about a tragedy, such as an accident or natural disaster where lives were lost, do I care about it, say prayers for the people, or see how I can help out?
2. Do I give of my time and efforts to help to make my family even stronger and happier?
3. Do I display *derech eretz* to people that I don't know very well, or are those people mainly invisible to me?

היום ארבעה וארבעים יום,
שהם ששה שבועות ושני ימים, לעומר

*(Ha'yom arba'a v'arbaim yom,
she'hem shisha shavuot u'shnei yamim la'Omer)*

"TODAY IS THE FORTY-FOURTH DAY,
OR SIX WEEKS AND TWO DAYS, OF THE OMER."

DAY 44

Gevurah sh'b'Malchut
(Strength/Discipline within Leadership/Nobility)

Malchut's display of sovereignty and dignity also projects an air of credibility and competency, supplying a sense of security and fairness to life situations and challenges. When augmented by _gevurah, malchut_ is enhanced with added determination, assurance, and the will to make and execute difficult decisions in order to accomplish worthy ends.

Nothing demonstrated Avraham's rectification of the attribute of *chesed* in the world more than the *Akeidah*, when he was commanded by God: "Take your son, your only one, whom you love – Yitzchak – and go to the land of Moriah; bring him up there as an offering upon one of the mountains which I shall tell you."[436]

Responding with complete obedience, Avraham demonstrated his unswerving devotion to God and showed that he could moderate his natural state of pure *chesed* with appropriate amounts of *gevurah. Gevurah* within *malchut* is what emerged from this trial.

No one was more beloved to God than Avraham. He was the inquisitive, brilliant child who deduced there was a Creator of the world by

436. *Bereshit* 22:2.

gazing at the star-studded heavens. He was the strong, gutsy idol-smasher, boldly rejecting his father's and his country's entire way of life. He was willing to stand alone and be perceived throughout his life as an *Ish Ivri*, the man who always stood on the "other side," protesting against the evils of his day.

As we learned during Week One when we examined the *sefirah* of *chesed*, Avraham was the dedicated advocate of a Creator who never spoke to him until he was 75 years old. Only then was he instructed by God: "Go for yourself from your land, from your relatives, and from your father's house to a land that I will show you."[437] For the duration of his life, he remained a loving servant of God, trusting in God with every step he took. He was the humble host who welcomed people from all walks of life, displaying genuine loving-kindness throughout his life, and earning the right to become the father of many nations, and especially the Nation of Israel.

But when required, he held back his love for his son in order to comply with God's command – a command that basically brought into question his entire understanding of a God who did not require human sacrifices, and who had promised him progeny through the very son that now was to be sacrificed. Still, he did not question it. Through his response, Avraham rectified the imbalance of *chesed* that resulted ten generations prior when Adam ate from the Tree of Knowledge of Good and Evil despite God's explicit command not to do so. Through his complete nullification of his own emotions and desires in deference to God's command, Avraham achieved *gevurah* within *malchut*.

Yitzchak also demonstrated *gevurah* within *malchut* – at the time of the *Akeidah* and at many other times in his life.

Earlier we learned that Yitzchak was satisfied with his mission of continuing the *mesorah* of his father and adhering steadfastly to it rather than charting his own course. By so doing, he ensured the continuity of the Jewish people and demonstrated *gevurah* within *malchut*.

Towards the end of his life, "blind" to the truth of Esav's character, Yitzchak decided to give this elder twin the blessing of the "firstborn." However, the moment he discovered Rivka had contravened his wishes and he had unintentionally given the blessing to Yaakov instead, Yitzchak immediately grasped the *emet* of the event. He both understood and accepted the outcome as coming directly from God. He refrained from

---

437. Ibid., 12:1.

displaying any form of personal agenda or preference, and simply deferred to the obvious will of God.

SELF-CONTROL AND *GEVURAH* WITHIN *MALCHUT*

In every situation where we display appropriate self-control over our thoughts, speech, and actions in order not to harm ourselves or another, we are living and breathing the air of what it means to demonstrate *gevurah* within *malchut*. This is so important that we recite the blessing each morning: "Blessed are you, Hashem, our God, King of the Universe, who girds Israel with strength." This blessing acknowledges that God has endowed us with the power to muster the necessary restraint whenever it is called for.

Those who are addicted to anything at all, but have managed to commit to change that and are recovering from their addiction, are exercising *gevurah* within *malchut*. Such people are saving their own lives as well as of all those whom they touch and affect. As recovering addicts will attest, it feels incredibly great to be in this mindset of *gevurah* within *malchut*, one day at a time, and day after day.

Those who struggle with a hot temper, or a quick tongue, or who are low on patience have to face the fact that *gevurah* within *malchut* might be lacking in their lives. It's simple – if we don't learn to control negative behaviors, we cannot achieve *gevurah* within *malchut*.

Self-control is also critical in how we use our God-given power of speech. Those who spread gossip or relish listening to *lashon hara* will not achieve a dignified *malchut* state of being. They demean themselves when they disparage others, or when they actively listen to those who do it. Under the laws of *shmirat ha-lashon*, both the speaker and listener of *lashon hara* are judged harshly – it is considered as if they committed murder with their words. Acts of *lashon hara* signify a total absence of the *sefirah* combination of *gevurah* within *malchut*.

Those who take advantage of others, manipulate others, or treat others in a discriminatory manner cannot achieve a *malchut* state of being. If they have a sense of entitlement about their possessions and forget to be grateful to God and to all the many people who made it possible for them to have what they have, they cannot achieve *gevurah* within *malchut*.

There are many examples of those who train themselves to embody *gevurah* within *malchut* at various times in their life, but only a rare few who can represent and express this *sefirah* at all times. Unfortunately, there are many whose behavior evinces a total lack of *gevurah* within *malchut*, a sign of deficiency in the maturity, functionality, and wellness of our society at large.

Just recall the incident of the adult men in Beit Shemesh, Israel, who spat at an eight-year-old girl on her way to school because they felt she wasn't dressed with sufficient modesty, and then try to imagine how disappointing such conduct must be to God. The lack of appropriateness in societal interactions needs to be rectified and quickly. It's time for us all to do our part. And we cannot let up no matter what – no excuse is acceptable.

"WITH STRENGTH, EIGHTY"

An urban legend has it that on his 80th birthday, the Pope invited the Chief Rabbi of Israel to Rome. Why? He wanted to understand the meaning of the phrase, "with strength, eighty" found in *Pirkei Avot*.[438]

So what does this text in the Mishna mean?

The body is not the same at 80. There are innumerable aches and pains in many places. Our body just cannot function the way it once used to. How are we to respond to the reality that aging is occurring?

This Mishna seems to be suggesting that this is the precise time to demonstrate *gevurah*. We are to tell ourselves that we won't let age prevent us from pushing forward in our efforts to accomplish all the things we can. Thank God that, at 80 years of age, we have been blessed by God to appreciate the many life experiences we had and to integrate them into a broad outlook and elevated state of being. At 80, we can better relate to each of the *sefirot* and balance them with the *sefirah* of *malchut*. At 80, we are blessed if we still have reserves of strength, vitality, vigor, and discipline to further energize our *malchut*.

But we have to make the effort. It is at 80 that we have to try to draw upon our *gevurah* to study Torah, volunteer, help others, exercise our minds, move our bodies to be active wherever and however we can. And to rectify what needs rectifying in this world so that *malchut* rules the day.

---

438. *Pirkei Avot* 5:21.

DISCUSSION TOPICS FOR *GEVURAH* WITHIN *MALCHUT*

For adults

1. Honestly, do I have an issue with speaking, or listening to, too much *lashon hara*? What do I plan to do about it?
2. How do I demonstrate respect for the authority of the rabbi of my synagogue? For my boss? For the police? For community leaders?
3. Can I name a family situation where I had the authority to act, but chose not to? Why did I make that choice? How did it turn out?
4. Do I tend to impose my will and authority on my children? My spouse? How do they react? What better approach could I take?

For children

1. In the last week, how did I demonstrate by my speech and actions that I respect the authority of my parents? My teachers? Our rabbi?
2. How did I display respect for God?
3. In the last week, did I say something bad about someone that got him or her in trouble?

היום חמישה וארבעים יום,
שהם ששה שבועות ושלושה ימים, לעומר

*(Ha'yom chamisha v'arbaim yom,
she'hem shisha shavuot u'shlosha yamim la'Omer)*

**"TODAY IS THE FORTY-FIFTH DAY,
OR SIX WEEKS AND THREE DAYS, OF THE OMER."**

DAY 45

Tiferet sh'b'Malchut
(Harmony/Truth within Leadership/Nobility)

When *malchut* is enhanced with *tiferet*, it becomes all the more beautiful, truthful, balanced, and harmonious in its overall stature and effectiveness. Wherever and whenever one is in a leadership role, whether at the head of a family, in a classroom, the workplace or the synagogue, or as the leader of a community, a government or a nation, *tiferet* within *malchut* facilitates calm, organized, clear, and open communications. In turn, this aids the achievement of common goals that all involved understand and accept, and where each is treated with dignity and respect.

If there is an imbalance in any situation for any reason, then we must employ an extra measure of *tiferet* – balance and truth. It may be that too much *chesed* was displayed and someone isn't getting the message. It may be that too much *gevurah* was displayed and someone else is being squelched. *Tiferet* within *malchut* helps us process and analyze experiences and relationships to correctly sort the possibilities and make choices that personify "truth." This results in harmony, balance, and beauty in relationships, personal life choices, roles of authority, and in all life experiences.

Tiferet within *malchut* keeps the two sides of the scale in balance as it promotes strong leadership with compassion, dignity, and harmony.

YAAKOV'S DREAMS

Yaakov's dream of speckled, spotted, and striped sheep was a clear revelation of *tiferet* within *malchut*. Let's recall the details:

After twenty-two years of living and working for his father-in-law, Lavan, Yaakov had a dream about "counting sheep," and realized how much of his life had become adulterated by materialistic concerns. His prior dream on his way to uncle Lavan's house, after having fled his brother Esav, was that of angels ascending and descending a ladder that reached up to the heavens. How far away from that mind-set had he traveled. His realization had to have been disconcerting to someone as spiritually elevated as Yaakov. To his credit, he got the message. In connecting all the dots, he realized that, if his family was going to be reared and influenced properly in all areas of what is holy, then leaving Lavan's environs was essential. He gathered his household together and departed.

Frankly, Yaakov had been there too long. But now he saw the light. As the head of the family, he accepted full responsibility for realizing that the environment in which his children were being raised had to change. They had to leave, or risk further influence by the deceitful Lavan and the rest of the society in Padan Aram, an influence which would be detrimental to the family mission of bringing the world to monotheism – the realization that there was only one God.

Returning home to Israel after more than two decades, Yaakov had to prepare himself for the reality that he would likely be facing his twin brother Esav who, the last time they crossed paths, threatened to kill him for "stealing" their father's blessing, a blessing that Esav claimed despite having sold his birthright to Yaakov earlier. We read in the Torah how carefully Yaakov planned and strategized for the encounter with his brother. Indeed, some Torah commentators suggest that their meeting is a prototype for how modern-day leaders of Israel should prepare themselves when they must meet with world leaders about matters affecting Israel.

Thanks to all his preparations, as well as his deeply felt prayers to God, the meeting went better than expected and, rather than trying to kill him, Esav invited Yaakov to live together with him. The Torah describes the dialogue:

Esav said, "Travel on and let us go – I will proceed alongside you." But, as with the decision to leave the environs of Lavan, Yaakov once again tapped into *tiferet* within *malchut* and responded to Esav, "My lord knows that the children are tender, and the nursing flocks and cattle are upon me . . . Let my lord go ahead of his servant; I will make my way at my slow pace according to the gait of the herd before me and the gait of the children, until I come to my lord at Seir."[439]

Yaakov's mastery of the *sefirah* of *tiferet* within *malchut* is nobly displayed in this interchange. He understood with crystal clarity that he could not physically be neighbors with Esav. Such proximity would have soon tainted the truth and harmony of God's plan for Yaakov and the Jewish people. It would have been an incompatible mixture, as Esav represented the world of *gashmiut* (physicality), while Yaakov represented *ruchniut* (spirituality), its opposite. They would not mix.

Yaakov delicately and respectfully let his brother know that he should go ahead without him. He understood that Esav and what he stood for would have apparent ascendency in world events at this time. But one day, even Esav would understand and concede that Yaakov's way of life is the ultimate truth and that only it will triumph.

Remember the final words of the *Aleinu* prayer:

> Then all humanity will call upon Your Name, to turn all the earth's wicked toward You. All the world's inhabitants will recognize and know that to You every knee should bend, every tongue should swear. Before You, Hashem, our God, they will bend every knee and cast themselves down, and to the glory of Your Name they will render homage, and they will all accept upon themselves the yoke of Your kingship that You may reign over them soon and for all eternity. For the kingdom is Yours and You will reign for all eternity in glory, as it is written in Your Torah: "Hashem shall reign for all eternity." And it is said: "Hashem will be King over all the world – on that day Hashem will be One and His Name will be One."

MESSAGE TO US

It is not easy to pick up and leave a life of material comfort such as that which Yaakov had with Lavan. Today, there are those who live in the convenience of America, Europe, or wherever, who cannot imagine saying good-bye to these comforts in order to say hello to a life in Eretz Yisrael.

---

439. *Bereshit* 33: 12–14.

It is not easy to shun what appears to be so shiny and alluring – and physical pleasures and the world of *gashmiut* is just that. It takes inner balance to understand what is truthful and lasting versus that which is temporal and passing like "dust in the wind." Sometimes we don't achieve that inner insight and do not find "truth" until we have experienced tests and trials, as Yaakov did.

The environment in which we live and what we permit ourselves and our families to be exposed to is a major factor in determining the sort of people we become. Each of us must "strive for truth," to borrow the title of Rabbi Eliyahu Dessler's outstanding book. When we achieve it in our lives, we must try to assist our children and loved ones to achieve it too. Those of us who are living a life as Lavan's neighbors and are not contemplating what ultimate effect his influence may have on our families need a loving, compassionate nudge to think again and consider making the journey home.

Indeed, we must pray that all Jews in the world choose to come to Eretz Yisrael and serve God in our Land. Each of us needs to do what Yaakov did, first with Lavan and then with Esav. We must move on and settle the Land and not allow our lives to become polluted with alien cultures and lifestyles. We, like Yaakov, need to display *tiferet* within *malchut* about this matter.

Indeed, years later, when Yaakov was about to go down into Egypt, knowing this was divinely ordained, he understood with complete *tiferet* within *malchut* that he had come to the culmination of his life's work. In referring to Yaakov's mission, the Torah uses his name Israel, and also employs it whenever he is acting on behalf of the nation and not only his family:

> So Israel set out with all that he had and he came to Beersheba where he slaughtered sacrifices to the God of his father Yitzchak. God spoke to Israel in night visions and He said, "Yaakov, Yaakov." And he said, "Here I am."

God then reassured him and told him not to be afraid of descending into Egypt, promising him that "I shall establish you as a great nation there. I shall descend with you to Egypt, and I shall also surely bring you up; and Yosef shall place his hand on your eyes."[440]

---

440. Ibid., 46:1–4.

Just as happened with his grandfather – whom the angel called twice, "Avraham, Avraham" and he responded, "Here I am" – Yaakov was called twice. It has always seemed to me that God calls out to us as well, even in the twenty-first century, if we but listen. Sometimes He calls us through a blessing, and sometimes through a test to help us discover our true self. When we respond, "Here I am" to God's call, we master *tiferet* within *malchut*.

HEROES OF THE HOLOCAUST

The reader will discern a theme running through the many stories for this Week Seven – stories of "everyday" people, who responded to God's call. Several of these will emanate from the actions of the victims of the Holocaust. Let me assure you that if each of the six million Jewish victims had time to write a letter which then survived the war, their last words and thoughts would have doubtless given us a lifetime of *chizuk*. In those messages that we do have and treasure, we can plainly see the *tiferet* within *malchut* of their lives.

The Holocaust was an evil of mind-numbing proportions. However, such great evil brought the good into relief. From the stories of the victims, we can perceive amazingly radiant displays of *tiferet* within *malchut*: truths finally understood; priorities clarified; identities accepted; nobility brought into relief. Bodies disintegrate but *neshamot* live forever – except those of the evil beasts who remain in a living Gehennom, never to appear again.

Janusz Korczak, a famous Polish-Jewish educator and author of children's books, ran an orphanage. When the orphans were sent to Treblinka for extermination, he voluntarily went with them. "Here I am." No more to say. Assignment understood and accepted. Mission accomplished. *Tiferet* within *malchut*.

Rabbi Dr. Solomon Schonfeld was only 26 years old, when he took it upon himself to organize a "Kindertransport" with the sole mission of saving Jewish children, mostly between the ages of 4 and 17. He had already taken over his father's pulpit in London when he assumed this additional mission, which sometimes required that he pass himself off as a British army officer. Due to his extraordinary efforts, approximately 10,000 Jewish children from Germany, Poland, Austria, and Czechoslovakia were rescued and transported to England. Writes Barry Davis in *The Jerusalem Post Magazine*:

> On one occasion, eager to get visas to Vienna for another group of *kinder*, Schonfeld walked over 30 kilometers to London Airport on a Shabbat to make sure the precious permits got to Austria on the evening plane.[441]

(Incidentally, from Austria there were adult Jews, called *begleiter*, who traveled with the children to England, but instead of saving themselves, returned to Austria to attempt to retrieve more children. Their sacrifice, *hod* within *malchut*, was a heroic part of "Kindertransport" as well.)

Rabbi Schonfeld, at great odds and risks, held high the eternal torch of *tiferet* within *malchut* to search out and save countless precious *neshamot* while most of the world's nations – including Western leaders who knew better – were indifferent to their plight and acquiesced to evil.

THE PROMISE OF SALVATION

Lest we wonder what playbook the Nazis used when they plotted their great evil, *Sefer Devarim* supplies the answer:

> Remember what Amalek did to you on the way when you were leaving Egypt . . . that he struck those of you who were hindmost, all the weaklings at your rear, when you were faint and exhausted, and he did not fear God. It shall be that when Hashem, your God, gives you rest from all your enemies all around, in the Land that Hashem, your God, gives you as an inheritance to possess it, you shall wipe out the memory of Amalek from under the heaven – you shall not forget![442]

God's command to the Jewish people is to wipe out Amalek. From those clear instructions we know that destruction of Amalek is imbedded in

441. Barry Davis, "A Hero Remembered," *The Jerusalem Post Magazine*, March 9, 2012, 18–20. David Kranzler's biography of Rabbi Schonfeld, *Holocaust Hero*, cites many more stories.

442. *Devarim* 25:17–19.

tiferet within *malchut*, because the light, truth, and harmony that comes from destroying evil from our midst completes the *sefirah* of *malchut*.

Thanks to *tiferet* within *malchut*, Amalek will not make it. Why? Because Amalek knew that God was with the Jewish people – Amalek knew that God has taken them out of Egypt and split the sea for them – and yet he attacked their most vulnerable ones. And this is why Amalek will be destroyed, while God will save the Jews.

On the seventh night after Pesach, the day that the splitting of the Red Sea occurred, we celebrate this truth. The Haftarah which we read in synagogue on the seventh day of Pesach week is from the end of the Second Book of the Prophet Shmuel. This Haftarah is a beautiful song composed by David in gratitude to God for saving him time and again from his enemies and their conspiracies. (Oddly, though, there is no mention of Pesach.) The song reads:

> Hashem is my Rock, my Fortress, and my Rescuer. God, my Rock, I take refuge in Him; my Shield and the Horn of my Salvation, my Stronghold and my Refuge, my Savior . . . In my distress I would call upon Hashem, and to my God I would call – from His abode He would hear my voice, my cry in His ears . . .
>
> And God thundered in the heavens, the Most High cried out . . . He drew me out of deep waters. He saved me from my mighty foe, and from my enemies for they overpowered me. They confronted me on the day of my misfortune, but God was my support . . . God recompensed me according to my righteousness; He repaid me according to the cleanliness of my hands. For I have kept the ways of God, and I have not departed wickedly from my God . . .
>
> With the devout You act devoutly, with the wholehearted you act wholeheartedly. With the pure You act purely, with the crooked You act perversely. You save the humble people, and Your eyes are upon the haughty to lower them. For You, God, are my lamp, and God will illuminate my darkness . . .
>
> God – His way is perfect: the promise of Hashem is flawless, He is a shield for all who take refuge in Him . . . You have given me Your shield of salvation, and Your humility made me great . . . I pursued my foes and overtook them, and returned not until they were destroyed . . . God lives and blessed is my Rock; and exalted is God, Rock of my salvation . . .

> Therefore, I will thank You, God, among the nations, and sing to Your Name. He is a tower of salvations to His king, and does kindness to His anointed one, to David, and to his descendants forever.[443]

On the seventh night after the Exodus, God destroyed the army of Egypt, the only other power which had a claim (due to the sale of Yosef) on the Nation of Israel. On this night, God reset everything making salvation possible. God's declaration to the world when He worked this open miracle is that the Jewish people belong to Him. Do not mess with the Jewish people. If you do, you will have Him to reckon with.

This is a perennial message to anyone who lays a claim to our Land or our People. The essence of the seventh day of Pesach is the absolute promise that we will be saved from our enemies. God will, at a time that He decides, obliterate our enemies. Not every Jew will survive, but the Nation of Israel will be saved.

This is an eternally powerful truth of *tiferet* within *malchut.*

443. II *Shmuel* 22:1–51.

DISCUSSION TOPICS FOR *TIFERET* WITHIN *MALCHUT*

For adults

1. Have I made the best choices in determining and refining the optimum environment for bringing up my children? What needs to change?
2. In my home environment, is there a good balance between organization and coziness?
3. When I delegate chores, do I do it in a way that ends up being a positive and successful experience for all involved?

For children

1. Do I take responsibility for making sure my bedroom, clothes, and backpack are clean, neat, and organized? Do I take responsibility for doing all of my homework and being prepared for tests, or do I rely too much on others?
2. Do I help make my home environment one of harmony, co-operation, and open communication?
3. Do I make good choices and carry through with them?

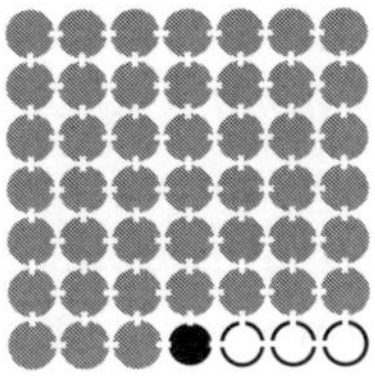

היום ששה וארבעים יום,
שהם ששה שבועות וארבעה ימים, לעומר

(Ha'yom shisha v'arbaim yom,
she'hem shisha shavuot v'arba'a yamim la'Omer)

"TODAY IS THE FORTY-SIXTH DAY,
OR SIX WEEKS AND FOUR DAYS, OF THE OMER."

DAY 46

Netzach sh'b'Malchut (Endurance in Leadership/Nobility)

Netzach is needed in combination with *malchut* when worthy situations, relationships, or goals require extra resolve, drive, and tenacity. This endurance is needed if we are to pursue goals and solutions in the face of all odds – even when others may be against us, even when a situation seems hopeless.

When *netzach* is combined with *malchut*, it must not be to pursue power, but rather to recognize that all success comes from God and must serve God's purpose. This must be our stance if we are to arrive at a powerful, mature, balanced, and considerate determination to ethically and humanely pursue goals and achieve positive outcomes. These outcomes contribute to wholeness, integration, and a healthy completeness in all matters and relationships.

INDIVIDUAL EXAMPLES

In Week Four's overview, we related the story Lt. Colonel Shahar Spada who was gravely injured, but persevered to return to the IDF in order to continue to serve and protect Israel. In addition to *netzach*, we can also view this remarkable leader through the lenses of the seven *sefirot* we have counted. Let's now take a closer look at Lt. Colonel Spada through the *sefirah* of *malchut*, which has integrated the previous six *sefirot*. This will help us to recalibrate our own attributes and, consequently, to grow in the areas that we now understand better. It will help us to see opportunities to crank up the frequency on some of our traits and tone it down on others – in order to achieve wholeness. We will thus be motivated to implement concrete changes in our lives.

First and foremost, Lt. Colonel Spada displayed countless acts of love (*chesed*) through his speech and actions – love for God, his wife, his daughters, his country, Israel, and the people whose lives he protected. He acted with *gevurah*, *tiferet*, and undeterred *netzach* at the highest of levels, when he overcame his severe injuries and endured twenty-six months of rehabilitation so he could be restored to the military duty, which he knew was his mission in life. When we recognize and focus on our mission with the same intensity, we reflect *tiferet*. It is with complete humility (*hod*) that Lt. Colonel Spada appreciated merely being able to stand on his own feet and be in the loving arms of the family God gave him. He was completely bonded (*yesod*) to his mission of defending the Land of Israel and its inhabitants because, as he said, "We have only one country." And, finally, what emerged in this remarkable leader? *Malchut*.

Consider his comments:

> "Respect is not guaranteed by rank. These marks on my shoulder don't mean a thing . . . Respect is earned . . . It's how you behave personally with the soldiers under your command that counts, the example you set. The ultimate worth of a commander is measured by how his soldiers conduct themselves in his absence."[444]

The author of *The Jerusalem Post* article about Lt. Colonel Spada, Yaakov Lappin, concludes: "It is difficult, if not impossible to hear Spada's story without being overwhelmed with a feeling of respect."

Remember 16-year-old David Feiglin, who lay in a coma after a serious auto accident until he awoke from it on Yom Kippur only to renew his faith in God? What about Tamar, Ro'ee, and Yishai Fogel who survived the terrorist attack that murdered their parents and three siblings in Itamar? Remember Dr. Viktor Frankl and Rebbetzin Esther Jungreis who lost

---

444. Lappin, Ibid.

members of their family to Nazi barbarism? All of these heroes displayed extreme levels of *netzach* within *malchut* at critical moments of their lives. May God always be with them in their courageous journey through life.

Another amazing model is Rabbi Noach Weinberg, the founder of Aish HaTorah, and a leader in the modern *ba'al teshuvah* movement, which he helped fashion and to which he dedicated his life until the day of his death on February 5, 2009. His goal was simple – to get young unaffiliated Jews to identify with the Jewish people. Through his tireless efforts and infectious love for all Jews, Reb Noach has taught tens of thousands of Jews around the world (through Aish HaTorah outreach centers) about their Jewish heritage and how to live a Torah life. His dedicated wife, Rebbetzin Denah Weinberg, founded EYHAT College of Jewish Studies for Women with now more than 2,000 alumnae.

This amazing couple has demonstrated tenacious endurance in their noble mission of helping others become committed Jews. Their display of *netzach* within *malchut* is palpable and lives on in the countless Jews they have affected.

WARTIME LEADERSHIP

Biographies of those who led their nations during wartime are often enlightening and sometimes inspiring.

For example, we learn much from the wartime conduct of General George Washington, who led a volunteer colonial army in the long fight for independence from Britain and who became a founding father of the United States of America. Later, when it was suggested by the newly-formed government that he be addressed as "His Majesty" or "His Highness," he objected and declined all such accolades.

He was not alone, the entire "band of brothers" that Joseph Ellis describes in his Pulitzer Prize winning work, *Founding Brothers*, was determined to establish a true, representative democracy and a unified republic.[445] It would not be a monarchy with absolute power in any single individual, even someone as key to its success as George Washington, the first President of the United States who exemplified *netzach* within *malchut* because of his worthy accomplishments and virtuous character.

And then consider Abraham Lincoln, the sixteenth President of the

445. Joseph J. Ellis, *Founding Brothers* (NY: Alfred A. Knopf, 2000), 145–148, 162, 168.

United States who suffered the crushing responsibility of serving as Commander-in-Chief during the Civil War (1861–1865). More lives were lost in that war than in any other war in the history of the United States (the lives of 750,000 soldiers and of an undetermined number of civilians). This was more than the number of US soldiers who lost their life in World Wars I and II combined. The depths of the tragedy of this war, the divisiveness it caused, the cost, the loss, the pain – where no family was spared at least one victim – were etched on the face of President Lincoln who looked as if he aged thirty years over the four years of the war. Lincoln's battle to save the union was for him a fundamental issue, as described by Doris Kearns Goodwin in *Team of Rivals*, where she quotes him as saying:

> "[It] is the necessity that is upon us, of proving that popular government is not an absurdity. We must settle this question now, whether in a free government the minority have the right to break up the government whenever they choose. If we fail it will go far to prove the incapability of the people to govern themselves."

Recalling that George Washington, the nation's first President, had forewarned the citizenry about the need to be vigilant against "the first dawning of every attempt to alienate any portion of our country from the rest or to enfeeble the sacred ties which now link together the various parts," Lincoln seemed to share this "mystical idea of popular government and democracy that propelled [him] to call forth the thousands of soldiers who would rise up to defend the sacred Union created by the Founding Fathers."[446]

On January 1, 1863, President Lincoln signed the Emancipation Proclamation announcing that all slaves within the rebellious states were freed effective immediately, and authorizing the recruitment of black soldiers into the Union army. Lincoln's comments on this day say it all, "I never, in my life, felt more certain that I was doing right, than I do in signing this paper . . . If my name ever goes into history, it will be for this act, and my whole soul is in it."[447] President Lincoln, a man who stood tall, carrying the arduous responsibility of life and death while building

446. Doris Kearns Goodwin, *Team of Rivals* (NY: Simon & Schuster Paperbacks, 2005), 356–357.
447. Ibid., 499.

and maintaining the promise of reuniting a nation that would come to represent freedom, peace, and security for all. If that is not *netzach* within *malchut*, I don't know what is.

It is worthwhile to contrast Lincoln's resolve with the lack of same displayed by Neville Chamberlain, the Prime Minister of Great Britain who failed, in the 1930s, to stand up to Adolf Hitler and, as a result, plunged the world into war. Chamberlain's weak-kneed and misguided strategy lacked any form of *netzach* within *malchut*. He mistakenly believed that Hitler could be placated. The rest is history.

One of the only leaders in Great Britain to publicly disagree with Chamberlain was Winston Churchill. When Chamberlain was proved wrong and forced out of office, Churchill became Britain's wartime leader and he fought to defeat the evil Nazi empire. It should be noted, however, that neither Churchill nor President Franklin Roosevelt would agree to destroy the railroad tracks leading to Auschwitz in 1944 when they were bombing other sites in the area, even though they knew that the tracks were used to transport Jews to this genocidal killing factory. Their purported rationale – that no efforts should be undertaken that would divert from winning the war – was a monumental, ethically-flawed decision that led to the continued operation of this death camp until later in 1945, when the Allied troops liberated it. Even though Churchill went to war against Hitler, due to his callousness, he doesn't rise to *netzach* within *malchut*; he lacked *chesed*, *tiferet*, and *hod*, which are essential components of *malchut*.

Lastly, we should take a proud look at Menachem Begin, who loyally served Israel from the time of its war for independence through its founding as a state. Begin was a passionate, brilliant, and sensitive leader in every role he played in his lifetime. He displayed amazing endurance – through his imprisonment in Russia, through his days of hiding in the underground during the British Mandate, through his service as a leader of an outspoken opposition under many prime ministers, and then finally as Israel's Prime Minister.

One of the most exciting books I have read in the recent years is Yehuda Avner's *The Prime Ministers*. Avner served under several prime ministers of Israel, and his historical narrative of the events of our modern history is riveting. Begin, his personal favorite, displayed *netzach* within *malchut* repeatedly. Avner relates that he was first introduced to this amazing man in 1947 by way of a poster on the wall of police station in then British-controlled Palestine in 1947. The poster read: "WANTED: Menachem

Begin, dead or alive, ten thousand pounds reward for information leading to his capture."[448]

Begin displayed enduring passion for the Jewish people and fought for the Land of Israel to be independent from foreign control. He played so many vital leadership roles, displaying *chesed*, *gevurah*, *tiferet*, *netzach*, *hod*, and *yesod* in so many of them.

Just imagine the restraint (*gevurah*), humility (*hod*), and bonding/foundation (*yesod*) it took for him to surrender, rather than order Irgun fighters under his command to defend themselves against their fellow Jews in the Altalena incident in 1948.[449] What was his rationale? This:

> "Now hear this each and every one of you, and hear it well. I live by an iron rule: a Jew must never lift a finger against a fellow Jew, NEVER. A Jew must never shed the blood of another Jew, NEVER. Twenty centuries ago we faced the bitter experience of the destruction of our Second Temple, the destruction of our capital Jerusalem. And why? Because of our senseless hatred of each other, a hatred that led to civil war and to our utter ruin: *bechiya ladorot* – generations of tears . . . Therefore, I say to you tonight, a curse on him who preaches civil war. Let his hand be cut off before he raises it against another Jew. There will never be a civil war in Israel – NEVER."[450]

And what about the deep and abiding love for Israel and Jerusalem he displayed during the Six-Day War in 1967. Despite being the head of the opposition Likud party, Begin lent his immediate, complete, and unequivocal support to then Prime Minister Levi Eshkol during this time. And he pressed Eshkol to ensure that the Old City of Jerusalem was restored to Jewish control. The words he used to persuade Prime Minister Eshkol were filled with passion, strength, balanced with the logic of truth:

> "Mr. Prime Minister, the question before us is of unprecedented historic consequence. This is the hour of our political test. We must occupy the Old City, in response both to the unheeded warnings we sent to King Hussein, and to the persistent Jordanian shelling

448. Yehuda Avner, *The Prime Ministers* (Jerusalem: Toby Press, 2010), 39.
449. See: http://en.wikipedia.org/wiki/Altalena_Affair.
450. Avner, *The Prime Ministers*, 80.

since. The United Nations Security Council is currently in session debating a ceasefire. If we do not act promptly we are liable to again find ourselves outside the walls of Jerusalem, exactly as happened in nineteen forty-eight when we lost the Jewish Quarter and all our holy sites, and the city was left divided – all because of a UN ceasefire. I therefore propose we take immediate military action to liberate the Old City."

Other cabinet members were both for and against. But Begin responded forcefully: "Our soldiers are almost in sight of the Western Wall. How can we tell them not to reach it? We have in our hands a gift of history. Future generations will never forgive us if we do not seize it."

Hours later in the middle of the night, Begin could not sleep. At 4:00 am he turned on a radio and the BBC was reporting that a UN Security Council ceasefire resolution was about to be voted upon. He phoned Eshkol immediately, urging, "We have no time left. I propose the army be ordered to enter the Old City forthwith, before it is too late."[451]

Avner reports that the cabinet convened at 7:00 am and, by unanimous decision, gave the order to immediately penetrate the Old City's walls, the troops to be spearheaded by a parachute brigade:

> Some three hours later, after intense combat, the brigade crashed through the Lion Gate, and shortly thereafter came the commander's message over the wire: "The Temple Mount is in our hands! The Temple Mount is in our hands!" Soldiers in their hundreds rushed to the Kotel, the Western Wall, and broke into choruses of *Yerushalayim Shel Zahav* ("Jerusalem of Gold") . . .
>
> "*Baruch Hashem*!" cried a jubilant Begin, and he proposed there and then that work begin on the reconstruction of the ancient Jewish Quarter which had been razed to the ground in the 1948 War of Independence, and whose inhabitants had either been killed, or taken prisoner, or expelled.[452]

451. Ibid., 157–59.
452. Ibid., 159.

Every time I walk into the Old City and go to the Kotel, I think of Begin's essential role in making it possible for millions of Jews to visit the holiest site we have. Begin was a leader who exemplified *netzach* within *malchut* on behalf of the Nation of Israel and the God of Israel. His perseverance, his vision, his goals and his mission combined in a splendorous display of all the *sefirot* suffused within *malchut*. This is what leadership and nobility is all about in this world.

JERUSALEM AS EMBODIMENT OF *NETZACH* WITHIN *MALCHUT*

The Holy City of Jerusalem (*Yerushalayim Ir HaKodesh*) is the only city in the world that embodies *netzach* within *malchut*. It is our eternal gift from God, the King of Kings. What does that entail? Perhaps the most touching definition of the meaning of Jerusalem, our Holy City, comes from Yehuda Avner in his book just mentioned above, *The Prime Ministers*. He writes about the first time he laid eyes on it in 1947:

> Jerusalem! Its individuality is unique . . . Something deep stirred within me when I entered it. I did not know what to call it then; I do not know what to call it now. It has the depth of an old masterpiece whose simplicity veils an immense sophistication. And like great music, its composition – the ancient and the modern, the religious and the secular, the Jews, the Muslims, the Christians and their multiple tones and variations, all somehow synchronize into an incongruous harmony . . . Yet, it is said that Jerusalem is the most disputed city in history; that more blood has been shed for Jerusalem than for any other spot on earth. Century after century, armies have fought to conquer and subjugate it: the Assyrians, the Babylonians, the Greeks, the Persians, the Syrians, the Romans, the Saracens, the Franks, the Arabs, the Turks, the Europeans, and again the Arabs. Nonetheless, throughout its three-thousand-year-long history, Jerusalem has been capital to no one but the Jews.[453]

When I read this I wondered how many of us can recall the month and year we first laid eyes on Jerusalem? Selected by God to stand and survive

453. Ibid., 38.

throughout history, Jerusalem has its place as the "highest city" on earth (as Rabbi Shlomo Carlebach used to call it). The enduring quality, centrality, and depth of Jerusalem is a majestic form of *netzach* within *malchut*.

A final word on Jerusalem. In *The Prime Ministers*, a story is told about Menachem Begin's attitude to the city. When he was about to meet with Prime Minister Margaret Thatcher of Great Britain, he was asked by a reporter if he planned to ask Mrs. Thatcher for her support in recognizing Jerusalem as Israel's capital. Begin's response: "No sir – under no circumstances." The reporter was obviously perplexed and asked, "Why not?"

Begin's answer illustrates his *netzach* within *malchut*, his enduring commitment to truth and integrity, and it illustrates how the eternality of Jerusalem lives in the heart and soul of every Jew:

> "Because, sir, Jerusalem was a Jewish capital long before London was a British capital. When King David moved the capital of his kingdom from Hebron, where he had reigned for seven years, to Jerusalem, where he reigned for thirty-three years, the civilized world had never heard of London. In fact, they had never heard of Great Britain."[454]

MAJOR TORAH THEMES AND *NETZACH* WITHIN *MALCHUT*

We obviously turn to Moshe, the Fourth Shepherd, who rectified the *sefirah* of *netzach*. Of the many examples of his *netzach* within *malchut*, we will focus on just one:

It was God's plan, before the Sin of the Spies, that Moshe should lead the Jewish people into Israel and then usher in the Messianic Era. But when the Spies caused the entire nation to balk, God decreed that all men over twenty would have to die first, and this would happen as the nation wandered the wilderness over forty years. God realized the people needed more maturing, that they still lacked the *emunah* required to live in the Land. And Moshe was burdened with the task of teaching them during this time.

Moshe had previously reacted with deep disappointment when the teaching role was foisted on him following the Israelite complaints about manna. Then he told God:

454. Ibid., 504.

> "Why have I not found favor in Your eyes, that You place the burden of this entire people upon me? Did I conceive this entire people or did I give birth to it, that You say to me, 'Carry them in your bosom, as a nurse carries a suckling, to the Land that You swore to its forefathers?' . . . I alone cannot carry this entire nation, for it is too heavy for me! And if this is how You deal with me, then kill me now, if I have found favor in Your eyes . . ."[455]

Notice that Moshe literally asked God to kill him, rather than force him to carry the load of teaching the entire Jewish people. This is how unpleasant the task seemed to him, but in the end he did it.

We learn a quintessential life lesson from all this. Namely, when we are given *yesurim*, trials and disappointments, we should shift gears and accept the will of God. If we do so, then these difficult moments will serve as our *kapparah*. And then we can thank God for providing a soul correction for our *neshamah* and also a course correction for our lives.

This is what Moshe did. And this is how he mastered *netzach* with *malchut*. He accepted his new and revised leadership role and mission for the subsequent thirty-eight years over which he came to embody each *sefirah* one by one. Consider the following:

- Moshe displayed *chesed* with the daughters of Zelophehad. As well, when he waited for Miriam while she was quarantined outside of the camp for speaking *lashon hara* about him.
- He displayed *gevurah* in confronting the rebellion of Korach.
- *Tiferet* was natural for Moshe. When God was going to destroy the Jewish people after the sin of the Golden Calf, Moshe implored Him to showy mercy and only punish the worst perpetrators.
- *Netzach* was Moshe's life story as demonstrated by his teaching the eternal Torah and oral tradition to the Jewish people until they were, in fact, ready to inherit the Land.
- *Hod* was displayed by Moshe at all times; he never took glory for himself and, as a result, he is described by Torah as the most humble person who ever lived.

455. *Bamidbar* 11:11–15.

- At the end of his life, Moshe gave in his final address to the Jewish people, which we know as *Sefer Devarim*. In it, he demonstrated *yesod* – his complete bonding with his people.
- And finally, Moshe's *malchut* shines forth eternally – he was the most important prophet who ever lived, the one and only person who merited to speak directly to God in an awakened state.

Moshe, a truly great and monumentally dedicated leader to whom we owe so much.

DISCUSSION TOPICS FOR *NETZACH* WITHIN *MALCHUT*

For adults

1. Can I describe two times in the last five years that I showed determination and endurance to reach a worthy goal that I set for myself? If not, what prevented me from crossing the finish line?
2. What current goal have I set for myself – be it in my personal life or my career? Have I set timetables and stepping-stones toward its accomplishment?
3. What worthy causes have I ever fought for? How did that make me feel?

For children

1. Do I feel enough confidence in myself to finish tasks? If not, whom can I talk to about this, and what can I do to change it?
2. What is the longest amount of time I have worked on a project or goal? Have I ever built something, or planted a garden and watched it grow, or wrote something carefully that expressed my emotions very thoroughly?
3. What is the most important achievement in my life so far? How do I feel about this achievement? Which strengths of mine did it take to do it? Were there times along the way when I thought it was too hard to finish? What kept me going?

היום שבעה וארבעים יום,
שהם ששה שבועות וחמישה ימים, לעומר

Ha'yom shiva v'arbaim yom,
she'hem shisha shavuot v'chamisha yamim la'Omer

TODAY IS THE FORTY-SEVENTH DAY,
OR SIX WEEKS AND FIVE DAYS, OF THE OMER.

DAY 47

Hod sh'b'Malchut (Humility within Leadership/Nobility)

Hod within *malchut* is knowing that everything that we accomplish or that happens to us in life comes from God. It is recognizing that every outcome is the very best outcome, and that all the talents, blessings, and successes that rain down on us come from God and are not the sole result of our hard work and endeavors. Armed with this *sefirah* combination, we approach all situations – and especially those where we are called upon to lead – with a humble self-awareness that helps us act with consideration of others and with *derech eretz*.

We are taught by our Sages that "the whole world would not have been created except for me."[456] Contemplating this privilege, that the whole world was created for each one of us alone, causes us to conclude that we need to be worthy of receiving this gift and fills us with *hod*. The only way we can be worthy is to align our true self – our "I" – with the "Great Essential I" (God). That is when we can be sure of doing the right thing, because our will is then aligned with His will, and we function as a ray of His light in fulfilling the mission for which we were created.

Judaism holds that each one of us is unique and created for a unique

456. *Shabbat* 30b.

purpose. The trait of *hod* within *malchut* helps us cultivate the necessary faith to understand and carry out God's will for us in a truthful, caring way, and to be grounded and dignified, displaying leadership and nobility as servants of God. Without this trait, we may be prone to arrogance in all its forms and can block our connection to our *neshamah*, leaving us conscious of only our physical body and missing God's constant intervention in our lives.

ACTS OF DIVINE INTERVENTION

Readers may recall the Icelandic volcanic eruption in 2010 that paralyzed much of world transportation and stranded millions of travelers, causing the loss of billions of dollars. But it was not just one unmitigated disaster; it was certainly part of God's plan for all those affected, as this story testifies:

> The story begins with a young yeshiva student, an 18-year-old Yerushalmi, who was mortally ill with fulminate hepatic failure. With little hope of receiving a liver transplant in Israel, Rav Avraham Firer [head of Ezra LeMarpeh, which provides medical assistance to the needy] sought to send the boy on an emergency flight to Brussels, the world center of liver transplants. The only problem, however, was that Brussels under no circumstances transplants non-EU patients, in order to save the scanty supply of livers for Europeans. Nevertheless, it was decided to send him to Brussels despite this knowledge. The young student had no choice but to include his name on the long waiting list for a liver transplant. In the meantime, he tried to maintain his learning despite the illness, consciously aware that it would take weeks, months, and even years till he will be able to be given a new liver. Many patients were on the waiting list, and his name was somewhere on the bottom . . . And when his turn would finally arrive, [the donated liver] had to completely match his blood type and other medical criteria. If not a perfect match, he'd need to continue waiting . . . for a miracle.
>
> However . . . Hashem had a different plan for this young yeshiva student and Hashem's loyal servants produced avalanches of hot ash, rock, and gas, causing Europe to completely shut down its skies into a no-fly zone. It was during this time that this young Yerushalmi was

> sitting in the yeshiva learning Torah in the capital of Belgium. During the course of the shut-down of airspace above Europe, a person died in the hospital in the capital of Belgium, a person who had agreed to donate his liver to anyone that might need it. Astonishingly, a liver was perfectly parametric for our young yeshiva student. Health authorities in Belgium began searching the liver transplant waiting list, but "unfortunately" not even one patient was able to fly into Belgium for the healthy liver due to the volcanic eruption. As they advanced further on the waiting list, they reached the young yeshiva student, but [the liver] was not offered to him due to his lack of citizenship. As the clock closed on the deadline for time within which the liver would still be viable, however, no one else was able to arrive in Belgium for the transplant except this young Yerushalmi [who was already there].
>
> With clear Divine Intervention, this budding *talmid chacham* received the liver . . . The enormity of this miracle was even greater after the successful transplant. The doctors said that the young student's liver was very deteriorated and diseased, and it was a matter of days before it would have stopped functioning completely. The doctors unanimously believe that if he had had to continue waiting for a transplant, he would not have survived.[457]

What a story. Can you find all the humility? There was the Rav who instructed the boy to go to Belgium even with the knowledge that, technically speaking, the boy would never qualify for a liver. Both the boy and the Rav displayed tremendous *hod* within *malchut* in acting upon the belief that God runs the world which He created. The boy displayed tremendous *emunah* by going to Belgium, enrolling in a new yeshiva, and continuing his learning while he waited for a miracle. *Tefillah*, *tzedakah*, and *teshuvah* were all deployed, as these are all essential components of God's system of deciding who is deserving of a miracle.

And what happened? A live eruption in a volcano that had lain dormant for over 150 years. A no-fly zone over all of Europe for days. A death in the country where the boy waited for a new liver. A perfect match. No

457. This story can be found on geulawatch@yahoogrouops.com, where it is attributed to www.bhol.co.il/news.

one else able to accept it. The hospital forced to give it to the only person eligible to receive it!

Why? Who can know the mission assigned Above to this young yeshiva student? Perhaps it was only to be the recipient of the liver from the donor who died, to help the donor with his *tikkun*. Perhaps it was to inspire the rest of us with his story of *emunah*. Perhaps it was a completely different mission which he will eventually discover.

But the lesson to us is clear, and it is best captured in the words of Ramban to his son: "In all your words, actions, and thoughts – at all times – imagine in your heart that you are standing in the presence of the Holy One, Blessed be He, and that His Presence rests upon you."

ALICE HERZ-SOMMER, AGE 109

Alice Herz-Sommer is famous. She is the subject of the book by Caroline Stoessinger *Lessons from the Life of Alice Herz-Sommer, the World's Oldest Living Holocaust Survivor: A Century of Wisdom*, the center of attraction of the documentary *From Hell to Paradise, or Chopin Saved Me*, featured in a video by Anthony Robbins, and interviewed by Barry Davis in *The Jerusalem Post Magazine* article, "100 Years of Music and Life, and Counting."

She was 42 years old and living in Prague, when she and her young son were sent to the Theresienstadt concentration camp. There her "job" was to play the piano for camp commanders and their families, and also, sometimes, for prisoners. On the Robbins video, a fellow prisoner recollects that Alice's music created "a Garden of Eden in hell." That is how she and her son survived. And ever since, music has continued to dominate her life. At the time of this writing she was 109 and going strong, continuing to practice piano every day, even though she has lost the use of one finger on each hand.

Alice's philosophy of life, as verbalized in the Robbins video, is simple: "Be Optimistic." Her mother taught her that complaining doesn't change people and "to be thankful for everything." Having lived through so much, she says that "everything is a present" and notes that it is important to appreciate such gifts as not being hungry, the sun, or a kind word. As well, she suggests, "every day put something in your mind to learn."

Alice makes a statement that on the surface will sound astonishing, but underneath it reflects the same philosophy that Rabbi Arush promotes in

The Garden of Emuna and in *The Garden of Gratitude*. She says she was "thankful" to have been in the camps, because she is "richer than others" for the experience. "Hatred eats the soul of the hater, not the hated . . . I know about the bad, but I look at the good thing."

We could each learn a great deal from Alice Herz-Sommer about *hod* within *malchut*. Despite experience with "the bad," she has chosen to live her life with nobility and dignity. The Nazis may have imprisoned her body, but no one could imprison her spirit. She vividly demonstrates how *hod* within *malchut* unwraps the gift of life.

THE MODEL OF AARON

In Week Five, we examined in detail the personality of Aaron, the Fifth Shepherd who rectified *hod*. And yet, despite his humility, he was a world-class leader. Consider this list[458] of testimonials to him from Jewish sources:

- "Three good leaders arose for Israel: Moshe, Aaron, and Miriam." (*Taanit* 9a)
- "There were seventy small courts over which Aaron was appointed."(Zohar 3:20:1)
- "The world exists only for the sake of Moshe and Aaron." (*Chullin* 89a)
- "Moshe and Aaron are equivalent to one another." (*Bereshit Rabbah* 1:15)
- "The merit of Moshe and Aaron was enough to redeem Israel." (*Shemot Rabbah* 15:3)
- "'Before I arose,' said Moshe, 'my brother Aaron prophesied . . . for eighty years.'"(*Shemot Rabbah* 3:16)
- "He loved peace and pursued it, loved people and drew them close to the Torah." (*Avot* 1:12)
- "'He did not interrupt his friend's words' – this refers to Aaron." (*Pirkei d'Rabbi Natan* 37:12)
- "When Aaron went on his way and a wicked person encountered him, [Aaron] greeted him. The next day, that man wanted to commit a sin, [but] thought, 'Woe is to me! How will I raise my eyes

458. This list has been excerpted from the *Encyclopedia of Biblical Personalities* (Brooklyn, NY: Shaar Press [in conjunction with Mashabim], 1994), 55–56.

afterwards and look at Aaron? I will be ashamed before him . . .'" (*Pirkei d'Rabbi Natan* 12:3)

- "Aaron tied a rope of iron about his waist and went around to all the houses of Israel. To whoever was ignorant he taught *Kriat Shema* and prayer, and to whoever could not learn Torah he taught [Torah]." (*Tanna d'Bei Eliyahu Rabbah*, ed. Meir Ish Shalom)
- "When Moshe spoke, Aaron would bend his ear to listen in awe, and Scripture considers it as if he heard [directly] from the Holy One, Blessed be He." (*Mechilta Bo* 3)

In his own right, Aaron was a spiritual giant as evidenced by the above. And yet, even though he was the older brother, we do not read in the Torah that he ever asked to pre-empt Moshe or be the leader of Am Yisrael. We do not read that Aaron ever once asked for greater or different responsibility other than that given him by God. We do not read that he wanted his job description re-written to include some of Moshe's responsibilities. We do not read that he was jealous or ever thought poorly of a single living human being. So humble was Aaron, he couldn't even bring himself to demand the death of those Jews who were reveling at the base of the Golden Calf.

Aaron mastered humility. He reflected this humility in all his actions. And he achieved the masterful perfection of *hod* within *malchut*.

HUMILITY, A RARE QUALITY

Humility has all but disappeared in the twenty-first century. Today, most people crowd the public forums to publicly and loudly claim credit, show disrespect for others, expose their lives (including intimate moments) on Reality TV and Facebook, or participate in incessant texting of all the details of their every day. Boundaries between modesty and humility versus arrogant public displays have virtually been obliterated.

Each of us has much work to do in order to acquire the trait of *hod* within *malchut* and, in so doing, to understand, experience, and perfect composure, serenity, discretion, modesty and most importantly "other focus" versus "self focus." Most of all, as a top priority, we must learn to always conduct ourselves, whether in private or public, in ways that will find favor in the eyes of God.

DISCUSSION TOPICS FOR *HOD* WITHIN *MALCHUT*

For adults

1. When I am playing a dominant role in a relationship (such as that of a parent, teacher, or boss) do I believe that I am superior to my subordinates (my children, students, or employees)? Does that help me to be more effective in my role?
2. Does the family dynamic in our family permit all members to play their role, be heard, participate, and feel that they are essential to the whole unit? If not, what can I do to improve this?
3. When I meet a person who has less formal education and a lower societal position than me, how do I feel inside?

For children

1. Do I get interrupted a lot when I try to speak in our home at dinner, or when I am with my friends, or at school? Do I feel as if my opinions are truly considered? How about me – do I interrupt others while they are talking and do I listen to what they have to say?
2. Is there any part of my life where I feel confident in my abilities?
3. Do I know my strong points and have I thanked Hashem for blessing me with the natural talents I have?
4. From where in my life can I learn that God is in complete control?

היום שמונה וארבעים יום,
שהם ששה שבועות וששה ימים, לעומר

Ha'yom shemonah v'arbaim yom,
she'hem shisha shavuot v'shisha yamim la'Omer

**TODAY IS THE FORTY-EIGHTH DAY,
OR SIX WEEKS AND SIX DAYS, OF THE OMER.**

DAY 48

Yesod sh'b'Malchut (Bonding within Leadership/Nobility)

The emphasis of *yesod* within *malchut* reinforces the ability of *malchut* to reach out to others in order to optimize relationships and create consensus. *Yesod* within *malchut* is a magnet that builds a solid, healthy foundation between self and self, self and other, and self and God. We are not meant to be an island. We are expected to show respect for others and to bond with them while honoring their boundaries. We are also expected to bond with Torah ideals and principles that have been given to us for eternity. When we do, we have entered the realm of *yesod* within *malchut*.

God tells us in *Sefer Vayikra* that, if we follow His decrees and observe His commandments, a number of benefits will accrue to us. Among these is God's assurance that "I will walk among you, I will be God unto you and you will be a people unto Me."[459]

Commenting on this verse, Rabbi Jeffrey Bienenfeld provides an important insight into *yesod* within *malchut* – especially regarding how our relationship with God works:

459. *Vayikra* 26:3–13.

> Now, what exactly does it mean when God promises to walk among us? The Seforno offers quite an uplifting interpretation. Once the Mishkan was constructed, God declared He would dwell therein. True. But could God be found elsewhere? Would God be my companion and friend? Would He be willing to walk with me, be present with me?
>
> Comes along this heartening promise and tells us that indeed all of the above is possible. The only caveat is a sincere willingness to adhere to God's *mitzvot* . . .
>
> When a person observes a mitzvah and is consciously aware of this deed, he . . . invites God into his/her life. And . . . God happily accepts the invitation.
>
> The more we invest our daily behaviors with this God awareness, the greater Hashem's Presence is felt, and with that Presence come many good things. We are gently pushed to see the bigger picture when weighted down with our problems; we are reminded of what is really important in life; we are consoled when many of our goals are not met. In short, feeling Hashem close up can make a real difference in our lives. And it all begins with a simple mitzvah observance. You pick the mitzvah, add some concentrated *kavanah* (intentionality), and God responds.[460]

Just how promptly God responds we see from the many stories in the Torah, relating the lives of our illustrious ancestors.

RIVKA'S ROLE

Often judged as sneaky and conniving for her role in diverting the blessing from Esav to Yaakov, Rivka actually executed an extremely difficult act of *yesod* within *malchut*, for she bonded deeply at that moment with what she accurately perceived was the destiny of the Jewish people. Indeed, she bonded more deeply with that vision than with her husband, Yitzchak, whom she decided to fool for the sake of this worthy cause.

By bonding with the future of the Jewish people, she also bonded with the foundation created earlier by her father-in-law Avraham. She understood more clearly than her husband what was his mission – to ensure the

460. Bienenfeld, *Chizuk*, May 17, 2012.

continuity of the *mesorah*. Rivka knew that Esav was not capable of this. She knew this mission would be fulfilled by Yaakov, who was highly qualified to bear this responsibility, although he would need more instruction at the yeshiva of Shem v'Ever, as well as seasoning by her brother, Lavan.

Torah commentators note that Yitzchak began to listen to Rivka after these events, thereby suggesting that he recognized what his wife had perceived much earlier. When she complained about not wanting Yaakov to marry the "daughters of Het," Yitzchak commanded Yaakov not to take such a wife, and "Yaakov obeyed his father and mother."[461] This suggest that Rivka and Yitzchak were finally of one mind in relating to their sons.

Through her crucial actions on behalf of the first Jewish family and its mission, Rivka demonstrated a gutsy, heroic version of *yesod* within *malchut* and enabled the continuation of the Divine plan for the Nation of Israel.

YOSEF'S RECTIFICATION OF *YESOD*

As discussed during Week Six of the Omer count, Yosef is the shepherd tasked with rectifying the *sefirah* of *yesod* that was damaged in Gan Eden when Adam and Chava cut themselves off from their true selves by eating from the Tree of Knowledge of Good and Evil and, by so doing, cut themselves – and humanity – off from God.

Thrown into Egypt, Yosef rose above all temptations and remained bonded to God. He remained devoted to his father's tradition. He raised his children with this heritage and ensured that they adhered to the family mission faithfully, thus continuing the legacy of the Jewish people. When he was reunited with his brothers after twenty-two years, he forgave what they did to him, once he discerned that they had all bonded with each other, despite their different mothers. This is the proof Yosef needed to know they had done complete *teshuvah*.

Further, as tempting as it may have been, Yosef never told his story of suffering to his father or anyone else. He never revealed to Yaakov the truth of how terribly the brothers had treated him, knowing the irreparable rift this knowledge would cause in the family.

No wonder Yosef was able to rectify *yesod* in the world. He understood its pure meaning and its relationship to everything – from the individual

461. *Bereshit* 27:46, 28:6–8.

to the eternal. Therefore, Yosef's life and relationships display an unconditional loyalty to God, to *Yiddishkeit*, to his family, and to the Jewish people. Yosef is the epitome of *yesod* within *malchut* which he embodied throughout his life.

ADVICE FROM RABBI YAAKOV AVIGDOR

An absolutely phenomenal book that all should read is *The Forgotten Memoirs: Moving Personal Accounts from Rabbis who Survived the Holocaust* by Esther Farbstein. In this book, Farbstein has collected moving and inspirational writings by rabbis who were liberated from Nazi labor and death camps. I selected one example here:

The writer, Rabbi Yaakov Avigdor, the Chief Rabbi of East Galicia, was one of the few survivors of the Jews of Poland. In 1941, he was forced to live in the Drohobycz Ghetto until he was eventually sent to the Plaszow concentration camp, and then on to Buchenwald. After the Allied liberation of the camps, he was active in helping to revive religious life for survivors and served as a *dayan* on the rabbinical court for Holocaust *agunot* (wives with husbands who could not with certainty be declared as dead, thus allowing their wives to remarry). Afterwards, he was a Talmud and Torah teacher in New York and eventually the Chief Rabbi of Mexico until his death in 1967. He was a prolific writer both before and after the war.

Farbstein names Rabbi Avigdor as being among the first to address Jewish heroism in the Holocaust from a broader perspective, including upholding ethical principles in the face of enormously harrowing tests. She sums up[462] Rabbi Avigdor's 1950 preface to *Chelek Yaakov* where he identifies three types of Jewish heroism:

- *The first type of heroism – "restraint"*

We have already discussed at length that it takes more strength to restrain oneself than to act. Restraint (*gevurah*) is not the result of submission, but rather is a choice motivated by a strong sense of responsibility. In the Drohobycz Ghetto, restraint was the result of a recognition that any rebellion would lead to the liquidation of the ghetto and the killing of all the

462. Esther Farbstein, *The Forgotten Memoirs* (Brooklyn, NY: Shaar Press, 2011), 42–61.

inhabitants. Writes Rabbi Avigdor: "We felt, intuitively, that we must not carry out the desires of the enemy, and we knew that our enemy's greatest desire was only that we should rise up and rebel – so that he would have an excuse to destroy us all . . . In the end, hundreds of thousands of Jews did survive . . . one must marvel at the great heroism and inhuman effort we made to restrain ourselves and to transcend our suffering and intense sorrow. Our hearts were buffeted by the storm and bleeding in pain, our hearts were bursting from pain and sorrow, the bile and bitterness overflowed – yet we did not say a single word. Has there ever been heroism such as ours?"[463]

- *The second type of heroism – "the fight to survive"*

On the part of the ghetto residents, this included both the consuming struggle to hide themselves and other Jews and also to find food. "Life in the ghetto was a tremendous miracle . . . Only the Jewish people, long-experienced in miracles, could exist under such circumstances for years. Hunger was rampant; mortality was ten or even twenty times greater than the norm. Epidemics of all kinds broke out there . . . Yet despite the harsh, bitter tortures, life was still precious to us: Everyone wanted to live, to persevere and live, to thwart the desires of the enemy who only wanted the Jews to die, to kill themselves . . . . Despite the poverty, hunger, and diseases, several hundred Jews succeeded in digging pits deep in the ground. They actually lived in the pipes, the sewers of the swampland, the conduits – for several months. This is valor at its highest, beyond human ability, more than any other nation on the face of the earth – that we managed to exist under such conditions."[464]

Beyond finding food and hiding places, the struggle to survive also included rabbinic decisions that, under these grave circumstances, certain *mitzvot* could be sacrificed in order to save a life. Rabbi Avigdor describes the unprecedented questions the rabbis of the ghetto were asked. He also explains his decision to permit a Jew to disguise himself as a Christian and to hide in a Christian home. He correctly describes all of these efforts as heroic expressions with the aim of facilitating the ultimate rescue of Jews,

463. Ibid., 57.
464. Ibid., 57–58.

the preservation of Jewish values and efforts to confound the plans of the Nazis.

- *The third type of heroism (displayed time and again) – "the preservation of values and of the image of God in humanity"*

Here, Rabbi Avigdor writes so beautifully: "We still searched for some meaning and purpose in the suffering and punishment. Thus from our miserable existences would rise a spark of hope, a flicker of optimism, and an inexhaustible source of heroism: not materialistic, earthy heroism but the kind of valor that allowed us to withstand all our trials and tribulations for the sake of eternal moral, ethical principles. We have done nothing of which to be ashamed. What has been done to us, shamelessly in front of the entire world, has never before in the history of humanity been perpetrated."[465]

Rabbi Avigdor, and all those whose heroic actions he described, indeed mastered *yesod* within *malchut*. All three types of heroism bonded the Jewish people and revived the Jewish spirit to preserve and prolong life. The heroes refused to be tragic victims, and they employed wisdom, insight, understanding, restraint, and loving-kindness even while enduring the tortuous pain and agony that would break the average person. They bonded with fundamental, eternal, ethical, and moral principles and emerged complete, whether they lived or died by Nazi hands. We owe them a debt of deep gratitude for teaching us how to survive and not give up.

465. Ibid., 59.

DISCUSSION TOPICS FOR *YESOD* WITHIN *MALCHUT*

For adults

1. How strong is the spiritual and emotional foundation of your home? How many hours a day do you spend on items of value – expressing gratitude and genuine respect toward others – versus on mundane topics or complaints?
2. Discuss with family members how the family as a whole might optimize the dynamic described above to make better use of each day, to strengthen and deepen the emotional bonds with each other and the spiritual bonds with God.
3. Select either your family or your work environment to answer this question: Do you feel that the members of your family (or work group) are going off in different directions, with some members not engaged in a focused way to help achieve a positive outcome for the group? What can you do about it?

For children

1. What does your family talk about during the dinner hour? What topics could you bring up that would help everyone in our family to grow both individually and with each other?
2. Do you race through prayers? Can God feel that you bond with Him if you rush to finish talking to Him?
3. Deep down, do you like yourself?

היום תשעה וארבעים יום, שהם שבעה שבועות, לעומר

Ha'yom tisha v'arbaim yom, she'hem shiva shavuot la'Omer

"TODAY IS THE FORTY-NINTH DAY, OR SEVEN WEEKS, OF THE OMER."

DAY 49

Malchut sh'b'Malchut (Leadership/Nobility within Leadership/Nobility)

***Malchut* within *malchut* is the pinnacle toward which we have been striving. It is achieved when we genuinely respect others in all realms of life, whether physical, emotional, or spiritual.**

What does this mean on the practical level? First, we have to be aware of our own special individuality in order that we might understand and fulfill our own unique mission in this world. Second, we must demonstrate respect and regard for other people, each of whom has a unique mission too – and, just like us, the potential for *malchut*. We must not, however, under any circumstances, court evil, and when it appears in the world, we must fight it in accordance with God's directives.

Malchut within *malchut* is the scope of the combined wisdom and understanding that we have achieved through the cultivation and integration of the *sefirot* of *chesed*, *gevurah*, *tiferet*, *netzach*, *hod*, and *yesod*. Whether it be in a very limited or wider area of responsibility, whether it would involve ourselves or other individuals, and whether it would or would not involve power, authority, and leadership, *malchut* within *malchut* needs to be manifested in this world. *Malchut* is a state of mind and self-composure that allows us to act with nobility and dignity both individually and in concert with others, in order to achieve outcomes that are worthy. It is an integrated balance that acts with *emunah* to achieve unity, light, and holiness at all times.

Tests? Ethical challenges? Temptations? Crises? *Malchut* within *malchut* is our "home base." It is where we are centered and whole, where we are grounded in a safe haven of security and conviction. It is being "Balanced to Win" at virtually all times.

Ain Od Milvado ("There is nothing but Him") is the thought that immediately comes into mind and, from that vantage point, we can make sure that all our actions are consistent with what is right and good in the eyes of God.

TORAH MODELS

God's overarching role of creating and providing for all of existence and all of the needs of every form of life in the entire world is the prime example of *malchut* within *malchut*. As well, the Torah gives us many examples of ordinary people whose actions define *malchut* within *malchut* and help us understand what this *sefirah* combination is all about. Let us consider a few of them:

Moshe: Moshe's farewell address to the Jewish people – better known as *Sefer Devarim* – reflects *malchut* within *malchut* like no other part of Torah.

Yehoshua: First, Yehoshua played an important role by learning in the tent of Moshe and then leading the Jewish people into the Promised Land. Then, upon assuming leadership, he fulfilled the command given to Moshe by God just before the Jewish people were to enter the Land: "When you cross the Jordan to the land of Canaan, you shall drive out all the inhabitants of the Land before you; and you shall destroy all their prostration stones; all their molten images shall you destroy; and all their high places shall you demolish. You shall possess the Land and you shall settle in it, for to you have I given the Land to possess it. You shall give the Land as an inheritance by lot to your families . . ."[466] Yehoshua was the leader who led the Twelve Tribes in the conquest of the Land, a task that took seven years. Yehoshua then apportioned the Land among the tribes which took another seven years. It is a tribute to all involved that there

466. *Bamidbar* 33: 50–54.

were no disagreements as to how any of this was to be accomplished. All were united in following the instructions of God as conveyed by Yehoshua. This showed that all achieved a *malchut* within *malchut* state of being.

David HaMelech: The last act of his life – when King David ordered his son Shlomo to be crowned and not any of his other children (whose actions had not made them worthy to be king) – was a decision that demonstrated *malchut* within *malchut*.

Moshe, Yehoshua, and King David rose to the elevated heights of emulating God's attribute of *malchut* within *malchut* by aligning themselves with God's light. They each epitomized serving their Master, King, and Savior without fault as they carried out their life missions on behalf of the Jewish people. May we all be worthy some day to serve God in an equally pure manner.

OUR NATIONAL AND INDIVIDUAL MISSION

The Torah states: "You are a holy nation to God. God chose you to be His special people."[467] This seems to be redundant, but Rashi explains that it is not, because there are two aspects of being a Jew, the national dimension and also the individual dimension. Both are very important.

First, we belong to a holy nation. Second, within that nation, we each embody a unique holiness, as unique as "individual diamonds" (to borrow the words of Rabbi Joseph B. Soloveitchik).[468]

But what happens when the needs and obligations of the individual Jew conflict with that of the collective Jewish nation?

Rabbi Yonason Sacks, the Rosh Yeshiva of Lander College for Men, notes that the Jewish law addresses this very question. For example, when a person is in mourning and sitting *shiva*, *halachah* demands that he stop when Yom Tov arrives. This is because Yom Tov is a time of being together *b'simcha* with other Jews, and the obligation of being part of the *klal* in this instance supersedes his individual obligation to mourn.[469]

Rabbi Sacks cites another example – that of the *metzora*, the person who by his sin of *lashon hara* (a sin of arrogance and superiority over others) found himself stricken with a disease akin to leprosy. The *metzora* had

467. *Devarim* 14:2.

468. Quoted by Rabbi Bienenfeld in his *shiur* on April 18, 2012.

469. Ibid.

to be quarantined and sent to live outside the Jewish camp/community for at least seven days, during which time he had to act like a mourner sitting *shiva*. Rabbi Sacks asks: What was the *metzora* mourning? And he answers: He was mourning the fact that part of himself – the part that used to belong to the community – was dead. (Indeed, the Gemara comments that four people are called "dead" in the Torah, including the *metzora*.)

Why is this? Because the sin he had committed, the sin of *lashon hara* fractures the *klal*. States Rabbi Sacks: "The *metzora*, by his arrogance and inability to refrain from speaking harmfully about others forfeits his collective sanctity."[470] So destructive is the *metzora* who shatters the collective that his state is not cancelled even when Yom Tov arrives. His punishment seems to underscore the high price of exclusion that he is required to pay for allowing his individual actions to harm the nation.

Serious contemplation of the *sefirah* combination of *malchut* within *malchut* cannot begin if we are engaging in *lashon hara*. Harming another person is a despicable act that is completely contrary to the magnificent splendor, truth, love, restraint, bonding, humility, foundation and dignity that *malchut* within *malchut* radiantly reflects in its completeness.

We are blessed to be part of a religion that considers each of us to be an individual diamond. We are blessed to be part of a religion that recognizes that the One God created everything that exists and that every single human being is created in the Divine Image, and as such possesses a beautiful *neshamah*. God, in His Perfection and Omniscience, gave all us humans the ability to freely choose to establish a close relationship with Him and to choose "good" and to do the "right" thing in every single life situation facing us. He also gave all of us a system of *teshuvah*, to correct mistakes we have made.

When we recognize that we are a part of the "Great Essential I," and when our thoughts, speech, and actions demonstrate our alignment with God, we achieve individual *malchut*. We become noble leaders of our lives, making choices that display our respect of God, ourselves, and others. Our conduct is befitting the shining individual diamond we were created to be.

Yes, we are "a holy nation to God . . . His special people,"[471] but this designation comes with responsibility. As such, we are meant to participate

470. Ibid.

471. *Devarim* 14:2.

in establishing and supporting our collective national mission of holiness, for God has also told us:

> "I am God; in righteousness have I called you and taken hold of your hand; I have protected you and appointed you to bring the people to the covenant, to be a light for the nations."[472]

Achieving this mission is *malchut* within *malchut* on a national scale.

We can only achieve our national mission of serving as a light unto the nations if we are united as a people. We already know from thousands of years of Jewish history what the consequences are when one group of Jews acts towards another with hatred and arrogance.

The fact that the Third Temple does not stand tells us that we have not yet rectified the sin of our forefathers and are likely contributing to it. Each one of us must, today and now, commit to changing this sad state of affairs. Let's not test God anymore, and let's hope God will not test us. Let's pray that the Mashiach comes speedily, in our days, Amen.

PERSONAL AFFIRMATION

Those of us who have mastered loving-kindness, restraint, harmony, endurance, humility, and bonding within the whole of their life's choices will automatically be living within the *sefirah* of *malchut* within *malchut*. Toward that goal, I propose the following personal affirmation to be recited daily:

- I want to eliminate Egypt from my mindset and I want to be free of what enslaves me from within. I have integrated the various *sefirot* into my life, feel "Balanced to Win" in my life's goals and dreams, and have recognized the power of each *sefirah*.
- If I have mastered *chesed* within *malchut*, I do not harbor absolute hatred in my heart or mind for another person or group. I may disagree with some or even all of their views. I may disagree with the choices that I see them making. I may not want them as my friends or invite them to my home. But, nevertheless, I will treat them with respect, because they, too, embody the image of God. However, I am

472. *Yeshayahu* 42:6.

permitted to hate evil and the evil action of others. I will pray for God to intervene and thwart all evil plots and schemes.

- If I have mastered *gevurah* within *malchut*, I apply strength, discipline, and restraint for the purpose of only achieving aims that are noble and dignified and that reflect a love and awe of Hashem.
- If I have mastered *tiferet* within *malchut*, I know how to harmonize *chesed* with *gevurah* in every situation in order to achieve a noble, dignified outcome for me and for others. I respect balance, not extremism, in all traits except two: anger, which I have been taught by our Sages to avoid completely; and humility, which I work to develop to the highest level.
- If I have mastered *netzach* within *malchut*, I demonstrate persistence in relationships, goals and causes that are noble and dignified.
- If I have mastered *hod* within *malchut*, I display complete *emunah* and work humbly to further aims, relationships, and causes that are noble and dignified.
- If I have mastered *yesod* within *malchut*, I continue to bond with others and cleave to God. As well, I play whatever role I can to help others achieve noble and worthy goals.
- If I have mastered *malchut* within *malchut*, I love myself, my neighbor, and God. As well, I am in an active relationship with God through regular *tefillah* and *teshuvah*. I awaken each day like a lion who cannot wait to serve Hashem, my God, my Master, My King, and My Redeemer. I display loving-kindness towards humanity. I foster love among others and remain loyal to my family. I appreciate the gift of life that I am given daily, regardless of my tests and challenges, knowing that everything that happens is a gift from God tailor-made to help me fulfill my earthly mission. And when God takes my soul from me, to reunite with Him, I will accept that He knows best and pray for His unending mercy to resurrect the dead with the coming of Mashiach.

Reading this affirmation daily will help keep us focused on what the state of being "Balanced to Win" feels like and how to achieve it.

DISCUSSION TOPICS FOR *MALCHUT* WITHIN *MALCHUT*

For adults

1. Do I act as if I love myself every day?
2. Am I in an active relationship with God, by way of *tefillah* and *teshuvah*?
3. Do I display a high level of *derech eretz* with all those I meet, including those with whom I don't have much in common?

For children

1. Can I list five words/phrases that describe how unique I am?
2. Have I thanked God for creating me exactly the way I am?
3. What three things might I like to do when I am older?

Conclusion

Just like our brothers and sisters did over 3,300 years ago – when they left the bondage of Egypt and made their way toward the encounter with God at Mount Sinai – we have prepared ourselves for 49 days. We gave thought to every day of the Omer count. We worked on each *sefirah* combination. We committed ourselves to change, growth, and self-improvement.

With this effort, we were able to break some of the chains that held us back, perhaps without our even being aware of our "enslavement." We plan to continue to work on ourselves for the remainder of the year until we are completely free. But now we have reached the point of being able to *truly* experience Shavuot *because* we have counted each day for seven weeks, and approached each corresponding *sefirah* in a meaningful way.

Having chosen to count the Omer in a meaningful way, we are not the same as we were 49 days ago. We know with greater accuracy and awareness what our strengths are. We also acknowledge with greater clarity and honesty the areas that we still have to work on. During this period, we have tried to reframe our thoughts, words, and actions into a more positive outlook on life and thus achieve a state of being "Balanced to Win." We have initiated some new behaviors. We feel a sense of balance and harmony. We are smiling more often and more freely. We feel better about ourselves today than we did 49 days ago because we have fine-tuned our motivations and behaviors. The Omer counting process has brought us closer to understanding our unique mission and fulfilling it. There is a positive shift in our "God awareness" whereby we recognize our need and desire to draw closer to God. We recognize that we are a ray of God's Infinite Light and that recognition makes us shine.

Those of us who have read this book with a partner or with our children, undoubtedly can point to a perceptible change in the dynamics that characterize our home environment. We now feel better about our relationships and communications. We are inspired to see this continue. There has been a shift in how often our family seems to be thinking and talking about God. We are more keenly aware that we control very little "except" whether or not we will "choose life." When we choose life, we are showering ourselves with *chesed* as well as being graced by Hashem's *chesed.*

Although some stressful and overwhelming events have occurred in our past and may occur in the future, we alone determine how to view all those events and how to behave if we are faced with anything similar in the future. We will certainly attempt to deploy the most effective mix of *chesed, gevurah, tiferet, netzach, hod, yesod,* and *malchut* along with a higher level of *emunah* than we may have in the past.

Parshat Bamidbar, which we read annually as we are completing the Omer count, describes another type of "counting" – a careful census taken of every individual from all Twelve Tribes before their entry into the Promised Land. The connection is telling. All the people were counted before they entered the Land, demonstrating that every person counts.

And so do we. Because we have finished our count of the Omer, we stand ready to face our destiny. As Rabbi Joseph B. Soloveitchik said, the *destination* of the Jewish people was Eretz Yisrael, but the *destiny* of the Jewish people was Mount Sinai. Now that we have counted the Omer for 49 days and worked on the *sefirah* combinations for each day, we, too, are ready to stand at Mount Sinai this year and receive the Torah. From slavery to freedom. Every Shavuot. Every year.

EACH YEAR ANOTHER CHANCE

I marvel at the inherent wisdom and beauty of the annual Jewish cycle of holidays that always seem to give each of us a "second chance." Inherent in the counting of the Omer each year is the opportunity, through self-reflection, to make needed changes and do *teshuvah.*

Underlying the theme of *teshuvah* is the practice of honest self-assessment that is part of the *Tachanun* in daily prayers and of our nightly *cheshbon hanefesh*, a practice suggested by our Sages. Still another source of *teshuvah* is the gift of counting the Omer to improve our *middot* through working on those of our character traits which are deficient or unbalanced.

Indeed, honest self-introspection and *middah* improvement, using the counting of the Omer as a guide, can become our secret channel to God. This is a pathway we elect to open if we want to attain the state of standing before God at Sinai once again.

At Sinai we each were so keenly aware that our *neshamot* were a part of God – that we must be holy because God is Holy and, therefore, we must act accordingly.

"You shall be holy, for I [God] am holy" is the opening verse of *Parshat Kedoshim*. Note that this verse is in the future tense: "You *shall* be holy . . ." What does this tell us? Only God is absolutely Holy, but still *we* are commanded to be holy like *Him*. It is an astonishing charge. We are being told that the desire for and struggle to achieve ethical/moral holiness *shall* be our lifetime goal. And that just by engaging in the struggle to overcome long-held habits and pursue the ethical path, we become transformed.

The Brisker Rav, the grandfather of Rabbi Joseph B. Soloveitchik, once shared that by nature he "was an intemperate and self-absorbed individual . . . [but] since my youth, I've worked *every day* to change and improve myself." On his tombstone, the inscription does not mention his extraordinary rabbinic genius and creativity in which he had no peer, but rather that he was an *Ish HaChesed*, a man of charity and kindness. That he was brilliant beyond description was a gift from God. No real credit here. That he struggled to become "holy like God," and that, as a result of his efforts, he became a towering ethical personality, this was to his *own* everlasting honor.[473]

The message for us is that transforming our natural character is a lifelong effort of extraordinary import. The journey to do so brings us closer to realizing the mission we were placed on earth to fulfill. The annual Omer count provides us a spiritually-based structure that facilitates these efforts. Let's remember that each of us was created with a unique combination of strengths that can inform and personalize our counting of the Omer to elevate us and our loved ones, and to improve our lives.

How do we know that such transformation is possible, that even if we are far from it, we are given many second chances by God? Here's a fascinating answer: The Torah relates that, while the Israelites were in the wilderness, some men had been contaminated by a human corpse so

473. Bienenfeld, *Chizuk*, April 27, 2012.

that they could not make the proper Pesach offering; they asked Moshe and Aaron if they could have a chance to rectify that omission. Moshe responded that he would ask God their question. God's response was yes – if one is unable to observe Pesach at the appropriate time in the month of Nissan, one can bring the Pesach offering and eat it with *matza* and *maror* a month later.[474]

Rabbi Jeffrey Bienenfeld gives over two remarkable lessons about this unique *halachah* in his weekly *Chizuk*:

> With *Pesach Sheni*, a powerful message was being telegraphed to all Jews for all time: There is such a thing as a second chance in life . . . Even if a person should feel contaminated, besmirched by transgression and misdeed (*tamei*), he can have a second chance to make things right. And, no matter how far a person may feel alienated from God, no matter the degree of estrangement, there will be another chance to come back, to come home. But there's something else. Something quite critical in all this . . . There can be/will be no second chance unless you ask for it . . .
>
> The entire *Pesach Sheni* begins with a beseeching plea – almost a respectful demand – demand from the People imploring Moshe to allow them to have this second chance. Had such an appeal not been forthcoming, no second chance, plain and simple . . . To paraphrase an adage from our Sages – "If you first open yourselves up to Me like the eye of a needle, then I will open for you the massive doors and spaces of all that is good and treasured."[475] Now, you can't beat that! The different areas of our life afford us all many second chances: there's always another chance to connect with our children; a second chance to deepen the love with our spouses; another chance to connect with our friends; a second chance to bond with our People and another chance to commit to a life of Torah. But spotting these special opportunities is not enough. Once discovered, you have to ask for them, beg for them, really want them, and then, with God's help, wonderful things will happen![476]

---

474. *Bamidbar* 9:1–14.
475. *Yalkut, Shir HaShirim* 247:988.
476. Bienenfeld, *Chizuk*, June 7, 2012.

Second chances are possible. We just have to really want them, and then we have to ask God directly for them, and then we have to make something out of them once they are granted to us. It seems like a win-win proposition.

TRANSFORMATIONAL TIME

The transformational time between Pesach and Shavuot is when God reveals to us His attributes with which He orders, sustains, and operates the world and all of creation. These attributes, or *sefirot*, are not transitory, but rather are permanent fixtures from which God's Omnipotence and Omnipresence flows. This "guidance system of principles" derives from the Divine will and helps us to emulate His ways at all times, and certainly throughout the 49 days between Pesach and Shavuot.

If we want to emulate God, one of the best ways to do it is by counting the Omer diagnostically to rectify each *sefirah* combination – to treat, heal, adjust, and practice our behaviors to conform with God's will. When we can successfully achieve this, we are able to actualize the purpose of our lives in a healthy, holistic, integrated way always aligned with God, the "Great Essential I."

Each year we count the Omer and resolve to carry our count into the year, much like we try to carry Shabbat into the week. This practice allows us to rise step-by-step, higher and higher toward God's attribute of *malchut* within *malchut* and align our will with His will. When we and our family and all Jews achieve this plateau, we not only access personal merit and reward in this world and the World to Come, but we also elevate the Nation of Israel so that we can fulfill our collective mission "to be a light for the nations."[477] We believe all the problems and wounds – both the personal and communal – can be ultimately solved and healed just by taking the *sefirah* count seriously. God has already set this gift on the table before us. All we need do is accept it and put it to good use, in order to receive God's bountiful blessings.

What are the blessings that come to us through the Omer counting process as described in this volume? I hardly know where to start – the glorious display of kindness and love, strength and discipline and restraint, balance and harmony, truth, endurance, splendorous humility, modesty,

---

477. *Yeshayahu* 42:6.

sublime serenity, bonding, foundation, security, wholeness, integration, leadership and kingship and dignity, all in the right amount and combination and at the right time! And we need every bit to properly fulfill our mission in this world to bring humanity toward the Final Redemption.

OUR MISSION

Rabbi David Aaron captures the nature of our mission most clearly in his book, *The Secret Life of God*:

> Everyone of us has a unique path waiting for us to journey upon. To find it we've got to get on the highway. Collectively we have a mission. It's the highway. The collective mission of human beings is to become more and more humane. Each nation has a mission. One nation may be responsible to lead the advancement of technology in the world. Another perhaps is meant to lead research and development in the field of medicine. Another perhaps is called upon to increase art and music. And yet another may be appointed to head up promoting the moral and ethical progress of the world. After we have accepted our mission as a member of the human race and our mission as a member of our specific nation, then we will be shown our individual mission.
>
> Until that time you should work at becoming a more decent human being and a better citizen of your nation. When you are on the public highway, God will lead to your unique path. In the world of business, if your company sends you on a mission, the boss generally stays at the office while you go off to accomplish the assigned task. But that's not the case when God sends you on a mission. God comes along. This is the meaning of the verse in Psalms 127: "If God doesn't build your house, your labor is for nothing." Now, you might think that if God is going to build your house, why should you have to labor at all? The Psalm is saying that you must labor nonetheless, but if you don't invite God into your work, your efforts will be worthless. You will not have the energy to achieve your task . . .
>
> This is what's unusual about our mission from God. The One who sends us joins us in our mission. But if we don't acknowledge His presence in our work, then we are powerless to truly succeed. The daily focus of our life should be all about inviting God to join us in

> the performance of our mission . . . Once you understand that life is a divine mission, you will realize that no one has a better or more important mission than you . . . If God is with us in our mission, then one person's mission cannot be more important than another's, because everyone's mission is actually God's mission.
>
> Real success does not depend on how much we accomplish on earth. And it does not have anything to do with how much attention the accomplishment gains in the public eye. What really matters is your intention and the quality of your deeds. Did you put your soul into your mission and live your life for God's sake, seeking to grow, striving to become better, concerned about improving yourself and the world? These sages understood that each and every one of us has a mission in life – a calling.
>
> The thing you must always remember is who is calling. God is calling you to be His agent on earth, and the mission He is asking you to fulfill is not only your mission but God's mission.[478]

Rabbi Aaron's advice for us individually as Jews and collectively as a Nation of Israel is vitally important for us to internalize as we take our "Omer counting lessons" and walk boldly into the remainder of the year applying these lessons to our lives.

WHEN WE ARE OFF-TRACK

Now, sometimes as we strive boldly forward, we might get off-track. It takes a lot of insight, courage, and humility to recognize that we are on the wrong path. It takes even greater courage and humility (*hod*) to admit that we aren't even on the highway. Finally, it takes a lot of strength and discipline (*gevurah*) and endurance (*netzach*) to turn our life around.

But if we are able to re-orient and recalibrate our "personal mission GPS system" and align it with God's collective mission for humankind, our reward will be great. To use language of the Omer count, we will bask in harmony, truth, and balance (*tiferet*), and bonding and foundation (*yesod*). If we can go further and continue our search process for self-awareness – discovering, refining, and perfecting our individual mission God assigned to us, and utilizing the Omer count – we can reach the

478. Aaron, *The Secret Life of God*, 44–47.

ultimate destination and dwell consistently in the *sefirah* of *malchut*. We will become "Balanced to Win."

There was a powerful introspective piece in *The Jerusalem Post Magazine* entitled "Lose Yourself," by Daniel Eisenbud, in which the author brilliantly captures the process of how to make a course correction when our personal mission GPS system appears off-track. Eisenbud begins by describing with fondness, his pivotal early childhood experiences as part of a group of pre-teen boys who played outside with each other in spare time. He writes:

> The game itself was always inconsequential, as long as the rules and teams were agreed by all to be fair . . . the best part, though, was that when our heads were in the game, it was like the space-time continuum simply stopped. We all "lost ourselves" in the best possible way, because we stopped thinking in terms of "me" and shifted our focus to the more empowering "us." Individuality took a backseat to the greater good, and self-serving showboats who only played for themselves were quickly identified and isolated . . . And through our hours and hours of collective interactions, we learned invaluable life skills – ranging from the importance of fair play to conflict resolution, respect, sacrifice, sportsmanship, brinkmanship, and even diplomacy . . . we understood that the team concept was the reason we had gathered and had so much fun in the first place . . . What I find most fascinating and rewarding about those bygone days is how relevant, instructive, and transferable the rules of the playground I learned as a child are as an adult. Even instrumental in finding greater meaning in our place in the world . . . our interactions and teamwork taught us a decidedly adult truism about life. Specifically, that the most liberating and empowering state one can actualize comes through understanding that true meaning and purpose can only be derived from beyond the self. In short, that by becoming part of something larger, you are set free from the prison of self-absorption.[479]

Then Eisenbud's personal mission GPS mis-fired, and here's what he discovered:

479. Daniel Eisenbud, "Lose Yourself," *The Jerusalem Post Magazine*, March 9, 2012, 36.

> There was a distinct, yet thankfully short-lived, period in my adult life when I forgot this valuable lesson. I had become a professional mercenary, playing for whatever team had the deepest pockets . . . During this time, any selflessness I once had took a back seat to my salary, expense account, 401(k), vacation prospects, quality of my apartment and dinner reservations. And it ate away at my soul. Indeed, after years of living for me, and me alone, there came a point when no amount of money or recognition could compensate for my undeniable emptiness . . . I came to realize in no uncertain terms that if I didn't learn to become a team player again, and channel my once-considerable potential for an "adult" cause that I actually believed in, I was destined to become a shell of my former self, and of what I could have been. This epiphany, coupled with the encouragement and strength of my beloved grandmother, Carola, is what ultimately led me to move to Israel to proudly join the most outnumbered team in history, and it's the most rewarding decision I've ever made . . .

Eisenbud concludes that Israelis have an "inherent understanding that they are in this fight together – as one, for better or worse – thus allowing them to not have to feel like they are so alone."

We are fortunate that this journalist shared his realization that he was neither on the highway nor even on the path. What about us? With effort and openness and sharing, we can turn the annual 49-day cycle of the Omer count into a similar tool, and we can – working with our family teams – experience what Daniel Eisenbud experienced during his formative years. Our counting the Omer together should likewise help us acquire exceptional patterns of behavior, so we can travel more securely down the highway, steering ourselves onto the path that leads us to completing our mission on earth.

TODAY IS A NEW BEGINNING

So much has unfolded and been revealed through these 49 days of the Omer count. We should feel refreshed, invigorated by a sense of renewal, cleansed from selfishness and discord, and ready to receive our holy Torah with eager anticipation.

Today is not just another day. Today is a new beginning. From today we can apply the lessons that can be so informative for us and formative for our children. We have embarked on a great and glorious journey that will take us through the landscape of time and history. Our journey has and will continue to expose us to countless people and events from whose stories we can extract bits of wisdom and gain better understanding how to elevate ourselves on this sojourn towards a more meaningful life.

I want to express my deep appreciation to you, my readers, for journeying together with me and delving into God's gift of counting the Omer. I also want to extend blessings for you and your family now and until next year, when I hope we will repeat this *Journey Together* again.

Please remember that countless others have done this before us. Our ancestors counted the Omer as, each year, they made themselves worthy to receive the Torah again, and we must do the same. Counting the Omer is a ticket to get onboard our destiny and discover the endless treasure that comes from living a life aligned with God's Oneness of which we are – yes we are! – an essential part.

Acknowledgments

Serving Hashem in oneness with my husband is the focus of my life. I thank Hashem for both the talents and the life experiences He has blessed me with, in order that I can aspire to discover and achieve my mission in His world.

My husband fills up the world with kindness, wisdom, focus, devotion, and goodness. My love and respect for him knows no bounds. His insights into Torah and all of life are gems of understanding that open windows of profound thought and discussion. His focused devotion to being an *Eved Hashem* while navigating *Olam Hazeh* serves as the greatest inspiration I have been blessed to receive. It is through the joint experiencing and processing of significant moments in our lives, including our Torah learning, that we have been able to achieve meaning, purpose, balance, and harmony in our own "journey together."

I was blessed with great parents who believed in my potential, a gift of incalculable dimension.

We are counseled in our tradition to seek extraordinary rabbis and teachers, and I have been blessed to have found them throughout my life. Each of you have had a profound and lasting impact on who I am striving to become and some of you are mentioned throughout *Journey Together*. Thank you for the light of understanding you have brought to the world. In particular I want to extend a special appreciation to the exceptional educators, Rabbi Jeffrey Bienenfeld and Rabbi David Aaron, who combine a complete love of teaching with a complete love of Torah and devotion to Hashem.

I want to express deep appreciation to Uriela Sagiv whose sensitive and keen editing skills are a perfect match for all my idiosyncrasies; she is not only a genuine talent but a pleasure to work with. As well, I want thank Tzvi Mauer and the entire Urim team for their consummate professionalism and expansive thinking, my brother-in-law for providing a visual image of how powerful it looks when a family gathers around to count the Omer together each night, which triggered the initial idea for this book within me, and our daughter Aviva, whose creative eye and unique imagination gave birth to the cover design of *Journey Together*.

There are others who have helped to make it possible that I could carve out moments of time to write this book. I thank Yonatan Debela and Claudia Perreault for their love and support – without their help in my life, *Journey Together* would still remain a dream.

My life has been blessed with a number of deeply meaningful friendships with rare and special people. The privilege to bond with each of you has helped to shape who I am striving to become. Each of you knows who you are and the role you have played in my life, and I want to thank you from the depth of my heart for being a person upon whom I can rely.

Pirkei Avot reminds us that we can learn something from all people, and indeed I have discovered that teachers and opportunities to learn surround my every waking moment. I thank Hashem for having given the opportunity to "encounter" each of these events and people that have shaped my life understanding and for having given me the senses to try to tap into the lessons that I am supposed to be learning if I want to fulfill the mission He has designed for me.

Bibliography

Aaron, David. *Endless Light: The Ancient Path of the Kabbalah to Love, Spiritual Growth, and Personal Power*. New York: Simon & Schuster, 1997.

Aaron, David. *The Secret Life of God: Discovering the Divine within You.* Boston: Shambhala Publications, 2004.

Adams, John. Letter criticizing the depiction of Jews by the French Enlightenment philosopher Voltaire, 1808. Jewish Virtual Library: A Division of the American-Israeli Cooperative Enterprise.

Adler, Elchanan. "*Derech Eretz Kadma LaTorah*: A Multi-faceted Perspective." Shavuot Bulletin of Yeshiva University's Center for the Jewish Future, 5772/2012, 5–12.

Arush, Shalom. *The Garden of Emuna: A Practical Guide to Life*. Jerusalem: Chut Shel Chessed Institutions, 2008.

Arush, Shalom. *The Garden of Wisdom: A Practical Guide to Happiness in Life*. Jerusalem: Chut Shel Chessed Institutions, 2012.

Arush, Shalom. *Women's Wisdom: The Garden of Peace for Women.* Jerusalem: Chut Shel Chessed Institutions, 2010.

Avner, Yehuda. *The Prime Ministers: An Intimate Narrative of Israeli Leadership*. Jerusalem: Toby Press, 2010.

Ben-Shahar, Tal. *Happier: Learn the Secrets to Daily Joy and Lasting Fulfillment.* New York: McGraw Hill, 2007.

Bienenfeld, Jeffrey. *Chizuk*, September 16, 2011; November 4, 2011; April 27, 2012; May 17, 2012; May 24, 2012; June 7, 2012.

Bienenfeld, Jeffrey. *On Sitting Shiva & Its Aftermath: Some Reflections. Ben Yerucham* (Jerusalem: 2012).

Brenner, Bayla Sheva. "Reaching the iPod Generation." *Jewish Action*, Summer 2011.

Briggs, Dorothy Corkille. *Your Child's Self-Esteem*. Garden City, New York: Doubleday & Company, 1970 and Dolphin Books Edition, 1975.

Burg, Steven. "Getting Their Attention: Keeping Our Kids on the Derech." *Jewish Action*, Summer 2011.

Chasidah, Yishai. *Encyclopedia of Biblical Personalities*. Brooklyn, New York: Shaar Press (in conjunction with Mashabim), 1994.

Collins, Jim. *Good to Great*. New York: HarperCollins, 2001.

Cordovero, Moshe. *The Palm Tree of Devorah* (*Tomer Devorah*). Jerusalem: Targum/Feldheim, 1993.

Cotler, Irwin. "The Unlearned Lessons from the Holocaust." *The Jerusalem Post Magazine*, February 10, 2012.

Cousins, Norman. *Anatomy of An Illness*. New York: Bantam Books, 1981.

Covey, Stephen R. *Living the 7 Habits: The Courage to Change*. New York: Fireside, 2000.

Dafni, Reuven, and Yehudit Kleiman. *Final Letters*. New York: Paragon House, 1991.

Davis, Barry. "The First Volunteers." *The Jerusalem Post Magazine*, June 29, 2012.

Davis, Barry. "A Hero Remembered." *The Jerusalem Post Magazine*, March 9, 2012.

Davis, Barry. "100 Years of Music and Life, and Counting." *The Jerusalem Post Magazine*, May 25, 2012.

Dessler, Eliyahu E. *Sanctuaries in Time* (adapted from *Michtav Me-Eliyahu* by Carmell, Aryeh). Jerusalem: Feldheim, 1994.

Dessler, Eliyahu E. *Strive for Truth!* Jerusalem: Feldheim, 1989.

Eglash, Ruth. "It Takes a Village." *The Jerusalem Post Magazine*, February 10, 2012.

Eisen, Yosef. *Miraculous Journey*. Jerusalem: Targum Press, 2009.

Eisenbud, Daniel. "Lose Yourself." *The Jerusalem Post Magazine*, March 9, 2012.

Ellis, Joseph J. *Founding Brothers: The Revolutionary Generation*. New York: Alfred A. Knopf, 2000.

Erikson, Erik H. *Childhood and Society*. New York: W.W. Norton & Company, Inc., 1963.

Farbstein, Esther. *The Forgotten Memoirs*. Brooklyn, New York: Shaar Press, 2011.

Feuer, Avrohom Chaim. *Iggeres HaRamban, Ramban: A Letter for the Ages*. Brooklyn: Mesorah Publications, 1989.

Feuer, Avrohom Chaim. *Tehillim Treasury: Inspirational Messages and Uplifiting Interpretations of the Tehillim of David*. Brooklyn: Mesorah Publications, 1993.

Frand, Yissocher. *Rabbi Yissocher Frand in Print* (written in collaboration with Yonoson Rosenblum). Brooklyn, New York: Mesorah Publications, 1995.

Frankl, Viktor E. *Man's Search for Meaning*. New York: Washington Square Press, 1985.

Friedson, Felice. "Every Second Counts." *The Jerusalem Post Magazine*, July 27, 2012.

Goldstein, Warren. "Purimshpiel, 1946." *The Jerusalem Post*, March 2, 2012.

Goodwin, Doris Kearns. *Team of Rivals: The Political Genius of Abraham Lincoln*. New York: Simon & Schuster Paperbacks, 2005.

Grizzard, Lewis. *My Daddy Was a Pistol, and I'm a Son of a Gun*. New York: Dell Paperback, 1986.

Haber, Yaakov (with Sedley, David). *Sefiros*. Israel: TorahLab, 2009.

Harkov, Lahav. "MKs Recall Victims in Memorial Ceremony." *The Jerusalem Post*, April 20, 2012.

Hasten, Josh. "The Heart of a Community." *The Jerusaelm Post Magazine*, March 9, 2012.

Hasten, Josh. "The New Palmach." *The Jerusalem Post Magazine*, June 29, 2012.

Hasten, Josh. "A Second Home." *The Jerusalem Post Magazine*, June 29, 2012.

Heller, Tzipporah. *Let's Face It! The 8 Essential Challenges of Living*. Jerusalem: Targum/Feldheim, 2005.

Hirsch, Samson Raphael. *Collected Writings of Rabbi Samson Raphael Hirsch*. Vol. 7, *Jewish Education*. Edited by Elliot Bondi and David Bechhofer. Jerusalem: Feldheim, 1997.

Horowitz, Isaiah. *Shney Luchot Habrit*. Vol. 3. Translated and annotated by Eliyahu Munk. Jerusalem: 1992.

James, Muriel, and Dorothy Jongeward. *Born to Win: Transactional Analysis with Gestalt Experiments*. Reading, MA: Addison-Wesley, 1971.

Johnson, Paul. *A History of the Jews*. New York: Harper & Row, 1987.

Jungreis, Esther. *The Committed Life: Principles for Good Living from Our Timeless Past*. New York: Cliff Street Books, 1998.

Jungreis, Esther. *Life Is a Test*. Brooklyn, New York: Shaar Press, 2006.

Kaplan, Aryeh. *The Infinite Light: A Book about God*. New York: National Council of Synagogue Youth, 1981.

Kitov, Eliyahu. *The Book of Our Heritage: The Jewish Year and Its Days of Significance*. Vol. 2, Adar-Nisan. Jerusalem: Feldheim, 1997.

Kolitz, Chaim. *Rabbi Akiva: Sage of All Sages*. Woodmere, New York: Bet-Shamai Publications, 1989.

Lappin, Yaakov. "Believing in Willpower." *The Jerusalem Post*, April 20, 2012.

Lau, Israel Meir. *Out of the Depths*. New York: Sterling Publishing Co., 2011.

Leichman, Abigail Klein. "Honoring Altruism." *The Jerusalem Post Magazine*, June 1, 2012.

Lieber, Moshe. *The Pirkei Avos Treasury*. Brooklyn, New York: Mesorah Publications, 1995.

Lopiansky, Ahron. "Remembering Rabbi Nosson Tzvi Finkel." *Jewish Action*, Summer 2012.

Luzzatto, Moshe Chayim. *The Path of the Just* (*Mesillat Yesharim*). Jerusalem: Feldheim, 1990.

Manolson, Gila. *The Magic Touch: A Jewish Approach to Relationships*. Southfield, MI: Targum/Feldheim, 2005.

McCullough, David. *John Adams*. New York: Simon & Schuster, 2001.

Meleck-Sodah, Racheli. "A Miracle Recovery." *The Jerusalem Post Magazine*, January 13, 2012.

Parsons, David. "An End to Exile." *In Jerusalem Magazine*, February 8, 2013.

Pliskin, Zelig. *Begin Again Now: A Concise Encyclopedia of Strategies for Living*. Union City, New Jersey: Gross Bros. Printing Co, 1993.

Pliskin, Zelig. *Conversations with Yourself*. Brooklyn, New York: Mesorah Publications, 2007.

Raz, Simcha. *A Tzaddik in Our Time: The Life of Rabbi Aryeh Levin*. Jerusalem: Feldheim, 1989.

Rosenblum, Jonathan. "Half Shabbos is No Shabbos." *Jewish Action*, Spring 2012.

Rosenblum, Jonathan. "My Brothers Do I Seek." *The Jerusalem Post Magazine*, January 6, 2012.

Rosenblum, Jonathan. "Rabbi Yosef Shalom Elyashiv: The Reward of Diligence." *The Jerusalem Post Magazine*, July 27, 2012.

Rozett, Robert. "The Complexities of Jewish Solidarity in the Holocaust." *The Jerusalem Post Magazine*, April 20, 2012.

Sacks, Jonathan. "Jewish Unity. It Starts With . . . You." *Jewish Action*, Summer 2012.

Scherman, Nosson. *Perek Shirah: The Song of the Universe, Translation and Insights*. Brooklyn, New York: Mesorah Publications, 2004.

Schneider, Sarah Yehudit. *You Are What You Hate*. Jerusalem: Devorah/A Still Small Voice, 2009.

Shapiro, David. *Rabbi Joseph B. Soloveitchik on Pesach, Sefirat ha-Omer and Shavu'ot*. Jerusalem: Urim Publications (in cooperation with the Rabbi Josef B. Soloveitchik Institute), 2005.

Sharon, Jeremy. "Bringing Kin Together." *The Jerusalem Post*, February 10, 2012.

Siegel, Bernie S. *Love, Medicine and Miracles*. New York: Perennial Library, 1988.

Siegel, Judy. "Young Mother from US with Terminal Illness Achieves Dream by Becoming New Immigrant." *The Jerusalem Post*, September 16, 2011.

Sofer, Barbara. "Adi Hudja's High Heels." *The Jerusalem Post Magazine*, October 26, 2012.

Sofer, Barbara. "The Human Spirit: Top 63 + 1 Reasons I Love Israel." *The Jerusalem Post Magazine*, April 29, 2011.

Sofer, Barbara. "Riding Through the Long Night." *The Jerusalem Post Magazine*, November 18, 2011.

Sofer, Barbara. "A Roll This Side of Heaven." *The Jerusalem Post Magazine*, December 24, 2010.

Soloveitchik, Joseph B. *Abraham's Journey: Reflections on the Life of the Founding Patriarch*. New York: Toras HoRav Foundation, 2008.

Soloveitchik, Joseph B. *Shiur in June 1974*, as reconstructed by Rabbi Avraham R. Besdin. Rabbinical Council of America.

Tatz, Akiva. *The Thinking Jewish Teenager's Guide to Life*. Southfield, MI: Targum/Feldheim, 1999.

Telushkin, Joseph. *Words that Hurt, Words that Heal: How to Choose Words Wisely and Well*. New York: William Morrow, 1996.

Twerski, Abraham J. *Addictive Thinking: Understanding Self-Deception*. Center City, MN: Hazelden Foundation, 1997.

Twerski, Abraham J. *Generation to Generation*. Brooklyn, New York: Traditional Press, 1987.

Twerski, Abraham J. *I'd Like to Call for Help . . . But I Don't Know the Number: The Search for Spirituality in Everyday Life*. New York: Pharos Books, 1991.

Twerski, Abraham J. "Securing Your Home in an Insecure World." *Jewish Action*, Summer 2011.

Twerski, Abraham J. "The Six Obstacles to Teshuvah." *Jewish Action*, Fall 2012.

Wachsman, Esther. "True Super Heroes." *The Jerusalem Post*, October 26, 2012.

Weiss, Stewart. "Between Two Sirens." *The Jerusalem Post Magazine*, April 27, 2012.

Weiss, Stewart. "The Fifth Candle." *The Jerusalem Post Magazine*, December 23, 2011.

Weiss, Stewart. "Shabbat – the Day of Text?" *The Jerusalem Post Magazine*, July 8, 2011.

Zakutinsky, Rivka. *Tachinas: A Voice From the Heart*. Brooklyn, New York: Aura Press, 1992.

Zaloshinsky, Gavriel (ed.). *The Ways of the Tzaddikim* (*Orchot Tzaddikim*). Jerusalem: Feldheim, 1995.

Index

C

D

E

M

Z

DAY	COUNT
1	TODAY IS THE FIRST DAY OF THE OMER.
2	TODAY IS THE SECOND DAY OF THE OMER.
3	TODAY IS THE THIRD DAY OF THE OMER.
4	TODAY IS THE FOURTH DAY OF THE OMER.
5	TODAY IS THE FIFTH DAY OF THE OMER.
6	TODAY IS THE SIXTH DAY OF THE OMER.
7	TODAY IS THE SEVENTH DAY, OR ONE WEEK, OF THE OMER.
8	TODAY IS THE EIGHTH DAY, OR ONE WEEK AND ONE DAY, OF THE OMER.
9	TODAY IS THE NINTH DAY, OR ONE WEEK AND TWO DAYS, OF THE OMER.
10	TODAY IS THE TENTH DAY, OR ONE WEEK AND THREE DAYS, OF THE OMER.
11	TODAY IS THE ELEVENTH DAY, OR ONE WEEK AND FOUR DAYS, OF THE OMER.
12	TODAY IS THE TWELFTH DAY, OR ONE WEEK AND FIVE DAYS, OF THE OMER.
13	TODAY IS THE THIRTEENTH DAY, OR ONE WEEK AND SIX DAYS, OF THE OMER.
14	TODAY IS THE FOURTEENTH DAY, OR TWO WEEKS, OF THE OMER.
15	TODAY IS THE FIFTEENTH DAY, OR TWO WEEKS AND ONE DAY, OF THE OMER.
16	TODAY IS THE SIXTEENTH DAY, OR TWO WEEKS AND TWO DAYS, OF THE OMER.
17	TODAY IS THE SEVENTEENTH DAY, OR TWO WEEKS AND THREE DAYS, OF THE OMER.
18	TODAY IS THE EIGHTEENTH DAY, OR TWO WEEKS AND FOUR DAYS, OF THE OMER.
19	TODAY IS THE NINETEENTH DAY, OR TWO WEEKS AND FIVE DAYS, OF THE OMER.
20	TODAY IS THE TWENTIETH DAY, OR TWO WEEKS AND SIX DAYS, OF THE OMER
21	TODAY IS THE TWENTY-FIRST DAY, OR THREE WEEKS, OF THE OMER.
22	TODAY IS THE TWENTY-SECOND DAY, OR THREE WEEKS AND ONE DAY, OF THE OMER.
23	TODAY IS THE TWENTY-THIRD DAY, OR THREE WEEKS AND TWO DAYS, OF THE OMER.
24	TODAY IS THE TWENTY-FOURTH DAY, OR THREE WEEKS AND THREE DAYS, OF THE OMER.
25	TODAY IS THE TWENTY-FIFTH DAY, OR THREE WEEKS AND FOUR DAYS, OF THE OMER.
26	TODAY IS THE TWENTY-SIXTH DAY, OR THREE WEEKS AND FIVE DAYS, OF THE OMER.
27	TODAY IS THE TWENTY-SEVENTH DAY, OR THREE WEEKS AND SIX DAYS, OF THE OMER.
28	TODAY IS THE TWENTY-EIGHTH DAY, OR FOUR WEEKS, OF THE OMER.
29	TODAY IS THE TWENTY-NINTH DAY, OR FOUR WEEKS AND ONE DAY, OF THE OMER
30	TODAY IS THE THIRTIETH DAY, OR FOUR WEEKS AND TWO DAYS, OF THE OMER.
31	TODAY IS THE THIRTY-FIRST DAY, OR FOUR WEEKS AND THREE DAYS, OF THE OMER.
32	TODAY IS THE THIRTY-SECOND DAY, OR FOUR WEEKS AND FOUR DAYS, OF THE OMER.
33	TODAY IS THE THIRTY-THIRD DAY, OR FOUR WEEKS AND FIVE DAYS, OF THE OMER.
34	TODAY IS THE THIRTY-FOURTH DAY, OR FOUR WEEKS AND SIX DAYS, OF THE OMER.
35	TODAY IS THE THIRTY-FIFTH DAY, OR FIVE WEEKS, OF THE OMER.
36	TODAY IS THE THIRTY-SIXTH DAY, OR FIVE WEEKS AND ONE DAY, OF THE OMER.
37	TODAY IS THE THIRTY-SEVENTH DAY, OR FIVE WEEKS AND TWO DAYS, OF THE OMER.
38	TODAY IS THE THIRTY-EIGHTH DAY, OR FIVE WEEKS AND THREE DAYS, OF THE OMER.
39	TODAY IS THE THIRTY-NINTH DAY, OR FIVE WEEKS AND FOUR DAYS, OF THE OMER.
40	TODAY IS THE FORTIETH DAY, OR FIVE WEEKS AND FIVE DAYS, OF THE OMER.
41	TODAY IS THE FORTY-FIRST DAY, OR FIVE WEEKS AND SIX DAYS, OF THE OMER.
42	TODAY IS THE FORTY-SECOND DAY, OR SIX WEEKS, OF THE OMER.
43	TODAY IS THE FORTY-THIRD DAY, OR SIX WEEKS AND ONE DAY, OF THE OMER.
44	TODAY IS THE FORTY-FOURTH DAY, OR SIX WEEKS AND TWO DAYS, OF THE OMER.
45	TODAY IS THE FORTY-FIFTH DAY, OR SIX WEEKS AND THREE DAYS, OF THE OMER.
46	TODAY IS THE FORTY-SIXTH DAY, OR SIX WEEKS AND FOUR DAYS, OF THE OMER.
47	TODAY IS THE FORTY-SEVENTH DAY, OR SIX WEEKS AND FIVE DAYS, OF THE OMER.
48	TODAY IS THE FORTY-EIGHTH DAY, OR SIX WEEKS AND SIX DAYS, OF THE OMER.
49	TODAY IS THE FORTY-NINTH DAY, OR SEVEN WEEKS, OF THE OMER.

יום	מספר	ספירה
1	היום יום אחד לעומר	חסד שבחסד
2	היום שני ימים לעומר	גבורה שבחסד
3	היום שלושה ימים לעומר	תפארת שבחסד
4	היום ארבעה ימים לעומר	נצח שבחסד
5	היום חמישה ימים לעומר	הוד שבחסד
6	היום ששה ימים לעומר	יסוד שבחסד
7	היום שבעה ימים, שהם שבוע אחד, לעומר	מלכות שבחסד
8	היום שמונה ימים, שהם שבוע אחד ויום אחד, לעומר	חסד שבגבורה
9	היום תשעה ימים, שהם שבוע אחד ושני ימים, לעומר	גבורה שבגבורה
10	היום עשרה ימים, שהם שבוע אחד ושלושה ימים, לעומר	תפארת שבגבורה
11	היום אחד עשר יום, שהם שבוע אחד וארבעה ימים, לעומר	נצח שבגבורה
12	היום שנים עשר יום, שהם שבוע אחד וחמישה ימים, לעומר	הוד שבגבורה
13	היום שלושה עשר יום, שהם שבוע אחד וששה ימים, לעומר	יסוד שבגבורה
14	היום ארבעה עשר יום, שהם שני שבועות, לעומר	מלכות שבגבורה
15	היום חמישה עשר יום, שהם שני שבועות ויום אחד, לעומר	חסד שבתפארת
16	היום ששה עשר יום, שהם שני שבועות ושני ימים, לעומר	גבורה שבתפארת
17	היום שבעה עשר יום, שהם שני שבועות ושלושה ימים, לעומר	תפארת שבתפארת
18	היום שמונה עשר יום, שהם שני שבועות וארבעה ימים, לעומר	נצח שבתפארת
19	היום תשעה עשר יום, שהם שני שבועות וחמישה ימים, לעומר	הוד שבתפארת
20	היום עשרים יום, שהם שני שבועות וששה ימים, לעומר	יסוד שבתפארת
21	היום אחד ועשרים יום, שהם שלושה שבועות, לעומר	מלכות שבתפארת
22	היום שנים ועשרים יום, שהם שלושה שבועות ויום אחד, לעומר	חסד שבנצח
23	היום שלושה ועשרים יום, שהם שלושה שבועות ושני ימים, לעומר	גבורה שבנצח
24	היום ארבעה ועשרים יום, שהם שלושה שבועות ושלושה ימים, לעומר	תפארת שבנצח
25	היום חמישה ועשרים יום, שהם שלושה שבועות וארבעה ימים, לעומר	נצח שבנצח
26	היום ששה ועשרים יום, שהם שלושה שבועות וחמישה ימים, לעומר	הוד שבנצח
27	היום שבעה ועשרים יום, שהם שלושה שבועות וששה ימים, לעומר	יסוד שבנצח
28	היום שמונה ועשרים יום, שהם ארבעה שבועות, לעומר	מלכות שבנצח
29	היום תשעה ועשרים יום, שהם ארבעה שבועות ויום אחד, לעומר	חסד שבהוד
30	היום שלושים יום, שהם ארבעה שבועות ושני ימים, לעומר	גבורה שבהוד
31	היום אחד ושלושים יום, שהם ארבעה שבועות ושלושה ימים, לעומר	תפארת שבהוד
32	היום שנים ושלושים יום, שהם ארבעה שבועות וארבעה ימים, לעומר	נצח שבהוד
33	היום שלושה ושלושים יום, שהם ארבעה שבועות וחמישה ימים, לעומר	הוד שבהוד
34	היום ארבעה ושלושים יום, שהם ארבעה שבועות וששה ימים, לעומר	יסוד שבהוד
35	היום חמישה ושלושים יום, שהם חמישה שבועות, לעומר	מלכות שבהוד
36	היום ששה ושלושים יום, שהם חמישה שבועות ויום אחד, לעומר	חסד שביסוד
37	היום שבעה ושלושים יום, שהם חמישה שבועות ושני ימים, לעומר	גבורה שביסוד
38	היום שמונה ושלושים יום, שהם חמישה שבועות ושלושה ימים, לעומר	תפארת שביסוד
39	היום תשעה ושלושים יום, שהם חמישה שבועות וארבעה ימים, לעומר	נצח שביסוד
40	היום ארבעים יום, שהם חמישה שבועות וחמישה ימים, לעומר	הוד שביסוד
41	היום אחד וארבעים יום, שהם חמישה שבועות וששה ימים, לעומר	יסוד שביסוד
42	היום שנים וארבעים יום, שהם ששה שבועות, לעומר	מלכות שביסוד
43	היום שלושה וארבעים יום, שהם ששה שבועות ויום אחד, לעומר	חסד שבמלכות
44	היום ארבעה וארבעים יום, שהם ששה שבועות ושני ימים, לעומר	גבורה שבמלכות
45	היום חמישה וארבעים יום, שהם ששה שבועות ושלושה ימים, לעומר	תפארת שבמלכות
46	היום ששה וארבעים יום, שהם ששה שבועות וארבעה ימים, לעומר	נצח שבמלכות
47	היום שבעה וארבעים יום, שהם ששה שבועות וחמישה ימים, לעומר	הוד שבמלכות
48	היום שמונה וארבעים יום, שהם ששה שבועות וששה ימים, לעומר	יסוד שבמלכות
49	היום תשעה וארבעים יום, שהם שבעה שבועות, לעומר	מלכות שבמלכות

About the Author

In *Journey Together*, Sarah Hermelin combines inspiring Torah examples and moving modern-day stories to truly "bring to life" the mitzvah of counting the Omer for the entire family – parents and children alike. The author's insights presented here flow out of three decades of experience in the areas of adolescent education, leadership training and development, management coaching and counseling, public speaking and business. Her formal schooling includes degrees in history, education, and counseling; she is also a graduate of Northwestern University's Executive Development Program. Projects which Sarah has both written and helped direct have won a number of Stevie Awards (the "Oscars" given out for the best productions in the business world).

Augmenting Sarah's diverse work experiences are decades of Torah learning and devotion to Eretz Yisrael and Am Yisrael. Her goal in writing this book is to make Sefirat HaOmer become a transforming experience for all Jewish families who take the time to read the *Journey Together* and apply its insights and lessons to their lives.

Sarah lives in Jerusalem with her family.